Isabella of France

Isabella of France
The Rebel Queen

Kathryn Warner

AMBERLEY

To John, with love and many thanks for everything

First published 2016
This edition published 2017

Amberley Publishing
The Hill, Stroud
Gloucestershire, GL5 4EP

www.amberley-books.com

British Library Cataloguing in Publication Data.
A catalogue record for this book is available from the British Library.

ISBN 978 1 4456 5242 9 (paperback)
ISBN 978 1 4456 4741 8 (ebook)

Typeset in 10.5pt on 13pt Sabon.
Typesetting and Origination by Amberley Publishing.
Family trees by Thomas Bohm, User Design, Illustrating and Typesetting.
Printed in the UK.

Contents

Acknowledgements

Thank you so much to my dear friends in Italy for making my book tour there so extraordinarily special and memorable and for all our great chats about Edward II and Isabella, especially Gianna Baucero, Claudia Bergamini, Ezio Candellone, Maurizio Girardi, Ivan Fowler, MariaRosa Gatti, Elena Corbellini, Elena Giacomotti, Mario Traxino, Enza Battaglia and Simone Bertelegni. Thank you also to Claudia Candellone, Angela Barbero Candellone, Gaia Portalupi, Gianni Marino, Gian Luca Marino, Fabrizio Zerbin, Caterina Costanza, Massimo Greppi, Maura Forte, mayor of Vercelli, Don Vincenzo Marchetti of Sant'Alberto di Butrio, Don Paolo Fontana of the cathedral archive in Genoa, Professor Renata Crotti of the university of Pavia, Maria Paola Invernizzi and Antonella Campagna of the university library of Pavia, Barbara Feltri, Anna Maria Soligno, Claudia Zanocchi, everyone else at the Auramala Project, the World of Tels and the Chesterton Association, and all the other lovely people who were so kind and welcoming to me in Vercelli and Pavia. A very special thank you to His Excellency the Archbishop of Vercelli, Father Marco Arnolfo, for so kindly allowing me to use his seminary as a venue for my talk about Edward II, for honouring me with his presence and for introducing my talk. A special thank you also to Monsignor Sergio Salvini, priest of the church of San Cristoforo in Vercelli, for his kindness and generosity and for making me an honoured guest at a concert held in his church. I can never thank my friends in Italy enough for their hospitality.

Thank you to my lovely friends for all your support, kindness, encouragement and knowledge: Rachel Fitzpatrick, Valentino Križanić Kovačić, Kyra Kramer, Ravi Kumar Mishra, Kasia Ogrodnik, Jen Parcell, Sami Parkkonen, Craig Robinson, Howard Sargent, Brian Stevenson, Gillian Thomson, Sarah Ursell, Brad Verity and Masud Vorajee. Thank you to everyone at Amberley and all the rest of you wonderful history-loving people on Facebook, Twitter and my blog.

A Note on Prices and Wages

At the start of the fourteenth century when Isabella arrived in England, the only coin in general circulation was the silver penny, which could be broken into two to make a half-penny or into four to make a farthing. The main unit of currency was the pound, consisting of 240d or 20s (a shilling was 12d), though it remained a purely theoretical notion for most people. The only way to transport large sums of money was in barrels containing thousands of pennies.

The mark was another unit of currency often used in accounting: it equalled two-thirds of a pound, or 13s 4d, or 160d. Ten marks was the equivalent of £6 and 66d; half a mark equalled 8s 6d.

A loaf of the cheapest bread cost a farthing, while a chicken, two dozen eggs and a gallon of ale each cost a penny. Labourers earned 1–1½d a day, craftsmen 3d, master craftsmen 6d, and sergeants-at-arms a shilling (12d).

An annual income of £40 qualified a man for knighthood. Isabella's income, as agreed between her father and husband, was set at £4,500 a year. By way of comparison, her uncle the earl of Lancaster, the richest man in England, earned £11,000 annually from five earldoms, and her nephew-in-law the earl of Gloucester, the second-richest man, earned £6,000.

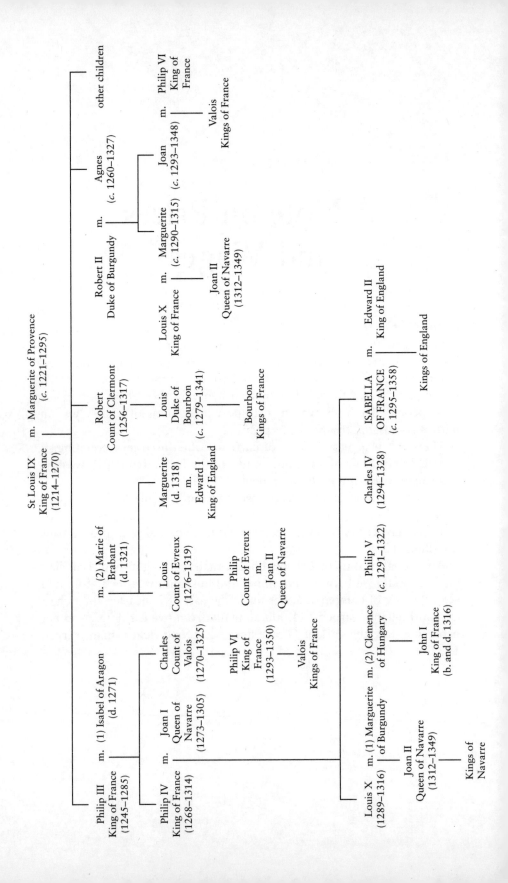

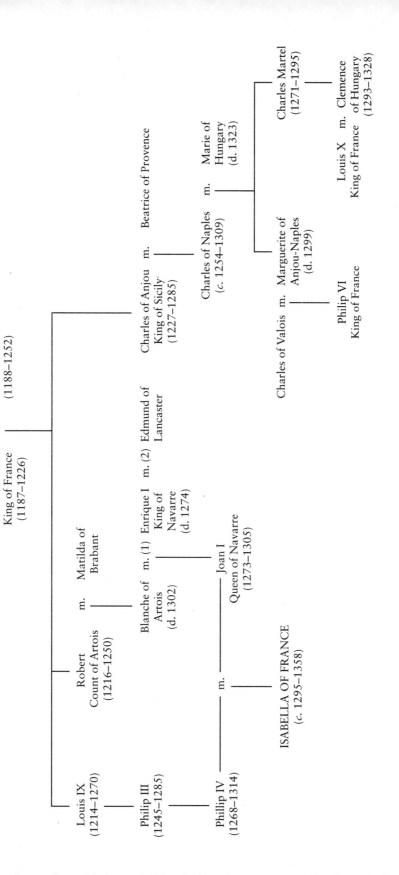

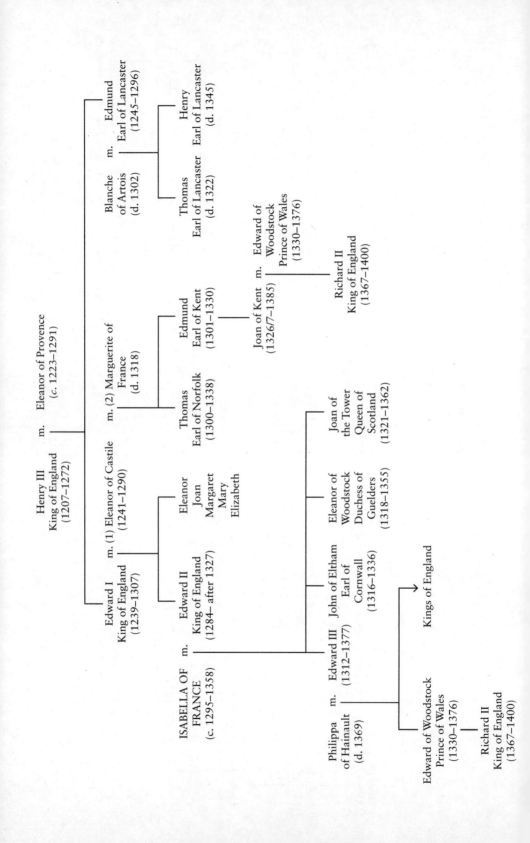

Henry III
King of England
(1207–1272)

m.

Eleanor of Provence
(c. 1223–1291)

Edward I
King of England
(1239–1307)

m. (1) Eleanor of Castile
(1241–1290)

m. (2) Marguerite of
France
(d. 1318)

Blanche
of Artois
(d. 1302)

m.

Edmund
Earl of Lancaster
(1245–1296)

Edward II
King of England
(1284– after 1327)

Eleanor
Joan
Margaret
Mary
Elizabeth

Thomas
Earl of Norfolk
(1300–1338)

Edmund
Earl of Kent
(1301–1330)

Thomas
Earl of Lancaster
(d. 1322)

Henry
Earl of Lancaster
(d. 1345)

ISABELLA OF
FRANCE
(c. 1295–1358)

m.

Edward III
(1312–1377)

John of Eltham
Earl of
Cornwall
(1316–1336)

Eleanor of
Woodstock
Duchess of
Guelders
(1318–1355)

Joan of
the Tower
Queen of
Scotland
(1321–1362)

Joan of Kent
(1326/7–1385)

m.

Edward of
Woodstock
Prince of Wales
(1330–1376)

Richard II
King of England
(1367–1400)

Philippa
of Hainault
(d. 1369)

m.

Edward III
(1312–1377)

Kings of England

Edward of Woodstock
Prince of Wales
(1330–1376)

Richard II
King of England
(1367–1400)

A List of European Royalty and the English Earls in the Early Fourteenth Century

Isabella of France (*c.* late 1295 – 22 August 1358), queen of England, lady of Ireland, duchess of Aquitaine, countess of Chester and Ponthieu: third but only surviving daughter of Philip IV, king of France, and Joan I, queen of Navarre

Edward II (b. 1284), often known as Edward of Caernarfon after his birthplace in north Wales: king of England, lord of Ireland, duke of Aquitaine, prince of Wales, earl of Chester and count of Ponthieu; marries Isabella on 25 January 1308

Edward of Windsor (1312–77), earl of Chester (1312), duke of Aquitaine and count of Ponthieu (1325), King Edward III of England and lord of Ireland (1327): eldest child of Isabella and Edward II; marries Philippa of Hainault in 1328

John of Eltham (1316–36), earl of Cornwall; **Eleanor of Woodstock** (1318–55), duchess of Guelders; **Joan of the Tower** (1321–62), queen of Scotland: the younger children of Isabella and Edward II

Edward of Woodstock (1330–76), prince of Wales and duke of Aquitaine: eldest son of Edward III and Philippa of Hainault, and Isabella's eldest grandchild; marries Joan of Kent; father of Richard II

Philip IV 'the Fair' (1268–1314), king of France from 1285; son of Philip III, grandson of Saint Louis IX; Isabella's father

Joan I (1273–1305), queen of Navarre and countess of Champagne, Brie and Bigorre in her own right; Isabella's mother

Edward I (1239–1307), king of England from 1272; Edward II's father

Eleanor of Castile (1241–90), queen of England; countess of Ponthieu in her own right; Edward II's mother

Philip III (d. 1285), king of France and **Henry I** (d. 1274), king of Navarre: Isabella's grandfathers

Isabel of Aragon (d. 1271), queen of France and **Blanche of Artois** (d. 1302), queen of Navarre and countess of Lancaster: Isabella's grandmothers

Henry III (d. 1272), king of England and **Fernando III** (d. 1252), king of Castile and Leon: Edward II's grandfathers

Marguerite of France (1278/79–1318), queen of England: half-sister of Philip IV and Isabella's aunt; second wife of Edward I and Edward II's stepmother; mother of Thomas of Brotherton, earl of Norfolk, and Edmund of Woodstock, earl of Kent

Marie of Brabant (1254–1321), queen of France: second wife of Philip III, stepmother of Philip IV and step-grandmother of Isabella; mother of Marguerite, queen of England and Louis, count of Evreux

Charles of Valois (1270–1325), count of Valois: brother of Philip IV and ancestor of the Valois dynasty of French kings; married to Marguerite of Anjou-Naples, then Catherine Courtenay and finally Mahaut de Châtillon; Isabella's uncle

Louis (1276–1319), count of Evreux: half-brother of Philip IV and Charles of Valois; married to Marguerite of Artois; Isabella's uncle

Edmund of Lancaster (1245–96), earl of Lancaster, Leicester and Derby: brother of Edward I, and uncle of Edward II; second husband of Blanche of Artois and stepfather of Isabella's mother Joan I of Navarre

Agnes of France (*c.* 1260–1327), duchess of Burgundy: youngest child of Saint Louis IX, Philip IV's aunt and Isabella's great-aunt; married to Duke Robert II of Burgundy (d. 1306); mother of Marguerite, queen of Navarre, Joan, wife of Philip of Valois and queen of France, Hugh V and Odo IV, dukes of Burgundy, and Marie, countess of Bar

Robert (1256–1317), count of Clermont: youngest son of Louis IX, brother of Agnes, and Isabella's great-uncle; married to Beatrice of Burgundy, heiress of Bourbon

Louis (*c.* 1279–1341), first duke of Bourbon: son and heir of Robert of Clermont and a first cousin of Philip IV; married to Marie of Hainault, aunt of Philippa of Hainault; a direct male-line ancestor via his son Jacques de Bourbon (1319-1361), count of La Marche, of Henry IV, who became the first Bourbon king of France in 1589

Louis (1289–1316), king of France and Navarre, count of Champagne: Isabella's eldest brother; succeeds his mother as Louis I of Navarre in 1305 and his father as Louis X of France in 1314; married to Marguerite of Burgundy and secondly Clemence of Hungary

Marguerite of Burgundy (*c.* 1290–1315), queen of Navarre: daughter of Duke Robert II of Burgundy and Agnes of France; granddaughter of Saint Louis IX and a first cousin of her husband Louis's father Philip IV; imprisoned for adultery in 1314, dies or is murdered in prison

Joan II (1312–49), queen of Navarre: only child of Louis X and Marguerite of Burgundy, and Isabella's niece; becomes Queen Joan II of Navarre in her own right in 1328; marries Philip, count of Evreux, son of Louis, count of Evreux

Charles II 'the Bad' (1332–87), king of Navarre and count of Evreux: son and heir of Joan II and Philip of Evreux; marries Joan, daughter of John II of France

Clemence of Hungary (also sometimes called Clemence of Anjou) (1293–1328), queen of France and Navarre: daughter of Charles Martel, titular king of Hungary, and Klementia von Habsburg, daughter of Rudolf I, king of Germany; marries Louis X in 1315

John I 'the Posthumous' (b. and d. 1316), king of France for five days: only child of Louis X and Clemence of Hungary

Philip (*c.* 1291–1322), king of France and Navarre, count of Poitiers: Isabella's second brother; becomes Philip V of France in 1316; married to Joan of Burgundy

Charles (1294–1328), king of France and Navarre, count of La Marche: married to Blanche of Burgundy, then Marie of Luxembourg and finally Joan of Evreux; becomes Charles IV in 1322, the last Capetian king of France; Isabella's third brother

Joan of Burgundy (1287/88–1330): queen of France; countess of Burgundy (the county of Burgundy is also known as the Franche-Comté and is separate from the duchy of Burgundy) and Artois in her own right; elder daughter and heir of Othon IV, count of Burgundy, and Mahaut, countess of Artois; married to Isabella's brother Philip V

Blanche of Burgundy (1295/96–1325/26): younger sister of Joan, above; the first wife of Isabella's brother Charles IV; imprisoned for adultery 1314, her marriage annulled 1322

Marie of Luxembourg (*c.* 1304–24), queen of France: daughter of Henry of Luxembourg, Holy Roman Emperor and king of Germany, and Margaret, sister of Duke John II of Brabant; sister of John 'the Blind', king of Bohemia; marries Charles IV in 1322

Joan of Evreux (*c.* 1310–71), queen of France: daughter of Louis, count of Evreux; marries her widowed first cousin Charles IV in 1324

Joan, duchess and countess of Burgundy, countess of Artois; **Marguerite,** countess of Flanders; **Isabella,** dauphine of Vienne; and **Blanche,** a nun: children of Philip V and Joan of Burgundy who survive into adulthood; Isabella's nieces

Blanche of France (1328–82), duchess of Orleans: daughter of Charles IV (born posthumously) and Joan of Evreux, and Charles' only child who lives into adulthood; Isabella's niece; marries Philip VI's second son Philip, duke of Orleans

Philip of Valois (1293–1350), king of France, count of Valois: son and heir of Charles, count of Valois and Marguerite of Anjou-Naples;

Isabella's first cousin; in 1328 becomes the first Valois king of France, Philip VI

Joan of Burgundy (*c.* 1293–1348), queen of France: married to Philip of Valois; daughter of Duke Robert II of Burgundy and Agnes of France, and granddaughter of Saint Louis IX; younger sister of Marguerite of Burgundy, queen of Navarre

John II (1319–64), king of France: son of Philip VI and Joan of Burgundy; married to Bonne (née Jutta), daughter of John 'the Blind', king of Bohemia; captured at the battle of Poitiers in 1356 by Isabella's grandson Edward of Woodstock and in captivity in England until 1360

Hugh V (d. 1315) and **Odo IV** (d. 1350), dukes of Burgundy: sons of Duke Robert II and Agnes of France; brothers of Marguerite and Joan of Burgundy; uncles of Joan II of Navarre. Odo marries Philip V's eldest daughter Joan of France in 1318

Eleanor (1269–98), countess of Bar; **Joan of Acre** (1272–1307), countess of Gloucester; **Margaret** (1275 – *c.* early 1330s), duchess of Brabant; **Mary** (1279–1332), a nun; and **Elizabeth**, countess of Holland and Hereford (1282–1316): Edward II's sisters who survive into adulthood

Joan of Valois (*c.* 1294–1342): second daughter of Charles of Valois and Marguerite of Anjou-Naples; sister of Philip VI; Isabella's first cousin. Married to William, count of Hainault and Holland; mother-in-law of Isabella's son Edward III

Philippa of Hainault (*c.* 1313/14–1369), queen of England: third surviving daughter of William, count of Hainault and Joan of Valois; marries Edward III in 1328. Her elder sister Margaret, born in 1311, marries Louis of Bavaria, future Holy Roman Emperor, in 1324

Catherine of Valois (*c.* 1303–46), titular empress of Constantinople in her own right as her inheritance from her mother; eldest daughter of Charles of Valois and his second wife Catherine Courtenay; half-sister of Philip VI. Marries Philip of Taranto, king of Albania and despot of Epirus, brother of her father's first wife Marguerite of Anjou-Naples and of Charles Martel, king of Hungary

Mahaut (1268/69–1329), countess of Artois in her own right: niece of Isabella's maternal grandmother Blanche of Artois, queen of Navarre; widow of Othon IV, count of Burgundy (d. 1302); mother of Joan and Blanche of Burgundy, who marry Isabella's brothers Philip and Charles

Robert of Artois (1287–1342): nephew of Mahaut; married to another Joan of Valois, second daughter of Charles of Valois and his second wife Catherine Courtenay

Blanche of Brittany (*c.* 1270–1327): mother of Robert of Artois; mother-in-law of Louis, count of Evreux; granddaughter of Henry III of England; sister of Duke Arthur II of Brittany and John of Brittany, earl of Richmond; Edward II's first cousin

Robert Bruce or Robert I (1274–1329): earl of Carrick, king of Scotland from 1306; married to the earl of Ulster's daughter Elizabeth de Burgh

David II (1324–71), king of Scotland from 1329; only son of Robert Bruce and Elizabeth de Burgh; marries Isabella's daughter Joan of the Tower in 1328

James II (b. 1267), king of Aragon, reigns 1291 to 1327; and his son **Alfonso IV**, born 1299, reigns 1327 to 1336

Fernando IV (b. 1285), king of Castile and Leon, reigns 1295 to 1312, great-grandson of Edward II's grandfather Fernando III; and his son **Alfonso XI**, born 1311, reigns 1312 to 1350

John II (1275–1312), duke of Brabant: nephew of Marie of Brabant, queen of France; uncle of Marie of Luxembourg, queen of France. Married to Edward II's third sister Margaret; their son is **John III**, duke of Brabant (1300–55), married to Marie of Evreux, daughter of Louis, count of Evreux and sister of Joan of Evreux, queen of France

Edouard I (1294/95–1336), count of Bar: son of Edward II's eldest sister Eleanor; married to Marie of Burgundy, daughter of Duke Robert II of Burgundy and Agnes of France

The English Earls in Edward II's Reign

Thomas of Brotherton (b. 1300), earl of Norfolk: elder son of Edward I and Marguerite of France; half-brother of Edward II, first cousin of Isabella; marries Alice Hales

Edmund of Woodstock (b. 1301), earl of Kent: younger son of Edward I and Marguerite of France, and Edward II's other half-brother; marries Margaret Wake; father of Joan of Kent, princess of Wales, and grandfather of Richard II

Thomas of Lancaster, earl of Lancaster, Leicester and Derby (b. *c.* 1278) and his brother and heir **Henry of Lancaster** (b. *c.* 1281): sons of Blanche of Artois and younger half-brothers of Queen Joan I of Navarre, and thus Isabella's uncles; also sons of Edward I's younger brother Edmund of Lancaster, and Edward II's first cousins. Thomas is married to Alice Lacy, daughter and heiress of Henry Lacy, earl of Lincoln; Henry to Maud Chaworth, niece of Guy Beauchamp, earl of Warwick and older half-sister of Hugh Despenser the Younger

Piers Gaveston, earl of Cornwall: a nobleman of Béarn in the English-ruled south-west of France, born in 1283 or earlier and the beloved of Edward II. Second son of Arnaud de Gabaston or Gaveston and Claramonde de Marsan. Marries Edward II's niece Margaret de Clare in 1307

Gilbert de Clare (b. 1291), earl of Gloucester and Hertford: son of Edward II's second sister Joan of Acre; Piers Gaveston's brother-in-law. Marries the earl of Ulster's daughter Maud de Burgh in 1308

Eleanor, Margaret and **Elizabeth de Clare** (b. 1292, 1294 and 1295): Gilbert's younger sisters and heirs, Edward II's nieces, married respectively to Hugh Despenser the Younger, Piers Gaveston, and the earl of Ulster's son and heir John de Burgh

Henry Lacy (b. *c.* 1250), earl of Lincoln and Salisbury. His heir is his daughter Alice (b. 1281), married to Thomas, earl of Lancaster

John de Warenne (b. 1286), earl of Surrey and Sussex. Married to Edward II's niece Joan of Bar; his heir is his nephew Richard Fitzalan

Joan of Bar (b. 1295/96), countess of Surrey and Sussex: only daughter of Edward II's eldest sister Eleanor; sister of Edouard I, count of Bar

Edmund Fitzalan (b. 1285), earl of Arundel. Half-Italian, grandson of the marquis of Saluzzo and nephew of the governor of Sardinia; married to Alice, sister of John de Warenne; their son and heir is Richard

Guy Beauchamp (b. *c.* 1270/72), earl of Warwick. One of the few English earls not closely related to Edward II by blood or marriage; maternal uncle of Hugh Despenser the Younger; marries Alice Toeni in *c.* 1309; their son and heir is Thomas

Humphrey de Bohun (b. *c.* 1276), earl of Hereford and Essex. Married to Edward II's fifth sister Elizabeth; their son and heir is John

John of Brittany (b. 1266), earl of Richmond. A grandson of Henry III of England via his mother, and Edward II's first cousin; also a second cousin of Isabella via their mutual great-grandfather King Theobald I of Navarre. Brother of Duke Arthur II of Brittany and uncle of Duke John III; never marries

Aymer de Valence (b. *c.* 1270/75), earl of Pembroke. Son of Henry III's half-brother William de Valence, and Edward I's first cousin; married firstly to Beatrice de Clermont-Nesle, daughter of the Constable of France, and then to Marie de Châtillon, daughter of the count of St Pol; dies childless and his successor as earl is his great-nephew Laurence Hastings

Robert de Vere (b. 1257), earl of Oxford, a political nonentity who plays no role whatsoever in Edward II's reign; married to Margaret Mortimer, aunt of Roger Mortimer of Wigmore (below)

Roger Mortimer, lord of Wigmore in Herefordshire, b. 1287: the baron with whom Isabella begins a relationship in about late 1325. Marries the heiress Joan Geneville in 1301, becomes 1st Earl of March in 1328

Hugh Despenser the Elder (b. 1261): brother-in-law of Guy Beauchamp, earl of Warwick, and stepson of Roger Bigod, earl of Norfolk (d. 1306); made earl of Winchester in 1322

Hugh Despenser the Younger (b. *c.* 1287/89): son and heir of Hugh Despenser the Elder. Marries Edward I's eldest granddaughter Eleanor de Clare in 1306, and is Edward II's nephew-in-law; is also the brother-in-law of Isabella's uncle Henry of Lancaster; later becomes lord of Glamorgan in south Wales and Edward's chamberlain and favourite

Timeline

1268: Birth of Philip IV of France

1270: Birth of Philip IV's brother Charles of Valois

1273: Birth of Joan I of Navarre

1274: Death of Henry I of Navarre, accession of Joan I

1276: Birth of Philip IV's half-brother Louis of Evreux

c. 1278: Birth of Isabella's uncle Thomas, earl of Lancaster

1278/79: Birth of Philip IV's half-sister Marguerite, queen of England

c. late 1270s/early 1280s: Birth of Piers Gaveston

c. 1281: Birth of Isabella's uncle Henry, earl of Lancaster

1284, 25 April: Birth of Edward II (of Caernarfon)

1284, 16 August: Wedding of the future Philip IV of France and Joan I of Navarre

1284, 19 August: Death of Edward of Caernarfon's elder brother Alfonso of Bayonne; four-month-old Edward becomes heir to the English throne

1285, 5 October: Death of Philip III, accession of Philip IV, aged seventeen

1287, 25 April: Birth of Roger Mortimer

c. 1287/89: Birth of Hugh Despenser the Younger

1289, 4 October: Birth of Louis X of France

1290, 28 November: Death of Eleanor of Castile, queen of England, Edward II's mother

c. 1291: Birth of Philip V of France

1291, May: Birth of Gilbert de Clare, earl of Gloucester, Edward II's eldest nephew

1292, October/November: Birth of Eleanor de Clare, Edward II's eldest niece

1294, 18 June: Birth of Charles IV of France

c. late 1295: Birth of Isabella of France

1294-96: Births of Edward II's nieces Margaret and Elizabeth de Clare and Joan of Bar

1298, August: Death of Edward's eldest sister Eleanor, countess of Bar

1299, June: Treaty of Montreuil, which arranges Isabella and Edward's future marriage

1299, 8 September: Wedding of Edward I and Marguerite of France

1300, 1 June: Birth of Edward of Caernarfon's half-brother Thomas of Brotherton

1301, 7 February: Edward of Caernarfon made prince of Wales and earl of Chester

1301, 5 August: Birth of Edward of Caernarfon's half-brother Edmund of Woodstock

1301, September: Wedding of Roger Mortimer and Joan Geneville

1303, May: Official betrothal of Edward and Isabella

1305, April: Death of Joan I of Navarre

1305, 23 August: Execution of Sir William Wallace

1306, 25 March: Coronation of Robert Bruce as king of Scots

1306, 22 May: Knighting of Edward of Caernarfon, Roger Mortimer, Piers Gaveston and Hugh Despenser the Younger

1307, 23 April: Death of Edward of Caernarfon's sister Joan of Acre, countess of Gloucester

1307, 30 April: Piers Gaveston's first exile from England

1307, 7 July: Death of Edward I, accession of Edward II

1307, 27 October: Funeral of Edward I at Westminster Abbey

1308, 25 January: Wedding of Edward II and Isabella of France

1308, 25 February: Coronation of Edward II and Isabella of France

1308, 25 June: Piers Gaveston's second exile

1311, 27 September: Publication of the Ordinances

1311, 1 November: Gaveston's third exile

1312, c. 12 January: Birth of Gaveston's daughter Joan

1312, 28 January: Birth of Isabella's niece Joan II of Navarre

1312, 19 June: Execution of Piers Gaveston

1312, 13 November: Birth of Edward of Windsor, later Edward III

1313, 23 May to 15 July: Edward II and Isabella visit France

1314, late February to late April: Isabella visits France and possibly breaks the adultery scandal of two of her sisters-in-law

1314, 20 April: Death of Pope Clement V

1314, 23 and 24 June: Battle of Bannockburn

1314, 29 November: Death of Philip IV, accession of Louis X

1315, 14 August: Death of Marguerite of Burgundy

1315, 19 August: Wedding of Louis X and Clemence of Hungary

1315-1317: Years of the Great Famine

1316, 5 June: Death of Louis X

1316, 7 August: Election of Pope John XXII

1316, 15 August: Birth of Isabella's second son John of Eltham

1316, 15 November: Birth of John I 'the Posthumous' of France

1316, 20 November: Death of John I; accession of Philip V

1318, 14 February: Death of Marguerite of France, dowager queen of England

1318, 18 June: Birth of Isabella's first daughter Eleanor of Woodstock

1319, 19 May: Death of Isabella's uncle Louis, count of Evreux

1321, 12 January: Death of Marie of Brabant, dowager queen of France

1321, 5 July: Birth of Isabella's second daughter Joan of the Tower

1322, 3 January: Death of Philip V, accession of Charles IV

1322, 13 February: Imprisonment of Roger Mortimer in the Tower

1322, 16 March: Battle of Boroughbridge

1322, 22 March: Execution of Thomas, earl of Lancaster

1322, 21 September: Wedding of Charles IV and Marie of Luxembourg

1323, 1 August: Escape of Roger Mortimer

1324, 26 March: Death of Marie of Luxembourg, queen of France

1324, 5 July: Wedding of Charles IV and Joan of Evreux

1325, 9 March: Isabella departs for France

1325, 12 September: Edward of Windsor departs for France

1325, October/November: Isabella refuses to return to Edward

c. late 1325 (before 8 February 1326): Isabella begins a relationship with Roger Mortimer

1325, 16 December: Death of Isabella's uncle Charles of Valois

Late 1325/early 1326: Death of Isabella's former sister-in-law Blanche of Burgundy

1326; 27 August: Betrothal of Edward of Windsor and Philippa of Hainault

1326, 24 September: Arrival of Isabella's invasion force in England

1326, 27 October: Execution of Hugh Despenser the Elder, earl of Winchester

1326, 16 November: Capture of Edward II

1326, 17 November: Execution of Edmund Fitzalan, earl of Arundel

1326, 24 November: Execution of Hugh Despenser the Younger

1327, 20 January: Abdication of Edward II

1327, 25 January: First day of Edward III's reign

1327, 1 February: Coronation of Edward III

1327, 21 September: Official date given for Edward II's death

1327, 20 December: Funeral of Edward II at St Peter's Abbey, Gloucester

1328, 25/26 January: Wedding of Edward III and Philippa of Hainault

1328, 1 February: Death of Charles IV

1328, 1 April: Birth of Charles IV's posthumous daughter Blanche; accession of Philip VI

1328, 17 July: Wedding of the future David II of Scotland and Joan of the Tower

1328, 12 October: Death of Louis X's widow Clemence of Hungary, dowager queen of France

1329, 7 June: Death of Robert Bruce; accession of David II

1330, 21 January: Death of Philip V's widow Joan of Burgundy, dowager queen of France

1330, 18 February: Coronation of Philippa of Hainault as queen of England

1330, 19 March: Execution of Edmund of Woodstock, earl of Kent

1330, 15 June: Birth of Isabella's eldest grandchild Edward of Woodstock, later prince of Wales, father of Richard II

1330, 19 October: Arrest of Roger Mortimer; Edward III takes over governance of his own kingdom

1330, 13 November: Edward III's eighteenth birthday

1330, 29 November: Execution of Roger Mortimer at Tyburn

1336, 13 September: Death of John of Eltham, earl of Cornwall

Early 1340s: Death of the former Edward II in Italy?

1346, 26 August: Battle of Crécy, victory of Edward III

1347–49: Black Death sweeps through Europe

1348, 12 September: Death of Philip VI's wife Joan of Burgundy, queen of France

1349, 6 October: Death of Joan II of Navarre; accession of her son Charles II 'the Bad'

1350, 22 August: Death of Philip VI, accession of John II

1355, 22 April: Death of Eleanor of Woodstock, duchess of Guelders

1356, 19 September: Battle of Poitiers, a victory for Edward of Woodstock; capture of John II of France

1358, 22 August: Death of Isabella of France

1358, 27 November: Isabella's funeral at the Greyfriars church in London

1362, 7 September: Death of Joan of the Tower, queen of Scotland

1369, 15 August: Death of Philippa of Hainault, queen of England

1371, 4 March: Death of Joan of Evreux, dowager queen of France

1376, 8 June: Death of Edward of Woodstock, prince of Wales

1377, 21 June: Death of Edward III; accession of his grandson Richard II

Introduction

London, Wednesday 24 September 1326, twentieth year of the reign of King Edward II

The hot summer of 1326, which had brought drought to England, was finally drawing to a close. Forty-two-year-old King Edward II was staying at the Tower of London with his household and the few important allies who still remained to him after almost two decades of misrule, favouritism, greed and ineptitude: Hugh Despenser the Elder, earl of Winchester; his son Hugh Despenser the Younger, lord of Glamorgan, the king's powerful chamberlain and perhaps his lover; Eleanor de Clare, Hugh the Younger's wife, the king's beloved eldest niece and, bizarrely, also perhaps his lover; Edmund Fitzalan, earl of Arundel; and Robert Baldock, chancellor of England. Despite the huge stress he was under, Edward II found time to reimburse the keeper of his private possessions 10*d* for four pairs of buckskin gloves which had been made for him for the coming winter, and gave 8*d* to a man who had brought him a gift of fish. The king himself went out to the Tower's postern gate, where he encountered a fisherman named Richard Marbon and paid him 3*s* for two fine salmon.[1]

Meanwhile, eighty miles away, a fleet of fewer than a hundred ships was landing somewhere along the River Orwell in Suffolk. No one at the time, least of all the oblivious Edward II, could have guessed that the landing of this fleet and the no more than 1,500 people who came ashore would spell his downfall; that these soporific days at the Tower were the last days of peace he would ever know; that soon he would be forced to flee from his capital, little more than a fugitive in his own kingdom; that within four months he would have lost his throne, forced to abdicate in favour of his teenage son. Even before he heard of the fleet's arrival three days later, however, Edward knew perfectly well who one of the leaders of the invasion in Suffolk was. His estranged wife and queen, Isabella of France.

Isabella of France (*c.* 1295–1358), who married Edward II in January 1308, is one of the most notorious women in English history. In 1325/26, sent to her homeland to negotiate a peace settlement to end the war between her husband and her brother Charles IV of France, Isabella refused to return to England. She began a relationship with her husband's deadliest enemy, the English baron Roger Mortimer, and with her son the king's heir under their control, the pair led an invasion of England which ultimately resulted in Edward II's forced abdication in January 1327. Isabella and Mortimer ruled England during the minority of her and Edward II's son Edward III, until the young king overthrew the pair in October 1330, took over the governance of his own kingdom and had Mortimer hanged at Tyburn and his mother sent away to a forced but honourable retirement. Edward II, meanwhile, had died under mysterious circumstances – at least according to traditional accounts – while in captivity at Berkeley Castle in September 1327.

Though she was mostly popular and admired by her contemporaries, her disastrous period of rule from 1327 to 1330 notwithstanding, Isabella's posthumous reputation reached a nadir centuries after her death when she was condemned as a wicked, unnatural 'she-wolf', adulteress and murderess by writers incensed that a woman would rebel against her own spouse and have him killed in dreadful fashion, or at least stand by in silence as it happened (the infamous and often-repeated 'red-hot poker' story of Edward II's demise is a myth, but widely believed from the late fourteenth century until the present day). Isabella's relationship with Roger Mortimer and her alleged sexual immorality, as well as her frequently presumed but never proved role in her husband's murder, became a stick often used to beat her with; a typical piece of Victorian moralising by Agnes Strickland declared that 'no queen of England has left such a stain on the annals of female royalty, as the consort of Edward II, Isabella of France'.[2] Strickland's work divided the queens of England, seemingly fairly arbitrarily, into the 'good' ones such as Eleanor of Castile and Philippa of Hainault, and the 'bad' ones such as Eleanor of Provence; Isabella of France, naturally, fell into the second category. Her reputation fared poorly between the sixteenth and nineteenth centuries, and well into the twentieth: in the early 1590s the playwright Christopher Marlowe called her 'that unnatural queen, false Isabel', a 1757 poem by Thomas Gray was the first to apply the ridiculous 'she-wolf' nickname (which had been invented by Shakespeare for Henry VI's queen Margaret of Anjou) to her, and in 1958, exactly 600 years after her death, Isabella was still being called 'the most wicked of English queens'.[3] The French nickname sometimes used for her, *la Louve de France* – the title of a 1950s novel about her by Maurice Druon – is simply the translation of the English word 'she-wolf' and has no historical basis whatsoever. (Although it is sometimes claimed nowadays that Edward II himself, or his favourite Hugh Despenser the Younger, called Isabella a 'she-wolf', this is not true; one fourteenth-century chronicler, Geoffrey le Baker, called her Jezebel, a play on her name, but otherwise no unpleasant nicknames for her are recorded until a few centuries after she died.) An academic work of 1983 unkindly calls Isabella a 'whore', and a non-fiction book published as late as 2003 depicts her as incredibly beautiful and desirable but also murderous, vicious and scheming, and claims without evidence that she 'had murder in her heart' towards her husband in 1326/27, called for his execution and was 'secretly delighted' when she heard of his death.[4] Her contemporaries were mostly kinder. With the notable exception of Geoffrey le Baker in the 1350s, who was trying to promote Edward II as a saint and who detested Isabella, calling her an 'iron virago' as well as 'Jezebel', fourteenth-century chroniclers generally treated her well, and it is certainly not the case, as is sometimes claimed nowadays, that they called her a 'whore' or anything equally ugly and harsh because of her liaison with Roger Mortimer. Most fourteenth-century chroniclers seem uncertain whether Isabella even had an affair with Mortimer at all, and a few depict the two merely as political allies and call Mortimer Isabella's 'chief counsellor', which may be a more accurate portrayal of their association than the romanticised accounts so prevalent in modern writing. In the late twentieth and twenty-first centuries, writers have mostly been keen to write Isabella sympathetically and rescue her from the unfair calumnies heaped on her head for so long – an impulse to be applauded – but in doing so have tended to go too far in the opposite direction. As a result, Isabella is depicted nowadays as a tragic, long-suffering victim of marital cruelty, impoverished and deprived of her children, who is miraculously transformed in 1326/27 into a strong, empowered feminist heroine bravely fighting to end the oppression of her husband's subjects and to get her children back. This is no more accurate than the old tendency to write her as an evil she-wolf.

Portrayals of Isabella of France down the centuries say far more about the societies that produced them and the prevailing attitudes towards women and their sexuality, in particular women who step outside the bounds of traditionally conventional behaviour, than they do about Isabella herself. For all the piles of chronicles, non-fiction books, novels, plays, poems and articles written about the queen over the last 700 years, have we come close to knowing the real Isabella at all, or has she only ever been an image of what we think she must have been like, formed from our own experiences and cultural expectations? Can we discover the real Isabella underneath the centuries of myth? The queen would surely not recognise herself and the events of her life in the way she has so often been portrayed: either as a malevolent and vengeful murderer, or as a despondent martyr treated appallingly for many years by her despised husband and his lovers, or as a time-traveller parachuted into the Middle Ages from the twenty-first century with modern attitudes towards sexual equality. Isabella was far more complex: neither wicked nor saintly, she was a fascinating human being with both excellent qualities and flaws, who did laudable things and other things not so praiseworthy. She was a product of her time and place – Europe in the fourteenth century – intensely proud of her royal birth and high position, steeped in Christianity, taught that she must marry in a political alliance to benefit her father's kingdom and happy to do so, taught also that she must obey her husband and bear his children.

Far too often, writers of non-fiction are prone to declaring what Isabella *must* have felt in a given situation when there are really no grounds for doing so. So we read that Isabella *must* have been disgusted and upset by her husband's relationship with Piers Gaveston, and she *must* have hated Gaveston, and she *must* have felt nothing but loathing and revulsion for her husband, especially after beginning a relationship with Roger Mortimer, whom she *must* have passionately adored, and that she *must* have wished fervently for Edward's death after his deposition and *must* have been delighted to hear about it. Such dogmatic assertions tell us little more than what the writer thinks he or she might have felt had they found themselves in Isabella's situation, and nothing about Isabella. We don't know for certain that she resented Piers Gaveston, or that she ever hated her husband and wished him physical harm, or even that she loved Roger Mortimer. Mere suppositions about Isabella and her thoughts and feelings have all too frequently come to be stated as though they are known fact, communicated to a writer 700 years later by mental telepathy or by the fortunate discovery of Queen Isabella's Secret Diary. It is important to remember that in the early fourteenth century nobody kept journals and private letters are few and far between, and therefore, although we know *what* people did, we can mostly only speculate as to *why* they did it. Their motivations and innermost thoughts, feelings and beliefs are, to a very great extent, hidden from us. This can be frustrating both for the biographer and the reader, but we should be very wary of making supposedly factual declarations about the personal feelings of a person who lived 700 years ago in a society very different to our own.

For centuries Isabella was depicted as evil – a ridiculous notion – but in more recent years the events of her life have been twisted and slanted almost beyond recognition in non-fiction and fiction to fit popular modern narratives. We have the soap-opera style, with salacious and mostly fictitious (though masquerading as factual) accounts of 'wife-swapping' among Isabella, her husband Edward, his chamberlain Hugh Despenser the Younger and Despenser's wife Eleanor de Clare, and forbidden, doubly adulterous but yearningly passionate romance between Isabella and Roger Mortimer. In this telling, any mistakes and errors of judgement on Isabella's part are made because of her claimed sexual infatuation with Mortimer; she is a woman who runs entirely on emotions and desires which she cannot or will not control. This analysis turns Isabella into a shallow creature living a one-dimensional existence, whose marriage of nearly two decades is never anything but profoundly unsatisfactory and whose husband is never anything but useless and hateful, and whose emotional life is reduced to a series of simplistic set pieces: she feels only contempt for Edward, hatred for his male favourites, lust for Mortimer. Secondly, we have the 'true confession' style, where 700-year-old events are forced to fit the modern genre which depicts how people overcome adversity such as poverty, addiction and abusive relationships. In this narrative, Isabella immediately after her marriage becomes the victim of ill-treatment at the hands of a negligent husband who has the temerity to prefer men to her, despite her great beauty and desirability (the fact that Isabella had only recently turned twelve when she married twenty-three-year-old Edward is underplayed in favour of presenting her as the victim of her husband's lack of due attention right from the start). As if that were not bad enough, Edward and his male lovers go out of their way for years on end to humiliate Isabella and even, in one case, sexually assault or rape her. After many years of misery, with her children removed from her custody to break her down still further and her husband threatening her with divorce, Isabella finally finds the strength and courage to strike back, escape from an unendurably bad marriage and take control of her own destiny. She discovers her long-suppressed sexuality, takes a virile, manly, exciting lover who is in every way superior to her weak and dismal husband and who adores her, gains revenge with his devoted help on the spouse and his male paramour who have so mistreated her, gets her children back, and everything ends happily ever after. At least, until Isabella's son has her lover executed. This inaccurate and anachronistic retelling involves grossly exaggerating the woes of Edward II and Isabella's marriage, which for many years (until admittedly it went horribly wrong) in fact shows all the signs of being a successful, mutually satisfactory and affectionate, even loving, partnership. It accuses a man of rape or sexual assault without a shred of real evidence. It romanticises a personal relationship, Isabella and Roger Mortimer's, about which we know very little, and mostly ignores the inconvenient fact that Mortimer himself was married throughout his association with Isabella, his wife Joan Geneville being shunted offstage and rarely mentioned except in rather disparaging terms as the matronly wife thrown over for the glamorous, sexy royal mistress. It minimises Isabella's bad choices during her unsuccessful period of rule for her underage son Edward III, and blames everything that went wrong during it on men around her who can handily be turned into scapegoats. The greatest scapegoat is usually Roger Mortimer himself, who within the space of a few pages passes from being a great romantic hero and the saviour of Isabella and England in general to being the cackling villain of the piece, bringing himself and Isabella down with his greed and tyranny. Meanwhile, the woman lauded to the heavens a few chapters earlier for being able to invade a kingdom and bring down a king suddenly becomes powerless to deal with a mere baron, allegedly because she is deeply in thrall to him sexually and emotionally. Depicting the queen as a helpless pawn of men, though certainly kinder than and preferable to the accusations of murderous malice thrown at her for so long, strips Isabella of her humanity. It absolves her of responsibility for her own actions and choices and removes her agency, and is as patronising and paternalistic as condemning her as a one-dimensionally wicked and sexually immoral 'she-wolf'. If Isabella is to be praised for her 'good' deeds and characteristics, she must be held equally responsible for her 'bad' ones, and not lauded as an empowered woman when doing something an author approves of but then painted as a dupe of unscrupulous men when doing something less laudable. Isabella was a very long way from being the notorious she-wolf of myth, but neither did she suddenly become a passive, compliant victim of men when things started going wrong during her regency. It dishonours her memory to paint her as one. It is unhelpful both to exaggerate her faults and claim that she was evil and depraved, and to ignore them or justify them as an understandable reaction to suffering she supposedly endured but which to a great extent is merely the invention of modern authors. Isabella was far more complex and fascinating than the currently prevalent myth of a much-wronged heroine flawed only by her need for a 'real man' in her life after many years of marriage to the inadequate Edward II.

Edward, undoubtedly one of the most unsuccessful kings England has ever produced and the first to suffer the ignominious fate of deposition, has rarely, in 700 years, been portrayed sympathetically, but in the twenty-first century he has been recast as an abusive husband, and the men he loved reduced to little more than caricatured moustache-twirling baddies whose main aim in life was to make Isabella suffer. Even in an age which likes to consider itself much more tolerant than the benighted past, Edward's strong emotional and perhaps physical need for men is frequently sneered at and deemed perverted, unnatural and an insult to Isabella's femininity, as though he chose his sexual orientation deliberately to spite her and could have stopped falling in love with men if he had simply tried hard enough. Isabella's rebellion against him is consequently presented as an inevitable consequence of Edward's failure or refusal to love her as she needed and deserved. Her association with Mortimer, which in all likelihood was a hard-headed and pragmatic political alliance, at least in the beginning, is written as a love affair for the ages between a neglected and hard-done-by wife and a man who is, conveniently, the exact opposite of her offensively gay husband. Isabella of France the politician, the invader of a kingdom, the daughter of the ruthless Philip IV, is reduced to a character in a tawdry melodrama who only really wants to find True Love Forever, and who 'succumbs' to and 'surrenders to the embraces' of a 'strong and lusty adventurer' as though she is the heroine of a 1950s Mills and Boon bodice-ripper.

It is hard to see how this new take on Isabella is any less problematic than the old 'she-wolf' routine, and the attitudes which see Edward II being written as a 'bad homosexual' who indulges himself in immoral relationships with other men and Roger Mortimer as the 'good heterosexual' who rescues Isabella from the horrid fate of being shackled to a vicious, effeminate and cruel pervert are wince-inducing. Earlier writers focused on her (presumed) adultery, casting her as a bad woman who loved sex and who came to a sticky end because of it; more modern writers applaud her as a good woman for looking for and finding true love. The association with Mortimer is tediously over-emphasised, perhaps because it provides a more satisfactorily romantic way of explaining Isabella's rebellion against her husband and her invasion of his kingdom than a desire for wealth and power. It is considered acceptable for men, but not women, to act in their own self-interest, and men, but not women, are assumed to be acting under their own agency at all times. Roger Mortimer's ambitions to regain his political position and the lands he had lost in 1322 are considered a good enough motive for him to invade Edward II's kingdom in 1326. Isabella also lost her lands, which were confiscated by Edward in 1324, and was deprived of her ability to intercede with her husband and thus lost her political influence, but this is rarely examined as a motive for her and Mortimer's invasion of 1326. Instead, it is sometimes claimed that she wished to liberate her husband's subjects, in particular women and children, from his tyrannical rule, which, given that she herself acted little better during her period of power and also imprisoned women and children, hardly seems very likely.[5] Any errors Roger Mortimer made are deemed to be entirely his own responsibility and are not explained away on the grounds that he had suffered terribly by being imprisoned, and no one claims that he invaded England, deposed Edward II and made himself the richest and most powerful man in the country simply because he was madly in love with Isabella and, in the grip of his infatuation with her, had little other choice than to do whatever she wanted and ordered. The same applies to Edward II, who is not exempted from criticism for the numerous instances of his misrule on the grounds that he was in love with Piers Gaveston and Hugh Despenser, yet it has been claimed that 'Isabella was a remarkable queen, a woman of outstanding ability, flawed by her infatuation with Mortimer'.[6] It is hard to imagine that anyone would write, 'Mortimer was a remarkable nobleman, a man of outstanding ability, flawed by his infatuation with Isabella.' (There is really nothing to suggest, except wishful thinking and romanticising, that either Isabella or Mortimer ever felt 'infatuation' for the other.) Certainly, no one would ever say that Roger Mortimer was the grossly maligned victim of circumstances and an unscrupulous woman, yet it has also been claimed that Isabella was a 'remarkable yet grossly maligned woman, who was the victim, not of her own wickedness, but of circumstances, unscrupulous men and the sexual prejudices of those who chose to record her story'.[7] Isabella was not a victim, either of the ever-useful 'unscrupulous men' who can generally be relied upon in narratives about her period of rule to be made to take the blame for everything that went wrong during it, or anyone or anything else. If she has been the victim of 'sexual prejudices', so too has her husband, a lover of men and women, though predominantly men. It seems fairly pointless to try to rehabilitate Isabella's reputation by enthusiastically maligning Edward II instead. It makes no sense to complain about the sexual prejudices she has faced while painting her husband's sexuality as abnormal and disgusting, or to perpetuate different sexual prejudices by turning a woman into the helpless victim of circumstances and nasty men while holding that the men themselves are fully responsible for their own actions at all times. Opining that a woman can be 'flawed' by her sexual desires while a man – or at least, a man presumed to be heterosexual – is not, is hardly a helpful analysis either.

We know little about Isabella's private thoughts, and in many ways her life serves as a blank canvas onto which fantasies of 'strong' and 'empowered' women can be projected. She is not alone in this. For example, Mary Boleyn – sister of Henry VIII's second queen, Anne Boleyn – about whom we know very little except the bare narrative of her life, has become remarkably popular in the last few years, thanks mostly to Philippa Gregory's bestselling novel about her. In online history forums, blog posts and social media, Mary is depicted as a remarkable, unconventional woman who had the courage to marry her second husband for love and was centuries ahead of her time in doing so. Praise is heaped on women of the past who are believed to have been liberated in an approved twenty-first-century fashion and to have broken the bonds of custom and followed their own path. Isabella of France chose her own lover – if her relationship with Roger Mortimer was indeed sexual – which in the pre-modern era caused many writers to denounce her venomously as an immoral scarlet woman and in the twenty-first century has led to a thousand books and online articles acclaiming her magnificence. Isabella is, like many other royal and noble women of the Middle Ages, often described nowadays as a 'pawn' because her marriage was arranged by her father and father-in-law and the pope. This rather ignores the fact that Edward II and other royal and noble men of the era had no say in whom they married either, yet men are never described as 'pawns' on these grounds. Edward and Isabella's marriage came about in 1299 as a means of making peace between their warring fathers, the kings of England and France, and it was fifteen-year-old Edward's fourth betrothal, the previous three also made in furtherance of his father's foreign policy and what suited England best at any given time. If Isabella was a mere pawn on the royal marriage market, then so too was her husband. Depicting medieval royal and noble women as unwilling pawns in a game of power politics played by men which has nothing to do with them, however kindly it may be meant, gives a disagreeable impression of fragile, submissive victimhood, which in Isabella's case at least is entirely unwarranted. Isabella was as well-versed in the game of politics as anyone, and certainly was not a feeble chess-piece manoeuvred by the hands of powerful men, anachronistically wailing, 'But I don't love him!' when informed that she will marry the future king of England, a scene so often repeated in historical fiction about medieval and Tudor women as to have become a cliché. Isabella had no concept of marrying a man she had chosen herself because she was in love with him. It is futile to pity her for not being allowed to exercise a choice which meant nothing to her and which she would likely not have wanted to take advantage of even if it did. It is not as though the daughter of the king of France and the queen of Navarre, if genuinely allowed to choose freely whom she wanted to marry, would ever have selected a carpenter or a latrine-cleaner or even a knight whom she would have considered so far beneath her as to make the idea of marrying him and sharing his bed revolting. There were few people in Europe whom Isabella would rather have married than the king of England: the ruler of a powerful country and as royal and well-connected as she herself was.

Much of what is written about Isabella of France today is either invention or exaggeration. Edward II removing her children from her; stealing her jewels or wedding gifts from her to give to his lover Piers Gaveston; abandoning her in tears when she was pregnant at Tynemouth in 1312 so that he could save his beloved Gaveston instead; Isabella taking a lover who fathers her eldest child Edward III; being buried next to Roger Mortimer or with his heart in a casket on her chest: all of these are myths, but have often taken on the status of fact and are frequently repeated as such. A great deal of what we think we know and what is often stated about Isabella and her life simply melts away when we turn to the primary sources. Isabella's children were not 'removed' from her cruelly and punitively but simply set up in their own households, as was entirely normal for royal children in the Middle Ages. The St Paul's annalist says merely that Edward II sent the gifts given to him by his new father-in-law Philip IV – given solely to him, not to him and Isabella jointly – to his regent Piers Gaveston in England, probably only to store safely for him. The St Albans chronicler, writing nearly 300 miles away and many years later, confused Isabella being at Tynemouth in 1312 with another occasion when she was there in 1322, and that time truly in danger. Isabella was buried at the Greyfriars church in London, Roger Mortimer nearly a hundred miles away at the Greyfriars in Coventry, and the heart laid on the late queen's chest was that of her husband, not Mortimer's. No one suggested that Edward II was not the father of Edward III until the end of the twentieth century, and the notion says far more about modern binary concepts of sexuality than it does about history. Although a few recent novels, films and online articles enthusiastically push the idea of Isabella taking a lover who fathers her son and appear to find it an appealing and romantic one, Isabella herself would be furious at the suggestion that she would ever have contemplated foisting a child of non-royal paternity onto the English throne.

We know little of Isabella's childhood before she married Edward II in 1308, and the last twenty-eight years of her life after her downfall from power in 1330 are also obscure. This book will therefore focus predominantly on events of 1308 to 1330, the most dramatic and well-documented of Isabella's life, when she moved from a position of loyal support for her husband to committing the extraordinary act of invading his kingdom, forcing his deposition and ruling, or partly ruling, the kingdom for her son. Part one of the book tells the story of the first few years of Edward II and Isabella's marriage, from 1308 to 1321, and what went wrong during Edward's reign. Part two is a detailed examination of the years 1322 to 1330, when Isabella slowly moved from loyalty to her husband to opposition, her regency of the late 1320s and her downfall in 1330. Part three provides an account of the last years of her life. It is time to examine Isabella of France and her actions properly, as neutrally as possible, without judging her but also without overly romanticising her, without whitewashing and also without blackwashing her, and bearing in mind that her familial, cultural and societal norms were very different to ours. It is time to cut through the myths, the simplistic stereotypes, the mess of stories invented about Isabella which bear little resemblance to reality, and do our utmost to discover the real person.

PART ONE

The Conventional Queen

I

My Lady Yzabel, Queen of England
1295–1308

On Thursday 25 January 1308 at the church of Notre-Dame in Boulogne, northern France, a glittering event took place: the wedding of the king of England and the king of France's daughter. It was attended by a whole host of European royalty and nobility, including the bride's father and her brother the king of Navarre, the king of Naples and Albania, the groom's sister and brother-in-law the duke and duchess of Brabant, the dowager queens of France and England, the duke of Burgundy and his brothers, and the counts of Valois, Evreux, Hainault, Flanders, Nevers, St Pol, Namur, Dreux and Savoy.[1] The bride wore a red cloak lined with yellow sindon, over a gown and tunic in blue and gold, with which she would be buried fifty years later. Her new husband wore a satin surcoat and a jewel-embroidered cloak, and both wore crowns studded with precious stones.

The groom, Edward II of England, was exactly twenty-three years and nine months old, born on 25 April 1284, and had succeeded his father, Edward I, as king of England six and a half months earlier. Isabella of France, the bride, was much his junior: she had only recently turned twelve at the time of her wedding, probably born sometime between late November 1295 and 24 January 1296. The sibling closest to her in age, the future Charles IV of France, was born on 18 June 1294, and had married Blanche of Burgundy at her mother Mahaut of Artois's castle of Hesdin the week before Isabella's wedding.[2] Previous queen consorts of England had been the daughters of kings, or of dukes or counts; Isabella went one better by being the child of parents who were both sovereigns in their own right. Her father, Philip IV, born in 1268, succeeded his father, Philip III, as king of France in 1285. Her mother, Juana or Joan I, born in January 1273, became queen of Navarre, a small kingdom in northern Spain, as an infant when her father, Henry I, died in July 1274. Joan I of Navarre and the future Philip IV of France married on 16 August 1284 when Joan was only eleven and Philip sixteen; they were second cousins, both great-grandchildren of Louis VIII of France and his famous queen, Blanche of Castile, regent of France for many years in the name of her son Louis IX. Isabella was the sixth of King Philip and Queen Joan's seven children. She had two older sisters, Marguerite and Blanche, who both died as small children or babies in 1294/95 and whom she therefore never had a chance to know. Her eldest brother, Louis, who succeeded his father as Louis X of France and his mother as Louis I of Navarre, was born on 4 October 1289. Three other brothers followed. They were Philip, born probably in 1291, who became Philip V of France and Philip II of Navarre; Charles IV of France, also Charles I of Navarre, born on 18 June 1294; and Robert, the seventh and youngest child, born probably in 1297, who died a few months after Isabella's wedding, when he was about eleven. Of the four children who lived to adulthood, all were crowned monarchs. Isabella's mother, Queen Joan I of Navarre, who was also in her own right countess of Brie, Bigorre and Champagne in the south of France, died in April 1305 in her early thirties, and was succeeded in her Spanish kingdom by Isabella's then fifteen-year-old brother, Louis; Joan's widower, Philip IV, never remarried. Isabella was born into the Capetian dynasty, which had ruled France since 987. Her brothers would be the last three Capetian kings of France.

We know virtually nothing about Isabella of France's childhood, her relationships with her parents and brothers, her education or whom she was close to in childhood, other than her nurse, the noblewoman Theophania de Saint Pierre, lady of Brignancourt, who accompanied her to England after her marriage. Even the queen's appearance is unrecorded, whether she was blonde, brunette or red-haired, slim or plump, though her beauty impressed her contemporaries: the annalist of St Paul's Cathedral, for example, called her 'a most elegant lady and a very beautiful woman'.[3] The chronicler Geoffrey or Godefroy of Paris, who saw Isabella when she and Edward II visited France in the summer of 1313 when she was seventeen, was, to put it mildly, extremely impressed with her. In his rhyming chronicle, Geoffrey called Isabella noble and wise, 'splendid of body and fine of heart', more beautiful than other women as the sun over the stars, the most beautiful woman of her era who could be found in the kingdom of France or in the Holy Roman Empire, and 'the fairest of the fair, the rose, the lily, the flower and the exemplar'.[4] Her father, Philip IV, was known to his contemporaries as *Philippe le Bel*, which in English is usually translated as Philip the Fair in the sense of 'handsome', and her brothers Philip V and Charles IV were known as *Philippe le Long* and *Charles le Bel*, which indicates that the family was tall and good-looking. (Her eldest brother Louis X's rather less complimentary nickname, *le Hutin*, means 'the Quarrelsome'.) Isabella's name in her own lifetime was spelt in a variety of ways: Isabell, Isabele, Ysabel, Ysabell and Yzabel, among others, and Geoffrey of Paris called her Ysabelot and Ysabiau, which sound like affectionate nicknames perhaps used by her family and later her husband. Geoffrey wrote Edward II's name as Oudouart and Odouard, and French scribes of the era spelt it Edouart, Edouwart, Edduvart and so on, which gives us a good idea as to how Isabella would have pronounced her husband's name.

Isabella lost her mother when she was nine and never had the chance to meet her grandfathers, Philip III of France and Henry I of Navarre, who died long before she was born. Her maternal grandmother, Blanche of Artois, queen of Navarre and countess of Lancaster, daughter of one of Saint Louis IX of France's brothers, was the only one of her grandparents still alive at the time of her birth. Blanche married her second husband, Edward I of England's brother Edmund of Lancaster, in 1276 and died in 1302; she was the mother of Isabella's uncles Thomas and Henry, both earls of Lancaster, who were to play significant roles in the lives of her and her husband. Isabella's great-grandmother Marguerite of Provence, widow of Louis IX, died in December 1295, around the time that Isabella was born, and Pope Boniface VIII gave their dynasty a great boon when he canonised Louis in 1297, so that Isabella grew up knowing that she had a saint as a near ancestor. Her step-grandmother Marie of Brabant, Philip III's second queen, must have been someone she knew well; Marie lived until 1321, and her daughter Marguerite, Isabella's aunt, was the stepmother of Isabella's husband, Edward II. Isabella would also have known her father Philip IV's uncle Robert, count of Clermont and the youngest son of Louis IX, who outlived Philip IV and lived until 1317, and Clermont's sisters Agnes, duchess of Burgundy and Blanche, the widow of Alfonso X of Castile's son Fernando de la Cerda, who both survived into the 1320s. Isabella came from a huge family: she had around thirty first cousins and her father, Philip IV, had at least fifty. Her husband, Edward II, was also born into a large family and was the youngest of his parents' at least fourteen and perhaps as many as sixteen children, though only six of the siblings outlived their mother, Eleanor of Castile, and just four (Edward, Margaret, Mary and Elizabeth) were still alive when their father, Edward I, died in July 1307. Edward II also had two much younger half-brothers, Thomas and Edmund, from his father's second marriage, who were the sons of Philip IV's half-sister Marguerite and thus two of Isabella's many first cousins.

Isabella's paternal grandmother, Isabel of Aragon, after whom she was presumably named, died following a fall from her horse on 28 January 1271. Barely even in her mid-twenties at the time of her death, Isabel was pregnant with her fifth child, who did not survive the accident. Two of her other children also died young, so that her only surviving offspring were Philip IV and his younger brother Charles, count of Valois. Isabel had been queen of France for a mere five months, since the death of her father-in-law, Louis IX, and the accession of her husband, Philip III, on 25 August 1270. Isabel of Aragon was one of the daughters of James I, king of Aragon, Valencia and Majorca and count of Barcelona, and his second wife, Violante, daughter of Andrew II, king of Hungary and Croatia. Via the Hungarian line, Isabella of France was the great-great-great-great-great-great-great-granddaughter of Harold Godwinson, the king of England killed at the battle of Hastings in 1066, whose daughter Gytha of Wessex married Vladimir Monomakh, grand prince of Kiev. Harold Godwinson's blood thus returned to the royal line of England when Isabella's son Edward III succeeded his father as king in 1327. Isabella was also descended from Frederick I Barbarossa, Holy Roman Emperor; Isaac Angelos, emperor of Byzantium; Henry II of England and his queen Eleanor, duchess of Aquitaine; Theobald I of Navarre, the Troubadour King; and Reynald de Châtillon, prince of Antioch, who appears as a character in the film *Kingdom of Heaven*. Royal to her fingertips and related to the great houses of Europe, all her life Isabella was well aware and intensely proud of her high birth and regal dignity, as befitted someone who was queen consort of England, sister of three kings of France, daughter of the king of France and the queen of Navarre.

In 1294, the year before her birth, Isabella's father, Philip IV, went to war with his kinsman Edward I of England over the latter's possession of Gascony, the remainder of the large territory in the south-west of France which Edward I had inherited from his father Henry III and ultimately from his great-grandmother Eleanor, duchess of Aquitaine and queen of England. In the June 1299 Treaty of Montreuil, which made peace between England and France, it was agreed that Isabella, then aged three, would marry Edward I's fifteen-year-old son and heir, Edward of Caernarfon, then count of Ponthieu and later prince of Wales and earl of Chester (1301), duke of Aquitaine (1306) and King Edward II of England (1307). He was her only fiancé and her only husband, and given her youth at the time of her betrothal, she can hardly have remembered a time when she didn't know that it was her destiny to marry him and become queen of England. Given Isabella's enormous pride in her royalty, it is likely that she was delighted at the prospect, and extremely unlikely that she would ever have wanted to marry and have children with someone who wasn't as royal as she herself. Edward of Caernarfon, a future king, son of a king, and grandson of two more kings (Henry III of England and Fernando III of Castile and Leon in Spain), fitted the bill perfectly, though had Isabella's older sisters Marguerite and Blanche survived infancy, one of them may well have married Edward instead. Isabella and her future husband were second cousins once removed – her great-grandmother Marguerite of Provence was the older sister of Edward's grandmother Eleanor of Provence, queen of Henry III – and were also related rather more distantly via common descent from Alfonso VIII of Castile and his queen Eleanor of England, daughter of Henry II and Eleanor of Aquitaine. Their confusingly tangled and inter-related family tree threw up other connections: Isabella's maternal grandmother, Blanche of Artois, queen of Navarre and countess of Lancaster, was Edward's aunt by marriage, and Isabella's aunt Marguerite married the widowed Edward I in 1299 and was Edward of Caernarfon's stepmother.

Edward I died near Carlisle on 7 July 1307 at the age of sixty-eight, on his way to a military campaign against Robert Bruce, who had had himself crowned king of Scots the year before. He bequeathed to his son and successor an unwinnable war and claims to overlordship in Scotland, vast debts as a result of the war, dissatisfied magnates and, despite Edward II and Isabella's betrothal, hostile relations with France and Philip IV. Isabella never met her husband's father and was never princess of Wales, as shown in the 1995 Hollywood film *Braveheart*, as she married Edward II a few months after his accession to the throne. (The only princess of Wales in the English royal family in the entire Middle Ages was Edward II's niece Joan of Kent, who married his and Isabella's famous warrior grandson Edward of Woodstock and was the mother of Richard II.) Neither can Isabella possibly have met Sir William Wallace, who had been executed on 23 August 1305 when she was only nine years old, and for him to be the father of her eldest son as shown in *Braveheart* would have required her to become pregnant while still a child in France and carry the infant for more than seven years: her first child was born on 13 November 1312. The film turns Edward II into an offensive caricature – a feeble, cowardly court fop whose male lover is thrown out of a window and who is cuckolded by the far more courageous and stereotypically masculine Wallace. A few novels, online articles and even works of non-fiction in the twentieth and twenty-first centuries have enthusiastically followed suit: the authors recognise the impossibility of Isabella's affair with Wallace but write Edward as being cuckolded by the far more courageous and stereotypically masculine Roger Mortimer instead, with modern stereotypes of how gay and bisexual men are thought to behave spilled onto the pages with wild abandon. Edward stamps his feet, snivels, throws tantrums, shrieks, flounces, whines, pouts and flutters his hands. He is frequently called effeminate and his relationships with men perverted, and it is implied that these relationships were abnormal. He is written in ways which feminise him and is compared unfavourably to Roger Mortimer, who is claimed to have been 'unequivocally heterosexual' as well as 'manly' and 'virile' and therefore apparently superior to Edward. It has been stated in another book published as non-fiction in the twenty-first century that 'Isabella had known only the smooth girlish hands of Edward upon her' and that he must have fantasised about Piers Gaveston while making love with her, while Roger Mortimer was a 'heated warrior who took her, roughly at first, then tenderly'.[5] Such grotesque portrayals and absurd flights of fantasy are as far from the truth as one can imagine. Edward II was in fact a good six feet tall and enormously strong: he was 'one of the strongest men in his realm', 'of outstanding strength' and 'great of strength' according to three fourteenth-century chroniclers, and many others who saw him and knew him wrote much the same thing.[6] He adored the outdoors and arduous physical exercise, he went swimming and rowing in rivers in winter, he dug ditches, did metalwork and thatched roofs, he was the kind of man who would go into a forge to chat to the blacksmiths or stop to talk to fishermen while sailing along the Thames whenever he felt like it. In short, Edward II was as far removed from the popular image of him as an effete, mincing court dandy with 'smooth girlish hands' as any man possibly could be. Although he certainly lacked ability as a military leader and strategist and tarnished his reputation forever by his crushing loss at the battle of Bannockburn in 1314, there is no doubt that he was courageous in battle, not a snivelling coward who ran away from a fight. Chroniclers also called Edward elegant and good-looking, and there is no reason whatsoever to assume that Isabella felt 'profound revulsion' for him at any time or that she shared the prejudices expressed by some writers towards him. If Isabella would not recognise herself in the way both her detractors and her fans have depicted her and the events of her life over the centuries, she certainly would not recognise her physically powerful husband in the ludicrous caricatures made of him in much writing – even, sadly, writing claimed as non-fiction – which say everything about unpleasant and unfortunately still prevalent attitudes towards gay and bisexual men and nothing at all about Edward II as he really was.

At his accession to the English throne in the summer of 1307, Edward was twenty-three and Isabella still only eleven, and he had no intention of postponing his sex life until his fiancée was old enough to become his wife in more than name. He had fathered, or at some point not long after his wedding to Isabella would father, an illegitimate son named Adam, who died in his early or mid-teens in 1322, though sadly the identity of Adam's mother has never been discovered by historians. Contrary to popular modern belief, Edward II was definitely not averse to women: as well as the relationship which produced his son Adam, he was later, curiously, said to have had a sexual, incestuous relationship with his eldest niece, Eleanor de Clare, and he and Isabella formed a partnership which for many years was far more successful than is commonly imagined nowadays. But there is little doubt that Edward was predominantly a lover of men, and by far his most significant relationship was the one he had with Piers Gaveston, a nobleman of Béarn in the English-ruled south-west of France, whom the king made earl of Cornwall and brought into the royal family by marriage to his niece Margaret de Clare in 1307.[7] Edward had known Gaveston since at least 1300 when he was sixteen and probably before, and there is every reason to suppose that he was the great love of Edward's life. Although Agnes Strickland claimed in the nineteenth century that Edward abandoned the continuation of his father's war in 1307 because he was desperate to marry Isabella as soon as possible, given Isabella's extreme youth and the fact that he had never set eyes on her before, coupled with his obsession for Piers Gaveston, this seems highly unlikely.[8] It is also most unlikely, however, that Edward was trying to wriggle out of marrying Isabella at the start of his reign, as one modern historian has suggested; infatuated with Gaveston he may have been, but he also knew he had no choice but to marry Isabella, or face war with Philip IV and the loss of his extensive lands in France.[9] Edward and Isabella's betrothal had been arranged as far back as the Treaty of Montreuil in June 1299 (and officially took place in May 1303) and was a political match at the highest level designed to consolidate peace and cordial relations between two powerful kingdoms.[10] The personal desires and wishes of the pair were irrelevant, and they both knew it.

In the first few months of his reign, Edward II negotiated with Philip IV over his marriage to Isabella, and on 24 January 1308, the day he arrived in Boulogne, promised to grant his new queen the northern French county of Ponthieu and its main stronghold of Montreuil-sur-Mer.[11] She would bring him no dowry except the return of Gascony, which Philip had confiscated from Edward I in 1294 and which was all that remained of the English kings' once vast territorial landholdings in France, and there were other important issues to be thrashed out, such as Isabella's income (settled at £4,500 a year). The two men agreed that Edward would arrive in Boulogne on 21 January 1308 and marry Isabella on the 24th. Edward in fact arrived in Boulogne three days late, almost certainly because of rough weather or contrary winds in the Channel – it was the middle of winter, after all – and not because he intended any insult to Isabella or the French in general, or was too engrossed with Piers Gaveston to leave on time.[12] He had scandalised his kingdom and upset his barons by appointing Gaveston, his closest friend and perhaps his lover, as regent of England during his absence abroad.[13] Appointing one of his young half-brothers, Thomas and Edmund, or his cousin the earl of Lancaster as regent would have been far more appropriate, but Edward cared little for proprieties when it came to promoting Gaveston's interests.

No record survives of Isabella of France and Edward II's first meeting or of their first impressions of each other. Numerous novels of the twentieth and twenty-first centuries depict Edward as bored and unengaged, thinking only of Piers Gaveston, and Isabella, at first thrilled with the good looks and fine physique of her new husband, increasingly hurt and baffled at the deadly insult to her femininity as he demonstrates a total lack of interest in her. We cannot know what really happened, though it is unlikely that Edward would have been discourteous to Isabella in front of her father, and we should bear in mind that she had only recently turned twelve and that Edward was at least eleven and a half years her senior. Even if she was more physically and emotionally mature than the average modern twelve-year-old, and there is no real evidence to suggest that she was, eleven years is such an age gap as to make it seem creepy and abusive if Edward had fallen instantly in love or lust with her. Edward may have found Isabella enchanting and been delighted to marry a bride so royally well-connected and pretty, or he may only have seen a pre-pubescent or barely pubescent girl who could be of little use to him politically or personally until she grew up. His behaviour towards her in the early years of their marriage indicates that the latter is far more likely to have been the case, which is hardly to be wondered at.

Nor do we know what Isabella thought of Edward, whether she found him attractive and what she thought of his rather eccentric personality. She may have been made aware of the fact that Edward enjoyed the company of his lowborn subjects such as carpenters, blacksmiths and fishermen and took part in the decidedly non-royal pastimes of thatching roofs, digging ditches, driving carts, swimming and rowing, which she probably found disquieting and perhaps even insulting to her regal dignity. It is also unclear whether Isabella knew of Edward's relationship with Piers Gaveston and how she felt about it if she did, or of the existence of her husband's illegitimate son Adam. The latter would at least have shown her that Edward was capable of fathering children and thus may not have been entirely unwelcome news. Whatever the couple thought of each other on this first occasion, presumably they could communicate without hindrance, as Edward's first language was Anglo-Norman, the variant of French then spoken by the English elite and not too different from Isabella's native Francien, the dialect of Paris and the Île-de-France. At any rate, it was in the interests of both of them to try to get on as well as they could. As far as either of them knew at the time, they would be married for the rest of their lives, and somehow they would have to find a way to make their relationship work. They had had no way of avoiding marrying each other and, now that it had taken place, they had no way of ending the marriage if they ever wanted to: an annulment from the pope would have been almost impossible to procure, and politically this would have been totally out of the question anyway. There was therefore little they could both do but make the best of the situation. The royal marriage may have been consummated once to make it legal and binding, but it seems unlikely, given Isabella's youth, that the couple had much of a sex life in the beginning. She became pregnant for the first time – that we know of, at least – four years later, when she was sixteen. This was a normal and humane delay, and it may be that Philip IV had demanded that regular sexual relations be delayed until Isabella was older, or perhaps Edward II made the decision not to expose his young wife to the risks of pregnancy and childbirth until her body was more developed. Edward's four sisters who became mothers were nineteen, twenty-one, twenty-five and again twenty-five when their eldest children were born, his three de Clare nieces all married at thirteen and had their first children at sixteen or seventeen, Isabella's mother, Joan I of Navarre, married when she was only eleven and bore her first child also at sixteen, and none of Isabella's three brothers' wives gave birth before they were in their late teens; delayed pregnancy and childbirth was entirely usual in both their families.[14]

Edward, with Isabella at his side, held splendid banquets in Boulogne on 28 and 30 January. On the 31st, she may have been present as he knelt to perform homage to her father in his role as duke of Aquitaine and count of Ponthieu, a county in northern France Edward had inherited from his long-dead half-Spanish half-French mother, Eleanor of Castile, and his grandmother Joan of Ponthieu, queen of Castile and Leon, the second wife of Fernando III. Edward II was not only a (Welsh-born) king of England, he was a peer of the realm of France and owed homage for his lands there to his overlord Philip IV, and he held other titles as well: as his wife, Isabella was now lady of Ireland, duchess of Aquitaine and countess of Ponthieu and Chester as well as queen of England (Edward did not use his remaining title, prince of Wales, after his accession). She probably took the chance at this time to observe the English noblemen who had accompanied Edward to France, men who would play important roles in her husband's life and hers: the king's brother-in-law Humphrey de Bohun, earl of Hereford; John de Warenne, earl of Surrey, the king's nephew-in-law though only two years his junior; Edward's cousin Aymer de Valence, earl of Pembroke, who was married to the French noblewoman Beatrice de Clermont-Nesle; the elderly Henry de Lacy, earl of Lincoln; and Guy Beauchamp, earl of Warwick, hostile to the king and especially to Piers Gaveston. In Boulogne she probably also saw and met the twenty-year-old English nobleman Roger Mortimer, lord of Wigmore in Herefordshire, with whom, although she couldn't possibly have known it, Isabella would bring down her husband nineteen years later.

Philip IV gave his daughter a magnificent trousseau to take to England, an inventory of which fortuitously still exists and is headed *Des joyauz et habillemens de ma dame Yzabel de France Royne d'Angleterre*, 'The jewels and clothes of my lady Yzabel of France, Queen of England' (Isabella was not a princess, a title for the daughters of kings which did not yet exist, and it is anachronistic to call her one). The numerous belongings she took to England with her included seven crowns and two gold circlets, one studded with precious stones; three head-coverings with rubies and emeralds; a belt of gold; two *fleur de lis* brooches also of gold; four basins for washing her hands, two for washing her hair and four more for washing in general; a golden chalice; 'a very beautiful cross of gold'; a large bowl and a decorative ship for collecting alms; two goblets for her private chamber and another goblet made of gold; curtains and tapestries for her chapel embroidered with the arms of France and England; a gilded jug for holding holy water, also for her chapel; a gown of crimson velvet with a mulberry over-jacket, and another gown of red samite (a luxurious heavy silk fabric); fifteen sets of hangings for her bed; and many other splendid and costly items.[15] The list of Isabella's possessions was printed in the original French in the *English Historical Review* of 1897 by Walter E. Rhodes, who claims that Edward II gave Isabella's jewels from it to Piers Gaveston and that Isabella quarrelled with Edward over it, a statement found in no primary source. The idea that Edward gave his wife's jewels or her wedding gifts to Gaveston is often repeated, but it is simply untrue, and was invented by Agnes Strickland in the nineteenth century. She wrote that when Piers Gaveston was banished from England later in 1308, Edward gave him 'all the jewels of which he was possessed, even to the rings, brooches, buckles, and other trinkets, which his young and lovely consort had at various times presented to him as tokens of regard'. Strickland cites no source for this allegation, and was confused about the chronology of events early in Edward's reign, believing incorrectly that Gaveston was exiled to his native Gascony in 1308, which he was not. The story that Edward gave Isabella's jewels to Gaveston, and even that Gaveston wore them in front of her to hurt and humiliate her, is still frequently repeated in the twenty-first century, but is pure fabrication.

The *Annales Paulini*, the annals of St Paul's Cathedral in London, are the sole origin for the claim made by Strickland and many other writers since, but say merely that Edward, while still in Boulogne, sent his own presents given to him by his new father-in-law – warhorses, a bed or couch, a ring and other jewellery – to his regent, Gaveston, in England.[16] It is not stated that Edward intended Gaveston to keep the items, and it is certainly not stated that any of the items thus sent belonged to Isabella or even to Edward and Isabella jointly. As a woman, Isabella would not have received warhorses from her father, and there is no reason at all to think that her husband gave any of her possessions to Gaveston at this time or any other. The *Annales* use the word 'gave' (*dedit* in Latin) to describe what Philip IV did with the presents to Edward, and 'sent' (*misit*) to describe what Edward himself did with them; most probably it simply means that Edward sent his wedding gifts to his regent and closest friend in England to store safely for him, and even if he did give them to Gaveston to keep, they were his own possessions and he could do what he liked with them. From this rather unexciting situation has arisen the popular modern myth that Edward II gave away his wife's wedding presents or jewels to his lover and thus upset her right from the start, and that their marriage began disastrously. Isabella's own jewels and clothes are in fact itemised separately in the inventory cited above, travelled with her to England, and remained entirely in her possession. Far from seeing her own things given to her husband's lover, Isabella in fact almost certainly received a magnificent wedding gift from Edward: a gorgeous and richly illustrated manuscript, including a calendar, scenes from the Old Testament and the texts of the Psalms in Latin and Anglo-Norman, which still exists in a library in Munich and is now known as the Psalter of Queen Isabella.[17] Another psalter now called the Queen Mary Psalter, which two hundred years later belonged to Isabella and Edward's descendant Mary I (1516–58) – the only other English monarch beside Edward himself to have a Spanish parent – is also likely to have belonged to Isabella and was perhaps commissioned by her.

The royal couple left Boulogne on 2 February 1308, and spent several days in the port of Wissant in modern-day Belgium, from where they sailed to England on the 7th; the delay was presumably due to bad winter weather in the Channel or a lack of wind.[18] The *Vita Edwardi Secundi* (Life of Edward II), the most thorough, reliable and useful chronicle for the reign, written by a clerk in the king's service who knew Edward and Isabella well, says that 'the king and his wife joyfully returned to England', which certainly doesn't hint at any conflict between the couple at the start of their marriage and indeed indicates that they were happy together at this time.[19] At just twelve years old, Isabella was now alone and away from her family with the unconventional man she would have to live with for the rest of her life, as far as she knew, and had to travel to a country she had never set eyes on before which she would have to make her home. As though this was not challenging and stressful enough, she was about to step into a swirling maelstrom of conflict between her husband, infatuated with Piers Gaveston beyond sense and reason, and his barons; just seven months into his reign, Edward II was already about to bring his kingdom to the brink of civil war.

2

Three People in the Marriage
1308–1311

Isabella may have been sad to leave her homeland, but it was not the last time she would see it; she was to visit France again in 1313, 1314, 1320 and 1325/26. On Wednesday 7 February 1308, the king and new queen of England sailed to Dover, and arrived in the middle of the afternoon, when Isabella saw for the first time the country where she would live for the remaining fifty years of her life. Waiting for Edward and Isabella were a number of the English nobility, including the two of the king's three surviving sisters who lived in England – Mary, a nun, and Elizabeth, countess of Hereford – and Henry of Lancaster, the younger brother of Thomas, earl of Lancaster.[1] The Lancaster brothers were Edward's first cousins, sons of Edward I's brother Edmund, and were also Isabella's uncles, the younger half-brothers of her mother, Joan I of Navarre (all three of them were children of Blanche of Artois, queen of Navarre by her first marriage and countess of Lancaster by her second). England and the English court perhaps did not feel too alien to Isabella, as she had other relatives there, including her aunt the dowager queen and her second cousin the earl of Richmond, and the English court and elite spoke French, although of course the vast majority of the population did not. Whether or to what extent Isabella learnt English is unknown.

Another person waiting at Dover, and one perhaps far more unwelcome to Isabella, was Edward II's beloved Piers Gaveston, Gascon-born earl of Cornwall, regent of England during the king's absence in France, and new husband of Edward's thirteen-year-old niece Margaret de Clare. Gaveston himself was somewhat older than the twenty-three-year-old Edward, then probably in his mid- to late twenties, and although no physical likeness or description of him exists, one later chronicler called him 'graceful and agile in body, sharp-witted, refined in manners, sufficiently well versed in military matters'. Others called him 'haughty and supercilious' but also 'very magnificent, liberal and well-bred', 'very proud and haughty in bearing' and 'a man of big ideas, haughty and puffed-up'. Gaveston's haughtiness would seem to be a given, and Edward's adoration of him went to his head and led him to act as though he were of higher birth and rank than he actually was, which aggravated his contemporaries beyond endurance: 'Indeed the superciliousness which he affected would have been unbearable enough in a king's son.'[2] Gaveston was not, however, the son of a woman burned alive as a witch; this story, often repeated in fiction featuring him as a character, was first invented by the antiquarian John Stow at the end of the sixteenth century. Gaveston's mother, Claramonde de Marsan, was in fact a noblewoman who died a natural death in late 1286 or early 1287.[3] Nor is there any reason to suppose that Gaveston was the Goddess-worshipper he is often written as, or that he was anything but a pious Christian, as everyone else in England and France was at the time. Contrary to what some fourteenth-century chroniclers and other writers since have believed, Gaveston was not of low birth but a nobleman, and his father and grandfathers were among the leading barons of Béarn (one of the old provinces of France, in the Pyrenees in the far south-west of the country, bordering Spain). If he had been of such lowly position as many writers since the fourteenth century have imagined, Edward I would never have placed him in his son the future king's household as Edward's companion alongside, among others, the future earl of Hereford, one of the earl of Ulster's daughters, two of the earl of Warwick's grandchildren and the earl of Gloucester's nephew.[4]

As soon as Edward landed at Dover and saw Gaveston waiting for him, he threw himself upon him and hugged and kissed him. In the early fourteenth century, such behaviour did not necessarily imply lust or love as we in modern times would assume, as it was a tactile age where kissing was a common greeting among men. The problem for Edward's contemporaries was not so much that he kissed Gaveston, but that he ignored his other barons to do so and did not hug and kiss them as well.[5] Although a scene depicting Isabella's horror at the sight of her husband's love and sexual desire for another man is a staple of novels featuring her, she almost certainly didn't see the two men's reunion, as she and Edward came ashore separately: 'The king touched at Dover in his barge ... and the queen a little afterward touched here with certain ladies accompanying her.'[6] She was soon to learn at first hand, however, what a huge role the Gascon played in her husband's life.

Isabella's attitude to Piers Gaveston is difficult to determine, and of course it may have altered and developed over time. It is often assumed that she must have hated and resented him, but there is no real evidence for this. Although Isabella certainly loathed her husband's later and much more powerful favourite Hugh Despenser the Younger, it does not automatically follow that she loathed Gaveston as well; Gaveston and Despenser were very different men, and Despenser gave Isabella ample reasons to hate and resent him, which Gaveston did not. Other than the rather awkward fact that he (presumably) stood higher in Edward's affections and favour than Isabella herself, Gaveston offered her no insult and did not threaten her position as Despenser later did. A letter Isabella supposedly wrote to her father, Philip IV, in 1308 stating that her husband was 'an entire stranger to my bed', calling herself 'the most wretched of wives' and accusing Gaveston of alienating Edward's affection from her is often cited as evidence of her hostile feelings towards him, but this letter was invented by the chronicler Thomas Walsingham at the end of the fourteenth century. Walsingham had no access to the queen's private family correspondence, and the letter merely demonstrates how Walsingham, writing many decades later, thinks Isabella should or might have felt, rather than how she necessarily did. Although Walsingham also claimed that Gaveston taunted Isabella (as he did several of the English earls) and made her the target of his sarcasm, this is extremely unlikely and not backed up by contemporary evidence.[7] Gaveston enjoyed poking fun at the powerful and the pompous, but despite the generally unremitting hostility towards him of fourteenth-century chroniclers, two of them do point out his excellent manners, and although Edward II's tolerance of Gaveston and his foibles was almost limitless, for Gaveston to taunt his royally born queen would surely have been a step too far. At just twelve, Isabella may have been unaware of any sexual dimension to the relationship between her husband and the earl of Cornwall – assuming there was one – or known of it and, pious Christian that she was, been horrified by it. Alternatively, she may have felt that a man threatened her less than a female lover might have. Gaveston's father, Arnaud, had escaped from Philip IV's custody in the 1290s when Philip was legitimately holding him as a hostage, and Gaveston himself had fought in Edward I's 1297 campaign in Flanders against Philip, so Isabella may have borne a grudge towards Gaveston and his family on behalf of her father. We simply do not know how she felt. Only three fourteenth-century chroniclers claim that Isabella was harmed in any way by Gaveston's presence in her life, and two of them (the St Albans *Trokelowe* chronicle and the *Polychronicon* of Ranulph Higden, a monk of Chester) were written much later and may have confused Gaveston with Edward II's later favourite Despenser the Younger, who certainly did damage Isabella's relationship with her husband and her position as queen.[8] The third, the more contemporary Westminster chronicle *Flores Historiarum*, is hysterically anti-Edward

II – it frequently screeches about his 'insane stupidity' and his 'wicked fury', for example – and cannot be taken very seriously as a reliable source for the queen's feelings about her husband's lover (or close friend or adopted brother or whatever he was).

It is difficult to get a sense of Isabella's personality and feelings in these early years of her marriage. Barely past puberty or perhaps still pre-pubescent, she was too young to play any role in politics, too young to be Edward's wife in more than name only, and too young to begin a family. Her correspondence from this period does not survive, and English chroniclers generally took little notice of Isabella this early on; in fact, they took little notice of her at all until 1325. To the author of the *Vita Edwardi Secundi*, Isabella was notable mostly as the daughter of the king of France and the future mother of Edward II's successor. On 14 May 1308, three months and nine days after her arrival in England, Edward granted Isabella all the revenues from his county of Ponthieu in northern France, his inheritance from his mother, 'for her personal expenses', as he had promised her father on 24 January.[9] By fourteenth-century standards, this hardly seems a particularly undue or unusual delay in granting Isabella an income, and it seems a little unfair to use it as evidence of Edward's neglect of or callousness towards his young queen, as it sometimes has been by modern writers.[10] As Isabella's aunt Marguerite, Edward's stepmother, held the dower lands which normally would have been granted to the queen, alternative arrangements had to be made, and Edward later granted Isabella the county of Ponthieu outright. That she already in 1308, despite her youth, was allowed to exercise some influence over the king is demonstrated by several entries on the Patent Roll in this period, when various criminals were pardoned at her request and two justices were appointed also at her request in Hertfordshire.[11] Isabella has been described by one modern historian as 'a relentless intercessor' with Edward II, and certainly he allowed her to start becoming one almost immediately after her arrival in England.[12] On 16 August 1308, Isabella and Edward jointly appointed a proctor in their county of Ponthieu, and in 1308/09, Isabella also used her influence with the chancellor of England and the keepers of the king's great seal on a number of issues such as commissions of *oyer* and *terminer*, charters and overdue payments.[13]

On Sunday 25 February 1308, the coronation of Edward II and Isabella of France as king and queen of England took place at Westminster Abbey. His parents, Edward I and Eleanor of Castile, had also been crowned jointly, in August 1274, but Edward II and Isabella would be the last couple crowned together until Richard III and Anne Neville in 1483, as all the kings of England in between were single at the time of their coronations. Isabella's uncles Charles, count of Valois – father of the Valois dynasty which ruled France for more than two and a half centuries – and Louis, count of Evreux attended, as did the youngest of her three brothers, the future Charles IV of France, who in February 1308 was thirteen going on fourteen. Also present were Edward's sister Margaret and brother-in-law John II, duke and duchess of Brabant in the Low Countries; his other two surviving sisters, Mary and Elizabeth, and their young half-brothers, Thomas of Brotherton and Edmund of Woodstock; his first cousin Duke Arthur II of Brittany and Arthur's brother-in-law the count of St Pol; and Amadeus V, count of Savoy. Finally, there was Henry of Luxembourg, who shortly afterwards was elected king of Germany and Holy Roman Emperor and who was married to Duke John II of Brabant's sister Margaret. Henry's daughter Marie would marry Isabella's brother Charles in 1322, and his son John 'the Blind', king of Bohemia, would fall at the battle of Crécy, the great victory of Isabella and Edward II's son Edward III, in 1346.

No expense had been spared for the coronation (which Edward II, saddled with massive debts of £200,000 inherited from his father, was forced to pay for with loans from Italian bankers) and it should have been a splendid occasion, but ended up a complete fiasco. Controversially, Edward allowed Piers Gaveston to play a major role in events: the Gascon carried the royal crown and walked directly in front of the king and queen in the procession into Westminster Abbey: the prime position. Isabella, walking with her husband just behind Gaveston along a cloth strewn with flowers, both of the royal couple barefoot in the February cold in a display of Christian humility and piety, was forced to observe Edward's favourite wearing royal purple in stark contrast to the other English nobles, dressed more appropriately in cloth-of-gold. Astonished witnesses described Gaveston as 'so decked out that he more resembled the god Mars than an ordinary mortal' and said that he was 'more splendidly dressed than the king'.[14] The way from Westminster Palace, where fifteen temporary timber halls and a fountain supplying wine had been constructed for the occasion, to the abbey was so choked with crowds that the king and queen had to leave the palace by a back door. The crowds inside the abbey were also so great that a knight named John Bakewell was crushed to death.[15]

Piers Gaveston also played an important role in the coronation ceremony itself. Although Isabella's uncle Charles of Valois placed the boot and spur on Edward's right foot, and the king's cousin the earl of Pembroke placed his left boot on, it was Gaveston who attached the left spur, to the anger of many, as these duties were of profound ritual importance. Contemporaries were so shocked by Gaveston's prominent role in events and his and the king's behaviour that it took all their attention, and Isabella's participation in her own coronation went almost unnoticed. Things went from bad to worse at the banquet held afterwards in Westminster Hall, where Edward, Gaveston, Roger

Mortimer and more than 250 other men had been knighted in a mass ceremony twenty-one months before. The food arrived late, long after dark, and was badly cooked and close to inedible: a huge embarrassment for Piers Gaveston, who apparently had organised the occasion. The *Annales Paulini* say that at the banquet Edward preferred the company of Gaveston to Isabella, and although perhaps it is understandable that he preferred to talk to a man he had known well for many years than to a young girl he barely knew, it was extraordinarily discourteous of him to ignore his wife and queen in such a way. To add insult to injury, Edward had ordered beforehand that the walls of the hall be decorated with tapestries featuring his own royal coat-of-arms and Piers Gaveston's, but not the French arms in honour of Isabella. Although he had ordered the tapestries before he had even met his queen, and thus probably had not intended to upset her – his eleven- or twelve-year-old fiancée had surely been little more than an abstract notion in his mind at the time – it was a very obvious and visual sign of his infatuation with the Gascon and nothing less than a public insult to Isabella, her family and her native country. It also demonstrates that Edward at this time had little or no interest in the pubescent girl he had recently had to marry – at least until she grew older – and didn't care who knew it, and is also a sign of precisely whom Edward considered to be his true consort at this time. It is not at all surprising that Isabella's two uncles and brother who were there and forced to endure the offence were furious, and one of the English earls had to be physically restrained from assaulting Gaveston. It is unlikely, however, that Isabella's uncles walked out of the banquet, as has sometimes been stated, which would have been a gross insult to Edward himself and one which, despite his intense provocations, they surely felt unable to offer to the English king in his own kingdom and at his own coronation.[16] Isabella's uncles returned to France shortly afterwards and allegedly complained to her father about her treatment and Edward's behaviour, telling him that Edward favoured Piers's couch over Isabella's, though this is only recorded by the annalist of St Paul's Cathedral, who surely had no real way of knowing what the king of France's brothers had told him about his daughter and son-in-law in private.[17] Edward had, before his accession, been on close and very amicable terms with the count of Evreux, the youngest of the French royal brothers, but with his actions at the coronation he ruined all that goodwill, while Charles, count of Valois had been hostile to England since Philip IV went to war with Edward I in 1294. Edward II's relations with Isabella's brother the future Charles IV would prove far from friendly after Charles succeeded to the French throne fourteen years later, and Charles observing Edward's antics at the coronation surely cannot have helped his brother-in-law's opinion of him. Whether Edward was actively trying to insult the French at his coronation or whether he simply didn't care is unclear, but alienating his powerful father-in-law, the king of France, was foolish. Although we do not know how Isabella felt at this time, it seems highly probable that she was extremely hurt and upset at Edward's appallingly rude and tactless conduct, and also probable that she was left with few good memories of the ceremony which made her the crowned and anointed queen of England and which should have been the happiest day of her life.

Parliament met soon after the coronation, and almost all the English barons, led by Henry Lacy, earl of Lincoln, demanded that Piers Gaveston be exiled from England for the second time (Edward I had banished him from the kingdom on 30 April 1307, but died on 7 July and Edward II immediately recalled Gaveston and made him earl of Cornwall). The king refused to do any such thing, put his royal castles on a war footing and spent Easter preparing himself militarily for possible action against his own barons, while they did likewise. Just months into Edward's reign, civil war loomed because of the king's passion for his favourite and his excessive favouritism towards him. Isabella's aunt the dowager queen Marguerite joined the opposition to Gaveston, and sent them money, as did Marguerite's half-brother Philip IV; a newsletter of 14 May 1308 declared that the French king would regard as his mortal enemy anyone who supported Gaveston.[18] Edward retaliated by seizing some of Marguerite's castles, and although the king and his stepmother had been on cordial terms before his accession, it seems that Marguerite's opposition to Gaveston at this time destroyed their relationship and that Edward never forgave her. Marguerite withdrew from court and, although she and Isabella remained on good terms, for the remaining ten years of her life she played little role in the lives of her niece and stepson. Edward II politely continued to refer to Marguerite in public as 'the king's mother', but this was mere convention; he also called Philip IV his 'very dear and beloved lord and father' in correspondence, even though it is probable that he disliked Philip.

The attitude of Isabella herself at this time is, predictably, hard to determine. A letter written sometime between late February and late June 1308 by a monk of Westminster named Roger de Aldenham, which relates to Gaveston's meddling in the abbey's affairs and taking the side of the abbot against the prior in an internal dispute, suggests that Isabella and Henry Lacy might be persuaded to write to Philip IV of France, Pope Clement V and the cardinals about the abbey dispute on the grounds of their hatred of Piers.[19] Aldenham also suggested that the story of Gaveston's interference in abbey affairs should be related to the countess of Hereford (Edward II's sister Elizabeth) and other confidantes of the queen, who would then tell Isabella. It is interesting to note that at least one contemporary thought that Isabella hated Piers Gaveston, though whether he had a sound basis for this declaration or was projecting his own feelings of dislike onto her is unknown (and Aldenham a year later had completely changed his mind about Piers, describing him as a man of good conscience). There is no evidence that Isabella was ever actually involved in this incident.[20] It is unlikely that, whatever her feelings, Isabella was seen as some kind of leader of the opposition to Gaveston, as some modern historians have suggested; at twelve she was still far too young for a group of much older and more experienced magnates to view her as a leader, though she may of course have devoutly wished for Gaveston's removal from her life and Edward's side, and privately shown her support to the magnates determined to exile him, especially given the public humiliation of seeing Gaveston rather than herself treated as her husband's consort at her coronation banquet.[21]

Edward granted Isabella the revenues of Ponthieu on 14 May. Throughout his reign he paid almost all her expenses himself, and gave her a large household of close to 200 people, much larger than that of previous English queens. The identities of her ladies-in-waiting and eight or so damsels first survive from 1311/12, and then included her husband's eldest niece Eleanor de Clare, who may have begun attending the queen soon after her arrival in England. Eleanor was the daughter of Edward II's second eldest sister, Joan of Acre, countess of Gloucester (who had died in April 1307) and was born in October 1292. She was only eight and a half years younger than the king and about three years older than Isabella herself. Eleanor had been married to Hugh Despenser the Younger since May 1306, and their first child was born in about 1308/09; her younger sister Margaret had married Piers Gaveston five days after their grandfather Edward I's funeral the previous autumn, and their youngest sister, Elizabeth, would marry the earl of Ulster's son and heir later in 1308, in a wedding attended by their uncle the king and probably the queen. Hugh Despenser the Younger at this time, despite being the king's nephew-in-law, was little more than an impoverished knight aged twenty or so, and no one, least of all Isabella herself, could have guessed at the power he would come to wield in later years as the king's last and greatest favourite and perhaps lover. Despenser's father, Hugh Despenser the Elder, however, was one of the very few men who remained loyal to Edward II and Piers Gaveston in 1308, and would indeed remain totally loyal to Edward for the entirety of his reign: the only high-ranking English nobleman to do so.

In June 1308, Edward finally and reluctantly accepted that he had no choice but to exile Gaveston, though he ensured that his dearest friend left England in honour with a large financial gift, numerous lands in his native Gascony and England to make up for the revoked earldom of Cornwall, and an appointment as the king's lieutenant of Ireland. Gaveston and his young wife, Margaret de Clare, sailed for Dublin from Bristol on 28 June 1308, a distraught Edward II present to wave them off. The king would spend most of the following year conniving to get him back, expertly playing his barons off against one another and manipulating the pope, Clement V, by giving bribes of land and cash to his relatives, so that he would take the King's side. Some contemporaries, unable to comprehend the hold Piers Gaveston had over Edward, called the Gascon a sorcerer, and declared that there were two kings in England and that Edward worshipped Piers as a god.[22] Others believed that Edward and Gaveston were adoptive brothers, and indeed the *Vita Edwardi Secundi* says that Edward referred to 'my brother Piers' in speech. This was perhaps how Edward, unable to acknowledge Piers publicly as his lover or partner, presented their attachment to outsiders, or perhaps he truly did consider Gaveston his brother. The real nature of their relationship cannot be known, but that Edward adored and was passionately devoted to Gaveston is beyond all doubt. The *Annales Paulini* claimed that Edward 'loved an evil male sorcerer more than he did his wife, a most elegant lady and a very beautiful woman'. Even the sober and measured author of the *Vita* wrote that 'Piers was accounted a sorcerer', as Edward was 'incapable of moderate favour, and on account of Piers was said to forget himself'.[23]

During the year of Gaveston's exile, Isabella and Edward spent most of their time together. On 1 March 1309, Edward gave her a cash grant of £1,122 and six manors in Cheshire and north Wales, and in a letter to Philip IV of 4 March, told his father-in-law that Isabella was in good health and 'will, God be willing, be fruitful'. This may indicate that Edward and Isabella had begun regular marital relations, though as Isabella was still only thirteen, it is more likely to be simply a pious wish that God would grant them children in the future. On the same day, Edward granted his queen the payment of queen's gold in his earldom of Chester, backdated to the time of their wedding.[24] That Isabella had a certain amount of influence over him at this time is apparent from a number of entries in the chancery rolls detailing various grants and pardons made 'at the instance of Queen Isabella'.[25] Edward and Isabella spent almost all of the first four months of 1309 at Edward's favourite residence of Langley in Hertfordshire, later known as Kings Langley, where there was a delightful manor house and Spanish water gardens which he had inherited from his mother and where he kept a camel, a lion and other exotic animals.[26] In December 1308, the king founded a Dominican friary at Langley, which was closed down during the Dissolution of the Monasteries 230 years later, by Edward and Isabella's descendant Henry VIII; Edward, like his mother, was devoted to the Dominican order of friars, the Blackfriars, while Isabella herself preferred the Franciscans, the Greyfriars. Their grandson Edmund, duke of York was buried at Langley Priory in 1402, and so was, for a few years until his body was moved to Westminster Abbey, their great-grandson Richard II.

Edward was still scheming to bring Piers Gaveston back from Ireland, where he was excelling in his role as lord lieutenant. The king promised to address his barons' many grievances with his rule if they consented to Gaveston's return, and sent envoys to the pope, who lifted the sentence of threatened excommunication imposed on Gaveston by the archbishop of Canterbury in June 1308 if he ever set foot in England again. Almost exactly a year to the day after they had left, Gaveston and his wife, Margaret de Clare, returned to England, and Gaveston was restored to the earldom of Cornwall in parliament. Edward II was overjoyed; Isabella was presumably less so. Edward had built up a considerable amount of goodwill among many of his barons over the previous year, especially from his nephew Gilbert de Clare, earl of Gloucester, nephew-in-law John de Warenne, earl of Surrey and cousins the earls of Pembroke and Richmond, but foolishly allowed Gaveston to destroy it when the favourite began giving some of his fellow earls insulting nicknames. Edward's first cousin and Isabella's uncle, the powerful Thomas, earl of Lancaster was named the Churl or the Fiddler; Lancaster's ally and Gaveston's most dangerous enemy, Guy Beauchamp, earl of Warwick was called the Black Dog of Arden; the king's cousin Aymer de Valence, earl of Pembroke was Joseph the Jew; Edward's brother-in-law Ralph de Monthermer, formerly earl of Gloucester, the Whoreson; and the elderly and apparently stout earl of Lincoln, Sir Burst-Belly. Edward and Gaveston spent Christmas 1309 at Langley 'making up for former absence by their long wished-for sessions of daily and intimate conversation'.[27] Presumably Isabella and Margaret de Clare were also present, though the *Vita* does not mention them.

Edward II's reign staggered from one crisis to another, mostly thanks to his infatuation with, dependence on, and excessive favouritism towards Piers Gaveston. In March 1310, a coalition of eight of the eleven English earls, the archbishop of Canterbury, ten bishops and thirteen barons, who called themselves the Lords Ordainer and were exasperated beyond endurance with the king, declared that they would undertake vital reforms of his household and, for the first time, threatened him with deposition if he refused to consent to this.[28] Until he and Isabella had a child, Edward's heir was the elder of his two half-brothers, Thomas, the first son of Edward I and Queen Marguerite, who was born in June 1300. (His brother Edmund was born in August 1301.) It is unlikely that the Ordainers really intended to replace Edward with a boy of less than ten and unclear exactly how they could legally or otherwise have achieved this, but the king could not ignore the threat, which would be raised against him again and again during his turbulent reign. Edward II either could not, or would not, be the king his subjects needed and wanted him to be, and persisted throughout his reign in his unconventional and unregal behaviour, though he was also capable of standing on his royal dignity whenever he felt like it. Isabella, though she may have been equally frustrated with her husband and the way he behaved, was also threatened by the Ordainers' warning. A royalist to the core, she was surely as furious as Edward that mere barons would dare to threaten his throne, and of course Edward's deposition would deprive her of her queenship. Her opinion on kingship and ruling had been formed by her autocratic father, Philip IV, but Edward II was a very different kind of man and king. In 1309, Edward had been furious with Philip, who had gone behind his back and recognised Robert Bruce as king of Scots, while pretending to Edward that he had not. Edward sent Philip a letter which opens abruptly with the line, 'To the king of France, greetings.' He usually addressed Philip as 'the most excellent prince' and 'his beloved father' (*patri suo karissimo*) and sent him 'very dear affection', and his failure to follow the conventional style of address on this occasion indicates that he was positively seething with annoyance.[29]

In the autumn of 1310, Edward decided to lead a campaign in Scotland against Robert Bruce, who had had himself crowned king in 1306. Many of Bruce's family and supporters, including his wife Elizabeth, his daughter Marjorie, two of his sisters and the countess of Buchan, who had crowned him king, remained in captivity in England; Bruce's young nephew Donald, earl of Mar had also been imprisoned as a child in 1306 by Edward II's father, but at some point in or before 1309 joined Edward's household and for the entirety of his reign and afterwards proved himself one of the wayward king's most devoted supporters. Edward I had died on his way to campaign against Bruce in 1307, but Edward II, thanks mostly to the political turmoil in England caused by himself and Piers Gaveston, cancelled campaigns he intended to lead in Scotland in 1308 and 1309. This had given Bruce breathing space to consolidate his position, attack his enemies and gain many new allies. Edward II, who had been taught since childhood that the kings of England were rightful overlords of Scotland and that the Scottish kings owed him homage for their kingdom, was accused by the Ordainers in 1310 of 'losing' Scotland, and he knew that defeating Bruce would strengthen his own position and put his barons in their place.

Isabella accompanied Edward, and they spent almost the whole period from the beginning of November 1310 until the beginning of August 1311 in the port of Berwick-upon-Tweed, which then belonged to England. Only three of the English earls went on the campaign with Edward: Gaveston, the earl of Cornwall; the king's nephew-in-law John de Warenne, earl of Surrey; and Edward's nephew and Gaveston's brother-in-law Gilbert de Clare, earl of Gloucester. Gaveston's wife, Margaret de Clare, also went with them and she and Gaveston spent the winter at Roxburgh, and conceived a child in or around April 1311. On the royal couple's way north, the king's wardrobe account records a payment of £1 to a woman Edward drank with on the way – a large sum, a few months' or perhaps a year's wages for her.[30] This was entirely typical of Edward, who throughout his reign enjoyed the company of his lowborn subjects. His contemporaries, and perhaps Isabella herself, found this incomprehensible and shocking. On 20 November 1310, Edward gave Isabella £87 10s as the first instalment on a repayment of a £1,000 loan she had made to him: Edward had given the money to Blanche of Brittany 'in aid of marrying a certain daughter of hers'. Blanche was Edward's first cousin, a granddaughter of Henry III of England and the sister of Duke Arthur II of Brittany and John of Brittany, earl of Richmond, and was also (confusingly) the mother-in-law of Isabella's uncle Louis, count of Evreux. The money probably related to the wedding of her daughter Marie of Artois and John, marquis of Namur, who in about 1320 would become the parents of Blanche of Namur, later queen consort of Sweden and Norway. An anonymous letter of 25 November 1310 said that Edward and Isabella were both in good health, but that trouble was stirring in England in the king's absence, and that the Lords Ordainer had 'each gone to his own district, having privily arranged to return together; so many fear evil'.[31] Another anonymous letter of 4 April 1311 stated that Edward and Isabella were still in good health, but that a 'secret illness' was much troubling Piers Gaveston when he went to visit them at Berwick.[32] Both Isabella and Edward seem to have enjoyed fine health all their lives. Edward is only known to have been ill once in his life, when he came down with tertian fever (i.e. malaria) shortly before he turned ten, and all the outdoor exercise he enjoyed, such as swimming, rowing, digging ditches and thatching roofs, must have kept him fit. Isabella too had an excellent constitution: she outlived all her siblings by a few decades, surviving into her sixties, and also rarely suffered from serious illness as far as we know. She seems to have been a fan of healthy eating, as during their long sojourn in Berwick, she ordered many thousands of pieces of fruit for herself and her household, predominantly apples, pears and cherries.[33]

In early February 1311, Edward's regent in England, Henry de Lacy, earl of Lincoln died, and Edward sent his young nephew the earl of Gloucester, not yet twenty years old, south to take de Lacy's place.[34] The earl of Lincoln's heir was his son-in-law Thomas of Lancaster, Isabella's uncle and Edward's cousin, who already held the earldoms of Lancaster, Leicester and Derby and now inherited those of Lincoln and Salisbury as well. Thomas of Lancaster, with his five earldoms, was massively influential and wealthy with an income of £11,000 a year (the highest in the country and more than double Isabella's), and strongly opposed to his cousin the king and Piers Gaveston. Although he was Isabella's uncle, there is no evidence that the two were fond of each other – the queen's extant accounts of 1311/12 show that she only wrote to him once that year, at the same time as she wrote to several other earls – and Lancaster's prickly personality ensured that he had few friends among the English nobility. His relations with the young earl of Gloucester, the second-richest man in England behind Lancaster himself, were so bad that an anonymous letter writer of 14 April 1311 stated that he feared a riot when both men arrived in London.[35] Thomas of Lancaster had, at the start of Edward II's reign, supported his cousin, and before Edward's accession the two had been close friends, but an argument between them in late 1308 drove Lancaster into opposition to the king, a position he maintained for the rest of his life. The two cousins came to loathe each other.

In August 1311, Edward II paid £120 for three fine horses for Isabella, bought for her in Yarmouth from an Italian named Rufus de Piacenza.[36] While in Berwick, Isabella enjoyed the entertainment of her Fool, Michael, for whom she spent 4s 4d on shoes and other necessities, and took an interest in a young Scottish orphan named Thomelyn (a common nickname at the time for men and boys called Thomas). 'Moved by pity of heart', she gave him four ells of blanket cloth and a hanging for his bed, and at York on the way back south bought him an alphabet so that he could learn his letters. A little later, she had him sent to London to live with a woman named Agnes, wife of her organist John.[37] The young queen, pious and compassionate, gave a gift of cloth-of-gold to a man named Richard, a colleague of her confessor, for him to lay over the body of his late mother, and in early September 1311 sent a man to enquire after the health of her messenger John Moigne, who lay ill at St Albans.[38] Edward and Isabella received sad news in August 1311: Edward's little half-sister Eleanor, youngest child of Edward I and Marguerite of France and just five years old, had died. Edward paid £113 for the expenses of her burial at Beaulieu Abbey in Hampshire.[39] When Eleanor had been only four days old, on 8 May 1306, her almost sixty-seven-year-old father Edward I opened negotiations for her future marriage to Robert, son and heir of Othon IV, count of Burgundy (the Franche-Comté) and Mahaut, countess of Artois.[40] Robert was to die unmarried and childless in 1317, leaving as his heir to Burgundy and Artois his elder sister Joan, who was married to Isabella's second brother, Philip, count of Poitiers.

Isabella was attended during this period, or part of it, by her husband's niece Eleanor de Clare, Edward I's eldest granddaughter, who herself was of high enough rank to employ and be attended by her own chamberlain, John de Berkhamsted. Eleanor appears first on the list of Isabella's ladies-in-waiting, under the name *Domina Alianore la*

Despensere, Lady Alianore Despenser, her married name. In July 1311, the queen paid for ale for Eleanor's breakfast, and later that year had to make alternative arrangements for Eleanor's transportation when 'the lord Hugh le Despenser her husband stole away from her her sumpter-horses and other carriage'.[41] Other high-ranking attendants of the queen included Isabella's kinswoman Isabella, Lady Vescy, and Alice, titular countess of Buchan in her own right, who was married to Lady Vescy's brother Henry, Lord Beaumont. Isabella also had eight damsels, which was a social rank and referred to women who were either unmarried or married to men who were not knights, and had nothing to do with their age. One of them was Alice Leygrave, formerly Edward II's wet nurse, called 'the king's mother, who suckled him in his youth', and another was Alice's daughter Cecily.[42] As Alice had been old enough to act as the future king's wet nurse in the years 1284/85, she must have been decades older than the young queen. The other six damsels were Joan and Margaret de Villiers, who presumably were either another mother-daughter pair or sisters, Joan Launge, Mary de Sancto Martino, Joan de Falaise and Juliana Nauntel, and Isabella sometimes sent them away from court on her business. Four of the eight had pages to assist them. Isabella sometimes arranged the marriages of her damsels to male members of her household: Margaret de Villiers married Odin Bronard or Bureward, one of the queen's squires, and the couple received an extraordinarily generous gift of £300 from Isabella; Joan de Falaise was married to the queen's tailor John de Falaise; and Joan Launge was the wife of John Launge, Isabella's steward. In June 1311, Isabella gave John and Joan Launge a manor in Ponthieu for life.[43] Isabella's tailor John de Falaise employed a remarkable fifty workmen to stitch, make, repair, beat and clean Isabella's clothes, wall hangings and cloths. In the year 1311/12, John and his workmen made fifteen robes, four cloaks, six bodices, six hoods, a tunic of 'Tartarin cloth of Lucca' and thirty pairs of stockings for the queen. They also made a new curtain for her chapel, two hangings and a pillow for her bed, and two coverings of scarlet, a fine and expensive woollen cloth.[44]

Edward II's Scottish campaign of 1310/11 achieved precisely nothing, and he failed even to engage Robert Bruce in battle, let alone defeat him. The period may, however, have been a satisfactory time for Edward and Isabella personally. Isabella turned fifteen in late 1310 and thus was rapidly coming to an age when she and Edward could begin a full marriage, and she and the king spent ten months together almost entirely without Piers Gaveston's presence. Parliament opened in London on 8 August 1311, though Edward, knowing or guessing that the Lords Ordainer had something deeply unpleasant in store for him, left Berwick-upon-Tweed only on 31 July or 1 August and arrived late. The Ordainers had finished their reforms of their household and presented them to him at parliament. There were forty-one Ordinances, and they limited Edward's regal powers severely, dictating among many other things that he must not declare war or even leave the country without his barons' consent and that his great household officials must be appointed by themselves, not Edward. The one which caused the king the greatest consternation, however, was the twentieth, which demanded Piers Gaveston's exile from England yet again. This time, the Ordainers closed the loophole by which Edward had formerly appointed Gaveston lieutenant of Ireland, and banished him from all of Edward II's territories – that is England, Wales, Scotland, Ireland, Ponthieu and even Gaveston's native Gascony. Edward predictably refused to exile his beloved, and, despite the limitations they placed on his power, promised that he would abide by all the other Ordinances if the barons would only revoke this one. They refused, and back and forth it went for many weeks, Edward alternating between hurling angry threats and insults at his barons and attempting to bribe them with promises of favours if they revoked the twentieth Ordinance. Finally he had no other choice but to give in, and the Ordinances were published in the churchyard of St Paul's Cathedral on 27 September. Gaveston was ordered to leave England from Dover by 1 November 1311, and would once again lose his earldom of Cornwall. His wife, Margaret de Clare, Edward's niece and the earl of Gloucester's sister, was allowed to remain behind in England and given some lands for her sustenance; she was six or seven months pregnant. Gaveston in fact left England several days late, on 3 or 4 November. Edward II, apparently unable to bear yet another parting from the man he loved, was not there to see him off.

In mid-October 1311, Isabella went on pilgrimage to Canterbury to visit the shrine of St Thomas Becket, whom both she and Edward revered. Although the *Vita Edwardi Secundi* says that Edward joined her, looking at his itinerary, this seems improbable.[45] Isabella paid £4 6s 8d for a gold nugget as an offering to Becket's shrine; this is the only jewel or cloth she paid for herself during the entire fifth regnal year of her husband, 8 July 1311 to 7 July 1312, the rest being taken care of by Edward.[46] At this time, she sent a letter to her receiver of Ponthieu 'concerning the affairs of the earl of Cornwall'.[47] This may indicate that she had agreed to help Gaveston financially during his exile, and in her naming of him as the earl of Cornwall, a title which had been stripped from Gaveston, we may see some sympathy on her part for him – or perhaps it demonstrates her great relief to see him go. Some weeks later, at Christmas, Isabella paid 27s to have all the forty-one Ordinances transcribed for her, though to what purpose is unknown.[48] In late October and early November Edward gave Isabella Eltham, a palace in Kent which had been given to him in 1305 by his friend Anthony Bek, bishop of Durham, and the only Englishman in history to be appointed patriarch of Jerusalem (who had died earlier in 1311), and custody of two manors in Kent and lands in Lincolnshire. Perhaps this was his way of expressing his gratitude for her support of Gaveston, or it may be evidence of his growing affection for and interest in her as she matured: she turned sixteen in late 1311.[49] Isabella went to Eltham on or before 11 October, several weeks before Edward officially gave it to her, accompanied by Eleanor de Clare, Edward's eldest niece and Gaveston's sister-in-law. The queen wrote to Edward on 28 and 29 October, the first time 'with haste', and also to his nephew-in-law John de Warenne, earl of Surrey, one of his few remaining allies among the earls. She also sent letters to her lady-in-waiting Isabella, Lady Vescy, a kinswoman of both herself and the king whom both Edward I and Edward II had appointed custodian of Bamburgh Castle in Northumberland; and to her father, Philip IV; her brothers Louis, Philip and Charles; her uncles the counts of Valois and Evreux; and to 'various other magnates and ladies' in France, unnamed. Her father also sent letters to her, and Isabella paid for the rental of beds and for firewood and transport for his messenger. While at Eltham, Isabella went hunting – she owned eight greyhounds – and spent 20*d* having her bathtubs repaired.[50] In October 1311, Edward granted her the wardship of the thirteen- or fourteen-year-old Thomas Wake, heir to the barony of Wake and to lands in four counties, whose father, John, had recently died; this meant that she would receive the income of the Wake lands until Thomas came of age at twenty-one.[51] Piers Gaveston, meanwhile, seems to have gone to Flanders, though this is uncertain and some of the Ordainers believed, rightly or wrongly, that he had not left England and sent men to the West Country to search for him.[52]

The Ordainers ordered the removal of other members of Edward's household in case they stirred him up to recall Gaveston once more.[53] Edward didn't need anyone to encourage him to do that; he was almost certainly already planning to bring Gaveston back, although it is extremely unlikely that Gaveston had already returned to England by Christmas and spent the festive season with the king, as several fourteenth-century chroniclers claim.[54] For the king to bring Gaveston back could hardly have been more foolish politically, yet Edward was desperate for him and evidently felt that he could not live without him. The *Vita* also states wrongly that Edward spent Christmas with Gaveston in York, but the king's itinerary and the queen's accounts show that he and Isabella were at Westminster, and that he borrowed 100*s* (£5) from her to play dice, a tradition of his on Christmas Eve or Christmas night.[55] During the festive period, Isabella sent gifts both to the 'countess of Cornwall' at Wallingford, who was her niece-in-law and Gaveston's wife, Margaret de Clare; and to Margaret's aunt, confusingly also called Margaret de Clare, the dowager countess of Cornwall.[56] Isabella wrote to the 'lady de Mortimer', who was probably either Joan

Geneville, wife of Isabella's future favourite Roger Mortimer, lord of Wigmore, or Roger's mother, Margaret Fiennes, and sent gifts of venison and cheese to Isabella, Lady Vescy.[57]

Edward left Westminster for Windsor just before New Year, and the queen had arrived at Windsor by 4 January. The royal couple exchanged gifts on 1 January, the Feast of the Circumcision, as was the custom at Edward's court: Isabella gave her husband unspecified 'precious objects', sent from Westminster to Windsor with her clerk William Boudon.[58] The king left his wife behind in the south of England temporarily, and, collecting his heavily pregnant niece, Margaret de Clare, from Wallingford Castle, rode very fast to Yorkshire at the beginning of January 1312. Piers Gaveston had, yet again, returned to England.[59]

3

An Heir is Born

1312–1314

Edward II met Piers Gaveston at Knaresborough, near Harrogate in Yorkshire, on or before 13 January 1312, having made the decision to meet him safely out of the way of the Lords Ordainer, who remained in the south of England. Gaveston's wife, Margaret de Clare, gave birth to their daughter Joan, named after Margaret's mother and Edward II's sister Joan of Acre, on or about 12 January in York, and Edward and Gaveston rushed from Knaresborough to York the following day to see them. It is possible that Gaveston had only intended to slip into England for a while to see his wife and newborn child, but Edward, who refused even to try to live without Gaveston's constant presence in his life, whatever the consequences, took that decision out of his hands and revoked his exile, restored him to the earldom of Cornwall and declared him 'good and loyal'.[1] The Ordainers were furious when they heard and cut off money to the king from the exchequer, so that Edward supposedly had to plunder towns and the countryside for sustenance and resources.[2] Isabella's reaction to the news, the third time that Piers Gaveston had returned to England from exile in four and a half years, is not recorded. She celebrated the feast of Candlemas, or the 'Purification of the Blessed Mary' as it was called in her Household Book, on 2 February 1312, and had her tailor John de Falaise make fifty gold knots 'to be fastened to the cloak of the queen's robe' for the occasion.[3] From the south, she sent her husband in York letters on an unrecorded date, and began making her way north to join him on or just before 7 February. Her journey took her through Newport Pagnell, Leicester, Nottingham, Doncaster and Pontefract.[4] Edward sent Isabella the expenses for herself and her retinue on the trip north on 10 February.[5] The queen kept in touch via letter with the earls of Gloucester, Hereford, Lancaster, Surrey and Pembroke, all of whom, except Surrey, were Ordainers, and also wrote to the countess of Pembroke, her fellow Frenchwoman Beatrice de Clermont-Nesle; she may have been attempting to maintain at least some kind of cordial relations between her husband and his furious earls, who gathered at St Paul's in London to discuss what should be done about Gaveston. Despite Isabella's efforts, five English earls – Lancaster, Warwick, Hereford, Pembroke and Arundel – bound themselves by oath to capture the royal favourite.[6] Isabella also wrote to her aunt the dowager queen Marguerite at her castle of Berkhamsted and to the king's sister Mary, a nun at Amesbury Priory in Wiltshire, perhaps to keep them informed about the current dire situation.

Isabella made her way north far more slowly than Edward had done, and her 200-mile journey took her more than two weeks at an average of about thirteen miles a day, a reminder of how painfully slow travel could be in the early fourteenth century, especially in winter. She kept in regular contact with Edward via her messenger John Moigne, and sent him a gift of a basket of lampreys.[7] The queen had reached Bishopthorpe, three miles south of York, on 21 February, and probably arrived in the city where Edward was still staying that day or the next; she was certainly there by the 24th.[8] She just missed the huge feast paid for by Edward to celebrate the birth of his great-niece Joan Gaveston, which took place on 20 February and cost the king forty marks (£26) for the minstrels alone, though may have seen Guillelmus, a minstrel sent to Edward by Isabella's eldest brother Louis, king of Navarre and count of Champagne, who performed for Edward and perhaps also herself on 23 February. In early March, Isabella and Edward received the news of the birth of the queen's niece Joan of Navarre, first and only child of Louis and his wife Marguerite, one of the daughters of Duke Robert II of Burgundy and Agnes of France, Saint Louis IX's youngest daughter. Queen Marguerite sent her usher Jeannot de Samoys to inform the king and queen of England of her daughter's birth.[9] Joan was born on 28 January 1312 and would become Queen Joan II of Navarre in 1328, having been passed over for the throne of France in favour of her two uncles Philip and Charles and their cousin Philip of Valois.

Isabella and Edward II's first child, Edward III, was born on 13 November 1312, which would place his conception very soon after the queen arrived in York (13 November minus thirty-eight weeks in a leap year is 21 February). Just over four years had passed since the couple's wedding, and Isabella was now sixteen and, evidently, fully mature and fertile. Edward II, from late 1311 onwards, demonstrated far greater interest in her than previously, now that she was old enough to be his partner in more than name only; she became his lover, his helpmeet and his loyal supporter, and Edward responded with affection, generosity and trust. Numerous books, films and online articles of the late twentieth and twenty-first centuries claim that someone other than Edward II was Edward III's real father, which is absolute nonsense with not a shred of evidence to support it. The king and queen were certainly together at the right time to conceive their son, and it is stretching credulity much too far to suggest that the young queen might have taken a lover without her husband or anyone else noticing. She had a household of close to 200 people and probably never spent a moment of her life alone. It is true that she had some kind of relationship with the baron Roger Mortimer much later, but this only began in late 1325, thirteen years after the birth of her eldest child and half a decade after the conception of her youngest, and when she and Mortimer were in France and beyond Edward II's influence. Mortimer was in Ireland in 1312 and in later years, and cannot possibly have been the father of Edward III or of any of Isabella's other children, being several hundred miles away from her when all of them were conceived.[10]

The notion that another man was Edward III's father is based solely on modern assumptions about Edward II's sexuality: that his love for men necessarily means that he must have been incapable of performing with women. Yet as we see from the existence of Edward's illegitimate son Adam, rumours of an affair with Eleanor de Clare, and a chronicle and poem written in his own lifetime which state that he loved Isabella, he was not at all averse to intimacy and relationships with women and none of his contemporaries said that he was. Fourteenth-century chroniclers and the many barons and bishops who forced Edward II to abdicate his throne to Edward III in 1327 were in no doubt whatsoever that the young king really was the son of the old king. In 1337, Edward III claimed the French throne from his mother's cousin Philip VI and began the Hundred Years War against France; Philip and the French would have loved nothing more than to be able to demonstrate that he was not the son of a king and merely the child of Isabella's lover, and thus discredit him and his claims entirely, but, as with the English barons who were happy to replace Edward II with his son on the English throne, there is not the slightest hint that such a notion ever crossed their minds. Had there been even the merest hint of gossip that Edward III was not Edward II's son, it would have eagerly been seized upon by the young king's enemies. There was not: the idea that anyone other than Edward II was the father of Isabella's eldest son was first invented in a novel published in 1985, 673 years later, and was popularised by the 1995 Hollywood film *Braveheart*, which impossibly makes William Wallace (executed in August 1305) the father of Isabella's child. The 1985 novel changes Edward III's date of birth by eight months, from November 1312 to March 1312, in order to accommodate the fiction that his real father was Roger Mortimer, though in fact this would still be impossible as Mortimer was also in Ireland nine months before March 1312, and

Isabella was with Edward in Berwick-upon-Tweed.[11] Other novels of the early twenty-first century and online articles have claimed that Edward III's real father was his grandfather Edward I, who died in July 1307 more than five years before the child was born and who never even met Isabella, or else that the father was an unnamed Scotsman, on the curious grounds that Isabella had been abandoned by her husband in Scotland at the time of her son's conception. Her own accounts and Edward II's itinerary prove conclusively that both of them were in York in February/March 1312, more than 100 miles from the Scottish border. Isabella in fact never set foot in Scotland, not counting the port of Berwick-upon-Tweed, which Robert Bruce, king of Scots, seized from Edward II in 1318 but was still in English hands when she stayed there.[12]

Although Edward and Isabella only had four children together – in contrast to Edward's parents who had at least fourteen or their son Edward III who had a dozen children with his queen, Philippa of Hainault – his grandparents Henry III and Eleanor of Provence had five children, of whom one died young, so a comparatively small number of offspring was not unprecedented in Edward's close family.[13] Isabella's brother Louis had only two children, and two of the four of Edward's sisters who married had one child and two children respectively. Edward and Isabella's elder daughter, Eleanor, also had only two children. Isabella apparently suffered a miscarriage in 1313 and may have had others, and either she or Edward II may not have been particularly fertile. The number of Edward and Isabella's children says little about the nature of their relationship or their sex life. Something of their feelings towards each other, however, is demonstrated by their conceiving their eldest child during Lent (Easter Sunday fell on 26 March in 1312), when intercourse was forbidden by the Church. This prohibition, for all that they were both pious and devout Christians, did not stop them sleeping together. Neither did Edward's relationship with Piers Gaveston impede his relationship with Isabella, nor that of Gaveston and his wife, Margaret, as both couples produced children in 1312.

Isabella's attitude towards royal children and paternity is demonstrated on two occasions. In 1314 when staying at her father's court, she almost certainly revealed to him that two of her brothers' wives were committing adultery, out of fear and anger that they would become pregnant by their lovers and endanger the French royal line. In 1329, when her son Edward III had to pay homage for his French territories to her cousin Philip VI, son of her uncle Charles, count of Valois and the first Valois king of France, she declared passionately, 'My son, who is the son of a king, will never do homage to the son of a count.'[14] Isabella's sense of royalty and her belief in the sanctity of royal descent was profound. She was not a woman who was even remotely likely to impose a non-royal child onto a throne, or a woman who would see anything but insult in the popular modern notion that she took a lover who fathered her eldest child, the king of England.

The king and queen remained in York together for most of the period until 5 April, though Edward made a brief trip to Scarborough for four days at the end of February, probably to check on the state of the castle, which he intended to provide a possible bolthole for Piers Gaveston should it come to that (as it did). Isabella, as she always did when they were separated, sent Edward letters via her messengers John de Noyun and William Bale; she wrote to him no fewer than three times during the four days they were apart.[15] On 5 April, Edward and Gaveston made their way north to Newcastle, leaving Isabella to follow more slowly behind them with her household. While in York, she gave cloths of gold to the church of the Franciscans (the Greyfriars or Friars Minor), her favourite order – decades later she would be buried in a Franciscan church – and to the abbey of St Mary.[16] Travelling through Thirsk and Darlington, Isabella rejoined her husband in Newcastle on or shortly after 22 April. No sooner had she arrived than she sent her squire John Nauntel (presumably the husband or a relative of her damsel Juliana Nauntel) back to York 'to look for certain secret things pertaining to the chamber of the said queen' which she had left behind there.[17] Isabella only stayed in Newcastle for some days, however, and soon moved on the nine miles to Tynemouth Priory. This may have been because Piers Gaveston was ill again – Edward paid two men ten marks each on 26 April for looking after him[18] – and because Isabella and Edward now knew that she was pregnant and wanted to keep her out of the way of any possible infection. The queen wrote to her father, Philip IV, and 'various other magnates of parts across the sea' on 27 April, which seems likely to be an announcement to her family and others of the happy news of her two-month pregnancy.[19] On Edward II's twenty-eighth birthday, 25 April 1312, he borrowed £40 from his friend, the wealthy Genoese merchant Antonio di Pessagno, to buy 'large white pearls' for Isabella, almost certainly his reaction to hearing the joyous news that his queen was expecting their child.[20] Indeed, both king and queen must have been delighted. Edward, however, was still so infatuated with Gaveston and determined to keep him safe whatever the cost that he had offered to recognise Robert Bruce as king of Scotland if Bruce agreed to shelter Gaveston in his kingdom: a truly extraordinary offer. An astonished Bruce declared that no trust could be put in the promises of a man as fickle as Edward, and refused.[21] Gaveston had by this point been excommunicated by the archbishop of Canterbury, Robert Winchelsey, an Ordainer and one of his most intractable enemies, because of his unlawful return to England.[22]

On 3 May, Edward and Piers Gaveston heard of the imminent arrival of one of their most dangerous enemies, Thomas, earl of Lancaster, the king's cousin and the queen's uncle. He had stealthily been making his way north, intending to seize and capture Gaveston, holding jousting tournaments along the way as a cover for assembling armed men.[23] His arrival took the king completely by surprise, and he and Gaveston fled to Tynemouth where they joined Isabella, escaping the earl by only a few hours. Lancaster seized their baggage train, though Edward recovered all his possessions, which included 'four silver forks for eating pears' and numerous horses, jewels and other precious items, a few months later.

The king and Gaveston were soon forced to leave Tynemouth and make for Scarborough in extreme haste, and their flight on this occasion has led to one of the most famous, or infamous, and often repeated stories about Edward II and Isabella: that Edward callously left her behind weeping at Tynemouth, unconcerned with her fate and interested only in protecting Gaveston, despite her pleas to him not to leave her. This story appears only in the *Trokelowe* chronicle written many years later and 270 miles away in St Albans, and the chronicler confused events in 1312 with another occasion when Isabella was in Tynemouth ten years later, and that time truly in danger of capture by the army of Robert Bruce (who was nowhere near the town in May 1312).[24] Isabella's extant household account shows that she also left Tynemouth on 5 May, and may even have sailed with Edward and Gaveston in their boat down the coast to Scarborough, a journey which took them five days and must have been cold and miserably uncomfortable. It is more likely, though, that Isabella travelled by land, deeming a journey on the bleak and chilly North Sea too risky and unpleasant given that she was in the first trimester of pregnancy. Members of her household certainly travelled by land to York, via Darlington (where they stayed on 11 May) and Ripon, twenty-five miles from York, which they passed through on the 12th. Most of Edward's own household, bar a handful of attendants he took with him, also left Tynemouth by land. Edward arrived in Scarborough on 10 May after a long sea journey, and left Gaveston in the castle there. The king then set out for York and arrived in the city on the 14th, having first made a brief visit to Gaveston's castle of Knaresborough, where most of his household had arrived several days before he did and were waiting for him. Far from Edward abandoning the tearful queen, they either travelled together from Tynemouth to Scarborough to York, or met in York only nine or so days after they had separated. Edward gave the controller of Isabella's household £20 on 16 May for the expenses of her journey, and her damsels, who had travelled by land with the rest of her servants, received 20*d* for the expenses of their own journey and that of their 'equipment' some weeks later.[25] It is absolutely clear that Isabella was not left behind, pregnant and weeping, at Tynemouth by a husband who had little concern for her welfare, and she left the town in such a hurry that some of her own possessions were left behind, as Edward's were, at 'Les Sheles' or South Shields, under the guard of four men.[26] Certainly, Edward and Isabella's arrival in York at almost exactly the same time means that it must have been well-planned and arranged.

The *Trokelowe* chronicle also claims that Isabella's uncle the earl of Lancaster sent her a letter promising her he would rid her of Gaveston's presence, but if he did so she ignored it and clung to her husband.[27] Even if she had remained in Tynemouth, she was in no physical danger from her uncle Lancaster or the other enemies of Gaveston. It seems clear that the St Albans chronicler confused events of 1312 with those of 1322, when Isabella did feel that she had been abandoned to danger at Tynemouth during a Scottish invasion of England and blamed, not Edward II himself, but his then favourite Hugh Despenser the Younger; the furious queen was to raise the issue against Despenser several times and took revenge for this and other humiliations she felt he had inflicted on her as soon as she was able. No northern chronicle even hints that Edward abandoned Isabella in tears in 1312, nor does the *Vita*, written by a clerk in Edward's service, nor Adam Murimuth who was also a clerk in Edward's service and wrote a chronicle, nor the writer of the Westminster chronicle *Flores Historiarum*, who loved Isabella and loathed Edward and seized every opportunity to criticise him. Although an earlier generation of writers accepted the story, and it is still sometimes found in books written by non-specialists and in novels, historians of the fourteenth century in more recent times have pointed out that the story is certainly untrue. Edward II's academic biographer Professor Seymour Phillips, for example, says firmly that 'the pregnant Isabella was not abandoned at Tynemouth', and the editors of her 1311/12 household book say, 'The story that Edward abandoned Isabella seems to be a most unlikely one,' and that the queen's household book 'gives us no support for any part of this story'.[28] There is absolutely no reason to accept the tale, and not a shred of evidence that Isabella was angry with Edward for supposedly abandoning her at such a vulnerable time, or that she wished to stay away from him; quite the opposite, though to be married to a king forced to skulk in a distant part of his kingdom and to flee in haste from one of his own subjects can hardly have given her much cause for pride and contentment. It would be most peculiar if Edward, having given Isabella a gift of expensive pearls only a few days earlier most probably because he had just heard the news of her pregnancy, would have carelessly abandoned her, weeping, to danger, and the story can be dismissed as the confusion of one later chronicler. It is unfortunate that is has so often been repeated in novels and non-fiction, and thus given an entirely false impression of Edward and Isabella's relationship. Humiliating though it surely was to be the consort of a king who had allowed himself to be manoeuvred into such a disastrous position and who felt himself in danger in his own kingdom from several of his subjects, there is no doubt that Isabella staunchly supported Edward in 1312.

On the day Edward II left Piers Gaveston at Scarborough Castle, 10 May 1312, four men arrived to besiege Gaveston there: the northern lords Henry Percy and Robert Clifford, and Edward's cousin Aymer de Valence, earl of Pembroke and his nephew-in-law John de Warenne, earl of Surrey. Both earls had formerly been close allies of the king and of Gaveston, but the royal favourite's unlawful return from his latest exile pushed them into opposition. With little other choice, trapped in a castle with few provisions, Gaveston surrendered to them nine days later. It was arranged on 28 May that the earl of Pembroke would take him south to Gaveston's own castle of Wallingford, and that his fate would be decided at the next sitting of parliament.

On 9 June 1312, the king and queen sailed along the River Ouse from York to Howden, past Selby; four boats carried Isabella, her damsels and squires and some of her possessions. In early summer, this may have been a warm and pleasant interlude for the royal couple, though Edward shortly afterwards wrote to Isabella's father, Philip IV, petulantly declaring that he was 'grievously annoyed' with his subjects.[29] On the same day 140 miles to the south, the earl of Pembroke and Piers Gaveston reached the Oxfordshire town of Deddington, only thirty miles short of Gaveston's castle of Wallingford, and Pembroke left Gaveston under guard there overnight while he went to visit his wife nearby. Gaveston was awoken the next morning by shouting: Guy Beauchamp, earl of Warwick, the enemy he had mocked as the Black Dog of Arden, had arrived with a large crowd of armed men and surrounded the priory where he was sleeping. They seized Gaveston, ripped the belt of knighthood from him, and forced him to walk barefoot and bareheaded through jeering crowds to Warwick Castle, nearly thirty miles away, finally allowing him to ride a horse to speed the rest of his journey. He was cast into a dungeon while the earl of Warwick waited for his allies Thomas, earl of Lancaster; Edward II's brother-in-law Humphrey de Bohun, earl of Hereford; and the earl of Surrey's brother-in-law Edmund Fitzalan, earl of Arundel to arrive and decide his fate. The earl of Pembroke, meanwhile, who had sworn an oath to protect Gaveston, tried desperately to persuade anyone he could to help the Gascon, but Edward II was far out of reach in Yorkshire and his nephew, Gaveston's own brother-in-law the earl of Gloucester, refused to help, even though Pembroke 'beseech[ed] him with tears' to restore Gaveston to him or he would lose his lands as per the oath he had sworn. Evidently even Gloucester was sick of Gaveston by now, and told Pembroke that the earl of Warwick 'did this with our aid and counsel'.[30]

On 19 June, one of the earl of Warwick's servants insolently told

Gaveston, 'Look to yourself, my lord, for today you will die the death.'[31] The earls had every intention of killing Gaveston; if they did not and merely exiled him, Edward would simply recall him and the whole cycle would begin again. When it came to the deed itself, the earl of Warwick lost his nerve and stayed in his castle, while the earls of Lancaster, Hereford and Arundel took Gaveston two miles along the road to Kenilworth until they reached Blacklow Hill, which lay in the vast territories of the earl of Lancaster. In the road, a Welsh man-at-arms ran Gaveston through with a sword, and cut off his head as he lay dying on the ground. The earls returned to Warwick Castle and simply left Gaveston's body where it had fallen, and it was found by a group of Dominican friars from Oxford, probably because someone had sent for them (the Dominicans were Edward II's favourite order, and in return supported him staunchly). The friars took Gaveston's remains the forty miles to their house in Oxford and embalmed him, though could not bury him in consecrated ground, as he had died excommunicate. Various precious jewels were found on Gaveston's body, including a diamond 'of great value' and an enormous ruby set in gold, worth £1,000 and a gift to him from Edward II.[32] Gaveston left his eighteen-year-old royal widow, Margaret de Clare, and their five-month-old daughter, Joan, who was his only legitimate child and heir and whom Edward II later betrothed to the earl of Ulster's eldest grandson. Joan Gaveston was fated to die on 13 January 1325, probably the day after her thirteenth birthday, and before her wedding could go ahead. Like Edward II himself, Piers Gaveston had also fathered an illegitimate child, Amie, about whom little is known except that she joined the household of Isabella's daughter-in-law Queen Philippa and had at least one child.

On the day of Piers Gaveston's death, Isabella, now about four months pregnant, was with Edward II at the royal manor of Burstwick near Hull.[33] Edward received the news of Gaveston's murder on 26 June after the couple had returned to York, a week after it happened, though who told him is unknown; perhaps the earl of Pembroke sent a messenger, or the Dominican friars who took care of Gaveston's body. A flurry of activity in the chancery rolls on 26 June demonstrates that Edward had just heard the news: he granted custody of Gaveston's castles at Wallingford, Knaresborough and Tickhill to three of his (Gaveston's) retainers, asked the mayor of London 'to take the city into the king's hands without delay and to guard it for the king's use' and to have the Tower of London fortified, and ordered the Ordainer William Martin to send 1,200 marks he had seized from one of Gaveston's servants to the earl of Pembroke. Pembroke was then to bring the money immediately to Edward.[34]

How Isabella reacted to Piers Gaveston's death cannot be known. Whatever her private feelings might have been, it is unthinkable that she would have gloated to Edward about the death of his beloved, and we can probably assume that she did her best to comfort him and expressed her sympathy and support. If nothing else, she knew that Edward would never forgive her if she openly demonstrated any pleasure at the killing. It goes without saying that she had nothing to do with Gaveston's death, and though it may not have been unwelcome to her, she had spent much time in Gaveston's company in the last few months and years and there is no evidence that she had protested about this or found it objectionable. As for Edward himself, his primary reaction to Gaveston's murder was utter rage. Distraught and bereft, deprived of the man he had known and trusted for half his life and whom he adored, he vowed revenge on the perpetrators, especially on his cousin Thomas, earl of Lancaster, whom he later came to hold chiefly responsible. The *Scalacronica* chronicle comments on the 'mortal hatred, which endured forever' between the king and the earl, and Edward finally gained his long-desired revenge on Lancaster ten years later when he had him executed.[35] For all of Piers Gaveston's superciliousness, haughtiness and talent for aggravating the barons beyond bearing, he had done nothing which merited the death penalty. He had been stripped of his earldom of Cornwall, and although Edward II had restored the title to him in January 1312, it is not clear if legally Gaveston was the earl of Cornwall at the time of his death; if he was, he was the first English earl to be executed since Waltheof was beheaded by William the Conqueror in 1076 (though Edward I had the Scottish earl of Atholl hanged in London in 1306). Gaveston's murder achieved little but open the door for other men, royal favourites, who would prove to be far more malign, and ensured a rift between the king and many of his barons which would never heal.

Edward II left York for London on 28 June 1312, two days after hearing of Gaveston's death, to hold his capital city against his enemies and to meet his trusted advisers to discuss the next course of action. He told Isabella to remain behind in York, to keep her out of the way of possible danger as the country teetered once again on the brink of civil war, but left her a gift of three golden brooches with rubies and emeralds, worth a total of £40.[36] She sent him a letter the day after his departure. During her stay in York, the queen remembered young Thomelyn, the Scottish orphan she had looked after in 1311 who was now living in London, and paid for 'little necessities' for him, including a plaster for a scab on his head.[37] The king arrived in London on 14 July and stayed at the house of the Dominican friars, where he made an impassioned speech condemning the way that some of his barons were behaving towards him, and asking the Londoners to keep the city closed to Gaveston's killers. Although London in the Middle Ages tended to be anti-royalist, the citizens agreed to do the king's bidding for once, and closed the city gates. The earls of Lancaster, Hereford and Warwick threateningly took an army to Ware in Hertfordshire, twenty miles from the city, and Edward forbade them from approaching him 'with horses and arms and a great body of armed men', as he had heard they were about to do.[38]

The situation did not, however, result in war, as close as it must have seemed to a fearful population in the summer and early autumn of 1312. Gilbert de Clare, earl of Gloucester, although he had refused to help Piers Gaveston in captivity at Warwick Castle, agreed to negotiate between Edward and the earls of Lancaster, Warwick and Hereford. Although Gloucester was still only at the beginning of his twenties in 1312, as the eldest grandchild of Edward I and scion of the ancient noble house of Clare he commanded a great deal of respect and esteem among the English barons, and his negotiations helped to calm matters considerably. Even so, as late as the end of September and beginning of October 1312, Edward II raised 1,000 foot soldiers in Kent and Sussex and refused to allow the barons' negotiators to stay in or even pass through London. He did, however, find some time to relax while in Canterbury in mid-August, and gave 3s to an Italian performer for 'making his minstrelsy with snakes in the presence of the king'.[39] John of Brittany, earl of Richmond, who was a first cousin of Edward and a second cousin of Isabella – he was a grandson of Henry III of England and a great-grandson of Theobald I of Navarre – also joined the negotiating team on the king's side. Isabella's father, Philip IV, sent his half-brother Louis, count of Evreux to help, and Pope Clement V sent his chamberlain Arnaud d'Aux, bishop of Poitiers, and Cardinal Arnaud Nouvel, priest of St Prisca. The baron Hugh Despenser the Elder, who despite being the widower of the earl of Warwick's sister always supported the king and was opposed to his brother-in-law politically, was also among those involved in proceedings on the king's side and one of Edward's most trusted advisers. Finally, a few days before Christmas 1312, the long negotiations bore fruit, and Edward II signed a peace treaty with the earls of Lancaster, Warwick and Hereford (the earl of Arundel, though seemingly present at Warwick Castle and at Gaveston's murder, is curiously not mentioned in the ongoing process afterwards). The earls were to make obeisance to Edward in his great hall at Westminster, 'with great humility, on their knees', and humbly beg him to forgive them and 'receive them into his good will'. The goods the earl of Lancaster had seized at Tynemouth were to be returned to Edward on 13 January 1313, though in fact he didn't receive them until 23 February.[40]

Edward sent an escort north for Isabella in late July 1312, evidently judging the situation to be safe enough by now for her to rejoin him. She travelled very slowly because of her pregnancy, and the couple were reunited in early September. Isabella dined with her uncle Louis of Evreux on 15 September, then retired to Windsor Castle.[41] She was accompanied by her husband, whose itinerary shows that he travelled to Windsor from Westminster on 17 September 1312 and stayed there with Isabella for almost the entire period until the end of November, bar a short return trip to Westminster at the end of October.[42] Rather curiously, on 9 November Edward took himself off to his palace of Sheen, twenty miles away. He returned to Windsor on 12 November, perhaps having received an urgent message that the queen had gone into labour. His departure to Sheen three days before this may indicate that Isabella's French physician, Master Theobald of Troyes, and Henri de Moderville, the personal surgeon of Philip IV himself whom the concerned king of France had sent to England to supervise his daughter's confinement, did not believe the birth to be imminent, and perhaps that the child was slightly premature.[43] Edward paid a Welsh musician named Coghin for entertaining him and Isabella at Windsor on 12 October, and eight days later granted 'our very dear consort' Isabella permission to make her will: as a married woman, she needed her husband's consent to make one, and it was a common thing for pregnant women to do in an age when pregnancy and childbirth were so risky. Edward, stating that 'because we know well that nothing is as certain as death, nor less certain than the hour at which it may come' – which may indicate that Isabella was enduring a difficult pregnancy – granted his queen all his county of Ponthieu, the lands of its principal stronghold of Montreuil-sur-Mer and all other lands she held and would hold in the future in England and France, and all the moveable goods, gold and silver vessels and jewels she owned wherever they were to be found. Finally, Edward added that 'by our leave and special consent' the executors of Isabella's will would be allowed to buy land worth £1,000 on which to build a hospital 'where poor people will be rescued, sheltered and laid in bed, for the safeguard of our souls', i.e. Isabella's and Edward's.[44] Isabella's will sadly does not survive, and Edward II never made one and is one of the few medieval English kings who died intestate. At Windsor the king and queen must also have received news of the death of Edward's brother-in-law Duke John II of Brabant in late October; Edward's twelve-year-old nephew John III, who would later marry Isabella's first cousin Marie of Evreux, succeeded as duke. Edward's kinsman King Fernando IV of Castile also died in the autumn of 1312, leaving his one-year-old son Alfonso XI to succeed him.

On Monday 13 November 1312, the feast day of Saint Brice, Queen Isabella gave birth to her and Edward II's first child, Edward of Windsor. Later King Edward III, he was destined to reign for fifty years, begin the Hundred Years War against France, see the first massive outbreak of the Black Death and be remembered as one of England's most accomplished kings. In the nineteenth century, Agnes Strickland curiously stated that the boy was born at exactly 5.40 a.m., citing *Foedera 1307–1327*, p. 187. This is merely a memorandum in French which was appended to several of the chancery rolls and which officially announced the boy's birth, and says only that 'Isabella, queen of England, consort of King Edward son of King Edward, bore the king his first-born son in the castle of Wyndesore [Windsor] the Monday after St Martin, in the year of grace one thousand three hundred and twelve, and in the sixth year of the king's reign'. It then goes on to state that the boy was baptised the following Thursday and lists the names of his seven godfathers. Nothing is said about the time of Edward of Windsor's birth, and no one in England in 1312 could have known (or cared) that it was precisely 5.40 a.m. anyway, even though this alleged 'fact' has found its way into numerous books ever since.[45] A delighted Edward II soon afterwards granted Isabella's steward John Launge and his wife Joan, Isabella's damsel, the astonishingly generous income of £80 a year – at a time when £40 a year qualified a man for knighthood – for bringing him news of the birth. This probably only means that John Launge had walked from one part of Windsor Castle to another to inform the king, unless it was he who had ridden to Sheen the day before to tell Edward of the impending delivery.[46] Edward II himself had had to wait until he was almost seventeen in 1301 before his father bestowed titles and lands on him, the principality of Wales and earldom of Chester; his and Isabella's son was a mere eleven days old when Edward granted him the entire earldom of Chester and the county of Flintshire in north Wales on 24 November 1312, except for the manor of Macclesfield, which Edward had formerly given to Isabella and which remained in her hands. On 2 December, Edward gave their son all the royal castles, lands and manors on the Isle of Wight as well.[47] Two fourteenth-century chronicles, the *Vita Edwardi Secundi* and *Trokelowe*, say that the birth of his son and heir went some way to assuaging the king's terrible grief over Piers Gaveston.[48] The author of the *Vita*, a clerk in Edward's service, wrote shortly afterwards, 'Our King Edward has now reigned six full years and has until now achieved nothing praiseworthy or memorable, except that by a royal marriage he has raised up for himself a handsome son and heir to the throne.' The author was terribly disappointed in Edward II, commenting, 'What hopes he raised as prince of Wales! How they were dashed when he became king!' and declaring that if Edward had not listened to the advice of evil men (such as Piers Gaveston) 'not one of his predecessors would have been more notable than he. For God had endowed him with every gift, and made him equal to or indeed more excellent than other kings.' Edward's curious and widely criticised fondness for outdoor pursuits, such as thatching, digging and rowing, also raised the *Vita* author's ire at this time: 'If only he had given to arms the labour that he expended on rustic pursuits, he would have raised

England aloft.'[49] Edward of Windsor, no doubt to the great relief of his subjects, did not inherit his father's enjoyment of such hobbies; he was a warrior through and through, and took after his grandfathers and his father's maternal grandfather, Fernando III of Castile and Leon, another great warrior king, far more than he did Edward II.

Isabella was probably still sixteen, but close to turning seventeen, when her eldest child was born. She must have been thoroughly delighted to have become the mother of the future king of England, and her husband's subjects shared her enthusiasm and expressed their joy that the succession to the throne was assured. According to the London annalist, the inhabitants of the city celebrated extravagantly, dancing in the streets and drinking free wine – scenes which were probably replicated up and down the country. A public holiday was announced in London on 14 November, the day after the birth, and services of thanksgiving were held at St Paul's Cathedral and Westminster Abbey.[50] Isabella's son had two great kings as grandfathers: Edward I of England and Philip IV of France; despite the general incompetence and eccentricity of his father, the boy's future probably seemed bright. Not counting his younger brother John, who died when he was only twenty in 1336, Edward of Windsor would be Philip IV's only grandson who lived past childhood. The *Vita* comments, 'There was born to the king a handsome and long looked-for son,' and goes on, 'Long live, therefore, the young Edward, and may he combine in his person the virtues that characterised in turn his forebears. May he follow the industry of King Henry II, the well-known valour of King Richard [Lionheart], may he reach the age of King Henry [III], revive the wisdom of King Edward [I], and remind us of the physical strength and comeliness of his father,' Edward II's robust physique and good looks apparently being his only positive characteristics in the mind of the author.[51] The royal baby was named Edward after his father or perhaps his grandfather Edward I, who had in turn been named after his father Henry III's favourite saint, Edward the Confessor (died 1066) in 1239, when the name had long fallen out of use in England and must have sounded terribly old fashioned. Isabella's uncle Louis of Evreux requested that the boy be named Louis in honour of his French ancestry and his saintly great-great-grandfather Louis IX, but the English nobles and Edward II refused.[52]

Three days after his birth, on Thursday 16 November, little Edward of Windsor was baptised in Windsor Castle by Cardinal Arnaud Nouvel of St Prisca, one of the envoys sent to England by Pope Clement V. He had seven godfathers: the pope's chamberlain and envoy Arnaud d'Aux, bishop of Poitiers; his great-uncle Louis, count of Evreux; two English earls, Pembroke and Richmond, kinsmen of his parents; Walter Reynolds, bishop of Worcester and future archbishop of Canterbury; John Droxford, bishop of Bath and Wells; and his father's close ally

Hugh Despenser the Elder, then aged fifty-one, whom young Edward was destined to see hanged at his mother's instigation less than fourteen years later. Edward of Windsor was given into the care of a wet nurse, Margaret of Daventry, whom he would remember devotedly for many years.[53]

Isabella's churching, the ceremony of purification after childbirth, took place on 24 December, forty-one days after the birth, which was a normal procedure in the royal family at the time. The king, queen and heir to the throne spent Christmas 1312 and most of January 1313 at Windsor; Edward II spent almost £1,250 on cloth for the three of them and their retinues for the festive season, and spent part of January in the park of Windsor Castle rather than in the castle itself, though to what purpose is not stated.[54] A peace treaty with Piers Gaveston's murderers had finally been signed in London on 20 December 1312, which stated that the men must make humble obeisance to the king at Westminster, though this did not happen until the following October. In January 1313, Isabella must have received the news that her sister-in-law Joan of Burgundy, wife of her second brother Philip, count of Poitiers, had given birth to their first son, also called Philip. Had he lived longer, the boy would have become king of France in January 1322, but sadly he was destined to die at the age of eight in 1321. Philip of Poitiers and Joan of Burgundy also had several daughters who lived into adulthood: Joan, duchess of Burgundy by marriage and countess of Burgundy and Artois in her own right; Marguerite, countess of Flanders; Isabella, dauphine of Viennois; and Blanche, a nun.

Isabella and Edward were temporarily apart in early February 1313, when the king was at Sheen in Surrey. Isabella went to her palace of Eltham in Kent, and their households stayed at Westminster.[55] The London annalist says that on 4 February 1313 the fishmongers' guild of London gave a pageant in Isabella's presence to celebrate the birth of her son and afterwards escorted her to Eltham, where her itinerary does indeed place her on 4 February. The queen then went to Canterbury to worship at the shrine of St Thomas Becket and give thanks for the safe delivery of her son.[56] On 23 February, with both of the royal couple back at Windsor, Edward II finally received his and Piers Gaveston's goods which his cousin the earl of Lancaster had seized at Tynemouth the previous May. The goods included gifts sent to Edward by his sisters and by the queen of Germany, probably Albert I of Habsburg's wife Elisabeth of Carinthia, 'a cameo in gold from Israel', 'a gold ring which St Dunstan forged with his own hands', two brooches which had been gifts to Edward from Isabella, and a belt 'decorated with ivory, notched with a purse hanging down from it, with a Saracen face'.[57] March, April and most of May 1313 passed quietly and peacefully, and Isabella and Edward spent the period at various royal castles and manors, though mostly at Windsor and Sheen. Their son Edward of Windsor had already been set up in his own household with his own officials and a guard of men-at-arms protecting him, and in June 1314 Edward rather tellingly moved his son's chief residence to Wallingford Castle, which had formerly belonged to Piers Gaveston. Isabella visited her son for four days at Bisham in Berkshire in May 1313, and in early August 1313 the king spent three days with him there.[58] The young earl of Chester also visited court on occasion.

On 23 May 1313, Edward and Isabella left England for an extended visit to her homeland. The occasion was the simultaneous knighting in Paris of her three brothers, Louis, Philip and Charles, and their cousin Philip of Valois, all of them future kings of France, and for Edward to engage in more of the usual endless negotiations with his father-in-law about his duchy of Gascony. Edward left his nephew Gilbert de Clare, earl of Gloucester, in England as regent, but took a large retinue with him, as did Isabella. Among those who accompanied her were her long-term companion Isabella, Lady Vescy, her cousin and Edward's; Louis Beaumont, brother of Lady Vescy and future bishop of Durham; Ida Clinton, who had been one of her ladies-in-waiting in 1311/12 and whose son William would much later become earl of Huntingdon and a close friend of Isabella's son Edward III; her physician Master Theobald of Troyes; and her damsel Alice Leygrave, formerly Edward II's wet nurse. Among those who went with the king were his brother-in-law Ralph Monthermer, widower of Edward's sister Joan of Acre and stepfather of the earl of Gloucester; Edward's kinsmen and his son's godfathers Aymer de Valence, earl of Pembroke, and John of Brittany, earl of Richmond; and his close ally Hugh Despenser the Elder and Despenser's son Hugh the Younger, the king's nephew-in-law, of whom Edward took no notice at all until at least 1317.[59] Also accompanying the royal couple was Edward's French niece Joan of Bar, the only daughter of his eldest sister Eleanor (d. 1298), and Henri III (d. 1302), count of Bar in eastern France.[60] Joan's brother was Count Edouard I, named after their grandfather the king of England, and she herself, born sometime in 1295 or 1296, was almost exactly the same age as Isabella and seventeen or eighteen in 1313. Despite her youth, Joan of Bar's marriage to John de Warenne, earl of Surrey had already broken down, and Edward II was paying her living expenses at the Tower of London, having sent men to fetch her from her husband's Yorkshire castle of Conisbrough some months before.[61] The earl of Surrey had fathered several children with his mistress Maud Nerford, and later tried unsuccessfully to annul his marriage to Joan and make his illegitimate sons his heirs. Tactfully, Edward left Surrey behind in England in May 1313 and charged him with keeping the peace during his absence.[62] Two days before he left, grateful for Surrey's loyal support of him, Edward ordered the bishop of

Norwich to defer the publication of excommunication for abandoning his wife and keeping a mistress.[63]

Edward casually disregarded the Ordinance which stated that he needed his barons' consent to leave his kingdom, had it proclaimed that he was travelling to France at the personal invitation of both the king of France and the pope and intended to return 'with the utmost despatch' on 24 June, and then said that 'God willing' he and Isabella would actually return on 7 July in time for parliament (they didn't).[64] Just before they sailed from Dover to Wissant, Edward granted favours to various people at Isabella's request, asked the constable of Dover Castle to give 6*d* each daily to six 'Saracens' who were staying there, and rather curiously gave a large gift of money to a Gascon called Richard de Neueby, 'who says he is the king's brother'.[65] This man and his claim to royal blood are never heard of again. The king and queen of England entered Paris in splendour on 2 June 1313, where they attended a banquet that evening hosted by Philip IV, and 'the whole city rose up and went forth to meet them'.[66] Also present in Paris were Isabella's uncles Charles of Valois and Louis of Evreux, Duke Hugh V of Burgundy who was her brother Louis of Navarre's brother-in-law, Edward II's cousin Duke John III of Brittany, and numerous counts of France and the Low Countries, including William III of Hainault and Holland, who was married to Isabella's cousin Joan of Valois.[67] Isabella probably also met her great-uncle Robert, count of Clermont, who had attended her wedding to Edward, and Robert's sisters Agnes, dowager duchess of Burgundy, and Blanche, widow of Alfonso X of Castile's son Fernando de la Cerda. These three were the last surviving children of Isabella's great-grandfather Louis IX (d. 1270), king of France and canonised as a saint in 1297, and Agnes was the mother of Isabella's sister-in-law Marguerite, queen of Navarre, and Duke Hugh V of Burgundy.

On Sunday 3 June 1313, the feast of Pentecost, Edward II knighted his brother-in-law Louis, king of Navarre and count of Champagne. The two young men were joined by Philip IV, and the three kings then knighted Louis and Isabella's brothers Philip and Charles, their cousin Philip of Valois, and about two hundred other young men. The luxurious splendour of Edward and Isabella's visit continued: on Monday 4 June they ate at a banquet given by her brother Louis of Navarre, and on the 5th Edward himself hosted a banquet at St-Germain-des-Prés, which was held in tents open to public view and hung with rich cloths. Torches, candles and lamps burned even in the middle of the day, attendants on horseback served the guests, Louis of Navarre's armourer created a 'castle of love' as the main attraction, and Edward gave a gift of £1 to the singer William Craddock who entertained them. Isabella ate again that evening when her father gave yet another feast at the Louvre for herself and her brother Louis's wife Marguerite of Burgundy, queen of

Navarre, both women wearing their regal crowns for the occasion.[68] They were joined by her other sisters-in-law Joan and Blanche of Burgundy (who were the daughters of Count Othon IV of Burgundy and Countess Mahaut of Artois, and married to her brothers Philip and Charles) and, confusingly, possibly another Joan of Burgundy, who was Queen Marguerite's younger sister (they were daughters of Duke Robert II of Burgundy and Isabella's great-aunt Agnes of France, and sisters of Duke Hugh V) who shortly afterwards would marry Isabella's cousin Philip of Valois, eldest son and heir of her uncle Charles, count of Valois. More banquets were to follow on Wednesday 6 and Thursday 7 June, hosted by Louis, count of Evreux and Charles, count of Valois respectively and attended by Edward and Isabella.[69]

The king and queen of England and their retinues certainly did not go short of food during their visit to France: as well as all the magnificent banquets they attended, Philip IV gave them ninety-four oxen, 189 pigs, 380 rams, 200 pike, 160 carp and eighty barrels of wine.[70] One wonders if the royal couple arrived back in England rather heavier than when they had left. On 7 June, Edward should have attended a morning meeting with Philip IV, but missed it because he and Isabella had overslept. The amused chronicler Geoffrey, or Godefroy, of Paris, a clerk who was an eyewitness to their visit to France and who provides a vivid description of it in his rhyming chronicle, gives their night-time dalliance as the reason, adding that it was hardly a wonder if Edward desired his wife, given how very beautiful she was.[71] When they finally managed to get out of bed on 7 June, the couple watched a parade of local citizens through Paris from the 'Île Notre Dame to the Louvre from the windows of Philip IV's apartments, and later saw it again from a tower in their lodgings at St-Germain, surrounded by a throng of ladies and damsels'.

Isabella and Edward left Paris on 10 June and travelled to Pontoise, about twenty miles away, where they spent what must have been a very difficult anniversary for Edward: 19 June 1313 marked exactly one year since Piers Gaveston had been murdered. Evidently not in the mood for wallowing in grief, the king of England paid tribute to Gaveston in his own unique way: he asked a performer named Bernard the Fool and fifty-four of his associates to dance for him naked, and gave them £2. Geoffrey of Paris writes of a near tragic situation which occurred while Isabella and Edward were at Pontoise, where they stayed from 10 to 30 June 1313.[72] The royal couple were sleeping in a silken pavilion when a fire broke out in their wardrobe during the night, and they lost many of their possessions. Luckily, Edward had the presence of mind to scoop Isabella up in his arms and rush outside with her, and managed to get them both to safety, though Isabella suffered burns to her arms for which she was still being treated months later with rose water, olive oil and lead plasters.[73] Geoffrey of Paris says that Edward 'was brave against the fire' and 'well proved himself bold by his actions', and that he saved members of his entourage as well, though he was 'completely naked' (*toute nue*) at the time. The poet comments that Edward 'saved her [Isabella] with his bravery' and that he was keen to rescue her above all else 'because he loved her with *amor fine*', which we can translate as 'fine love' or 'courtly love'. Finally, Geoffrey comments that 'love made him [Edward] do it'.

Coupled with Geoffrey's statement that Edward and Isabella overslept and caused Edward to miss a meeting with Philip IV, and the fact that on this occasion they were sleeping together naked, and that they watched a parade in Paris together from their chambers and so on, we can see that the couple were taking pleasure in each other's company during the visit, and apparently enjoying an active sex life. Unfortunately, English chroniclers took little interest in the personal relationship of their king and queen and thus rarely recorded any aspects of it, except much later when it had gone badly wrong, so we have no way of knowing if their behaviour in France was the norm. There is no real reason, however, to suppose that it was not. Edward and Isabella spent most of their time together – where Isabella's itinerary can be established, it almost always coincides with Edward's, and their households often merged together – and on the rare occasions when they were apart, they sent each other letters. Sadly, these mostly do not survive (their existence is attested to by payments to messengers for delivering them), but several which do survive reveal that Edward called Isabella 'dear heart' while for her part she addressed him as 'my very sweet heart', 'my very dear and dread lord' and 'my gentle lord'. As late as February 1326, after their marriage had broken down and Isabella had refused to return to Edward because of her fear of his powerful favourite Hugh Despenser, she was still referring to her husband as 'our very dear and very sweet lord and friend', which is most unconventional – conventional would be simply 'our very dear lord' – and hints at her strong feelings for him.[74] Other evidence also indicates that the royal couple were on very good terms in 1313 and spent much time together: in that year, Isabella interceded with Edward (on behalf of other people) eleven times, compared to only three occasions in 1312 when Edward was distracted with Piers Gaveston's murder and its aftermath. The numbers for 1314 and 1315 are ten and nine. Extant household accounts of 1311, 1313 and 1315/16 reveal that the king and queen spent almost all of their time together.[75]

It is common in the twenty-first century to depict Isabella as the victim of marital neglect and even cruelty, and to assume that she and Edward always disliked each other and that their marriage was little more than an unhappy tragedy in which Isabella endured considerable emotional pain and humiliation for many years. The testimony of Geoffrey of Paris, who saw them together, shows that this view is inaccurate: he does not in any way hint that he thought Isabella was suffering in her marriage, or that he or anyone else believed that Edward was neglecting her or behaving badly towards her in any way or not treating her with the courtesy, respect and affection she deserved. Indeed, Geoffrey even states outright that Edward loved Isabella and that he bravely saved her life and was deeply concerned about her safety. Geoffrey wrote his chronicle in or before 1316 and died around 1320, long before the royal relationship went spectacularly wrong, and thus did not write with hindsight, knowing what later became of the couple. His chronicle and much other evidence indicates that the popular modern notion that Edward and Isabella's marriage was a disaster from start to finish simply holds no water. Both of them seem to have made an effort to make their relationship work as well as possible. Edward had a strong emotional and perhaps sexual need for men for most of his life from his teens onwards, yet simply because he loved men such as Piers Gaveston and, later, Roger Damory and Hugh Despenser the Younger does not necessarily mean that he could not or did not love his queen as well. Isabella for her part cannot have found it easy to live with someone as fiercely emotional, erratic and eccentric as Edward, and may ideally have preferred a very different kind of man to be her husband and lord, but she showed Edward considerable affection and loyalty for many years, which says a great deal about her interpersonal skills. Her behaviour in the 1320s indicates that she was distraught about and mourned sincerely for the breakdown of a marriage in which she had previously been happy, and that, thanks to the intrusion into it of a third party, she felt that she had lost the husband she loved.

Edward and Isabella spent the early days of July 1313 at Poissy, south of Pontoise and to the west of Paris, apparently in no hurry to return to England and the parliament which was supposed to start on 8 July at Westminster.[76] Poissy was the birthplace of Isabella's sainted great-grandfather, Louis IX, who had been born exactly seventy years to the day before Edward II, on 25 April 1214. Philip IV was with them, and gave Edward a gift of four horses and armour.[77] The couple left Poissy on 10 July and travelled back to Montreuil-sur-Mer and Boulogne via the town of Hesdin, where they visited Mahaut, countess of Artois in her own right and countess of Burgundy by marriage to her late husband, Othon IV. Mahaut and Othon were the parents of Joan and Blanche of Burgundy, married to Isabella's brothers Philip and Charles. Mahaut ordered a team of painters to wash the paintings in her great chapel, vaulted chapel, 'Indian chamber', 'hall of shields' and the rather intriguingly named 'chamber of pigs' before their arrival. The carriage transporting Isabella's damsels broke down between Beauvais and Boulogne, delaying their return to England with the queen as they were forced to wait for repairs.[78] Isabella and Edward missed the 29 July 1313 wedding in Paris of their kinsman Philip of Taranto, king of Albania, prince of Achaea and Taranto and despot of Epirus, and Isabella's young first cousin Catherine of Valois, the eldest daughter of her uncle Charles, count of Valois and his second wife, Catherine Courtenay. Catherine of Valois was titular empress of Constantinople in her own right as her inheritance from her mother, who had died in 1307. Philip of Taranto was also extremely well connected: his many brothers included Charles Martel, the titular king of Hungary; Robert 'the Wise', king of Naples, titular king of Sicily and Jerusalem, and duke of Calabria; and Louis, bishop of Toulouse, canonised as a saint by Pope John XXII in 1317. Another of Philip of Taranto's siblings was Marguerite of Anjou-Naples, countess of Anjou in her own right and the first wife of Catherine's father, Charles of Valois (which meant that Catherine married the uncle of her older half-siblings). Philip was a quarter of a century older than Catherine, who was only ten or twelve at this time, and had accused his first wife, Thamar Angelina Komnena, of adultery with no fewer than forty men and imprisoned her. She died in prison in 1311. The king and queen of England apparently met Philip of Taranto before the wedding, however, as he asked Edward to intervene with the pope and cardinals on some business relating to his older brother Robert, king of Naples. Edward, owing to the 'diverse troublesome words' contained in Philip's letters on his brother's behalf, hedged, and asked his chancellor for advice on his return to England.[79] Philip later sent Edward a talented violist named Robert Daverouns, perhaps in gratitude for Edward's offer to help; Edward, who loved music and spent huge sums on minstrels, gave Daverouns a generous gift of £5.[80] Edward and Isabella also just missed the July 1313 wedding of Isabella's first cousin Philip of Valois (Catherine of Valois's eldest half-brother) and her first cousin once removed Joan of Burgundy, granddaughter of Saint Louis IX and sister of Isabella's sister-in-law Marguerite, queen of Navarre.

The king and queen of England landed at the port of Sandwich around vespers, or sunset, on Monday 16 July 1313, and unhurriedly made their way through Kent to Westminster, spending two nights at the archbishop of Canterbury's manor of Sturry on the way (currently the archbishopric lay vacant, Edward and Gaveston's enemy Robert Winchelsey having recently died). On 27 July, Edward gave Isabella the Oxfordshire manor of Woodstock, where a royal palace stood which would later be the birthplace of their elder daughter, Eleanor, and of their renowned grandson Edward of Woodstock, the 'Black Prince', father of Richard II.[81] The couple spent much of late summer and early autumn at Windsor, though both of them visited their son at nearby Bisham at different times and Isabella spent several days at Chertsey Abbey in Surrey, where she sent a letter to Edward relating to their county of Ponthieu on 11 August. She addressed him as 'my very dear and dread lord' and 'my gentle lord'.[82] Isabella may have conceived a child and miscarried while she and Edward were together in late summer or early autumn, as a purchase of pennyroyal is recorded as being made for her in or shortly before November; the traditional medicinal use of pennyroyal is to increase uterine contractions and menstrual flow, and it was used after miscarriages to clear the womb of any infection (though in modern times is considered too dangerous to use for this purpose). Isabella also seems to have had trouble with insomnia at this time, as a payment of 20*d* was made for 'women's [breast] milk, on several occasions' to give her. This was sometimes mixed with the juice of opium poppies to induce sleep.[83] The account of payments made for medicine for Isabella says that *Madame la Reyne*, 'my lady the queen', was ill at Westminster in November and into the second week of December. This, presumably, was partly on account of the burns she had suffered during the fire at Pontoise in June, the miscarriage she had probably suffered, and her insomnia. On 14 November, Edward gave her the manor of High Peak in Derbyshire and two manors in Nottinghamshire.[84] That Isabella was very close to Edward in late 1313 and early 1314 and had ample access to him to ask him for favours on behalf of other people is shown by the numerous grants and pardons the king granted 'at the request of Queen Isabella' or 'at the instance of Queen Isabella'.[85] Edward gave his wife another wardship in early 1314, that of John de Bohun, son and heir of James de Bohun and a relative of his brother-in-law Humphrey de Bohun, earl of Hereford.[86]

On 16 October 1313, Edward II finally came to terms in public with the men who had killed Piers Gaveston, and they submitted to him on their knees at Westminster Palace; he raised them and kissed them one by one and absolved them, though as his later actions proved, he had not forgiven them at all and was still bent on revenge. Officially, at least, he pardoned them and more than 350 of their adherents 'of all causes of rancour, anger, distress, actions, obligations, quarrels and accusations, arisen in any manner on account of Piers Gaveston, from the time of our marriage with our dear companion, our very dear lady, Lady Isabella queen of England', a formulation which, as with so much else in 1313, reveals Edward's huge affection for his queen.[87] To mark their reconciliation, the king invited the barons to a banquet, and the following day they reciprocated.[88] In the middle of December 1313, Edward made a flying visit to Ponthieu to discuss some Gascon-related issues with his father-in-law Philip IV, and spent Christmas with Isabella at Westminster.[89] The king ordered the sheriffs of Kent, Surrey and Sussex to buy eighty oxen, 100 pigs, 300 sheep and large quantities of wheat, malt and oats for the use of Isabella's household over the festive period.[90]

On 17 February 1314, Isabella and Edward attended the enthronement of the new archbishop of Canterbury, Edward's friend and ally Walter

Reynolds, formerly bishop of Worcester and one of their son Edward of Windsor's seven godfathers. Edward had probably been delighted to hear of the death, on 12 May 1313, of the previous archbishop, Robert Winchelsey, who had been one of his and Piers Gaveston's most stubborn enemies and who had excommunicated Gaveston for returning to England from his third exile in 1312. Winchelsey's funeral had taken place in Canterbury on 23 May 1313; although Edward was in the city on the 20th and 21st, he pointedly decided not to postpone his and Isabella's trip to France for a day or two and stay in Canterbury to attend the funeral, but set off with her to Dover.[91] In late February 1314, the king and queen spent some time at the royal manor of Hadleigh in Essex, then separated: Edward returned to Westminster, and Isabella made her way to Dover, from where she was to sail once again to France. It had been agreed that she would discuss some Gascon-related issues on which her husband and father had been unable to agree on Edward's two trips to France in 1313, and would present various petitions on her husband's behalf at the next meeting of the Paris *parlement*.[92] Isabella took a splendid entourage with her, and twenty-six ships and thirteen barges were needed to transport them all across the Channel; among them were her husband's nephew Gilbert de Clare, earl of Gloucester, Isabella Vescy and her brother Henry Beaumont, the royal physician Theobald of Troyes, the queen's lady-in-waiting Ida Clinton, and her damsel Alice Leygrave. Isabella went to France with almost £5,000 to pay her expenses, a remarkably large sum which was more than her entire annual income.[93] During her absence overseas, Edward granted her the reversion of the magnificent Leeds Castle in Kent, which had once belonged to his mother, Eleanor of Castile, and was now held by his stepmother, the dowager queen Marguerite (though years later he changed his mind and gave it to the steward of his household, Bartholomew, Lord Badlesmere).[94]

Isabella sailed from Dover on 28 February and first travelled to Boulogne, where she made an offering at the church where she and Edward had married six years before, and passed through Crécy, a village in Ponthieu where their son Edward III would win a resounding victory in a battle against her cousin Philip VI of France thirty-two years later. She travelled slowly to Paris, reaching the city on 16 March, and stayed at the lodgings at Saint-Germain-des-Prés in which she and Edward had stayed together the year before. She wrote to her husband on the 18th, and on the same day paid the man who had taken care of her fifteen greyhounds during the journey to Paris. The pious queen took the opportunity to visit numerous shrines during her visit, and purchased fur and a hanging (for a wall or for her bed) which was worked with images of baboons.[95] In October 1307, her father, Philip IV, had had the French members of the wealthy and influential military monastic order the

Knights Templar arrested, imprisoned and tortured on the grounds of their alleged heresy, sodomy, idolatry and other crimes such as urinating and spitting on the Cross. He pressed other European monarchs to do the same with the Templars in their own countries, including the new English king Edward II, who protested vociferously but eventually, faced with a papal bull ordering him to arrest the Templars in England, had no other choice but to comply. However, Edward allowed many of the English Templars to escape, ordered the ones who were imprisoned to be treated and fed well, and granted them their usual wages of 4*d* a day while in prison.[96] On 15 March 1314, the evening before Isabella arrived in Paris, her father had the Templar Grand Master, Jacques de Molay, and his associate Geoffroy de Charnay burned alive on a massive pyre on an island in the middle of the river Seine. Molay was then in his seventies and had been in prison for six and a half years. He is said to have screamed out a curse from his pyre, challenging Philip and Pope Clement V, who had helped the French king suppress the Templars, to meet him before God's tribunal within a year, though this story almost certainly was written with hindsight and is unlikely to be true. Clement was dead in little over a month; Philip before the end of the year as well.

It is probable that while she was in France, Isabella discovered that Marguerite and Blanche of Burgundy, respectively the wives of her eldest brother, Louis, king of Navarre, and third brother, Charles, count of La Marche, had been conducting extramarital affairs with the d'Aulnay brothers, Philip and Gautier, and informed her father. It is not certain that she did, but several fourteenth-century chroniclers thought that she had, and it would perhaps be a little too much of a coincidence that she just happened to be in Paris at the time that the scandal broke. On 6 April 1314, a payment was made to several boys carrying torches who escorted Isabella after dark to her father's palace on various occasions, which, accurately or not, certainly sounds rather cloak and dagger.[97] Whether Isabella did tell her father, or the news came out in some other way, it transpired that Queen Marguerite and Countess Blanche had been meeting their lovers at the Tour de Nesle, a tower in Paris, where they had dined with the d'Aulnay brothers and afterwards committed adultery with them. Joan of Burgundy, older sister of Blanche and wife of Isabella's second brother, Philip of Poitiers, was not accused of having a sexual affair with anyone, though did apparently know what was going on and ineffectually begged the women to stop, but did not tell anyone. Joan was temporarily imprisoned in 1314 but released after her father in law's death later in the year. She remained married to Philip for the rest of his life, and was queen consort of France between 1316 and 1322.

If Isabella did break this scandal, as a few chroniclers claim she did, her motives were almost certainly not vindictive. She was the daughter of two sovereigns and had been raised with a sacred sense of royalty, and therefore would have been profoundly disturbed at the notion that her sisters-in-law might foist a child not of the royal bloodline onto the French throne.[98] Given that Isabella much later, beginning in about 1325, herself became involved in some kind of extramarital relationship with Roger Mortimer, her actions here might seem hypocritical. Yet in 1314 Isabella could not have foreseen that almost a dozen years in the future she would find herself in a similar position to her sisters-in-law, and may in addition have thought in late 1325 that as she had already borne Edward II's children some years before, over whose paternity there was no doubt whatsoever, she was committing a much lesser sin than that of Marguerite and Blanche. It is also not certain that Isabella's relationship with Mortimer was sexual and it may have been merely a political alliance, whereas there is little doubt that Marguerite and Blanche of Burgundy were sleeping with the d'Aulnay brothers. The severe punishment meted out to the two women and the d'Aulnays suggests that the evidence against them was undeniable. Philip IV would not have imprisoned his first cousin Marguerite of Burgundy, whose royal mother and Philip's own aunt, Agnes of France, was still alive, and proclaimed two of his sons as cuckolds before the whole of Europe had he not been certain of Marguerite and Blanche's guilt. A rather later and mostly unreliable French chronicler claims that Isabella spotted what was going on when she gave her sisters-in-law a gift of purses during her and Edward's visit to Paris in 1313, and on her second visit in 1314 saw the d'Aulnay brothers wearing them.[99] The story may (or may not) have some truth in it, but Philip IV would have required far more compelling evidence than this to imprison a woman who was Saint Louis IX's granddaughter and a crowned and anointed queen. The idea has been put forward that Isabella was deliberately trying to discredit her sisters-in-law in order to make their children illegitimate and thus improve her own son's chances of inheriting her father's throne one day.[100] This theory credits Isabella with foreknowledge which she could not have had, and a disagreeable and highly improbable amount of cynical and callous manipulation; as early as 1314 she could not possibly have guessed that her brothers would eventually all die young and without male heirs. Given that the three men were only aged between twenty and twenty-five in 1314, she knew they had ample time to remarry and father more sons, even if she had connived at their wives' imprisonment. The idea that she was acting in her son's interests regarding this matter as early as 1314 derives from historians' knowledge that Edward III did claim the throne of France in the 1330s, and assumes that the queen might have planned for this eventuality for more than twenty years. It further assumes that as Isabella supposedly played a role in the murder of her husband, Edward II, in 1327, she must therefore have been capable of just about anything, and is simply a form of the unpleasant old idea that she was an evil and manipulative 'she-wolf'.

Marguerite and Blanche of Burgundy, weeping, their heads shaved, were sentenced to life imprisonment in Château Gaillard, the grim and forbidding fortress in Normandy built in the 1190s by King Richard the Lionheart of England. Their lovers suffered a far worse fate: they were castrated and their genitals thrown to dogs, flayed, and broken on the wheel, before decapitation mercifully put an end to their dreadful torment. The later English chronicle *Scalacronica* claims that one of the brothers escaped to England, but was captured in York and sent back to France, though the story is unconfirmed by any other evidence.[101] Blanche of Burgundy was only about eighteen or nineteen in 1314, and had given birth to her son, Philip – who died as a child a few years later – mere weeks before her arrest. Her husband, Charles, must surely have wondered if the boy was really his, and a question mark also hung over the paternity of Louis of Navarre and Marguerite of Burgundy's daughter, Joan, though as the girl had been born in January 1312 and was thus conceived in about April 1311, it seems likely that she was indeed Louis's daughter. It would seem rather improbable that Marguerite had been carrying on with a lover undetected for an entire three years, and Louis did accept and acknowledge Joan as his own child. The marriages of Louis and Marguerite and Charles and Blanche were not annulled; Louis had to wait until Marguerite's death in August 1315 before he could marry again, and Charles remained married to the captive Blanche until September 1322, after he succeeded to the French throne and finally managed to persuade Pope John XXII to annul their marriage. Even then, annulment was granted on the grounds of spiritual affinity – as Blanche's mother, Countess Mahaut of Artois, was Charles's godmother – and not because of Blanche's adultery.[102] Blanche of Burgundy was finally released from prison in 1325 and died, her health broken, sometime in late 1325 or early 1326, still aged only thirty. Marguerite of Burgundy became queen consort of France, at least in name, on the death of her father-in-law Philip IV in November 1314, but was never crowned or acknowledged as such.

Only a few months after the magnificence of Philip IV's feasting and celebrations to mark the knighting of his three sons and nephew, the reputation of the French royal family lay in scandalous tatters. King Philip was in his mid-forties in 1314, and had three healthy sons aged between twenty and twenty-five to succeed him. No one could have guessed that within fourteen years all of them would be dead without male heirs, that the throne of France would pass to another dynasty, and that in the 1330s, Philip's English grandson would claim the French throne and begin a war between the countries which would last for more than a hundred years.

4

The King's Defeat
1314–1316

Isabella travelled back to England through her and Edward's northern French county of Ponthieu, and on 23 April 1314 entertained her brother Charles of La Marche and her uncle Charles of Valois at Abbeville, the capital of Ponthieu. Throughout her stay in France she had corresponded regularly with her eldest brother, Louis, king of Navarre, and wrote to him again and to Edward II's cousin Blanche of Brittany on the 24th.[1] If her brothers Louis and Charles were angry with her for exposing the adultery of their wives, there is no sign of it. Isabella arrived back in England a few days after her husband's thirtieth birthday on 25 April 1314, made a brief pilgrimage to the shrine of St Thomas Becket in Canterbury, perhaps to give thanks for her diplomatic successes regarding certain Gascon issues in Paris, then set out to join Edward in the north, having received a rather peculiar gift of a porcupine from an unknown donor at Dover.[2] In May and June 1314, Isabella's diplomatic career continued: she mediated on behalf of her husband's nephew Count Edouard I of Bar, brother-in-law of John de Warenne, earl of Surrey. Edouard had been captured and taken prisoner by Ferry IV, duke of Lorraine; Isabella, who was still only eighteen years old, may have been instrumental in the settlement between the two men reached on 21 June.[3]

Pope Clement V had died on 20 April 1314 while Isabella was on her way back to England from Paris, and, much to the consternation of Edward II and no doubt herself, the cardinals would not elect another pope until more than two years had passed, and then only because Isabella's brother Philip of Poitiers locked them in a room in Lyons and refused to let them out until a new pope was chosen. Edward, in the spring and early summer of 1314, was preparing a massive military campaign in Scotland. Since his pointless and entirely unsuccessful last venture there in 1310/11, Robert Bruce had gone from strength to strength. More and more of the Scottish nobility flocked to his side and Philip IV of France had acknowledged him as king, though Robert was still under sentence of excommunication (which was periodically renewed by two popes) because of his 1306 murder of his rival John 'the Red Comyn', lord of Badenoch, in the Greyfriars church in Dumfries. Pope Clement V had never recognised Bruce as king, and many of his family, including his wife Elizabeth de Burgh and his young daughter Marjorie, were still held in captivity in England, but within his own kingdom he was gradually becoming the master. He and his chief lieutenants James Douglas and Thomas Randolph captured several English-held fortresses in Scotland in the years 1312 to 1314 and razed them to the ground to prevent them being recaptured. Although Bruce failed in several attempts to seize the vital port of Berwick-upon-Tweed, and also failed to capture the English border town of Carlisle in 1315, he and his allies carried out numerous raids on the north of England, carrying off crops, livestock and goods unless the local inhabitants paid them to go away. They raised a considerable amount of money in so doing – as much as £20,000.[4] Edward II made some attempts to strengthen the defences of the north of England but ultimately did little to protect his northern subjects from the raids, and they suffered terribly.

Edward Bruce, Robert's only surviving brother – the other three had been executed by Edward I in 1306/07 – began besieging Stirling Castle in June 1313. This was the most important stronghold still held by the English, as it commanded the River Forth and access to the northern Lowlands and Highlands. Edward Bruce came to an arrangement with Stirling's constable, Sir Philip Mowbray, that if an English army did not relieve the castle within a year and a day, Mowbray would surrender the castle to him. This was a challenge that even Edward II could not ignore, and so he began raising a massive army to march north. Thanks to the political turmoil he had created in England, only three of the English earls accompanied him to Scotland: his nephew Gilbert de Clare, earl of Gloucester; his cousin Aymer de Valence, earl of Pembroke; and his brother-in-law Humphrey de Bohun, earl of Hereford, who had submitted to Edward the previous October and received forgiveness for his part in Piers Gaveston's death in June 1312. Even John de Warenne, earl of Surrey, usually an ally of the king, did not attend the campaign – perhaps he was distracted by his ongoing marital woes with the king's niece Joan of Bar and his relationship with his mistress Maud Nerford – and Surrey's brother-in-law Edmund Fitzalan, earl of Arundel followed his lead and also stayed at home. Edward's cousin and deadliest enemy, Thomas, earl of Lancaster also remained in England and raised an army, not to take against Robert Bruce, but to protect himself from the English king should Edward prove victorious. Other English noblemen did flock to join the king, however: his kinsman Henry, Lord Beaumont; Robert, Lord Clifford; Thomas, Lord Berkeley and his son and grandson; the steward of Edward's household Sir Edmund Mauley; Roger Mortimer of Chirk and his nephew Roger Mortimer of Wigmore; and the brilliant Sir Giles Argentein, said to be the third greatest knight in Europe behind the Holy Roman Emperor Henry of Luxembourg and Robert Bruce himself. Also present in Edward's army was the young John Comyn, whose father John 'the Red Comyn' had been killed by Bruce in 1306.

The rich baggage train taken by Edward II to Scotland was said to stretch back twenty leagues and consisted of 216 carts drawn by 424 horses and 880 oxen containing jewellery, fine wines, costly plate and napery, and this was not all he and his noblemen took: the personal possessions of the earl of Hereford alone filled an entire ship.[5] Before Edward left England, he ordered the mayor of London to issue a proclamation forbidding 'rumpuses with large footballs' in public fields, an early reference to the enormously popular sport of later centuries.[6] Isabella accompanied Edward as far north as the port of Berwick-upon-Tweed, then still in English hands, though for only four years more until it fell to Robert Bruce. She took with her a wooden altar 'bound with iron bands in the manner of a coffer', which could be easily packed up and carried by a sumpter-horse, 'for the celebration of masses before the queen'. This had been made for her by one John Fraunceys (whose name means 'Frenchman') of London, and cost 26*s* 8*d*.[7] Isabella, like her husband, was conventionally pious; both of them gave 7*d* a day each in oblations, and Isabella offered gold on three of the great Marian festivals – the Conception, Nativity and Assumption of the Blessed Virgin.[8] She surely owned holy relics as well; Edward II certainly did, and inherited from his father, and passed on to his and Isabella's son Edward III, a large number of them, including a thorn from the Crown of Thorns 'in a gold box ornamented with diverse precious stones', a fragment of the True Cross, the blood and a bone of St George, the blood and hair of St Stephen, a tooth of St Edward the Confessor, and sundry relics from other saints including John the Baptist, Mary Magdalene, Agatha, Agnes, Jerome, James the Less and the 11,000 virgins.[9]

With her sister-in-law Elizabeth, countess of Hereford, whose husband Humphrey de Bohun was fighting in Edward's army, Isabella eagerly awaited the news of the king of England's victory. It must have seemed inconceivable, given the enormous size of Edward's army and the relative wealth and power of England compared to that of Scotland, that Edward could do anything but win, even given his lack of military experience and expertise. Isabella must have been horrified when on 27 June, three days after the battle, Edward II returned to Berwick, not at the head of a glorious victorious army but in a fishing boat with a mere handful of attendants, shattered, defeated and humiliated. He had lost the battle of Bannockburn, his cavalry bogged down on the field and unable to make any headway against Robert Bruce's schiltrons (tight, roughly circular formations of infantry holding long pikes with sharpened steel points). The king had been dragged off the field, protesting, by his kinsman the earl of Pembroke, when Pembroke realised the battle was lost, and had had to gallop hard the sixty or more miles to the safety of Dunbar Castle to avoid capture by Robert Bruce's lieutenant James Douglas. Edward vowed to found a Carmelite friary in Oxford to give thanks for his escape, and did so in February 1318 when he granted the order his Oxford palace of Beaumont.[10]

Worst of all, Edward's twenty-three-year-old nephew Gilbert de Clare, earl of Gloucester, the greatest nobleman in England behind Edward himself and his cousin Thomas of Lancaster, lay dead on the battlefield. Dead, too, were Robert, Lord Clifford, Sir Edmund Mauley, Sir Giles Argentein, five hundred other noblemen and knights, and thousands of English footmen, their bodies piled so high in the Bannock stream that it was said a person could cross it and keep their feet dry. Also fallen in battle was the Scottish nobleman John Comyn, who had been so keen to avenge his father's murder on Robert Bruce. Comyn's young widow, Margaret Wake, sister of Isabella's ward Thomas, Lord Wake, later married Edward II's half-brother Edmund of Woodstock, earl of Kent and was the maternal grandmother of Richard II. Edward's brother-in-law the earl of Hereford and the Scottish earl of Angus were taken prisoner at Bannockburn; in order to secure their release, Edward had to free all the Scottish prisoners in England, who included the bishop of Glasgow, Robert Bruce's wife Elizabeth de Burgh (daughter of the earl of Ulster and sister of the dead earl of Gloucester's wife, Maud de Burgh) and his daughter Marjorie, his sisters Mary and Christina, and his nephew Donald, earl of Mar, who, however, chose to remain in England and for many years was one of Edward II's most loyal supporters. The prisoners were exchanged in October 1314.[11] Edward's vast baggage train and lavish possessions also fell into the hands of the Scots, who welcomed the great windfall, and a Carmelite friar and poet named Robert Baston, presumptuously taken to Scotland to make verses about the English king's great victory over Bruce, was taken prisoner and made to write about the Scottish victory instead.[12]

The defeat was greeted with absolute horror and disbelief in England: 'O day of vengeance and disaster, day of utter loss and shame, evil and accursed day, not be reckoned in our calendar,' laments the author of the *Vita Edwardi Secundi*. 'An evil, miserable and calamitous day for the English,' agrees *Lanercost*.[13] Something of the frustration of Edward's contemporaries with him for losing the battle of Bannockburn is apparent in the *Vita*'s remark that 'if he had habituated himself to the use of arms, he would have exceeded the prowess of King Richard [the Lionheart, elder brother of Edward's great-grandfather King John]. Physically this would have been inevitable, for he was tall and strong, a fine figure of a handsome man.'[14] One of Edward's own household, a messenger called Robert de Newington, remarked in July 1314 that nobody could have expected the king to win a battle when he spent all his time idling, digging and thatching when he should have been hearing Mass. Robert was arrested for his 'irreverent and indecent words' about Edward (though failed to explain how listening to Mass would have helped the king win the battle). It was true that the king preferred to thatch, dig and go swimming than to practise feats of arms – he never even jousted, that most beloved pastime of royal and noble men in the fourteenth century, including his own son Edward III – and so he lost a battle whose name has reverberated down the centuries as one of England's most mortifying military defeats ever. Robert de Newington was finally released from prison on 29 November 1315 on mainprise (i.e. bail) in the name of Walter Reynolds, archbishop of Canterbury, and at Isabella's request. Presumably she recognised the futility of imprisoning a man who only said what many others were thinking.[15] In January 1315, a goldsmith of London named John Bonaventure was arrested and charged with saying 'certain evil and shameful things about the king' (he was found not guilty), and in December 1315 a clerk named Thomas de Tynwelle was overheard declaring loudly in a public park in Oxford that Edward II was not his father's son, and was arrested but also later acquitted.[16] Tynwelle perhaps only meant that Edward II was a very different man to his father, which was certainly true, but foreshadowed an occasion in 1318 when a tanner from Exeter would claim in public that he, not the king, was the real son of Edward I.

Isabella must have been distraught to hear of her husband's defeat at Bannockburn and perhaps humiliated as well, though at least she had the comfort of knowing that her husband had fought bravely in the battle, 'like a lioness deprived of her cubs' according to one chronicler.[17] Her father and brothers did not impress as military leaders either: Philip IV's commander Robert of Artois had lost the battle of Courtrai or the 'Battle of the Golden Spurs' in 1302, and in 1315 her brother Louis X would lead a campaign in Flanders that proved an absolute disaster. As always, she showed Edward her support, tended to his wounds herself, and even cleaned his armour.[18] Edward borrowed forty marks from Isabella, given to him by the keeper of her wardrobe, to buy clothes for three knights from Germany and the Low Countries who had fought for him at Bannockburn and turned up at Berwick on 28 June disguised as paupers, presumably in a successful attempt to evade capture after the battle.[19] The king's privy seal was left behind on or near the battlefield, and so Isabella immediately lent him her own so that government business could continue.[20] Robert Bruce courteously returned Edward's seal and his shield, demanding no payment for them, sent back to the king with the captured Roger Mortimer (either Isabella's future favourite Mortimer of Wigmore, or his uncle Roger Mortimer of Chirk) when he was released.[21] Bruce personally kept an overnight vigil over the body of Gilbert de Clare, earl of Gloucester, his second cousin and his wife Elizabeth de Burgh's brother-in-law, and returned it and the body of Robert, Lord Clifford, the second-highest ranking Englishman to fall at Bannockburn, back to England with full honours and also no payment demanded.

The queen travelled from Berwick to York with her husband; they arrived on 17 July and parliament opened on 9 September. Even more humiliation was piled on Edward. The earls of Lancaster and Warwick, Thomas of Lancaster and Guy Beauchamp, who had refused to fight for their king in Scotland, gloated over his defeat and interpreted it as a result of Edward's failure to abide by the Ordinances of 1311 (the reforms of the royal household to which they were both dedicated and which Edward loathed). The army the earl of Lancaster had raised at his Yorkshire stronghold of Pontefract was used to force Edward to accept the wholesale removal of officers of his household and their replacement by men sympathetic to Lancaster, and a reduction in his income to a mere £10 a day. Edward 'refused nothing to the earls', being in no position to, and was also forced to promise to abide by the hated Ordinances in good faith. The earl of Lancaster also ordered the king's second cousin Henry, Lord Beaumont, who had fought for Edward at Bannockburn and who was also a kinsman of Isabella, to be removed from court. Isabella had helped her husband to the best of her ability since Gaveston's death, and even her own uncle Lancaster came to regard her as an enemy. He ordered her income to be reduced as well, although Edward did his best to help her with grants from his own limited resources.[22]

In late 1314 came a great shock for Isabella: her father, Philip IV, died on 29 November, at Fontainebleau. He was only forty-six years old and had been king of France for twenty-nine years, since the death of his father, Philip III, in 1285. Philip IV's enemy Bernard Saisset, bishop of Pamiers, described him as 'neither a man nor a beast, but a statue', and also likened to him to an owl, because he had a habit of sitting and staring at people but not speaking (either deliberately to make them uncomfortable or because he was painfully shy).[23] Philip added a codicil to his will the day before his death – Isabella is not mentioned in his main will and Edward II in neither the will nor the codicil – leaving several items to 'our beloved daughter the queen of England'. They were two rings, one containing a large lodestone and one set with a ruby called 'the cherry' which she had previously given to him. Philip also left a valuable cup given to him by 'beloved Ysabel, queen of England, our beloved daughter' (*carissima Ysabella Regina Angliae carissima filia nostra*) to the convent of Poissy, and a golden fleur-de-lis to the church of St Mary in Boulogne, where Isabella and Edward had married in January 1308.[24] Edward II had heard of the death of his father-in-law and second cousin by 15 December, when he ordered both English archbishops, all the bishops and twenty-eight abbots to 'celebrate exequies' for him.[25] Philip was succeeded as king of France by his eldest son, Louis X, already king of Navarre since his mother Joan I's death in 1305, and still married, at least in name, to the adulterous and imprisoned Marguerite of Burgundy. On his deathbed, the old king told his twenty-five-year-old son and successor, 'I love you above all others.'[26] Philip was buried at the basilica of Saint-Denis in Paris, the royal necropolis where almost all of the kings of France for a thousand years were buried. Isabella did not attend her father's funeral, perhaps because of the difficulty of winter travel and because she had already been to France that year and spent time with him.

Isabella and Edward were at Edward's favourite residence of Langley near St Albans on 6 December 1314, the feast day of St Nicholas, and Edward gave £2 to Robert Tyeis, who served as 'boy-bishop' in his chapel on that day. After several weeks at Langley, they spent the festive season at Windsor, and Edward played the game of 'tables' on Christmas Eve with members of his entourage.[27] Piers Gaveston was much on the king's mind: on 27 December, Edward gave the chancellor and scholars of Oxford University £20 to pay for Gaveston's soul, and for only twenty-eight days that month gave the two custodians he had appointed to watch over Gaveston's remains the large sum of £15.[28] Edward did not forget Isabella at this time, however: on 26 December he gave her the Kent manor of 'Maundeville by Eltham', near the palace he had given her in 1311.[29] On 2 or 3 January 1315, Edward finally had Gaveston buried, a little over two and a half years after his death, at Langley Priory in Hertfordshire, which the king himself had founded in 1308. The *Vita Edwardi Secundi* states that he had delayed the burial for so long because he had vowed to avenge himself on Gaveston's killers before he committed Gaveston's body to the ground, but Edward was in such a weak position in late 1314 and early 1315 that even he must have realised that revenge would have to wait for quite a while.[30] Isabella attended Gaveston's funeral; it is unfortunate that we cannot know her feelings as she watched his embalmed remains being lowered into his tomb and saw her husband's grief. Edward had spent considerable sums of money between June 1312 and January 1315 on cloths to adorn Gaveston's coffin and on wax for candles to burn perpetually around it, and after the burial would continue to spend much more money on rich cloths to be laid on the tomb and for prayers to be said for Gaveston, for which he paid regularly for the rest of his reign.[31]

Edward's demands for these prayers could be onerous: in the spring of 1317 he asked Tupholme Abbey to take in a former servant of his who was retiring, and they told him, 'Although they would gladly obey him in all things, their very small income is already heavily burdened with the charge of finding a chaplain to say Mass for the soul of Sir Piers Gaveston.'[32] Also in 1317, Edward ordered the convent of Thame to take on six additional monks to celebrate divine service daily for the souls of Gaveston and Edward's ancestors.[33] Edward spent over £4 on having Gaveston's remains transferred the forty or so miles from Oxford to Langley at the end of 1314, £300 on three cloths of gold for dressing the body, and just under £80 on food and wine for the attendees. He also paid for three pavilions (presumably where the guests would eat) to be transported from London to Langley.[34] Gaveston's widow, Edward's niece Margaret de Clare, and their not quite three-year-old daughter Joan presumably attended. Certainly present were Edward's fourteen-year-old half-brother Thomas of Brotherton, displaced as heir to the throne by the birth of his nephew Edward of Windsor in 1312 and made earl of Norfolk shortly afterwards; Edward's brother-in-law Humphrey de Bohun, earl of Hereford, rather bravely as he had been present at Gaveston's death; Aymer de Valence, earl of Pembroke, who had tried to save Gaveston; four bishops, fourteen abbots and large numbers of Dominican friars; Henry, Lord Beaumont; and Edward's friend and close ally Hugh Despenser the Elder and Despenser's son Hugh the Younger, the king's nephew-in-law.

Edward II and Isabella spent virtually all of the year 1315 together, including a month at Langley in June/July, and from 10 to 12 June went on pilgrimage to the Canterbury shrine of a saint they both venerated and often visited, St Thomas Becket. The *Scalacronica* says that in 1315 Edward 'tarried in the south, where he amused himself with ships, among mariners, and in other irregular occupation unworthy of his station, and scarcely concerned himself with other honour or profit, whereby he lost the affection of his people.'[35] The king gave £1 on 14 June to three sailors 'for their labour in taking a whale, lately caught near London Bridge', which may be the whale supposedly eighty feet long which had made its way up the Thames in 1309.[36] On 28 April 1315, Edward regranted Isabella the manor and castle of High Peak, and throughout the year continued to grant land, favours and pardons to many people at her request, demonstrating that people petitioned her to intercede with the king for them, that she was glad to do so, and that she had ample access to Edward to bring the matters to his attention.[37] Guy Beauchamp, earl of Warwick died on 12 August 1315, only in his early or mid-forties, leaving his eighteen-month-old son Thomas – named after the earl of Lancaster – as his heir. Many decades later the gossipy and unreliable chronicler Thomas Walsingham claimed that Warwick was poisoned by friends of Edward II in revenge for his part in Piers Gaveston's death, though this seems very unlikely. It is also unlikely, however, that Edward grieved much for Warwick, the 'Black Dog of Arden' as Gaveston had called him.

1315 would be a horribly disastrous year in the history of northern Europe. It barely stopped raining all that year or the next, and the subsequent floods meant that crops lay saturated and useless in the fields, and livestock drowned. So bad were the conditions that the years from 1315 to 1317 are remembered as those of the Great Famine, when 5 per cent or even more of the population of England and the rest of northern Europe died of hunger, malnutrition and disease. The price of basic foodstuffs rose so tremendously that few people could afford to pay for them, and any bread which was available contained minimal nutrients and barely satisfied hunger as the grain was so waterlogged. A couple of small onions cost the equivalent of half a day or even an entire day's wages for most people. The St Albans chronicler *Trokelowe* says that when Edward and Isabella passed through the town between 10 and 12 August, even they had trouble finding enough food for their households. *Trokelowe* and the *Vita* say that people resorted to stealing and eating dogs, horses and other animals, and, one hopes with great exaggeration, even children.[38] The famine was the worst anyone had seen for a hundred years or more, and the situation in the northern port of Berwick-upon-Tweed was particularly bad: Sir Maurice Berkeley, keeper of the town, wrote to Edward II several times between October 1315 and February 1316 to tell him that 'no town was ever in such distress', and that if the king didn't send help immediately Berwick would be entirely lost to famine. Berkeley ended one letter by saying, 'Pity to see Christians living such a life.'[39] A 'severe pestilence' also swept through the stricken country; bodies were so numerous they could hardly be buried. [40] Isabella and Edward could do little but watch helplessly as the greatest natural disaster of the early fourteenth century unfolded in all its horror. Edward ordered his magnates to limit the number of courses they ate at table, and passed regulations limiting the prices of various basic foodstuffs – no more than 1*d* for two dozen eggs, 1½*d* for a fat chicken and 12*s* for a live fat cow, for example – but these proved unsuccessful and only resulted in traders refusing to sell what they had at an artificially low price, and were abolished a few months later.[41]

On 14 August 1315, aged just twenty-five, Isabella's sister-in-law Marguerite of Burgundy, the nominal queen consort of France and Navarre, died in prison at Château Gaillard in Normandy. The cause of her death is unknown for certain, but it is possible that she was murdered, as her death was very convenient for her husband, Louis X. It is also possible, however, that Marguerite died as a result of harsh treatment: she had no decent clothes to wear and was imprisoned in a high tower with little shelter from the elements.[42] Marguerite left her only child, Joan of Navarre, then three; her brother Odo IV, duke of Burgundy since the death of their brother Hugh V three months before; and her sisters Joan, the wife of Philip of Valois, a future queen of France, and Marie, wife of Count Edouard I of Bar and Edward II's niece by marriage. Only five days after Marguerite's death, Louis X married his second wife, Clemence of Hungary, also sometimes known as Clemence of Anjou. She was the daughter of Charles Martel, titular king of Hungary, and a niece of Philip of Taranto, king of Albania, and Robert 'the Wise', king of Naples; on her mother, Klementia von Habsburg's side, she was a granddaughter of Rudolf I, king of Germany. As a great-granddaughter of Saint Louis IX's brother Charles of Anjou, king of Sicily, she was Louis X and Isabella's third cousin. The marriage of Louis X and Clemence had been arranged with the aid of Charles of Valois, whose first wife, Marguerite of Anjou-Naples, was the sister of Charles Martel and who was thus Clemence's uncle as well as Louis's. Louis and Clemence were crowned king and queen of France at Rheims a few days after their wedding.

In the autumn of 1315, Edward II went on holiday: in September/October he spent time in the Fens in Cambridgeshire and Norfolk, swimming and 'rowing about on various rivers' with a large group of his lowborn subjects.[43] The eccentric king loved water, a normal enough state of affairs in later centuries but most peculiar to the fourteenth-century mind; the *Brut* chronicle states that he 'loved to go by water' and that women in Scotland knew of his love of rowing and made a mocking song about it in the aftermath of his defeat at Bannockburn.[44] In February 1303, a teenaged Edward had gone swimming in the Thames at Windsor with his fool Robert Bussard. The winter conditions on that occasion did not put him off, and neither did the awful wet weather which dominated the autumn of 1315.[45] Edward thoroughly enjoyed the company of carpenters, fishermen, blacksmiths and the like, though the nature of his associations with such men is uncertain; perhaps he simply felt he could relax and be his own unconventional self around his subjects as he could not among his nobility. There is no reason to assume that he enjoyed 'being promiscuous with low-born men' (though of course we cannot prove that he did not) as one modern writer has suggested. The men named as his lovers who are said to have received 'substantial sums' as 'hush money' after spending two weeks in his company and allegedly having sex with him were simply Edward's own chamber valets and are frequently named as such in his household accounts. The king's staff were paid two or three times monthly, which explains these men being paid for time spent 'in the king's company' for the previous two weeks; this formulation was often used when members of the royal household were receiving their wages and certainly does not imply anything 'euphemistic', as suggested.[46] The rather later chronicler Ranulph Higden declared that Edward II 'forsook the company of lords, and fraternised with harlots, singers, actors, carters, ditchers, oarsmen, sailors, and others who practise the mechanical arts'.[47] The *Lanercost* chronicle says that Edward 'devoted himself privately from his youth to the arts of rowing and driving chariots, digging pits and roofing houses; also that he wrought as a craftsman with his boon companions by night, and at other mechanical arts, besides other vanities and frivolities wherein it doth not become a king's son to busy himself'.[48] A year or two after Edward's swimming and rowing holiday in the Fens, the new pope expressed regret to the archbishop of Canterbury that Edward still indulged himself in 'childish frivolities'.[49] It is reasonable to assume that Isabella shared this opinion, but if she ever expressed it to Edward, he took no notice.

It is unclear whether Isabella accompanied Edward on his holiday to the Fens; if not, they were reunited sometime in late October 1315 when the king passed through Nottingham and arrived at the royal hunting lodge of Clipstone in Nottinghamshire, where he and Isabella spent all of November and most of December 1315 and January 1316, including Christmas. Sometime in about mid- to late November, they must have conceived their second child, who was born on 15 August 1316. As with their first son, Edward of Windsor, it is certain that they were together at the right time to conceive their second. While at Clipstone, Edward heard that a member of his own household named John the Irishman had abducted Maud, Lady Clifford, widow of Robert Clifford killed at Bannockburn, and taken her to Barnard Castle in County Durham. Edward sent four knights, including his good friend Sir William Montacute, and thirty-six squires and men-at-arms to rescue her. They did so with minimal fuss, and shortly afterwards Maud Clifford romantically married Sir Robert Welle, one of her rescuers. The couple failed to secure Edward's permission for their marriage, however, and rather less romantically he temporarily seized Maud's lands and fined them £100.[50] On 28 November 1315, Edward marked the twenty-fifth anniversary of the death of his mother, Eleanor of Castile, queen of England and countess of Ponthieu. Something the royal couple had in common was that they had both lost their mothers when they were young: Edward when he was six, Isabella when she was nine. Early April 1315 had been the tenth anniversary of the death of Joan I of Navarre, and now Isabella, who turned twenty at the end of 1315, had lost her father too.

By late 1315, it appears that Edward II was falling for another man: a rather obscure knight of Oxfordshire who had been in the retinue of Edward's nephew the earl of Gloucester and who had fought bravely at Bannockburn. His name was Sir Roger Damory or d'Amory. Earlier in

1315, Edward had ordered Damory to stay at court with him, and by the end of the year the knight had grown close to the king. A series of grants of lands, money and appointments flowed Damory's way from late 1315 until well into 1317.[51] Damory would come to wield an influence over the king out of all proportion to his rank and position, and a malign influence at that. Since Piers Gaveston's death three and a half years previously, Edward had had no man in his life, but that now changed, and for the rest of his reign one man or another would dominate his favour. Isabella, however, does not seem to have been hostile to Roger Damory, and indeed gave him some splendid gifts for his chapel: a 'chasuble of red cloth of Tarsus sprinkled with diverse flowers of Indian colour, together with alb and amesse, stole and maniple, and two frontals of the same sort'.[52] Perhaps she had grown used to her husband's emotional need for a man in his life, and perhaps she did not consider Damory a threat to her position as queen or to her personal relationship with Edward. Damory's elder brother Sir Richard Damory was appointed 'keeper of the body of my lord Sir Edward, earl of Chester'; in other words he became the guardian of Isabella's elder son, the future king, in or before 1318.[53] There were two other men who also grew very close to Edward II in the mid-1310s and who came to wield considerable authority beyond their rank at court. The three were collectively called 'worse than Piers [Gaveston]' by the *Flores Historiarum*.[54] The other two were Sir Hugh Audley, a household knight of Edward's since 1311, and Sir William Montacute, who came from an old noble family of Somerset and had been knighted with Edward and Roger Mortimer in 1306, and who would be appointed steward of the king's household in 1316. Audley was a close relative, via his mother, Isolde Mortimer (though precisely how is unclear), of Isabelle's future favourite Roger Mortimer of Wigmore. Montacute was married to Elizabeth de Montfort, and their second but eldest surviving son, William, would much later become a close personal friend of Isabella's son Edward III and be made earl of Salisbury by him in 1337. The nature of Edward II's relationships with Roger Damory, Hugh Audley and William Montacute is impossible to determine for certain, and whether he had sexual or romantic relations with one or more of them, or simply enjoyed ties of close friendship and trust and perhaps leaned on them emotionally, we cannot know.

Edward and Isabella left Clipstone on 25 January 1316 (their eighth wedding anniversary) and arrived thirty miles away in Lincoln on the 27th, the day of the opening of the parliament which, in the words of the *Flores*, Edward had 'ridiculously caused to be summoned' there.[55] The king and queen stayed in the dean of Lincoln's lodgings, and Edward announced that he wished parliamentary proceedings to pass as speedily as possible, to ease the burden placed on the city by the presence of so many people demanding food; the Great Famine still held England in its deadly grip. His cousin and Isabella's uncle Thomas, earl of Lancaster however, thwarted his wish and didn't arrive at parliament until 12 February, when to the king's huge annoyance he finally gained an official position as the chief of Edward's council. Lancaster had dominated the government since the York parliament of September 1314, but after his appointment strangely took little further part, preferring to stay at his favourite residence of Pontefract in Yorkshire, where Edward and his council were forced to communicate and negotiate with him as though he were another king.[56]

One attendee at the Lincoln parliament of early 1316 was Roger Mortimer, lord of Wigmore in Herefordshire and Isabella's future favourite. Mortimer was then twenty-eight and was busy building a large family with his wife Joan Geneville, heiress to numerous lands in several countries: they ultimately had eight daughters and four sons. He spent much of the 1310s in Ireland, at times as Edward's lieutenant (Piers Gaveston's position in 1308/09) and sometimes as his justiciar, and came to Lincoln to pass on grim news: Edward's army had suffered a catastrophic defeat at the battle of Kells the previous December, to Robert Bruce's brother Edward, who would be crowned high king of Ireland later in 1316. And more bad news reached Edward during parliament. His niece Elizabeth de Clare, widow of the earl of Ulster's eldest son and heir John de Burgh, had been abducted from Bristol Castle and forcibly married to Theobald Verdon, also justiciar of Ireland and widower of Roger Mortimer's sister Maud. The furious king fined Verdon £1,000 for marrying Elizabeth without his consent, which Verdon never paid as he died only five months later. Elizabeth, third daughter of Edward's much older sister Joan of Acre, was born in September 1295 and was thus just a few weeks older than Isabella, and the two women were close. Another member of their circle of friends was Elizabeth's cousin Joan of Bar, countess of Surrey, also a niece of the king and the same age as Isabella and Elizabeth. Elizabeth and her older sisters Eleanor, wife of Hugh Despenser the Younger, and Margaret, widow of Piers Gaveston, were joint heirs of their brother Gilbert de Clare, earl of Gloucester, killed at the battle of Bannockburn in June 1314. Gloucester's widow, Maud de Burgh, however, was still claiming to be pregnant with her late husband's child. Given that almost twenty months had passed since Bannockburn, Hugh Despenser the Younger naturally did not believe her, and at the Lincoln parliament demanded that he and his wife Eleanor be granted their third of the vast de Clare inheritance. He had only a tiny income and no political influence at all, despite being the king's nephew-in-law and the son of one of his most loyal supporters, and was desperate for both. Edward II, who would continue to receive the huge income from the late earl of Gloucester's lands in England, Wales and Ireland until his putative child came of age, was most reluctant to admit that there was no heir of the earl's body, and so ordered two royal justices to tell Despenser that he should have applied for a writ to have the countess's belly inspected and that Maud's pregnancy was 'well-known in the parts where she lives' and he could not therefore gainsay it.[57] Despenser's reaction to these farcical statements is unfortunately not recorded, though he did commit violence in front of the king in the middle of Lincoln Cathedral during parliament by punching the baron John Ros repeatedly in the face after he heard that Ros had tried to arrest Sir Ingelram Berenger, one of his father's retainers. Despenser's amusingly implausible excuse when arrested was to claim that he had merely held out his arm to defend himself when Ros 'taunted him with scandalous words' and 'outrageous insults' and made as if to rush at him with a dagger, and that he accidentally hit him over and over in the face.

One final piece of bad news which reached Edward II at Lincoln involved an uprising in south Wales: Llywelyn Bren, lord of Senghenydd and Meisgyn, sick of the tyranny of the royal official Sir Payn Turberville and accused of sedition by him, attacked Caerphilly Castle, which had once belonged to the earl of Gloucester and had been built by his father Gilbert 'the Red' de Clare in the 1270s. Edward sent men to put down the rising and to capture Bren, including his brother-in-law Humphrey de Bohun, earl of Hereford, Roger Mortimer and his uncle Roger Mortimer of Chirk, Isabella's uncle Henry of Lancaster (the earl of Lancaster's younger brother), and the king's current favourite Roger Damory. Pointedly, Edward did not send Hugh Despenser the Younger, who had always followed the political lead of his uncle Guy Beauchamp, earl of Warwick, and whom the king disliked and distrusted, even though Despenser and his wife Eleanor de Clare were in line to inherit Caerphilly when Edward finally gave up pretending that the dowager countess of Gloucester was pregnant. The campaign against Bren was successful, and he and his six sons were captured and sent to the Tower of London.

There was, however, finally some excellent news, at least for the royal couple personally: Isabella and Edward now knew that she was pregnant again, and by the end of parliament on 20 February she had probably just passed the end of her first trimester. On 22 February 1316, Edward asked the dean and chapter of the church of St Mary in Lincoln to 'celebrate divine service daily for the good estate of the king and Queen Isabella and Edward their first-born son, and for the souls of the king's ancestors and heirs, and of all Christians'. The reference to 'first-born son' indicates that the king knew there would be a second child.[58] On 27 March, Edward gave £20 to John Fleg, horse dealer of London, for a bay horse 'to carry the litter of the lady the queen' during her pregnancy, and also paid almost £4 for pieces of silk and gold tissue and flame-coloured silk to make cushions for Isabella's carriage so that she could travel in greater comfort.[59] In April 1316, Isabella and her son Edward of Windsor received green silk lined with miniver (expensive white fur made from the ermine) from her husband's wardrobe, and at Pentecost 1316 the royal couple and their infant son wore robes lined with silk.[60]

Isabella's sister-in-law Elizabeth, countess of Hereford and dowager countess of Holland, youngest of the daughters of Edward I and Eleanor of Castile, died on 5 May 1316. She was only thirty-three, and died shortly after giving birth to her tenth child, who also died. Elizabeth left her widower – her second husband, Humphrey de Bohun – and seven children, including two future earls of Hereford, the earl of Northampton, the countesses of Devon and Ormond and the peculiarly named and obscure Aeneas. Only two of Edward II's numerous sisters – he had at least eleven, of whom many died young – now remained alive: Margaret, the widowed duchess of Brabant, who seems never to have visited England again after attending Edward and Isabella's coronation in 1308; and Mary, a nun at Amesbury Priory. Edward and presumably Isabella attended Elizabeth's funeral at Walden Abbey in Essex on 23 May; Elizabeth was only twenty months older than Edward and the two had always been close, and in 1308 Elizabeth had been named as one of Isabella's 'confidantes' and so was apparently also on excellent terms with the queen.[61]

Exactly a month after Elizabeth's death came even worse news for Isabella: her eldest brother, Louis X of France and Navarre, died at Bois de Vincennes on 5 June, at the age of only twenty-six, supposedly from drinking chilled wine after playing a vigorous game of *jeu de paume* (an early form of tennis), or perhaps more likely of a sudden infection. Edward II had written to Louis and his wife Clemence of Hungary on 17 May, less than three weeks before Louis's sudden death, asking them to strive to continue their friendly relationship with him. His clerk who wrote the letter, apparently unfamiliar with Clemence's unusual name, made the embarrassing error of addressing the letter to her as 'the most excellent lady, Lady Elizabeth' (perhaps he had the recent death of Edward's sister on his mind).[62] Two funerals were held for Louis X at the basilica of Saint-Denis, the first two days after his death and one somewhat later after his brother Philip, count of Poitiers returned to Paris from Lyons.[63] Isabella did not attend either funeral, but she was about seven months pregnant and was thus unable to make the journey across the Channel. Louis's widow, Queen Clemence, was also pregnant, the baby due in November 1316; the French nobility and populace waited eagerly for the birth of the child who, if male, would immediately become their new king. In the interim period, Isabella's second brother, Philip of Poitiers, acted as regent of the kingdom. On

7 August 1316, Edward II gave a generous gift of twenty marks to the messenger who brought him and Isabella news of the birth of Philip and Joan of Burgundy's second son, Louis, who would die in early 1317.[64]

Also on 7 August 1316, the cardinals in Avignon finally elected a new pope after a delay of well over two years, the conclave having begun on 1 May 1314, a few days after Clement V's death. Philip of Poitiers, sent to the conclave as an emissary by his brother Louis X in March, locked the cardinals in the house of the Dominican friars in Lyons on 28 June when he returned to Paris after Louis's death, leaving them there under guard and finally forced to decide.[65] Their choice was Jacques Duèse, cardinal-bishop of Porto and a Gascon, as Clement V had also been, who chose the name John XXII. Edward II sent gifts worth a staggering £3,387 to the new pope, including a cope 'embroidered and studded with large white pearls', several golden ewers, thirteen golden salt cellars, numerous golden dishes and bowls, a golden basin and a golden chalice. The enormous sums of money spent on gifts for John XXII included £300 for an incense boat, a ewer and a 'gold buckle set with diverse pearls and other precious stones' to be sent in Isabella's name, and 100 marks for another cope embroidered by Roesia, wife of London merchant John de Bureford, also sent in the queen's name.[66] The gifts were intended, at least in part, as a bribe to encourage John XXII to treat Edward favourably in his disputes with Scotland. Around this time, Edward demonstrated his generosity by giving £500, an enormous sum, to Isabella's former nurse Theophania de Saint Pierre, lady of Brignancourt.[67]

The king and queen spent most of the period from April to July 1316 together at Westminster, though made a quick trip around 20/21 June to the archbishop of Canterbury's manor of Mortlake in Surrey, where Isabella petitioned John Sandal, chancellor of England, on behalf of a man named Isambard de St Blimont.[68] On 23 July 1316, the king and the very pregnant queen left Westminster and rode the dozen miles to her palace of Eltham in Kent, which Edward had given Isabella in 1311. He left her there on 26 July and rode north, intending to lead a military campaign to Scotland, which he soon postponed, and then inevitably ended up cancelling (the Scots invaded England as far south as Richmond in Yorkshire and the Furness peninsula in Lancashire in the summer of 1316, and according to the *Lanercost* chronicle carried off numerous goods and men and women as prisoners).[69] The king arrived in York on 16 August and stayed at the house of the Franciscan friars, accompanied by his niece Margaret de Clare, Piers Gaveston's widow, who was then living in his household. As Margaret was one of the three co-heirs of her fantastically wealthy brother the late earl of Gloucester, and as her sister Elizabeth had been abducted and married without the king's permission some months before, no doubt Edward wanted to keep a close eye on her. Sometime in August, Edward met his cousin and Isabella's uncle Thomas, earl of Lancaster in York, and they had a furious row.[70] The two most powerful men in the country had once been close allies and affectionate relatives, but those days were long since over, and they loathed each other. Lancaster's responsibility for the murder of Piers Gaveston was something Edward could never forgive.

On 15 August 1316, Isabella gave birth to her second son, John, at Eltham Palace. For the entirety of his rather short life – he was destined to die at only twenty, unmarried and childless – the boy was known as John of Eltham, and would be made earl of Cornwall when he was twelve in 1328. It was conventional at the time to name the second son after his maternal grandfather, which would have been Philip in this case, after Philip IV. Isabella, however, chose the name John, presumably in honour of the new pope, John XXII, news of whose election in Lyons on 7 August must have reached her around the time she gave birth. It is interesting and possibly rather revealing that she chose not to name her son after her father, especially as she and Edward later decided to follow convention and named their two daughters after their mothers, Eleanor of Castile and Joan of Navarre. Isabella immediately sent her steward Eubolo Montibus the almost 250 miles to York to inform her husband, and Edward II – this would be the only occasion on which he was not nearby when one of their children was born – reacted with elation. He gave Montibus a gift of £100 for bringing him the news, and on 24 August asked the Dominican friars of York to say prayers for himself, 'our beloved consort Isabella, queen of England, Edward of Windsor our elder son, and John of Eltham our younger son, especially on account of John'.[71] The St Albans chronicler comments on the king's joy on the birth of his second son; he and Isabella now had the proverbial heir and spare, and the succession to the English throne seemed assured. [72] Edward had a piece of Turkey cloth and a piece of cloth-of-gold delivered to Eltham to cover the font in the chapel during John's baptism, and ordered Isabella's tailor to make her a robe from five pieces of white velvet for her churching ceremony forty days after birth. At the end of July, Isabella sent her messenger Godyn Hautayn with letters to John Salmon, bishop of Norwich, and her uncle Thomas, earl of Lancaster asking them to stand sponsor (i.e. act as godfathers) to her soon-to-be-born child, but Lancaster failed to show up for the ceremony, which was a gross insult.[73] This is probably because the already tense relationship between Edward and Lancaster had deteriorated still further. The *Flores* claims that Edward armed himself against his cousin, and that his fear of Lancaster was the reason for the king's postponement of the 1316 campaign to Scotland.[74] Whether that is true or not, Edward was concerned enough about Lancaster's hostility to summon Isabella to him in York with all speed, fearing for her safety. The queen travelled very fast: on 22 September she was at Buntingford in Hertfordshire, 175 miles from York, and must have been reunited with Edward soon after the 27th, as on that date the king paid her messenger William Galayn £1 for informing him of her imminent arrival.[75] The king and queen spent most of October and November 1316 in York, where Edward busied himself arranging a future marriage for his great-niece Joan Gaveston (which never went ahead as she died young), who, since the death of her uncle the earl of Gloucester at Bannockburn and as the current sole heir to her mother Margaret de Clare, was a very attractive marital prospect, although still only four years old. On 23 November 1316, Edward appointed Roger Mortimer of Wigmore 'keeper of the land of Ireland, and the king's lieutenant there'.[76]

The bishop of Durham, Richard Kellaw, died on 9 October 1316. Edward II put forward a candidate for the bishopric: Thomas Charlton, keeper of his privy seal and brother of his then chamberlain John Charlton. Fierce politicking ensued. The earls of Lancaster and Hereford supported their own candidates, and so too did Isabella, who desired the election of Louis Beaumont, who had accompanied her to France in 1314 and who was the brother of Henry, Lord Beaumont, and Isabella, Lady Vescy. The monks of Durham elected a man of their own choice, Henry Sanford, but Isabella refused to accept this and begged Edward on her knees that he would push for Louis Beaumont's election. He agreed to do her bidding and abandoned his support for his own candidate, being persuaded also by Beaumont's brother Henry that if Louis became bishop of Durham, he would be 'a defence like a stone wall' against the Scots in the north. Isabella's attempt was successful, and John XXII duly appointed Louis Beaumont to the vacant bishopric in early 1317, even though he could barely speak or read Latin.[77] The *Lanercost* chronicler calls Louis 'a Frenchman of noble birth, but lame on both feet, nevertheless liberal and agreeable'; he and his siblings Henry Beaumont and Isabella Vescy née Beaumont, who used their mother's name, were the children of Agnes Beaumont, viscountess of Beaumont-au-Maine, and Louis Brienne, son of John Brienne, king of Jerusalem.[78] With the episode, Isabella had shown that she could influence her husband and that he was willing to be persuaded by her. No shrinking violet, she was not afraid to be seen to oppose her husband's choice in public and to push forward her own; she would do the same thing some years later in 1319 when the bishop of Rochester died. Edward promoted Hamo Hethe, and Isabella her confessor John Puteoli. On this occasion Edward's candidate won the day, despite the queen's attempts to have Puteoli appointed, and Pope John XXII marvelled that Isabella would dare to write to him against her husband's wishes.[79] Edward did not express any displeasure with her behaviour, however, and seems to have accepted Isabella expressing her own opinion and her involvement in politics and episcopal elections, at least in public. He himself told her in December 1325 that 'sometimes the king has addressed to her, in secret, words of reproof, by her own fault, if she will remember, as was befitting, without other hardship'.[80] To a modern audience Edward's need to offer 'reproof' to his wife 'by her own fault' sounds horribly patronising, but by fourteenth-century standards Isabella was bound to listen to and obey her lord and husband, and at least Edward did it in private and 'without other hardship', which presumably means that he only talked to her and did not back up his reprimands with any violence or threats of such (as would, unfortunately, have been his right).

The disastrously unhappy marriage of Edward's niece and Isabella's friend Joan of Bar and John de Warenne, earl of Surrey reached a nadir in the autumn of 1316. Surrey decided to try to have their marriage annulled so that he could marry his mistress Maud Nerford instead and make their sons his heirs. He began legal action against Joan, who was cited while in Isabella's presence in the lower chapel of Westminster Palace.[81] Edward II did his best to steer the difficult course between loyalty to his niece and loyalty to a steadfast, politically useful ally. In August 1316, he allowed Surrey to surrender his lands to him, and granted them back with reversion to John and Thomas, two of his sons by Maud – meaning that he accepted Surrey's illegitimate children as his heirs.[82] On the other hand, Edward paid all Joan's legal costs, and appointed his clerk Master Aymon de Juvenzano 'to prosecute in the Arches at London, and elsewhere in England' on his niece's behalf from 10 July to 26 November 1316. In November 1316, Joan left to go abroad, probably to stay with her brother Edouard, count of Bar, and Edward gave her more than £166 for her expenses.[83] Joan seems never to have been a lady-in-waiting to Isabella as her cousin Eleanor de Clare was, but the two women were on excellent terms, and Joan was to accompany Isabella abroad in 1325.

On 15 November 1316, Louis X of France's widow, Clemence of Hungary, gave birth to her husband's eagerly awaited child. It was a boy – Isabella's nephew – and he became king of France as soon as he drew his first breath: John I, 'the Posthumous'. Isabella's brother Philip of Poitiers was to continue as regent during his nephew's minority. Queen Clemence perhaps also named her child in honour of the new pope John XXII, or after her sister-in-law Isabella's three-month-old son, John of Eltham; the name John was most unusual in the French royal family at this time, and it would have been far more conventional to call the boy after his grandfather Philip IV or his father, Louis X. Sadly, the baby king died when he was just five days old, though there is no reason to assume foul play or poison, as has sometimes been suggested; the rate of infant mortality was heartbreakingly high. A crisis thus arose in France. Next in line to the throne was Louis X's other child,

Joan of Navarre, John I's half-sister and now four years old. Joan's mother, Marguerite of Burgundy, had been imprisoned for adultery and a question mark necessarily hung over the child's paternity, though Louis X had accepted her as his daughter. At a *parlement* held in Paris, Joan of Navarre's uncle Duke Odo IV of Burgundy spoke on her behalf and appealed for her to be crowned queen of France. However, the powerful Charles, count of Valois, brother of the late Philip IV, supported his nephew Philip of Poitiers, and so, understandably, did Mahaut, countess of Artois, mother of Philip's wife Joan of Burgundy. The party of Philip of Poitiers won the day, and Isabella's second brother was duly crowned King Philip V of France at Rheims on 9 January 1317 with Joan of Burgundy at his side. Philip invited Isabella and Edward to attend, but Edward politely declined, probably in an attempt to postpone his duty of having to kneel to the new king of France, now his overlord for his territories of Gascony and Ponthieu in that country, and pay homage to him. Edward had managed to avoid paying homage to Louis X as Louis's reign had been so short, and successfully delayed the ceremony of homage to Philip until the summer of 1320; as all the English kings did, he loathed having to kneel to another person, even if he were doing so in his position as duke of Aquitaine and count of Ponthieu, not as king of England.[84] On 23 January 1317, Edward sent a rather extraordinary letter to his chancellor John Sandal and his treasurer Walter of Norwich, stating, 'The king has heard that Sir Charles, count of La Marche, the king's brother[-in-law], claims to have his purparty [share] of the realm of France by succession of heritage by the death of his nephew [John I]; and the king should have his purparty also according to the laws and customs of those parts by reason of the queen of England, his consort.'[85] This was in response to a letter to him from his vassal in Ponthieu, John, lord of Fiennes, informing him of a rumour that the kingdom of France would be partitioned.[86] Edward ordered the chancellor and treasurer to attend a meeting of his great council and advise him on the matter, but unsurprisingly nothing came of it. Edward and Philip V seem to have been on amicable terms, as brothers-in-law at least, if not as kings: shortly before his accession, the French king sent Edward bunches of new grapes, and a year later a box of rose sugar.[87] Just four weeks after Philip V's coronation, his and Isabella's great-uncle Robert, count of Clermont, the last son of Saint Louis IX and Marguerite of Provence, died at the age of sixty-one and was buried at the convent of the Jacobins in Paris. Clermont and his son Louis, made first duke of Bourbon in 1327, are considered the founders of the House of Bourbon that, 272 years after Clermont's death, would become the ruling dynasty of France when their descendant Henry of Bourbon, king of Navarre and later of Spain too, succeeded as Henry IV.

Shortly after Philip V's coronation, a general assembly of clergy, nobles, citizens and academics set out a general principle that a woman could not succeed to the French throne. This was codified into the *lex Salica* or Salic law in the reign of King Charles V (1364–80). It was agreed in 1317 that Philip V's niece Joan of Navarre would marry her cousin Philip of Evreux, son and heir of Philip IV's half-brother Louis, count of Evreux, while her uncle Duke Odo IV of Burgundy would marry Philip V and Joan of Burgundy's eldest daughter, yet another Joan, who was born in 1308. Odo and the younger Joan's wedding duly went ahead, and on her mother the dowager queen's death in 1330, Joan of France became countess of Burgundy and Artois in her own right and was already duchess of Burgundy by marriage. Her disinherited first cousin Joan of Navarre, meanwhile, was granted a generous financial settlement, and it was agreed that the county of Champagne, once held by her paternal grandmother Queen Joan I of Navarre, would revert to her if her uncle Philip V died without male heirs (as he did). Joan of Navarre was again passed over for the French throne in 1322 when Philip V died with four daughters but no surviving sons, and her last uncle became Charles IV. She became Queen Joan II of Navarre in her own right in 1328 when Charles IV died; his heir to the throne of France, his cousin Philip of Valois who became Philip VI, had no claim to the kingdom, as he was not a descendant of Joan I.[88] Joan II of Navarre passed on her claim to the French throne to her eldest son and heir Charles II 'the Bad', king of Navarre and count of Evreux (b. 1332), a rival and sometime ally of Edward II and Isabella's son Edward III of England during the Hundred Years War. Isabella of France and Edward II's marriage, intended to make peace between two powerful countries, ultimately ensured instead a war between them which would last for more than a century.

5

The Impostor

1317–1319

Isabella and Edward spent Christmas 1316 at Nottingham, New Year 1317 at the hunting lodge of Clipstone, and the whole of February, March and much of April 1317 at the royal manor of Clarendon in Wiltshire. On 21 March at nearby Amesbury Priory, Edward's niece Elizabeth de Clare gave birth to her daughter Isabella Verdon, posthumous child of her husband Theobald, who had abducted her from Bristol Castle in February 1316 and who died eight months before their daughter's birth. Edward sent a silver cup with stand and cover worth £1 10s as a christening gift for his great-niece, and Isabella Verdon was named after Queen Isabella, her godmother. The sub-sheriff of Wiltshire John Harnham escorted the queen from Clarendon to Amesbury, where she lifted her baby namesake from the font during the christening ceremony.[1] Edward II visited Elizabeth at Amesbury while she was pregnant or even just after she gave birth, and put pressure on her to marry his latest favourite, Roger Damory, whom he tactlessly took with him. As one of the three heirs of the earl of Gloucester and with dower and jointure lands from two previous husbands, Elizabeth was among the wealthiest women in the country and a great marital prize that the king was determined to secure for Damory. Whatever her feelings about marrying an obscure knight, Elizabeth accepted; she really had no other choice. Sometime in late April or early May, she married Damory at Windsor Castle, and at about the same time her sister Margaret, Piers Gaveston's widow, married Sir Hugh Audley, another of the king's three current court favourites, in the presence of the king and queen. Roger Damory and Elizabeth de Clare had one child, Elizabeth Damory, later Lady Bardolf and heir to Damory's few landholdings, while Hugh Audley and Margaret de Clare also had only one daughter,

Margaret Audley, later countess of Stafford and ancestor of the Stafford dukes of Buckingham, and sole heir (after her half-sister Joan Gaveston's death in 1325) to Margaret de Clare's third of the enormous de Clare inheritance.

Alice Lacy, daughter and heiress of the late earl of Lincoln and married to Isabella's uncle Thomas, earl of Lancaster, left her husband and her unhappy marriage in early May 1317 with the aid of John de Warenne, earl of Surrey, who sent one of his household knights to a manor where Alice was staying in Dorset to fetch her to his castle of Reigate in Sussex. The earl of Lancaster accused his cousin the king and his favourites Damory, Audley and William Montacute of plotting with the earl of Surrey to snatch Alice away from him, which may or may not be true. The Westminster chronicle *Flores Historiarum*, always anti-Edward II, claims that the abduction came about as a result of Edward's 'violent boiling anger' towards and extreme envy of the earl of Lancaster, while the much more measured *Vita Edward Secundi* reports without comment Lancaster's belief that Edward had connived at the earl's wife leaving him and the *Bridlington* and *Anonimalle* chronicles say that Alice left her husband voluntarily and that the earl of Surrey took her under his protection.[2] Although Thomas had fathered at least two illegitimate sons, he and Alice had no children, and his heir was his younger brother Henry, Isabella's other Lancaster uncle and a far less thin-skinned and difficult character than his brother. Henry and his wife Maud Chaworth, niece of the late earl of Warwick and the older half-sister of Hugh Despenser the Younger, had a son and six daughters – Isabella's first cousins.

In April 1317, Edward asked for a dispensation from Pope John XXII for his and Isabella's two sons, Edward of Windsor, now four and a half, and John of Eltham, eight months, to make future marriages with girls with whom they shared a set of great-great-grandparents.[3] The marriage of their elder son, the future king, was of particular importance. And almost three years after his nephew the earl of Gloucester had fallen at Bannockburn, the king finally gave up the pretence that Gloucester's widow, Maud, was pregnant, and ordered the earl's vast lands in England, Wales and Ireland to be divided among his sisters, Eleanor, Margaret and Elizabeth, and their husbands, Despenser the Younger, Hugh Audley and Roger Damory.[4] The spring of 1317 saw the abduction of an English nobleman on the continent: Aymer de Valence, earl of Pembroke, when returning to England in early May from an embassy to the pope in Avignon on Edward's behalf, was captured and imprisoned in the county of Bar in eastern France. This almost certainly took place on the orders of Edward II's nephew Edouard, count of Bar – who had himself been taken prisoner by the duke of Lorraine three years before – who was angry at the treatment of his sister Joan at the hands of her husband the earl of Surrey. It may be that Pembroke had presented a petition to the pope requesting the annulment of Surrey and Joan's marriage.[5] As soon as Edward heard the news, on 10 May 1317, he sent letters to his nephew Edouard, his brother-in-law Philip V of France, Isabella's uncles the counts of Valois and Evreux, the dukes of Brittany (John III) and Burgundy (Odo IV), almost two dozen other noblemen, and – significantly – Joan of Bar herself, asking them to do their utmost to procure Pembroke's release.[6] This major diplomatic effort had the desired effect, and Pembroke was released by mid-June.[7]

The never-ending struggle with Scotland continued throughout the 1310s. Despite Edward's defeat at Bannockburn, he had not recognised Bruce as king of Scots and never would. In the north of England, some of Edward's subjects grew tired of his inability to protect them from frequent Scottish raids, and sometime in 1316 or 1317 attempted to launch an invasion of Fife, which failed. Many of them drowned on the way back to England.[8] On 1 January 1317, Pope John XXII confirmed a two-year truce between Edward and Robert Bruce, calling Edward 'our dearest son in Christ, Edward, illustrious king of England', and Bruce 'our beloved son, the noble man, Robert de Bruce, holding himself king of Scotland'. On 17 March, John exhorted Edward to make peace with Bruce, and appointed two cardinals to travel to England and negotiate between the two kings.[9] On 28 March, however, having met the earl of Pembroke and other envoys sent to him by Edward, the pope changed his mind and once again excommunicated Robert and his brother Edward Bruce and all those who were hostile to Edward II or invaded his kingdom, saying that Robert was 'unjustly pretending to occupy the throne of Scotland'.[10]

Edward's dire relations with his powerful and supremely rich cousin and Isabella's uncle Thomas, earl of Lancaster worsened still further throughout 1317. Lancaster loathed Edward's current three favourites and demanded that they be sent away from court. He even accused Roger Damory and William Montacute of trying to kill him, and claimed that he had intercepted letters Edward II had sent to Scotland, asking the Scots to come and help him kill his cousin.[11] Edward refused to expel his friends and refused to act in regard to the abduction, voluntary or otherwise, of Lancaster's wife Alice Lacy. Damory, Audley and Montacute did their utmost to stir things up between the king and his cousin, selfishly counselling the king to remain hostile to Lancaster. They 'intrigued against the earl as best they could', and the *Flores* calls them 'men who stir up discord and many problems for the kingdom daily attending the lord king, continually supporting his arrogance and lawless designs'.[12] Pope John XXII tried to heal the breach between Edward and Lancaster and urged the king not to allow any 'backbiter or malicious flatterer' to bring about disunity between himself and Lancaster.[13]

Edward did not listen. He was incapable of distinguishing between good and bad advice, tended to act impulsively on whatever information the last person had given him, always believed what people he was fond of told him and could not or would not take their own self-interest into account, and generally showed little if any good or balanced judgement. Although these middle years of his reign were comparatively peaceful, that is purely relative; the situation with Scotland and Robert Bruce which Edward could neither resolve nor leave alone dragged on and on, his conflict with his cousin Lancaster threatened everyone – the king and the earl both took to marching around the country with large numbers of armed men, civil war constantly threatening to break out – and the Great Famine was not yet over and numerous people were still suffering terribly from hunger, malnutrition and diseases associated with them. Fortunately, the weather improved in 1317 and the harvest also, and the grip of the famine loosened slowly.

Isabella and Edward seem to have been on good terms in 1317, though if she gave him advice about coming to terms with her uncle Lancaster and how this would be better for everyone, and how it would be sensible not to show so much favouritism towards the three men doing their utmost to make the situation worse, he did not listen to her. The king and queen spent the period from mid-April to mid-May 1317 at Windsor. Edward II turned thirty-three on 25 April, while Isabella had turned twenty-one probably at the end of 1316. On 4 April, Edward asked the Dominican friars of Pamplona in Aragon to pray for 'the good estate of the king, Queen Isabella, Edward of Wyndesore his elder son, and John of Eltham his younger son'. The previous Pentecost, 1316, he had sent the Dominicans of Pamplona £20 to pay for three days' entertainment for themselves, one day as a gift from himself, one from Isabella and one from Edward of Windsor (John of Eltham had not yet been born).[14] On 22 April 1317, Edward gave Isabella the castle, town and honour of Wallingford, and on 25 July, while they were staying in Nottingham, also gave her 'all the king's castles, towns, manors, lands and tenements' in Cornwall.[15] That Wallingford and Cornwall had once belonged to Piers Gaveston and that Edward was willing to give them to his wife is perhaps indicative of the position she now held in his heart. It is also telling that in the remaining fourteen and a half years of his reign after Gaveston's death, Edward II never gave the earldom of Cornwall to another person, not even to his younger son, John of Eltham (who did ultimately receive it in 1328, but from his mother, not his father), or Edmund of Woodstock, the younger of his half-brothers, to whom he granted the less prestigious earldom of Kent in 1321. It is as though in Edward II's mind, the earldom of Cornwall belonged to Gaveston and could not be given to anyone else. As late as June 1326, only months before his forced abdication, Edward was still ordering various convents to have prayers said for Gaveston.[16] It seems reasonably certain that Edward loved Isabella, and it is beyond all doubt that he adored Piers Gaveston and remembered him frequently for many years after Gaveston's death.

Edward and Isabella spent a month in May/June 1317 at Westminster, where Edward paid four men for singing before himself and perhaps the queen in his chamber and had a crown made for himself especially for the Nativity of St John the Baptist, one of his favourite saints, on 24 June.[17] On 7 July 1317, ten years to the day after his father, Edward I's death, Edward founded the King's Hall at the University of Cambridge. In 1546 it was incorporated into Trinity College, the new foundation of his and Isabella's descendant Henry VIII. Edward also founded Oriel College at Oxford in 1326. His ally Walter Stapeldon, bishop of Exeter and treasurer of England, founded Exeter College at Oxford in 1314; another ally, Hervey Staunton of the King's Bench, founded Michaelhouse at Cambridge in 1324 (also incorporated into Trinity College in 1546); and his niece Elizabeth de Clare founded Clare College at Cambridge in 1338. King's Hall, Cambridge, maintained thirty-two scholars. Edward gave books on canon and civil law worth £10 to his new foundation, which Isabella later confiscated and presumably kept for herself; in the early 1330s, their son Edward III compensated the college for the loss.[18] Edward II also once borrowed books – the lives of St Thomas Becket and St Anselm – from the library of Canterbury Cathedral, and failed to return them.[19] Both Isabella and her husband liked books. Edward could certainly read and perhaps also write, and probably Isabella could too. The earliest extant example of a king of England's handwriting is their son Edward III's, in a letter to John XXII in which *Pater Sancte* ('Holy Father' in Latin) is written in his own hand, which dates from 1329 or 1330. There is evidence that Edward's favourite Hugh Despenser the Younger could read and that Edward's sister-in-law Margaret Wake, countess of Kent was able to write, and if these two members of baronial houses could do so, it seems likely (though not certain) that the royally born and educated Isabella had been taught to do so as well.[20] Edward II owned a few books, including a romance bequeathed to him by his grandmother Eleanor of Provence, another romance about Tristan and Isolde which he gave to Hugh Despenser the Younger in 1326, a history of the kings of England in Latin, a biography of St Edward the Confessor and a Latin book called *On the Ruling of Kings*.[21] Isabella, who had ample leisure time as dowager queen for the last twenty-eight years of her life, owned more, which passed at her death in 1358 to her two surviving children, Edward III, king of England, and Joan of the Tower, queen of Scotland, and she has been reasonably called a 'bibliophile'. Among many other books, she owned eight romances, a 'great book' bound with white leather about the deeds of King Arthur, an encyclopedia of ancient history, a book of homilies in French, an unspecified 'picture book' and an unidentified 'story of hermits', and a Bible in French, in two volumes.[22] In late 1315, Edward II paid £5 for a book about the life and deeds of his father Edward I to be made for him, and in 1326 paid his painter Jack of St Albans to illustrate a book Jack was making for him about the earls, lords and knights of England.[23] Isabella, for her part, commissioned an illustrated book on an unknown topic and paid 14s for it near the end of her life, with an extra payment to Richard the Painter for azure paint to be used in it.

Pope John XXII sent two cardinals to England in 1317 to negotiate between Edward and Robert Bruce, and they arrived in Canterbury on 24 June, the Nativity of John the Baptist. They were Luca Fieschi, an Italian nobleman by birth who was a distant cousin of Edward's and always acknowledged as such, and the pope's own relative Gaucelin Duèse. The two cardinals never met Bruce, however: he refused to allow them to enter his kingdom unless they acknowledged him as king of Scotland, which they would not do. On their way to Durham in September 1317 to attend the consecration of Louis Beaumont, the new bishop of Durham, in the company of Beaumont's brother Henry, Cardinals Fieschi and Duèse were attacked, robbed and briefly imprisoned by a knight called Sir Gilbert Middleton. On their release, the cardinals excommunicated Middleton, and a furious and embarrassed Edward II, declaring Middleton and his companions to be 'the sons of iniquity', sent fourteen of his squires to capture and arrest him and take him to the Tower of London.[24] Middleton was given a terrible death by hanging, drawing and quartering on 24 January 1318, the first man to suffer this penalty during Edward's reign. (The second would be the Welsh nobleman Llywelyn Bren, who had rebelled in Glamorgan in 1316, but suffered his gruesome fate sometime later in 1318; Hugh Despenser the Younger removed him from the Tower of London and took him to Cardiff to have him executed, without the king's permission.)

Edward II tried, however reluctantly, to come to terms with his turbulent cousin the earl of Lancaster in the summer of 1317, and he and Isabella travelled to Nottingham, where the king had summoned Lancaster to attend a meeting on 18 July. Lancaster failed to appear, although the king and queen waited for him for three weeks; Edward sent a letter remonstrating with him, and Lancaster sulkily replied that he would not attend the king unless Roger Damory, Hugh Audley, William Montacute and John de Warenne, earl of Surrey were removed from court.[25] Isabella and Edward gave up waiting for the earl and left Nottingham on 7 August 1317 to travel slowly to York, passing through the small Nottinghamshire village of Shelford on the 8th, where the king distributed 5s 6d in oblations at the church; the heart of his nephew

Gilbert de Clare, earl of Gloucester, killed at Bannockburn three years before, was interred there.[26] The royal couple stayed at Somerton Castle in Lincolnshire and then for a few days at the Gilbertine priory of St Catherine's in Lincoln, where the body of Edward's mother, Queen Eleanor, had rested in 1290 before her funeral cortège wound its way to Westminster Abbey. They had had little choice but to take the more easterly route to York: Thomas, earl of Lancaster had blocked their way by placing armed men on the roads south of the city. Edward was utterly furious that one of his subjects would dare to impede his and his queen's travel through their own kingdom, and would raise the issue against Lancaster years later.[27] Edward and Isabella managed to arrive safely in York in early September, spent time with the two cardinals Luca Fieschi and Gaucelin Duèse, and sent envoys to the earl of Lancaster to try to make peace with him so that yet another campaign in Scotland which Edward was intending to lead could go ahead – 'a love-day without the clash of arms', as the *Vita* puts it. Lancaster refused, claiming that Edward wanted to 'have his head or consign him to prison', but then finally agreed to meet the king in October 1318.[28] Sometime while they were together in York in September 1317, Isabella and Edward must have conceived their third child, who would be born on 18 June 1318.

On the way back to London, the king and queen passed through Pontefract, which was the favourite residence of the earl of Lancaster. Lancaster had now removed his soldiers from the roads and bridges so that Edward and Isabella could travel without impediment, but did his utmost to make the situation even worse by leading his men out to the top of his castle ditch and jeering at the king and queen as they rode past. Edward, understandably incensed at this appalling rudeness and already persuaded by one of his friends – probably Roger Damory – that Lancaster was preparing to attack him and that he should attack first, was only just talked out of leading an assault on Pontefract Castle by the sensible Aymer de Valence, earl of Pembroke, who fortunately retained some influence over the king.[29] The royal party arrived safely in London in mid-October 1317 without further incidents, but the earl of Lancaster continued to make trouble: he seized Knaresborough Castle, formerly Piers Gaveston's, in Yorkshire, and Alton Castle, formerly Theobald Verdon's, in Staffordshire; the loathed royal favourite Roger Damory was custodian of both. Lancaster also sent his knights and men to take over the Yorkshire castles of John de Warenne, earl of Surrey, the king's nephew-in-law whom he considered another of his deadly enemies, and the property of Surrey's mistress Maud Nerford. Edward II sent out ineffectual orders telling him to desist, but Lancaster had gone far beyond listening to his despised cousin, and it wasn't until January 1318 that he handed over the castles he had seized to the king's men.[30] The earl of Lancaster must have been furious when on 15 November

1317, Roger Damory, Hugh Audley and Hugh Despenser the Younger and their wives, Eleanor, Margaret and Elizabeth de Clare, finally received their division of the lands which had belonged to the late earl of Gloucester. Their new wealth catapulted all three men to the forefront of the nobility, and made Damory a much more powerful enemy. And although no one at the time could have known it, this marked the start of the rise to power of Hugh Despenser the Younger, the man who would bring down Edward II and the man whom Isabella would come to hate above all others.

On 22 November 1317, Edward gave Isabella all the houses in London which had been given to him by his friend the rich Genoese merchant Antonio di Pessagno, whom he had appointed steward of Gascony earlier in the month (Pessagno sent Edward a gift of two camels in return).[31] As always, Isabella made numerous requests to Edward on behalf of other people throughout 1317, which he granted.[32] Isabella, now about three months pregnant, spent Christmas 1317 at Westminster with her husband. She received an enamelled silver-gilt bowl with foot and cover from him, worth £17, while her sons Edward of Windsor (aged five) and John of Eltham (aged sixteen months) received rings from their father, as did the king's nieces Margaret and Elizabeth de Clare. Edward's five-year-old great-niece Joan Gaveston received a gold ring with two emeralds and three pearls worth 32s from Edward, and another gold ring with six emeralds, worth twenty marks, went to his sister Mary, a nun with no vocation, who was five years older than the king and of whom Edward was extremely fond.[33] Pope John XXII once more excommunicated 'all those who invade the realm of England or disturb its peace' on 29 December 1317, a reference to Robert Bruce and his allies.[34] On 27 December, Edward gave Isabella all the lands and tenements which had once belonged to Theobald Verdon, who had abducted his niece Elizabeth de Clare and married her in February 1316, including Verdon's main seat of Alton in Staffordshire, recently seized by her uncle Thomas of Lancaster but returned to the king's custody.[35] Isabella also received the wardship of Verdon's four daughters and co-heirs, the eldest three of whom were Roger Mortimer's nieces and the youngest, Isabella, was the king's great-niece and her own goddaughter. Verdon's lands and the custody of his daughters had formerly been in the hands of Edward's favourite Roger Damory; this may be a sign that Edward was somewhat losing interest in the knight, though Damory did remain fairly close to the king for a while longer. Certainly the king chose to enrich Isabella considerably at Damory's expense, which can only have pleased her. The queen received sad news at the end of 1317, however: her former nurse Theophania de Saint Pierre died shortly before 27 December.[36]

On 14 February 1318, the dowager queen Marguerite, Edward's

stepmother and Isabella's aunt, died at her Wiltshire castle of Marlborough, in her late thirties (she was only about five years older than Edward, and years younger than some of her other stepchildren). She left her two sons, Thomas of Brotherton, earl of Norfolk, aged seventeen, and Edmund of Woodstock, later earl of Kent, aged sixteen, whom Edward II appointed as executors of her will.[37] The king sent two pieces of Lucca cloth to lie over his stepmother's body at Marlborough on 8 March, and visited her remains at St Mary's church in Southwark on the 14th. He bought six pieces of Lucca cloth for himself and two pieces each for his sister Mary and Roger Damory when they attended Marguerite's funeral at the Greyfriars church in London on 15 March. Isabella is not mentioned as receiving the cloth or as attending the funeral, which either means that any cloth purchased for her appeared in her own household accounts for this year, which do not survive, or that she did not attend her aunt's funeral, perhaps because her five-month pregnancy was causing her problems.[38] The dower lands Marguerite had held passed by right to Isabella. Edward, anxious that his wife should receive them as soon as possible, ordered the treasurer and barons of the exchequer 'to postpone all excuses and omit all other affairs' on 23 February and grant Isabella 'the dower assigned to her at the church door when the king married her'.[39] She now had an annual income of £4,500, in accordance with the arrangement Edward's father, Edward I, had made with her father, Philip IV, when negotiating the marriage.[40] On 6 March 1318, Edward granted Isabella the entire land of Ponthieu and the town of Montreuil and all its profits for life, over and above the assignments made to her in dower,[41] and on 20 March he asked the Italian banking society the Bardi to pay Isabella fifty marks (£33) a week for her household expenses, and acknowledged that he still owed her £7,030 'for diverse causes', part of which was perhaps the remainder of the loan she had given him a few years before for the wedding of his cousin Blanche of Brittany's daughter.[42] From 23 to 27 March 1318, Edward and presumably Isabella as well were guests of the king's niece Elizabeth de Clare, then about seven months pregnant, and her third husband, the royal favourite Roger Damory, at Clare Castle in Suffolk. Two months later, Edward gave Damory's messenger a massive £20 for bringing him news of the birth of Damory and Elizabeth's daughter Elizabeth Damory, half-sister of Queen Isabella's goddaughter Isabella Verdon, born the year before.[43]

At the Oxfordshire palace of Woodstock, which Edward had given her some years before, Isabella gave birth on 18 June 1318 to their third child (Edward's fourth, including his illegitimate son, Adam). It was a daughter, and they named her Eleanor after her paternal grandmother, Eleanor of Castile, queen of England and countess of Ponthieu, following contemporary convention. Edward had been on pilgrimage to Canterbury but arrived at Woodstock on the day of his daughter's birth, and paid 500 marks, or £333, to 'Lady Isabella, queen of England, of the king's gift, for the feast of her purification after the birth of Lady Alienora her daughter' (the name Eleanor in the fourteenth century was spelt Alianore or Alienora).[44] Little Eleanor of Woodstock was placed in the household of her older brothers, Edward of Windsor and John of Eltham, and cared for by a nurse named Joan du Bois.[45] Edward granted Eleanor and John of Eltham the manor of High Peak and the income from nine other manors, formerly in Isabella's hands, for their sustenance; the queen consented to give up her manors in order to provide an income for her two younger children, and in return received the entire county of Cornwall from her husband.[46] In February 1318, Edward had ordered four men to launch an inquiry about recent shipwrecks in Cornwall, and to find out who had carried away goods cast ashore there since the previous 25 July, the day he had granted the royal lands, manors and castles in the county to his wife. He declared that 'wreck of sea ought now to belong to the king and Queen Isabella' and goods taken away by anyone else rightfully belonged to her and should be returned to her.[47] Some months later, several men in Cornwall were charged with trespass against Isabella, which presumably relates to her right to receive goods from shipwrecks in the county.[48]

Edward and Isabella left Woodstock on 27 June 1318, only nine days after she had borne their daughter – which implies that the birth had been an easy one – and set off for Northampton, where the king had summoned a meeting of his great council. This meeting is famous mostly for the appearance of a royal impostor known as John of Powderham, a tanner from Exeter, who came before the king and told him that he was the rightful son of Edward I and that he, Edward II, was a mere impostor and a peasant. John claimed that as he lay in his cradle as a baby, he had been attacked by a wild sow and injured, and that his nurse, too terrified to tell Edward I what had happened to his son and heir, had secretly swapped him for a local child of low birth. Edward II, who never lacked a sense of humour, greeted John and his announcement with the ironic words 'Welcome, my brother', though went on to tell John, 'Thou hast not a drop of blood from the illustrious Edward [I], and that I am prepared to prove against thee.'[49] According to the *Anonimalle* chronicle, Edward thought that it would be an excellent idea to make John a court jester, and summoned his parents from Exeter to have them questioned about his real background.[50] Several English magnates, not named and considerably less amused than the king, ordered John to be hanged; the trial probably took place under the king's steward William Montacute and sentence was carried out sometime between 20 and 24 July 1318, and John's body remained on public view for long afterwards.[51] It is unclear whether Edward and Isabella witnessed the execution, as they left Northampton on 21 July and returned to Woodstock for a few days. Edward himself may have found the situation entertaining or at least pretended to, but Isabella certainly did not: the *Vita Edwardi Secundi* says that John of Powderham's claims 'annoyed the queen unspeakably'.[52] It is extremely unlikely that Isabella believed that her husband was of low birth and that John's claims were in any way true, but for a woman with her deep sense of royalty to be married to a king who opened himself up to such claims, with his love of rustic pursuits and the company of the lowborn, must have disturbed and upset her greatly. That John's claims became the talk of the kingdom and that many people believed him 'all the more readily because the said lord Edward [II] resembled the elder lord Edward [I] in none of his virtues' made the situation even worse, and Isabella surely felt profoundly humiliated.[53] Edward II was a crowned and anointed king, son of a king and grandson of two more, yet often behaved as though he had, indeed, been born into a peasant family. Her feelings and John of Powderham's claims to be the rightful king of England made no difference whatsoever to the eccentric Edward, however, who laughed them off and continued behaving as he always had. The author of the *Vita* wrote in 1318, 'Neither has our King Edward who has reigned eleven years and more, done anything that ought to be preached in the market place or upon the house-tops.'[54]

In early August 1318, the king finally made peace with his turbulent cousin Thomas, earl of Lancaster at the instigation of a coalition of magnates including the earls of Pembroke and Hereford and various bishops, who were sick of the lawlessness in England engendered by the hostility between the two men and their refusal to work together. The *Vita* says that Isabella was also instrumental in the peace settlement between her husband and her uncle.[55] Now in her early twenties, Isabella was truly coming into her own as a mediator and a political player. She had successfully negotiated with her father in 1314 on her husband's behalf, she had probably been involved in the release of the count of Bar from the duke of Lorraine's custody that year, and she publicly opposed her husband's wishes in 1316 and 1319 regarding the election of two bishops and was met with tolerant acceptance from him and, on one occasion, a willingness to change his mind and promote her candidate in place of his own. Edward and Thomas of Lancaster met in a field in Leake, Leicestershire, on 7 August 1318, in the presence of numerous earls, bishops and magnates, and the king gave his cousin a fine palfrey horse in recognition of his 'great love' for his cousin, as Walter Reynolds, archbishop of Canterbury, put it (though 'great hatred' would have been far more accurate).[56] Edward agreed to uphold the hated Ordinances of 1311 while Lancaster was threatened with sanctions if he continued to hold armed assemblies. Lancaster also demanded the removal from court of Roger Damory, Hugh Audley and William Montacute, and, surprisingly, Edward readily agreed – surely a sign that he had grown tired of the three men, even Roger Damory, who had once meant so much to him and on whom he appears to have depended emotionally in many ways. Montacute was removed from his position as steward of the king's household and appointed steward of Gascony instead; he died there in 1319. Audley and Damory were still the king's nephews-in-law and still wealthy by right of their wives, Margaret and Elizabeth de Clare, but their access to the king was now far more limited.

On 21 November 1318, Edward II granted his Oxford palace of Beaumont to the Carmelite order, as he had sworn to do after Bannockburn, and in return asked the friars to celebrate divine service 'for the good estate of the king and Queen Isabella and their children so long as they shall live, and for their souls after death'.[57] The king received excellent news from Ireland: Robert Bruce's brother Edward (who must have been named in honour of Edward I, Edward being an extremely uncommon name in Scotland at the time) had been defeated at the battle of Faughart in October and killed, and his head was sent to Edward II. The victor of Faughart was John de Bermingham, one of the many sons-in-law of Richard de Burgh, earl of Ulster – as Robert Bruce himself was – and Edward later made him earl of Louth in gratitude. Unfortunately, Robert Bruce had managed to seize the vital port of Berwick-upon-Tweed earlier in the year, and although Edward II summoned the earl of Lancaster and many other nobles to muster and to regain the port, the conflict and final resolution with Lancaster meant that the expedition was cancelled until 1319, giving Bruce far more time to strengthen the town's defences. Pope John XXII excommunicated Robert, whose army invaded Yorkshire in May 1318 and carried off numerous prisoners to Scotland yet again.[58] Roger Mortimer of Wigmore was granted 2,000 marks in late 1318 out of 6000 marks which Edward owed him for his service in Ireland; Mortimer was accompanied in that country by his wife Joan Geneville, with whom he seems to have had a close relationship. They had married as far back as 1301 when he was only fourteen and she fifteen, and she brought him numerous lands in England, Wales, Ireland and Gascony as her inheritance from her grandparents. Mortimer's father, Edmund, had died in 1304 when Mortimer was seventeen, and the same year Edward I gave his wardship and the custody of his lands to, of all people, Piers Gaveston, at the request of Edward of Caernarfon, now Edward II.[59]

On 6 December 1318, the four leading members of Edward II's household (his steward, chamberlain, treasurer and controller) formulated a Household Ordinance, detailing the roles and responsibilities of his many hundreds of staff. It is the second oldest royal Household Ordinance extant in England, after one made in 1279 for Edward's father. Isabella had her own household and so is only mentioned in passing in the document, simply as *ma dame*, 'my lady', entitled, as were the king and any lords dining with him, to 'four good courses and no more' at dinner, while the rest of the king's household had to make do with three. The king had his own personal cooks as well as squires to serve him at table, whose responsibilities included cutting his meat and serving him from his cup, and probably Isabella had the same. All food and drink, including a gallon of ale per day plus an allowance of wine for higher-ranking staff (who were also given candles or torches for their bedchambers), was provided for free in the king's household, as were all clothes, which were generally given out twice a year at Christmas and Pentecost and were colour co-ordinated – so that, for example, one summer the squires would be in red and black, the valets in striped blue, and so on. The lower ranks of staff received a cheaper quality of material and less-good fur, and also were not entitled to eat roast meat as their superiors were, but only the boiled kind. Wages were generous by the standards of the day, with valets receiving 3*d*, squires 7½*d* and sergeants-at-arms 12*d* daily, and the staff were entitled to take holiday leave on occasion with the king's permission, though their families were not allowed to accompany them or even to follow behind the court as the king travelled around the country. To ease the burden on any local district of so many hundreds of people requiring food and accommodation, Edward II rarely spent more than a handful of nights in the same place; he and his retinue, and Isabella's, were always on the move. Edward had a personal bodyguard of twenty-four archers on foot, and also thirty sergeants-at-arms 'who shall daily ride armed before the king's person'. The king was to nominate four of the sergeants-at-arms to sleep outside his bedchamber, had a porter 'who will guard the door of there where the king sleeps', and also had at least six valets who spent the night inside his chamber, except, one assumes, on the nights when he slept with Isabella (or anyone else with whom he might have had a sexual relationship). Edward rewarded these six valets financially in 1326 for their efforts in waking and obeying his commands whenever he himself awoke during the night. As well as the four sergeants-at-arms sleeping outside his chamber, the other twenty-six, when they were at court, were ordered to 'lie in the hall beside, to be nearby when the king needs them'.[60] Isabella, for her part, was closely attended by her eight or so damsels, who also slept in her chamber or nearby, and the king and queen spent every moment of their lives surrounded by servants. Usually, Edward and Isabella each had their own suite of rooms at the manors where they stayed; at the manor of Burgh in Suffolk, for example, there was a chamber for the king adjoining a 'great hall covered with shingles', and a chamber for the queen with its own chapel and a private bridge leading from her chamber to the park. Another bridge to the park was located near the bakehouse, and there was a 'chamber for the knights', another large chapel, a watchtower within the moat, and a 'great chamber' outside the moat with two garderobes, or toilets.[61] At the royal manor of Clarendon in Wiltshire, where Isabella and Edward spent much time in the middle years of his reign, an inquisition of 1315 revealed that Edward had a chamber with its own chapel nearby, while Isabella had chambers, plural, with their own passage and 'pentice' (covered walkway) towards the hall and her chapel. A 'chamber of the king's children' is also listed, with a passage, a pentice and a staircase connecting it to the king's chamber. Clarendon was said to be in urgent need of almost £2,000 worth of repairs in 1315, the numerous defects having been 'caused by long neglect of roofing'.[62]

In late 1318, Edward II's nephew-in-law Hugh Despenser the Younger replaced John Charlton as his chamberlain, a very powerful position as he controlled access to the king in person and in writing. Despenser was soon to exploit his power to the hilt, and to force people to bribe him in order to speak to the king. According to the later chronicler Geoffrey le Baker, Edward was displeased at Despenser's appointment as he loathed him, which is probably an exaggeration, but it does seem as though Edward had never much liked or trusted Despenser and had rarely shown him any favour at all, even though Despenser's father, Hugh Despenser the Elder, was one of the king's closest friends and allies (albeit twenty-three years his senior) and Despenser's wife, Eleanor de Clare, was Edward's oldest and favourite niece. Despenser the Younger was about thirty in 1318 and already had about half a dozen children with Eleanor. He was the nephew and grandson of earls of Warwick; Roger Bigod, the earl of Norfolk, who died in 1306 was his step-grandfather; the earl of Gloucester who fell at Bannockburn was his brother-in-law; and Edward I had arranged Despenser's marriage to the king's eldest granddaughter in 1306. Despite his excellent family connections to wealthy high-ranking noblemen, however, Despenser himself was comparatively impoverished. He owned no lands at all before 1317 and his father had had to give him the issues of half a dozen of his manors early in Edward II's reign to provide him with at least some income. Edward seized these manors early in 1310 when Despenser went abroad without his permission to take part in a jousting tournament in Mons.[63] It is often believed and stated that Despenser rose in Edward's favour around the time of Bannockburn or even before, which ignores the existence of Roger Damory, Hugh Audley and William Montacute and their importance at court between about 1315 and 1318, and the theory that Despenser had become close to the king as early as 1314 is refuted by Edward's refusal to partition the lands of the late earl of Gloucester until almost three and a half years after Gloucester's death; had Despenser already been in his favour then, Edward would have fallen over himself to give him the lands as soon as possible. Despenser followed the political lead of his maternal uncle Guy Beauchamp, earl of Warwick, rather than his royalist father, and was physically attacked by members of Edward's household irate at his opposition to the king in or before 1311, when the Lords Ordainer complained about it to Edward (though given that Despenser himself assaulted the baron John Ros at the 1316 Lincoln parliament, he was probably capable of giving as good as he got).[64] To what extent Isabella knew Despenser before 1318 is unclear, though she must have been aware of him as her chief lady-in-waiting's husband, her own husband's nephew-in-law and, in the confusingly tangled and interrelated family tree of the English and French royalty and nobility of the early fourteenth century, also as the brother-in-law of her uncle Henry of Lancaster. Despenser would, a few years later, intrude into Isabella's marriage to such an extent that she would hold him responsible for destroying it, and she would come to hate him as she hated no other person and avenge herself on him in the most savage and bloody manner possible.

6

The Contrariants
1319–1321

Isabella and Edward spent the first half of 1319 in York, where parliament took place in May. The Westminster chronicle *Flores Historiarum* reports that Isabella gave birth to a daughter, Joan, while they were there. This is certainly possible, though if Isabella did bear a daughter in 1319, the child must have died young. It is perhaps more likely, though, that the author of the *Flores* was thinking of Isabella and Edward's daughter Joan of the Tower, who was born in 1321 and later became queen consort of Scotland, and wrongly believed that she had been born two years earlier. If another daughter Joan, who died young, was indeed born to Isabella and Edward II in 1319, no other evidence exists to confirm it. As he often did, Edward asked Dominican friars to pray for himself, Isabella and their children in January 1319, this time in Marseilles, and at different times made the same request to Dominicans meeting in Paris, Rouen, Citeaux, Florence, Venice, Barcelona and Vienna.[1] In late 1318 and again in late 1319, the king corresponded with William, count of Hainault and Holland, regarding the possible future marriage of his and Isabella's elder son, Edward of Windsor, and the count's eldest daughter, Margaret – not his daughter Philippa, who did marry Edward III in 1328 and become queen of England, as is often assumed.[2] William of Hainault's wife and the mother of Margaret and Philippa was Isabella's first cousin Joan of Valois, one of the many daughters of her uncle Charles, count of Valois. This meant that her son and Joan's daughters were second cousins and thus needed a dispensation from the pope to marry, which Edward II asked John XXII to issue. Margaret of Hainault, eldest daughter of Count William and Joan of Valois, was born on 24 June 1311, so was a little older than Edward of Windsor, born on 13 November 1312, while her sister Philippa was born in about 1313 or 1314.[3] Edward sent Walter Stapeldon, bishop of Exeter and future treasurer of England, as his chief envoy to Hainault, and Stapeldon wrote a famous description of the girl he saw: he said that her hair was 'between blue[-black] and brown' (though this has also been translated as 'between blonde and brown'), that her eyes were 'brown and deep' and that all her body and limbs were 'of good form' but that her teeth were not particularly white.[4] Isabella's uncle Louis, count of Evreux, half-brother of her father Philip IV and full brother of the late Queen Marguerite, died on 19 May 1319, aged forty-three. He left as his heir, his son Philip, who later became king-consort of Navarre by marriage to his cousin Queen Joan II of Navarre and was the father of Charles II 'the Bad', king of Navarre and count of Evreux. One of Louis of Evreux's daughters, Joan, became queen of France in 1324 on marriage to Isabella's brother Charles, and another, Marie, was married to Edward II's nephew Duke John III of Brabant.

1319 was a mostly quiet year in England. On 20 July, Edward II asked the two archbishops and all the bishops of England to pray for him as he set off to lead the siege of the port of Berwick-upon-Tweed, captured by Robert Bruce the previous year, but in the end dithered in Newcastle for much of the summer and didn't arrive in Berwick until 7 September. Given the importance of recapturing the port, even the earl of Lancaster co-operated with the king for once and went to the siege. Only Edward II could have been so incompetent as to lead a siege and forget to take siege engines and diggers with him, both of which he belatedly had to ask his chancellor to bring to Berwick on 9 September, though in fairness no one who accompanied him to the port remembered either.[5] The king kept himself amused in Berwick: he ordered his hunting dogs sent from Wales and had two of his falcons brought from London, and paid two minstrels sent to him by Isabella's brother Philip V for their performance.[6] The king's chamberlain Hugh Despenser the Younger was also present at the siege of Berwick, and told the sheriff of Glamorgan in south Wales, which Despenser now owned as the major part of his wife, Eleanor de Clare's share of her brother the late earl of Gloucester's inheritance, that 'the earl [of Lancaster] behaved in such a way that the king took himself off with his army, to the shame and damage of us all. Wherefore we very much doubt if matters will go as well for our side as necessary.'[7] He was right. The siege, predictably, ended in total failure, and Berwick remained in Scottish hands until Isabella and Edward's son Edward III took it back in 1333. As a decoying tactic, Robert Bruce's closest two allies and chief lieutenants, James Douglas (who had followed Edward all the way to Dunbar after the battle of Bannockburn) and Thomas Randolph, led an army into England and reached as far south as Boroughbridge, a few miles from York. An army hastily cobbled together by the archbishop of York, Edward II's friend and ally William Melton, was heavily defeated near the village of Myton-on-Swale on 12 September and around 5,000 men were killed or drowned in the River Swale. When the news reached Berwick two days later, the earl of Lancaster gave up and left the siege in disgust.[8]

The presence of the victorious Scottish army in Yorkshire almost led to disaster for Isabella, who was staying at one of the archbishop's manors, either Brotherton, a village twenty miles to the south-west of York where her brother-in-law and first cousin Thomas, earl of Norfolk had been born in 1300, or Bishopthorpe, just south of the city. She and Edward must have thought she would be safe there, about fifty miles south of Berwick, but a captured Scottish scout revealed a plan that James Douglas, taking a force of ten thousand men (which is surely a gross exaggeration of the type so often found in medieval chronicles), was intending to seize her and kill anyone else they encountered unawares. Capturing Isabella was surely intended to keep the queen of England as a hostage until her husband agreed to recognise Robert Bruce as king of Scotland and give up all his claims to be overlord of the kingdom.[9] The *Vita* remarks that hardly anyone believed the spy's story, but to be on the safe side the archbishop of York, the chancellor of England John Hothum, the sheriff and burgesses of York and any able-bodied men in the city capable of carrying weapons, even monks, went out to Brotherton or Bishopthorpe and escorted Isabella from there to the city, where she would be much safer inside the walls. From York, the queen was taken by water to Nottingham, well beyond the reach of any Scottish force. The *Vita*'s author repeats a common rumour of the day, which he appears to believe, that Thomas, earl of Lancaster had received £40,000 from the Scots to betray his niece's location to them and to 'lend secret aid' to them, which included ordering his men not to assault the city walls of Berwick and allowing the Scots to march home without challenge.[10] The story that he had contrived at Isabella's capture seems very unlikely, and Lancaster defended himself by blaming Hugh Despenser the Younger for betraying the queen's whereabouts to the Scots instead. This hardly seems any more likely and probably represents the earl's awareness that Despenser was growing closer to Edward II, abandoning his former opposition to the king and alliance with the barons hostile to Edward, and might prove to be a dangerous enemy to Lancaster himself.[11] According to the *Flores Historiarum*, who calls the two men 'despicable parasites', Edward II promised to make Despenser keeper of Berwick Castle once the town fell and Roger Damory constable of the town itself, thus presumptuously handing out favours before he had even regained Berwick (if the story is true, Edward, it seems, had learned nothing from his overwhelming defeat at Bannockburn and his useless Scottish campaign of 1310/11).[12] From this allegation, it would seem as though Roger Damory was still close to Edward in the autumn of 1319, though the stream of gifts and appointments to him had long since dried up. Although it is not visible to us from contemporary records, beneath the scenes there must have been furious jockeying for position and the king's favour during the period from 1318 to 1320. Despenser emerged the winner, having somehow persuaded a man who had never previously liked or trusted him to lean on him politically and emotionally far more than Edward ever had on Damory, while Damory himself and the king's other former favourite Hugh Audley were soon to become Edward's enemies. Edward still had Piers Gaveston much on his mind in 1319: during the siege of Berwick he ominously announced, 'When this wretched business is over, we will turn our hands to other matters. For I have not forgotten the wrong that was done to my brother Piers.'[13] This was an obvious threat aimed at his cousin the earl of Lancaster and demonstrates that more than seven years after Gaveston's murder Edward still had revenge in mind. This same year, Edward paid for a turquoise cloth to cover Gaveston's tomb at Langley Priory.[14]

Meanwhile, the real culprit who had informed the Scots of Isabella's location was probably one Sir Edmund Darel, formerly a household knight of Edward's, who seems to have been arrested in York six months later and accused of betraying the queen, but had to be released for lack of evidence.[15] A furious and mortified Edward gave Isabella jewels and other gifts in an attempt at consolation.[16] In the last three months of 1319, he also gave her several manors in Suffolk, granted her the right to 'receive the corn sown' in various manors she had earlier received as part of her dower, and exempted all her lands from a tax he was levying, ordering his collectors to restore to her anything they might accidentally have taken.[17] Thomas Randolph and James Douglas, the man who had supposedly hatched the plot to seize Isabella near York, invaded the north of England again in late 1319, laid waste to much of Westmorland and Cumberland, and returned to Scotland with 'a very large spoil of men and cattle'.[18] Edward II therefore granted powers on 1 December to a number of men, including Hugh Despenser the Younger and Aymer de Valence, earl of Pembroke, to make a truce with Robert Bruce, and they successfully negotiated one which would run until Christmas 1321.[19] Isabella and Edward spent Christmas 1319 at York, where Edward had invited the master and scholars of his 1317 foundation at the University of Cambridge, King's Hall, to join them; most of them arrived late. The queen received jewels and other expensive gifts from her husband. In January 1320, the royal couple spent a few days at the Yorkshire castle of Knaresborough, which had once belonged to Piers Gaveston and where some years before Edward had ordered the constable of the castle to make a pentice or covered walkway between his chamber and the kitchen, as though he was getting peckish during the night.[20]

In early 1320, the king began making preparations for himself and Isabella to travel once again to France; he owed homage for Gascony and Ponthieu to her brother Philip V, and could put off the duty he hated no longer, having done so for three years. Parliament opened at York on 20 January, and Edward told his magnates that he and the queen had arranged to meet Philip at Amiens (seventy-five miles north of Paris) on 9 March. The king sent a letter to Philip on 19 February to confirm their meeting, and sent out commissioners to find lodgings in Amiens for himself and Isabella, along with the large retinues they would take with them. He also sent his half-brother Edmund of Woodstock, who was Isabella and Philip V's first cousin via his mother, Queen Marguerite, to France to arrange a safe conduct for them to travel.[21] During the 1320 York parliament, Edward forgave his new-beloved Hugh Despenser the Younger for his attack on John Ros at the Lincoln parliament four years earlier, and pardoned him the huge fine imposed on him at that time, of which Despenser had never paid a penny. Despenser was rising ever higher in the king's affections.

Isabella and Edward left York on 29 January 1320 and made their way towards London, where they arrived on 16 February; the mayor and other senior officials of the city met them at Kilburn.[22] On the way, they passed through Pontefract, where Isabella's uncle the earl of Lancaster spent most of his time. Lancaster and his men once again jeered at them as they passed, though on this occasion Edward did not rise to the bait and threaten to attack the castle but sensibly ignored his cousin (though he did not forget or forgive the insult).[23] The king and queen spent most of March and early April 1320 in Kent, including a few days at the archbishop of Canterbury's manor of Sturry and two weeks at Isabella's palace of Eltham, while they waited for a safe conduct from Philip V so that they could travel through his realm. One was issued on 24 March and sent to them, and Edward had already appointed his kinsman Aymer de Valence as keeper of the realm in his absence and evidently was fully expecting to leave England, but for some reason he and Isabella did not set off for France but rather returned to Westminster on 7 or 8 April. Probably Philip's letters of safe conduct had not reached them, and they gave up waiting.[24] In the October 1320 parliament, Edward blamed his failure to travel on 'various obstructions and excuses on the part of the king of France'.[25]

The royal couple finally departed for Isabella's homeland on 19 June 1320, the eighth anniversary of the death of Piers Gaveston and the seventh of Edward's paying fifty-four entertainers to dance naked for him in Pontoise, and sailed from Dover to Wissant. With Edward went his ruthless and ambitious chamberlain Hugh Despenser the Younger, but also Roger Damory, who was still just about clinging onto royal favour. Aymer de Valence, earl of Pembroke remained behind in England as regent. Also accompanying the king were his chancellor; his loyal young ally Donald, earl of Mar and Robert Bruce's nephew, who had made the choice to return to England and remain with Edward in 1314 after the English king sent him home to Scotland after Bannockburn; the earl of Angus, Robert Umfraville, another of the Scottish noblemen who lived in England by choice; the earl of Pembroke's nephew and co-heir John, Lord Hastings; the future earl of Salisbury William Montacute, whose father of the same name had been a close friend and household steward of Edward II and who had died in Gascony the year before; and Andrew Harclay, sheriff of Cumberland and future earl of Carlisle. Among her attendants, Isabella took her fellow Frenchwoman Beatrice de Clermont-Nesle, countess of Pembroke and wife of Aymer de Valence. Beatrice was the daughter of Raoul, great chamberlain and later constable of France, and Alix de Dreux, viscountess of Châteaudun.[26] Countess Beatrice would die later in 1320, and Edward II sent 'five pieces of silk cloth, embroidered with birds' to lie over her body at the church of Stratford in London on 14 September.[27] Another noblewoman who died sometime in 1320 was Maud de Burgh, dowager countess of Gloucester, widow of Edward's nephew Gilbert de Clare, daughter of the earl of Ulster and sister of Robert Bruce's wife Elizabeth, who took her reasons for faking a three-year pregnancy to the grave. Maud's dower lands were shared out among her sisters-in-law, Eleanor, Margaret and Elizabeth de Clare, and their husbands, Hugh Despenser the Younger, Hugh Audley and Roger Damory, making each couple richer by about £900 a year. Before their departure to France, Edward once again granted Isabella the manor of High Peak and the income from various other manors 'to hold in aid of the expenses of John, the king's son, and Eleanor his sister, the king's daughter'.[28] This may indicate that the households of Isabella's two younger children, John of Eltham, now almost four, and Eleanor of Woodstock, who turned two in June 1320, were now attached to her own household, rather than to their older brother, Edward of Windsor's as they had been previously. The households of younger royal children in the fourteenth century, those who were not the king's direct heir, were sometimes loosely attached to the queen's own household, though Isabella was of course not and was never expected to be the full-time primary carer of her children. At various times, it appears that the younger children travelled around with their mother's household, and at others were left at a royal residence under the care of trusted guardians appointed to look after them and visited sometimes by their parents.[29] Edward II's half-brothers, Thomas and Edmund, had not lived with their mother, Queen Marguerite, but were given their own household and servants from an extremely young age – when Thomas was barely six months old and Edmund even younger – by their father, Edward I.[30]

Isabella and Edward travelled once again through their county of Ponthieu and the town of Crécy, whose name their son Edward III would make famous down the centuries by his great victory there in 1346, and arrived in Amiens on 27 or 28 June. Isabella was reunited with her brother Philip V and her sister-in-law Joan of Burgundy for the first time since she had visited Paris more than six years previously and perhaps betrayed Joan's adulterous younger sister Blanche to her father, Philip IV. One wonders if there was any animosity in June 1320 between Joan, who had also spent time in prison in 1314 while the adultery was investigated, and Isabella. The two women now met as equals, both of them queens, and were probably both present to witness Edward II's liege homage to Philip V before the high altar of the cathedral in Amiens on 29 June 1320. Some days later during a meeting between the two kings and their councils, Philip demanded that Edward take an oath of personal loyalty to him as well; Edward vehemently refused and, with an eloquent and spontaneous speech explaining why he would never do such a thing, reduced Philip and his advisers to stunned silence. The matter was quietly dropped.[31] Edward, in 1320, was showing signs that he could be a most capable and involved ruler when he chose: during the parliament held in Westminster some months later, the bishop of Worcester, Thomas Cobham, told Pope John XXII and Cardinal Vitale Dufour that Edward 'bore himself honourably, prudently and with discretion'. Cobham also commented that Edward 'bore himself splendidly ... contrary to his former habit rising early and presenting a nobler and pleasant countenance to prelates and lords'. Cobham added that the king was 'thus giving joy to his people, ensuring their security, and providing reliable hope of an improvement in behaviour'.[32] Chronicler Nicholas Trevet agreed: Edward 'showed prudence in answering the petitions of the poor, and clemency as much as severity in judicial matters, to the amazement of many who were there'.[33] A speech given at the opening of parliament on the king's behalf declared that Edward had 'a great desire and longing to do all the things that pertain to a good lord to the profit of his realm and his people'.[34] Of course, the 'amazement' of the attendees and Cobham's comments about Edward's 'former habit' of getting up late and his 'improvement in behaviour' show that most of the time he could scarcely be bothered, and his belated desire to be a 'good lord' to his people was far too little and far too late. Edward II's problem was not lack of ability, but lack of interest. The rather later *Scalacronica* chronicle, written by the son of a man who had fought for Edward at Bannockburn and later served in the retinue of Hugh Despenser the Younger and who thus knew the king well, uniquely calls Edward 'wise' (and also 'amiable in conversation' and 'gentle').[35] The king's contemporaries found him intensely frustrating; the comment by the *Vita* that he could have 'raised England's name aloft' had he applied himself to military matters with the same enthusiasm as he did to his rustic pursuits, and the statements of Thomas Cobham and Nicholas Trevet in 1320, show that they knew he could be an excellent ruler and war leader if he exercised his considerable talents, but he did not.

Edward dined with Philip V on 1 July and on the 3rd hosted a feast with Philip and other magnates, before the animosity of the meeting where his brother-in-law demanded an oath of personal loyalty to him soured the visit.[36] He and Isabella held another banquet in a pavilion at Amiens on 8 July – it is easy to gain the impression that all the royal English couple did on their visits to France was eat – and were entertained there by minstrels, led by Edward's king of heralds, Robert Withstaff. Edward rewarded the performers with the very large sum of £20.[37] The king and queen spent the following two days at the abbey of Notre-Dame du Gard, ten miles north-west of Amiens, and several days in Abbeville, the capital of their county of Ponthieu, before sailing back to Dover on Tuesday 22 July 1320 and spending several days at the royal manor of Havering-atte-Bower in Essex. The mayor and citizens of London rode out from the city to greet them 'in fine style' in early August, 'dressed in clothes appropriate to their office'.[38] While they were at the Hertfordshire manor of Langley between 10 and 17 August, Edward's half-brother and Isabella's first cousin Thomas of Brotherton, earl of Norfolk, now twenty years old, visited them to ask his brother's advice about his marriage.[39] King James II of Aragon had proposed his daughter Maria, widow of Edward's kinsman Pedro of Castile (killed at the battle of Vega de Granada in 1319) as Norfolk's bride, but in 1321 reported that she had decided to become a nun and that he did not think he would be able to change her mind.[40] The earl of Norfolk subsequently married, probably in 1321, Alice Hales, daughter of the coroner of Norfolk, who was an odd choice for a man who was son and brother of kings of England and grandson and nephew of kings of France. The date of the wedding is unknown; if Edward and Isabella sent the king's brother a wedding gift, it is not recorded, and like everyone else they were surely baffled at and perhaps scornful of Norfolk's choice of bride. Isabella sent two petitions on 19 August and 5 September 1320 to a clerk named William Airmyn (whom she would later support in his election as bishop of Norwich), asking for his help in securing the release from prison of her valet Godyn or Godard Hautayn, who had asked for her help earlier in August.[41] She and Edward spent a week in early September at the royal manor of Clarendon in Wiltshire and travelled as far west as Canford Magna and Sturminster Marshall in Dorset. They returned to Westminster in early October for the opening of parliament on the 6th, and around this time must have conceived their youngest child, Joan, who was born on 5 July 1321 and who, at the age of eight, would become queen consort of Scotland when her five-year-old husband succeeded his father as king.

It was at this parliament Edward II demonstrated that, when he chose, he could be far more than the incompetent, uninterested and inept ruler he had shown himself to be during the thirteen years of his reign since his father had died on 7 July 1307. 1320 would be the highest point of his reign. The day after parliament ended, Edward took a step which would result in the exile of his friends the Despensers, prove his excessive partiality towards Hugh Despenser the Younger, and take him along a path which would ultimately destroy his and Isabella's marriage and lead the queen to a point where she felt she had no choice but to turn against her own husband, lord and king.

It all began with the peninsula of Gower in south Wales. The lord of Gower at this time was William Braose, a baron who had no son to inherit the land. Braose's son-in-law John, Lord Mowbray; Edward II's brother-in-law Humphrey de Bohun, earl of Hereford; Hugh Despenser the Younger; Roger Mortimer of Wigmore and his uncle Roger Mortimer of Chirk all claimed that Braose had offered to sell the reversion of Gower to them.[42] On 26 October 1320, the day after the Westminster parliament ended, Edward II ordered his officials to take Gower into his own hands after learning that John Mowbray had taken possession of it; this was almost certainly done with the intention of granting it to Despenser the Younger.[43] The *Vita* comments that Edward 'promoted Hugh's designs as far as he could', and numerous other contemporaries realised, to their horror, that history was repeating itself yet again and that their king was prepared to ride roughshod over the rights of many in order to please his latest male favourite.[44] By 1320, Hugh Despenser had come to wield excessive influence over Edward; he had won the battle with Roger Damory to gain the king's favour, and in and after 1320 it appears that Edward was almost as infatuated with Despenser as he had been with Piers Gaveston. It is uncertain whether the two men had a sexual relationship and what the true nature of the bond between them was. The *Lanercost* chronicle calls Despenser the 'king's right eye' and the *Flores* says that he led Edward around as though he were teasing a cat with a piece of straw.[45] Unlike Gaveston, who had rarely meddled in government business, Despenser was a politician through and through and was not content with gaining lands, titles and money; he wanted to rule England. This, then, was where Gaveston's murder had ultimately led: to the king falling in love with or otherwise being deeply involved with a man who would prove to be far more dangerous than Gaveston had ever been. And unlike the Gascon Gaveston, Despenser was an English nobleman and an insider, related by blood or marriage to all the important people in the realm, with ambitions to be as wealthy and powerful as possible, which he admitted to the sheriff of Glamorgan in a letter of 1321: 'We command you to watch our affairs that we may be rich and achieve our ends.'[46] The later chronicler Geoffrey le Baker considered him 'another king, or more accurately ruler of the king ... he frequently kept certain nobles from speaking to the king'. When Edward was receiving noblemen in his presence, Baker claims that Despenser 'threw back answers, not those asked for but to the contrary, pretending them to be to the king's advantage'.[47] Despenser's behaviour in the king's chamber was widely known and widely disapproved of; the _Brut_ chronicle says he 'kept so the king's chamber that no man might speak with the king ... the king himself would not be governed by no manner of man, but only by his father [Hugh Despenser the Elder] and him' and the _Anonimalle_ says 'no man could approach the king without the consent of the said Sir Hugh' and calls him haughty, greedy, arrogant and even evil, 'more inclined to wrongdoing than any other man'.[48]

Not content with the enormous landholdings in south Wales and England which had come to him in 1317 and 1320 as his wife Eleanor de Clare's inheritance from the earl of Gloucester, Despenser tried to take over some of the lands belonging to the other two de Clare sisters and their husbands, Hugh Audley and Roger Damory, as well. _Lanercost_ says that 'being a most avaricious man, he had contrived by different means and tricks that he alone should possess the lands and revenues, and for that reason had devised grave charges against those who had married the other two sisters'. The _Vita_ confirms that Despenser 'set traps for his co-heirs; thus, if he could manage it, each would lose his share through false accusations and he [Despenser] alone would obtain the whole earldom [of Gloucester]'.[49] As early as December 1317, only a month after the partition of the de Clare inheritance, Despenser tried to persuade the tenants of Gwynllwg, which bordered his own lordship of Glamorgan and which passed to Margaret de Clare and Hugh Audley, to swear homage and fealty to him instead of to Audley. Edward II heard of it and, not yet enamoured of Despenser, ordered the men of Gwynllwg to pay homage to the county's rightful owner.[50] Despenser withdrew from the county, but had not given up; in May 1320, by now high in the king's favour, he forced Audley and his wife, Margaret, to exchange Gwynllwg for some of Despenser's English manors of lesser value.[51] According to the Tintern version of the _Flores_, Despenser also tried to gain control of some of Roger Damory's lands in south Wales, but Damory successfully resisted him.[52] Edward attempted to mollify Roger Damory on the same day that he ordered Gower to be taken into his own hands by giving him the backdated wages he was owed as the former keeper of Knaresborough Castle; as so often with Edward, this was too little, too late, and Damory was soon to join the burgeoning opposition to Edward and Despenser.[53]

The other lords of the English–Welsh borderlands were also furious that the king had meddled in the affairs of the March, where by ancient custom they could enter into their lands, as Mowbray had, without needing the king's licence, and where an old saying stated, 'The king's writ does not run in the March'. They conveniently forgot, however, that the lords of the March had been granted extra privileges and freedom in return for protecting the border with Wales during the centuries when Wales and England had been hostile. Since Edward I had conquered north Wales in the 1280s, however, guarding the border was no long necessary, and the Marchers thus had rights which lords in England did not have with no extra responsibilities to justify them. The Marchers who turned against the king and Despenser in 1320/21 were John, Lord Mowbray; the king's brother-in-law Humphrey de Bohun, earl of Hereford; Roger, Lord Clifford, whose father had been killed fighting for Edward at Bannockburn; Roger Damory and Hugh Audley; Maurice, Lord Berkeley, of Berkeley Castle in Gloucestershire; Edward's former chamberlain John Charlton; John, Lord Hastings, nephew and one of the co-heirs of the childless earl of Pembroke; the king's cousin and Isabella's uncle Henry of Lancaster, younger brother of the earl of Lancaster; and Roger Mortimer of Chirk and his nephew Roger Mortimer of Wigmore. Now thirty-three, Mortimer of Wigmore and his wife, Joan Geneville, had returned to England permanently from Ireland in 1320. The leader of the Marcher opposition to the king was Thomas, earl of Lancaster, who had few interests in the Marches but was always glad of any chance for conflict with his hated cousin Edward. Lancaster loathed Hugh Despenser the Elder, for obscure reasons, and was willing to set aside his hatred for Roger Damory and make common cause with the royal favourite he had so long despised and feared in order to bring the Despensers down.[54]

Christmas 1320 passed uneasily, with the Marcher lords gradually leaving court and returning to their own lands: 'The barons departed full of indignation, and meeting in Wales, they unanimously decided that Hugh Despenser must be pursued, laid low and utterly destroyed.'[55] Edward and Isabella spent the festive season at Marlborough in Wiltshire, and the king spent almost £60 on the celebrations for Christmas and Epiphany.[56] The queen turned twenty-five in or around late 1320, and was in the first trimester of her fourth pregnancy (or at least, the fourth pregnancy which resulted in a living child). Although there is no hint of conflict between Edward and Isabella at this time or until several years later, the queen can hardly have been pleased at the rise of Hugh Despenser in her husband's affections. She had been only sixteen when Piers Gaveston was killed; she had tolerated Roger Damory, Hugh Audley and William Montacute, whom she seems never to have considered a threat to her; but she may have realised as early as 1320 that Hugh Despenser might prove to be a danger to herself and her position as queen and as Edward's wife. Once again, her husband was demonstrating that he 'loved too exclusively a single individual' and that he was 'passionately attached to one person, whom he cherished above all, showered with gifts and always put first; he could not bear being separated from him and honoured him above all others'.[57] After almost thirteen years of marriage, Isabella may well – however reluctantly – have come to terms with the fact that her husband loved men and could not live without one in his life for long, even though he surely loved her too, in his way.

On 12 January 1321, Isabella's step-grandmother Marie of Brabant, dowager queen of France, died, having outlived all three of her children – Marguerite, queen of England, Louis, count of Evreux, and Blanche, duchess of Austria – and her stepson Philip IV. Marie was the second wife of Philip III, and had been a widow for three and a half decades. Six days after her death, Hugh Despenser the Younger sent a letter to his sheriff of Glamorgan telling him that 'envy is growing, and especially among the magnates, against us [Despenser], because the king treats us better than any other' (writing 'we' and 'us' was a convention in letters of the era, and is not an example of Despenser using the royal plural).[58] After Christmas and New Year at Marlborough in Wiltshire, the king and queen returned to Westminster and arrived there on 17 January 1321. On 8 February, Edward attended a mass at Stratford in London, in honour of the late Beatrice of Clermont-Nesle, countess of Pembroke, and the following day rode to the royal manor of Havering-atte-Bower to attend the wedding of one of his great-nieces. This was Isabella Despenser, eldest daughter of Hugh Despenser the Younger and Eleanor de Clare, who was eight (and presumably named after her paternal grandmother, Isabella Beauchamp, rather than the queen) and marrying the seven-year-old Richard, son and heir of Edmund Fitzalan, earl of Arundel.[59] The earl of Arundel's career had followed a rather remarkable trajectory: present at Piers Gaveston's death in June 1312, he was now one of the king's closest allies, and Edward had forgiven him completely for any role he might have played in Gaveston's death. Isabella probably travelled with her husband, assuming that her five-month pregnancy allowed her to do so. They spent the second half of February 1321 at Westminster.

Edward left Westminster on 1 March 1321 with Hugh Despenser, and they made their way slowly west towards Gloucester, intending to sort out the situation with the furious Marcher lords. Isabella apparently remained behind, though both of Edward's half-brothers, Thomas and Edmund, went with him.[60] According to the *Vita*, the Marchers asked Edward to send Despenser away from him and have him put on trial to answer their complaints against him, and declared that if he refused they would renounce their homage and fealty to Edward and no longer have him as their king.[61] Yet again, the threat of deposition was held over Edward II's head. The king ordered the Marchers to come to him at Gloucester on 28 March, but they refused as long as Hugh Despenser remained in his company, thereby moving from hostility and truculence to open defiance of their king.[62] On the day he arrived at Gloucester, 27 March, and again on 13 April, Edward sent letters to the earl of Hereford, Roger Damory, Roger Mortimer, John Hastings, John Charlton and – in a transparent and fruitless attempt not to be seen to be taking sides – Hugh Despenser, ordering them not to make armed assemblies and disturb the peace.[63] He also dealt with some marital business, and wrote to John XXII asking him to grant a dispensation for the marriage of his widowed cousin the earl of Pembroke to another of his cousins, Marie de Châtillon, daughter of the count of St Pol and great-granddaughter of Edward's grandfather Henry III of England; her sister Mahaut was the much younger third wife of Isabella's uncle Charles of Valois. In November 1320, Edward had written again to the pope to ask for a dispensation for his and Isabella's elder son, Edward of Windsor, to marry Margaret, eldest daughter of William, count of Hainault and Holland.[64] Evidently, however, William had grown lukewarm on the alliance, and Edward wrote a frustrated letter to him on 30 March 1321, saying that he would go ahead with other marriage plans for his son if he did not hear from William by 8 July that year. He had already written to King James II of Aragon two days earlier regarding a possible marriage between Edward of Windsor and James's youngest daughter, Violante, who was born in 1310 and was thus slightly older than her putative fiancé.[65] Nothing would come of these negotiations, and Violante of Aragon later married Philip, despot of Romania, son of Philip of Taranto, king of Albania, and his adulterous and imprisoned first wife, Thamar Angelina Komnena. Edward also wrote to Philip of Taranto's elder brother Robert 'the Wise', king of Naples, Sicily and Jerusalem, while at Gloucester at the end of March, regarding the abduction by their brother John of Gravina, duke of Durazzo, of Matilda of Hainault, princess of Achaea. Edward asked Robert to ensure that John freed Matilda and allowed her to complete her marriage to Hugh de Palicia, to which she had been travelling when John of Gravina captured her.[66] The king ordered the abbot and convent of St Peter's Abbey in Gloucester to maintain a chapel called 'la Charnelle' in their cemetery, and to find three chaplains 'to celebrate divine service daily in the said chapel for Queen Isabella, whilst alive, and for the souls of the king and queen afterwards'.[67] Neither he nor Isabella could have known then that only a few years later he would be buried at St Peter's (now Gloucester Cathedral).

Having, as usual, achieved very little, Edward returned to Westminster to be reunited with Isabella, now seven months pregnant, on 7 or 8 May 1321, spending several nights at her Wiltshire castles of Devizes and Marlborough on the way. On 2 May, presumably with her permission, he had appointed Hugh Despenser the Elder as custodian of the castle of Marlborough.[68] The *Vita* says that Edward 'returned to London with his own Hugh [Despenser the Younger] always at his side'; the intimacy between the two men which is apparent from this carefully-worded statement must have distressed the queen.[69] Before the oblivious king and his favourite had even returned to the capital, the Despenser War had begun on 4 May, when the Marcher lords attacked the lands of the younger Despenser in south Wales. They indulged themselves in looting, destruction, theft and even the murder of some of Despenser's officials on a grand scale, and also attacked the lands and towns of himself and his father, the elder Despenser, throughout England; the elder Hugh later claimed losses of £38,000 on his sixty-seven manors, while his son lost goods to a claimed value of £14,000.[70] Even the author of the *Vita*, who loathed the Despensers and their greed, criticised the Marchers' actions, and their violence and vandalism had a dire effect on the economy of south Wales: the prior and convent of Brecon told Edward II that they had become 'greatly impoverished' thanks to the trouble in the region, and the 'poor people' of Swansea, which was one of the younger Despenser's towns besieged and attacked by the Marchers, petitioned the king for his help.[71] Although short in duration, the Despenser War was terrifically violent, and the *Brut* chronicle says, 'When the king saw that the barons would not cease of their cruelty, the king was sore afraid lest they would destroy him and his realm.'[72]

Edward II, doing his best to deal with a situation his excessive favouritism had helped to create, left several envoys sent to him by Isabella's brother Philip V waiting for several weeks, too busy to summon them to him. He did, however, find time to give money to a messenger who brought him news of the birth of another of his great-nephews, the future Count Henri IV of Bar, son of Edward's nephew Edouard I – only son of his eldest sister, Eleanor, and brother of Joan, countess of Surrey – and his wife Marie of Burgundy.[73] Marie was one of the daughters of Agnes of France and Duke Robert II of Burgundy, and sister of Duke Odo IV and the disgraced Marguerite, Isabella's adulterous sister-in-law who had died in prison in 1315. Edward sent a spy, his household steward Bartholomew, Lord Badlesmere, to Sherburn in North Yorkshire, where the Marcher lords were meeting Thomas, earl of Lancaster. Badlesmere switched sides and joined the Marchers, which would later prove to be an astonishingly unwise move on his part. He was one of the many men whom the earl of Lancaster detested and Edward now also loathed him for his betrayal, and he was destined to die a horrible death for his abandonment of the king.[74] After the assembly at Sherburn, the Marchers travelled south to attend the parliament which was due to take place in London, looting and pillaging far and wide as they went, and not only from Despenser manors: John, Lord Mowbray, and others stole goods from the church and inhabitants of a town in

Yorkshire, for example, and adherents of Roger Mortimer robbed and destroyed houses in Oxfordshire.[75] The 'poor people' of Hugh Despenser the Elder's manor of Loughborough in Leicestershire later petitioned the king, saying that the earl of Lancaster's adherent Sir Robert Holland and many armed men stole their goods, chased them from their homes and occupied the town, so they dared not return for three months. Although the Marcher lords' brutal vindictiveness was aimed at the Despensers, it was the poor and innocent who suffered most.[76]

On Sunday 5 July 1321, Isabella gave birth to her youngest child at the Tower of London, a girl she named Joan after her mother, Queen Joan I of Navarre. Edward II, also in the city barely a mile or two away, granted a man named Robert Staunton a respite of £80 on a loan of £180 he owed to the exchequer for the simple expedient of 'his bringing news of her [Isabella's] delivery of Joan, the king's daughter'.[77] The king arrived at the Tower on the 8th and stayed with Isabella and their child for six days; on the day of Joan of the Tower's birth, he had authorised the foundation of several houses for teaching logic and theology at Cambridge University.[78] On 11 July, Edward wrote to the chancellor of England ordering him to release from Newgate prison one Henry Basset, imprisoned there on a charge of receiving a silver hanap stolen from Isabella by one of her own household.[79] The Marchers arrived outside the city on 29 July, two weeks late for parliament, but the citizens refused to admit them; they therefore placed their armies at strategic intervals around the city walls to prevent the king and Hugh Despenser the Younger leaving. The Marchers entered London on 1 August, and according to the *Annales Paulini* threatened that they would burn the city from Charing Cross to Westminster unless Despenser ceased sailing along the Thames, meeting Edward at night and urging him to delay any agreement with them.[80]

Edward's allies the earls of Pembroke, Richmond, Surrey and Arundel brought the Marchers' demands to him: he must send both Hugh Despensers into perpetual exile, and if he did not he would be deposed. The king's cousin the earl of Pembroke told him, 'Consider, lord king … the power of the barons; take heed of the danger that threatens; neither brother nor sister should be dearer to thee than thyself. Do not therefore for any living soul lose thy kingdom,' and, quoting the Bible, 'He perishes on the rocks that loves another more than himself.' Edward refused, stating that it would be unjust and contrary to his coronation oath to exile the Despensers without giving them a chance to be heard (and he had a point; they had not even been accused of any crime which merited permanent exile from their homeland and perpetual disinheritance, let alone convicted). Edward would not listen to Pembroke and his other allies who told him that he simply had to accede to the Marchers' demand, and thus Isabella herself intervened:

only weeks after she had given birth to their youngest child, she went down on her knees and begged Edward to exile the Despensers.[81] She probably only did so to help her husband and to break the deadlock, given that the capital was surrounded by numerous armed men who had shown themselves willing to resort to violence, plunder and even murder, and she surely realised Edward had no other choice but to agree and wanted to give him an opportunity to save face after his consistent, futile refusals. Finally accepting that he indeed had no choice, Edward agreed, but swore to his ally Hamo Hethe, bishop of Rochester, that within half a year he would bring the Despensers back to England and that the whole world would hear of his revenge on his enemies and tremble.[82] He was as good as his word. As for Isabella, when Hugh Despenser the Younger returned to England only months later from his supposedly permanent exile, he determined to make her pay for persuading the king to send him away. The final chapter in Edward II's turbulent reign, and the destruction of the king and queen of England's hitherto successful marriage, would soon begin.

PART TWO

The Rebel Queen

7

Three People in the Marriage (Part 2)

1321–1322

Edward II, for all his laziness and lethargy when it came to government business, proved himself a man of strong and instant decisiveness when it came to his male favourites (it seems that he could be stirred into action only when his emotions were involved). 1321 proved no different, and immediately he began plotting to bring the Despensers back. Hugh the Younger became a pirate in the English Channel, but returned to England illegally during his exile and almost certainly met Edward in Kent and Sussex to plan their next moves and their revenge on their enemies. For all that she despised Despenser, Isabella was her husband's loyal ally in the autumn and winter of 1321: between 3 and 24 August and again between 23 October and 5 November, Edward granted her custody of his great seal and thus gave her control of his chancery, demonstrating the great trust he placed in her.[1]

Edward and Hugh Despenser the Younger, perhaps also in consultation with Isabella, devised a plan which centred on the king's former steward Bartholomew, Lord Badlesmere, who had switched sides to the Marchers. Badlesmere, a great landowner in Kent, was geographically isolated from his new allies, and his lands or castles could easily be attacked by a royal force, whereupon the Marchers would feel obliged to come to his aid – one of Badlesmere's daughters was married to Roger Mortimer of Wigmore's eldest son and heir, and Badlesmere was the uncle by marriage of Roger, Lord Clifford – and would thus be in armed rebellion against their king. This would give Edward an excuse to attack them as well. Edward no doubt saw using Badlesmere as an unwitting dupe in his plan to avenge himself on his and Hugh Despenser's enemies as a kind of poetic justice and revenge for Badlesmere's being a turncoat. The king, however, needed an excuse to act against Badlesmere, and thus asked Isabella to demand a night's accommodation at Badlesmere's Kent castle of Leeds, expecting his former steward to refuse and thus give him a good reason to attack the castle. On or shortly before 13 October 1321, Isabella, having been on pilgrimage once again to Canterbury, duly stopped at Leeds Castle and asked for admittance for herself, her household and her military escort for a night's accommodation, as was her and Edward's right as king and queen to demand wherever they went in their kingdom. (The usual route from Canterbury back to London went nowhere near Leeds, so clearly Isabella was in on the plan.) Bartholomew Badlesmere was absent, but his wife was staying at the castle, and fell into the king's trap by refusing to admit the queen and asserting that she must seek accommodation elsewhere.[2] Lady Badlesmere was born Margaret de Clare, and was the first cousin of Edward II's nieces Eleanor, Margaret and Elizabeth de Clare. In 1319 she had been taken prisoner and her servants assaulted by a large group of men at Cheshunt in Hertfordshire, and was rescued the following day by, of all people, Hugh Despenser the Younger, her cousin Eleanor's husband.[3] Some of Isabella's servants tried to force entry into Leeds Castle, and six of them were killed.

Edward II, who must have been delighted that his plan was working, feigned outrage at the insult to his consort, and on 17 October 1321 ordered the sheriff of Kent to take the *posse comitatus* ('county force') and all the knights and footmen of his jurisdiction to Leeds, 'which is held against Queen Isabella by men of the household of Bartholomew Badlesmere'.[4] Six days later, the king also ordered the sheriffs of Sussex, Surrey, Hampshire and Essex to muster knights and footmen 'with horses and arms and as much power as possible', and the city of London also sent five hundred men to the siege of Leeds.[5] All the English earls alive in 1321 joined the siege except Lancaster and Hereford, who were on the Marcher side; the obscure Oxford, who played no role whatsoever in Edward's reign; and Isabella's son the earl of Chester, who was not yet nine. Present were the king's half-brothers and Isabella's first cousins, Thomas of Brotherton and Edmund of Woodstock, earls of Norfolk and Kent; Pembroke, Richmond, Surrey and Arundel; and the Scottish earls of Atholl and Angus, David Strathbogie and Robert Umfraville, who lived in England and who loyally supported Edward. Another Scottish earl, Donald of Mar, the king's close ally and friend even though he was Robert Bruce's nephew, may also have joined; he certainly took part in the king's subsequent campaign against the Marcher lords. Edward himself arrived on 26 October, and, apparently bored, had his hunting dogs sent to him.[6]

Bartholomew Badlesmere, meanwhile, begged his new allies, the

Marchers, to take their armies and relieve the siege of Leeds, which put them in a very awkward position. Despite their actions against the Despensers and their threats to depose Edward, the Marchers were reluctant to take up arms against their king. Neither were they willing to be seen to acknowledge Badlesmere and his wife's insult of Isabella, and indeed two chroniclers say that they refused to go to Leeds out of respect for the queen.[7] Thomas of Lancaster also ordered his allies not to go to the hated Badlesmere's aid.[8] At any rate, it soon became a moot point: Leeds fell after a siege of only a few days, and thirteen of the garrison were hanged shortly afterwards on Edward II's orders, an act of which the author of the *Vita*, at least, approved: 'Just so as no one can build castles in the land without the king's licence, so it is wrong to defend castles in the kingdom against the king.'[9] The Marcher lords travelled instead to Yorkshire and met the earl of Lancaster, probably at Pontefract, on 29 November 1321. They sent Edward a petition accusing him of supporting Despenser the Younger in his piracy and in his attempts to persuade the king to attack the peers of his realm, and asked Edward to respond by 20 December 1321. He informed them that he had no intention of doing so and that imposing such a deadline on him gave the impression that he was the earl of Lancaster's subject, not vice versa.[10] After the meeting at Pontefract, the Marchers returned to the west of England with a large armed force.[11]

Edward was determined to lead a campaign against the men who had dared to force him to exile the two Hugh Despensers, and on 30 November, the day after the meeting at Pontefract, began to make preparations. Isabella, still supporting her husband, allowed the custody of her castles at Marlborough and Devizes to be given to two of Edward's men, Oliver Ingham and Robert Lewer, on 5 December 1321. At the same time, Edward ordered these two men to arrest a dozen of the Marchers, seize their goods and commit them to prison, including Bartholomew Badlesmere and the king's former favourites Roger Damory and Hugh Audley (but not the queen's future favourite Roger Mortimer).[12] On 8 December and on Christmas Day, the king issued safe conducts to the two Hugh Despensers so that they could return to England.[13] Isabella probably remained at Langley for Christmas 1321, while Edward had already set off for the west accompanied by the earls of Norfolk, Kent, Pembroke, Richmond, Surrey, Arundel, Atholl and Angus; he spent the festive season at Cirencester in Gloucestershire. On 10 December, he had written to his chancellor Walter of Norwich, asking him to 'provide sixteen pieces of cloth for the apparelling of ourselves and our dear companion [Isabella], also furs, against the next feast of Christmas', also ordering thirteen more pieces of cloth and linen for Isabella and her damsels, which cost him a total of £115.[14] Isabella's brother Philip V of France died on 2 January 1322, probably aged only thirty; leaving four daughters and no surviving sons; he was thus succeeded by their sole remaining brother, twenty-seven-year-old Charles, count of La Marche and now Charles IV of France and Charles I of Navarre. Charles was, after almost eight years, still reluctantly married to his adulterous wife, Blanche of Burgundy, younger sister of Philip V's widow, Joan. Later that year, Charles finally managed to persuade Pope John XXII to annul the marriage on the grounds of spiritual affinity – Blanche's mother, Mahaut of Artois, being his godmother – and two weeks after the annulment was granted he married eighteen-year-old Marie of Luxembourg, daughter of Henry, Holy Roman Emperor and king of Germany, who had attended Edward and Isabella's coronation in 1308. Blanche of Burgundy remained in prison.

Despite having an army almost four times the size of the king's, the Marcher lords refused to engage Edward II in battle in early 1322, and fled from him, pillaging and burning the Gloucestershire countryside as they went and holding the bridges over the River Severn against him. As soon as Edward had left Worcester on 7 January 1322, his former great favourite and nephew-in-law Roger Damory recaptured it for the Marchers, but they seemingly had no strategy except to avoid the king for as long as possible. Around this time, the king took to calling his enemies the 'Contrariants'. They were hoping for the powerful earl of Lancaster's aid, but although he began besieging the royal castle of Tutbury in Staffordshire shortly before 10 January, presumably because its constable William Aune was a close ally and friend of the king, he sent them no help. The Marchers retreated up the western side of the Severn, burning the bridges as they went to prevent Edward and his army crossing, but still not daring to confront him directly. Roger Mortimer, his uncle Roger Mortimer of Chirk, and the king's brother-in-law Humphrey de Bohun, earl of Hereford, fresh from attacking Hugh Despenser the Younger's Worcestershire castles of Hanley and Elmley, went to the Shropshire town of Bridgnorth and 'made a serious attack upon the king. They burned a great part of the town and killed very many of the king's servants.'[15] Edward II ordered the constable of Bristol Castle on 15 January to arrest the Mortimers, the earl of Hereford, Roger Damory, Hugh Audley and his father, Bartholomew Badlesmere and eleven named others, who had beaten, wounded and killed townspeople, stolen 'garments, jewels, beasts and other goods', and imprisoned people 'until they made grievous ransoms'.[16] The author of the *Vita* says bitterly that in 1322 the Marchers, or Contrariants, 'killed those who opposed them, [and] plundered those who offered no resistance, sparing no one'.[17]

After Edward reached Shrewsbury on 14 January and finally gained the west bank of the Severn, he offered a safe conduct to several Contrariants – though pointedly excluded the detested Bartholomew

Badlesmere by name – to go and treat with him. His brother-in-law the earl of Hereford refused to go, but Roger Mortimer of Wigmore and his uncle Roger Mortimer of Chirk met the king at Shrewsbury. On 22 January, the two men 'deserted their allies, and threw themselves on the king's mercy'.[18] The *Vita* goes on to say that the other Contrariants were astonished and tearful at this desertion, but in fact the Mortimers had little choice but to submit to Edward: Sir Gruffudd Llwyd, a staunch ally of the king, and Robert Lewer had been giving them a taste of their own medicine by attacking their lands and seizing Welshpool, Chirk and the castle of Clun, which they had captured the previous year from their kinsman and enemy Edmund Fitzalan, earl of Arundel (who was the grandson of Mortimer of Chirk's sister). The Mortimers' men were deserting them, they were running out of money and being squeezed between two forces – Edward's on the east side of the Severn and his allies on the west side – and their lands were being occupied and burnt. The royalists also seized the Marcher castles of Holt and Bromfield, which belonged to the earl of Lancaster, which meant that he was now in no position to come and help the Marchers – if he had ever had any intention of doing so – and which was also a factor in the Mortimers' submission.[19] On 13 February, the earl of Surrey, Robert Lewer and others took the two men to be imprisoned in the Tower of London, 'lest repenting of what they had done they should return to their baronial allies'.[20] Although the royal clerk and chronicler Adam Murimuth and the *Anonimalle* chronicle claim that the Mortimers were fooled into going to the king when the earl of Pembroke lied to them and pretended that Edward would pardon them, and were thus unjustly imprisoned, this seems most unlikely. Given the numerous crimes they had committed and encouraged in the previous nine months – homicide, assault, theft, plunder, vandalism, false imprisonment and extortion – their fate was not undeserved, and surely they were hardly naïve enough to expect the king to let them go without charge.[21] The 'community of Wales' presented a petition to Edward later in 1322, saying that they had heard the Mortimers' lands would be restored to them, and because of the threats the two men had made against them, the Welshmen would be ruined and no longer able to live on their lands if this were true. They asked Edward not to give the Mortimers their lands and lordships back, or the Welshmen would defend themselves against the two if necessary. Edward assured them that the Mortimers would remain in his keeping.[22]

On 14 July 1322, the two Roger Mortimers were sentenced to death by the mayor of London, three justices of the court of Common Pleas and the chief baron of the exchequer. Edward II commuted the punishment to lifelong imprisonment eight days later, which would prove to be one of the worst mistakes he ever made.[23] It is often stated that Isabella must have pleaded with him to spare the life of her future favourite, but there is no evidence for this and it is mere assumption based on knowledge of her later relationship with Mortimer. There is no reason at all to suppose that she had any kind of association with Mortimer as early as 1322, or favoured him in any way. Why Edward did change his mind is uncertain, especially as Hugh Despenser the Younger loathed Mortimer and their families had had a feud since they were on opposing sides of the baronial conflict in England in the 1260s, but possibly it was on account of Mortimer's former closeness to Piers Gaveston, who had become his guardian when Mortimer's father, Edmund, died in 1304, when he was seventeen, and because of Mortimer's longstanding loyalty to and support of the king for almost fifteen years. Mortimer of Wigmore was granted 3d a day for his sustenance while he remained in prison and his uncle 6d, and was accompanied during his incarceration by at least one squire, Richard of Monmouth (he was a nobleman and hence his captivity was considerably less harsh than that of a man of lower birth would have been).[24] Mortimer of Wigmore's wife, Joan Geneville, spent the remainder of Edward's reign under house arrest, firstly in Southampton, where she was sent on 4 March 1322, with eight servants and a small income from the king of sixty-two marks a year to feed and clothe herself and her servants.[25] Two of Mortimer's sons, the eldest of whom was in his late teens in 1322 and married to one of Bartholomew Badlesmere's daughters, were imprisoned at Windsor Castle, another was held in Hampshire, while the fourth, Geoffrey, was on the continent and thus escaped Edward's vengeance.[26]

Hugh Despenser, father and son, returned to England in triumph and were reunited with Edward on 3 March 1322, a little over five months since the Marcher lords had forced the king to exile them permanently. Edward must have been overjoyed – Isabella and most of her husband's subjects considerably less so. On the day he met the Despensers, Edward asked the Dominicans of Vienna to pray for himself, Isabella and their children.[27] Hearing that the king was advancing towards them, his cousin Thomas, earl of Lancaster and his allies broke the siege of Tutbury Castle and began to make their way back towards Lancaster's favourite stronghold of Pontefract. They encountered part of the royal army at Burton upon Trent, where a few days of inconclusive skirmishing took place between the two forces. Roger Damory, once so beloved of the king, was fatally wounded in a clash with Edward's army, and was left behind in the town when the Contrariants fled. On 11 March, Damory was condemned to a traitor's death by the chief justice Geoffrey le Scrope and Thomas of Brotherton, Edward II's half-brother and the marshal of England, though Edward respited the punishment on the grounds that he had given Damory his niece in marriage and that he had once loved him well.[28] Damory, however, died of his wounds at Tutbury Priory on 12 March; Edward had already moved on to Derby and was not present at his deathbed, and the king's feelings about his former beloved dying in rebellion against him must remain a matter for speculation. Damory left his widow, Elizabeth de Clare, the king's niece; and his almost four-year-old daughter and heir, Elizabeth. Even before her husband's death, Elizabeth de Clare was captured at Usk in Wales and sent to the abbey of Barking with her young children, Elizabeth Damory and the queen's goddaughter Isabella Verdon, where she learned of Damory's demise.[29] Elizabeth may have been pregnant at this time or had recently given birth to a child who did not survive (as her daughter Elizabeth Damory was certainly Roger Damory's only living legitimate child): there are references in 1322/23 to a wet nurse serving her daughter, and Elizabeth Damory, born in May 1318, would then have been too old to need one.[30] The king had more or less forced his niece to marry Damory in 1317, taking advantage of her vulnerability while she was pregnant or when she had recently given birth, and now had her arrested and held in a form of captivity, again while she was vulnerable. On 16 March, he informed the abbess of Barking that his niece was not to 'go out of the abbey gates in any wise'. Elizabeth's vast lands reverted to her on Damory's death and she once more became a highly desirable commodity on the marriage market, and Edward also ordered her not to marry without his consent (still only twenty-six and widowed for the third time, Elizabeth lived for almost forty more years and never married again).[31] Edward released her a few months later and restored her Welsh lands to her on 25 July and the English and Irish ones on 2 November 1322, having paid £74 for her expenses at Barking.[32]

After much deliberation, the remaining Contrariants decided to leave Pontefract and try to flee to the earl of Lancaster's stronghold of Dunstanburgh in Northumberland. They had only reached the town of Boroughbridge, thirty miles from Pontefract, where the Great North Road met the River Ure and which had once, rather ironically, belonged to Piers Gaveston, when they were caught and forced into battle by Sir Andrew Harclay, sheriff of Cumberland, and Sir Simon Warde, sheriff of Yorkshire. According to the *Flores Historiarum*, Isabella played an important part in this, writing to Harclay and Warde to order them to cut off the fleeing rebels.[33] The battle of Boroughbridge on 22 March 1322 ended in a resounding victory for the royal army – Edward II himself was not present – and in the death of the king's brother-in-law the earl of Hereford, killed horribly when a lance was thrust up his back passage by a soldier hiding under the bridge. Edward's cousin and Isabella's uncle the earl of Lancaster was captured, while numerous noblemen and knights who had fought on the losing side tried to flee the country by throwing away their fine clothes and possessions and disguising themselves as beggars or friars. The *Vita* comments, 'Their caution was of no avail, for not a single well-known man among them all escaped. O calamity! To see men lately dressed in purple and fine linen now attired in rags and imprisoned in chains!' The author, however, who disliked the baronial rebels even more than he disliked the Despensers, immediately goes on to describe the royalist victory as, 'A marvellous thing, and one indeed brought about by God's will and aid, that so scanty a company should in a moment overcome so many knights.'[34]

Twenty or twenty-two noblemen and knights were executed in the weeks after Boroughbridge, including Roger, Lord Clifford; John, Lord Mowbray; Sir Jocelyn Deyville; Sir Henry Montfort; Sir Henry Wilington; Sir Henry Tyes; and six of the earl of Lancaster's knights.[35] Bartholomew, Lord Badlesmere, captured by Edward's Scottish ally Donald of Mar while hiding at a manor belonging to his nephew the bishop of Lincoln, Badlesmere's nephew, was the only Contrariant given the atrocious traitor's death of hanging, drawing and quartering, as a warning to those who would betray the king; the others were merely hanged, and their bodies displayed in public until 1324, when several of the English bishops begged Edward II in parliament to allow them decent burial at last (which he did).[36] By far the most important man to be executed was Thomas, earl of Lancaster, Leicester and Derby and steward of England, grandson and nephew of kings of England, brother-in-law and uncle of kings of France and of the queen of England, son of the queen consort of Navarre. Thomas was given a mock trial in his own castle of Pontefract after being taken there by water from York; according to the pro-Lancastrian author of the *Brut* chronicle, who wished to portray him as a saint, Lancaster was abused and had snowballs thrown at him by a baying mob on his way.[37] When the earl arrived at Pontefract, a triumphant Hugh Despenser the Younger hurled 'malicious and contemptuous words' in his face.[38] Lancaster was said to have had a tower built at the castle in which to hold Edward II captive for the rest of his life once Lancaster managed to defeat his hated cousin; instead he was imprisoned there himself.[39]

A tribunal of seven earls – Kent, Pembroke, Richmond, Surrey, Arundel, Angus and Atholl – as well as Edward II, the two Hugh Despensers and the royal justice Robert Malberthorpe, sat in judgement on Lancaster. Four of these men were close relatives of Lancaster, and three had once served in his retinue. Unsurprisingly, they condemned him to death, and the long list of charges against him went all the way back to 1312, and included Lancaster's seizure of Edward's and Piers Gaveston's possessions at Tynemouth that year, and his jeering at the king as Edward passed through Pontefract in 1317. Some weeks earlier, Edward's friend and ally William Melton, the archbishop of York, had discovered letters exchanged between Lancaster and other Contrariants and Robert Bruce's adherent James Douglas, inviting Douglas and his men to come to England and ride with the Contrariants against their king: clearly treason. Lancaster used the conceited pseudonym 'King Arthur'.[40] Edward deliberately arranged Lancaster's execution as a parody of Piers Gaveston's, and numerous contemporary chroniclers pointed out that the king executed Lancaster in revenge for his execution of Gaveston in 1312, which the author of the *Vita* thought was 'perhaps not unjust'.[41] The *Brut*, meanwhile, says that 'the cursed Gascon', i.e. Gaveston, had brought Lancaster to his predicament, while *Lanercost* and the *Anonimalle* point out the parallels between Gaveston's execution and Lancaster's.[42] Rather than simply having his cousin beheaded inside the castle, Edward had him taken out to a small hill, as Gaveston had been executed on Blacklow Hill, forced to ride on the back of a 'worthless mule' and with a bent old chaplet on his head. The greatest nobleman in the realm, uncle of the queen of England and the king of France, was made to kneel facing towards Scotland, in a pointed reminder of his treason, and beheaded with two or three strokes of the axe.[43] It had taken Edward II just under ten years to do it, but finally he had gained revenge on his cousin for killing Piers Gaveston. According to the *Vita* and the Sempringham annalist, Edward commuted Lancaster's sentence of hanging, drawing and quartering to mere beheading out of respect for his cousin's royal blood, while the *Brut* says he did this out of love for Isabella; both interpretations are certainly possible, though perhaps Edward also intended Lancaster's death to mirror that of Gaveston (run through with a sword and beheaded) as closely as possible.[44] Three days later, on 25 March 1322, Edward II wrote to Pope John XXII to inform him of his victory against the Contrariants; John congratulated him, advised him to ascribe the victory to God and, far from asking Edward to cease the executions as two modern writers have claimed, excommunicated the English magnates who opposed the king.[45]

It is usually assumed that Isabella remained in the south of England while her husband campaigned against the Contrariants, and usually also assumed that she must have been horrified and upset when she heard sometime later of the execution of her own royal uncle the earl of Lancaster. A letter written at this time by Edward's squire Oliver de Bordeaux to John of Brittany, earl of Richmond, however, indicates that in fact she was not in the south: Oliver told Richmond that the king and queen 'were well and hearty, thank God' on St Cuthbert's day, which is 20 March. This implies that he saw the royal couple together. Edward's itinerary shows that he arrived at Pontefract on 19 March 1322, so if Isabella was with him the following day, she was certainly at Pontefract as well and therefore apparently also in the castle when her uncle was sentenced to death and executed on the 22nd.[46] There is no way of knowing if she was distressed about Lancaster's death or not (though the *Vita* does say it was not a wonder that she disliked

Despenser the Younger, 'through whom her uncle perished'), nor can we know if she was, as has been claimed, a shocked and 'helpless bystander as these horrors unfolded', i.e. the executions of the Contrariants.[47] For all we know, she may – being the staunch royalist that she was – have thoroughly approved of the executions of men who committed treason against the king. Sometime in 1322 Isabella received a petition from a woman, Joan Knovill, whose Contrariant husband, Bogo, was imprisoned at York Castle and who was pleading for his release, and duly passed it onto Edward for his consideration, but this does not necessarily mean that she disapproved of the deaths or thought they were brutal 'horrors'. Edward II did eventually pardon Knovill.[48] Edward himself released men accused of taking part in the Despenser War of 1321 or in his subsequent campaign against the Contrariants if he thought the evidence against them was too flimsy, and pardoned over a hundred of the earl of Lancaster's adherents within weeks of the earl's execution.[49] Many dozens of men were imprisoned, however, and were forced to acknowledge huge debts to the king which they had no chance of paying. A small number of men managed to flee the country and lived in exile on the Continent, including Sir John Maltravers, who was destined to play an important role in Edward's life in 1327.

The most unpleasant aspect of Edward II's behaviour after his victory against the Contrariants in 1322 was his imprisonment of their wives or widows and children, at least for a while. Aline, widow of John, Lord Mowbray, was imprisoned in the Tower of London even before her husband was executed in March 1322, though was released in June 1323, and Bartholomew Badlesmere's widow, Margaret, was also released from the Tower of London on 3 November 1322 and given 2s a day by the king for her expenses for the rest of his reign.[50] Edward's arbitrary vindictiveness towards the defeated Contrariant faction ensured that in and after 1322, England was full of desperate, disaffected men who hated him, and contemporary chroniclers called him 'a man of great vengeance' and bewailed 'the excessive cruelty of the king and his friends', meaning the Despensers.[51] The king allowed his niece Margaret de Clare to plead with him to spare the life of her husband, Hugh Audley, his former cherished friend who had fought against the royal army at Boroughbridge, and Audley would be the only one of the royal favourites who survived Edward's reign; it was a dangerous occupation. Margaret de Clare herself was sent to live at Sempringham Priory in Lincolnshire, where she arrived on 16 May 1322. Edward granted her three servants and a generous enough allowance of 5s, but ordered her not to leave the convent and kept her rich inheritance in his own hands. Presumably her young daughter Margaret Audley, later countess of Stafford, accompanied her, though her elder daughter, Joan Gaveston, remained at Amesbury Priory in Wiltshire, where she died in January

1325.[52] Margaret's elder sister Eleanor, meanwhile, the king's favourite niece and wife of his powerful and wealthy favourite and chamberlain Hugh Despenser the Younger, grew ever closer to Edward, to the point where one chronicler even claimed that they were having an incestuous affair.

Eleanor de Clare and her husband, Despenser the Younger, profited greatly from the defeat of the Contrariants, being granted numerous confiscated lands, though Despenser did not receive his late brother-in-law's earldom of Gloucester as he had wished. Hugh Despenser the Elder, now sixty-one, was made earl of Winchester, while Andrew Harclay, victor of Boroughbridge, became earl of Carlisle (though would hold the title for less than a year, being executed for treason in March 1323). Edward II also finally managed to revoke the hated Ordinances of 1311 at the 1322 York parliament. Isabella, however, did not benefit in the slightest: her husband gave her no confiscated lands and no wardships, and most notably of all, although she had always frequently pleaded with Edward on behalf of petitioners, in 1322 and 1323 virtually no intercessions on her past are recorded in the chancery rolls or in documents at the National Archives (Joan Knovill's being one exception). It gives the curious impression that the queen of England had suddenly died or retired to a convent.[53] Isabella is barely mentioned at all on the Patent Roll in 1322 and 1323, only appearing when her parks at Havering-atte-Bower in Essex and at several of her manors in Cornwall and Hertfordshire were broken into and some of her goods stolen, and in late 1322 when she went on pilgrimage.[54]

Although we cannot know, in the absence of private letters or any other kind of real evidence, what happened at this time, there is a strong impression of a sudden crisis in the royal marriage. The previous autumn, 1321, Edward had trusted Isabella enough to give her custody of his great seal twice; in March 1322 she had supported her husband by ordering the sheriff of Yorkshire to cut off her uncle the earl of Lancaster and the other Contrariants' escape to Dunstanburgh; and she had apparently been present at Pontefract Castle when Edward had Lancaster condemned to death. If she raised a word in protest against this or against Edward's other executions, or failed to show him her support and loyalty in any way, there is not the slightest sign of it. Yet Isabella suddenly disappears almost entirely from the records. It may be that Hugh Despenser, who evidently had not forgiven Isabella for going down on her knees and persuading Edward to exile him and his father in August 1321, even though Edward had really had no other choice and Isabella was simply giving him a chance to save face, was whispering in the king's ear that Isabella was not to be trusted. Despenser resumed his place as the king's chamberlain, and in and after 1322 became the most important and powerful man in England, the real ruler of the country and even wealthier than his brother-in-law the earl of Gloucester had been. Edward, seemingly infatuated, allowed Despenser to do whatever he wanted, and what he wanted was to become rich and hold as much land as possible by whatever means necessary. Despenser forced his sister-in-law Elizabeth de Clare to exchange her valuable Welsh lordship of Usk for his lordship of Gower (which had started the Despenser War of 1321 in the first place and which Edward granted him in 1322 after their defeat of the Contrariants). He subsequently deprived her of Gower as well, with the connivance of the king, who not only did not lift a finger to help his widowed niece but actively colluded in her plight. According to one document of the Duchy of Lancaster now held in the National Archives, the Despensers and Edward blamed Isabella's aunt by marriage Alice Lacy, widow of Thomas of Lancaster – even though the couple had been estranged since 1317 – for the death of her husband, and threatened to have her burned alive. Alice was forced to acknowledge a huge debt of £20,000 to the king and to sign over many of her lands to him.[55] In 1325, Despenser the Younger imprisoned Elizabeth Comyn, niece and one of the co-heirs of the late earl of Pembroke and daughter of John 'the Red Comyn' whom Robert Bruce had killed in 1306, until she agreed to sign over several of her manors to him and acknowledge an enormous debt of £10,000 each to him and his father.[56] There were numerous other examples of Despenser and his father taking over any lands they felt like with the aid and support of the king; Edward II, the man who loved digging ditches and thatching roofs and swimming with his lowborn subjects, became a tyrant, trampling over the rights of many to please and enrich his beloved Hugh. Despenser most probably did not, however, have a woman called 'Lady Baret' tortured into insanity, as was claimed at his trial in 1326; this is not mentioned by any fourteenth-century chronicler nor confirmed by any other evidence, and appears to be, at the very least, a gross exaggeration, and perhaps an outright invention by his enemies, including Isabella (it is not even entirely clear who 'Lady Baret' was: presumably the widow or mother of Sir Stephen Baret, a Contrariant executed in 1322).[57]

It does seem, however, that Despenser came between the royal couple in and after 1322 and persuaded Edward that he should not trust Isabella any more, and perhaps not even see her or spend time alone with her. The royal couple had no more children after Joan of the Tower was born in July 1321, and although this may simply have been the result of the declining fertility of one or both of them, it seems more likely that their intimate marital relationship had come to an end, or at any rate had became extremely infrequent. Hugh Despenser the Younger and his wife, Eleanor de Clare, did continue producing children in the 1320s, and Despenser and Edward II may – or may not – have been sexual partners as well. It is impossible to know the true nature of the two men's relationship, though it certainly seems as though Edward was infatuated with Despenser. Peculiarly, it may even be that in the 1320s the king had an affair with Eleanor de Clare, his own niece, as well. One Flemish chronicler stated outright that they did and that Eleanor was imprisoned after Edward's downfall in case she was pregnant by him. The later English chronicler Henry Knighton made the rather cryptic comment that when Isabella was in France in 1325/26, Eleanor was treated as though she were queen. The evidence of Edward II's extant household accounts indicates that uncle and niece were remarkably close in 1325/26 and perhaps before, though the records are fragmentary and it is hard to tell. They spent much time together that year and often sent each other letters and gifts when apart, and Edward paid Eleanor's living expenses at the royal palace of Sheen for a while. In the 1320s, he owned a ship named after her, *La Alianore la Despensere*.[58] Even if the two were not having a sexual and incestuous relationship, it is easy to understand why some contemporaries thought that perhaps they might have been. It is impossible to know the true nature of Edward's relationships with both Hugh Despenser and Eleanor de Clare, but the king refused to give up Despenser even after Isabella's invasion of 1326, and sacrificed everything for him, even his marriage. His adoration of and infatuation with Hugh blinded him to what he was doing: breaking the law to please and enrich him and even threatening his own niece Elizabeth de Clare. This is difficult to explain except by assuming blind passion and the king's strong emotional need for a man which had manifested itself for most of his life from his teens onwards. In 1326, the annals of an abbey in Devon revealingly referred to Edward and Despenser as *rex et maritus eius*, 'the king and his husband'.[59] It could be argued that Isabella, who later described Despenser as an intruder who had come between herself and her spouse, believed that the two men had a sexual and romantic relationship.

Whatever was going on, and whoever was or was not sleeping with whom, years later Isabella would blame Hugh Despenser for destroying her marriage and would take bloody revenge on him. It seems as though, beginning in the spring of 1322, she no longer had much or possibly any access to her husband, either as her partner or as her king. This obviously distressed her terribly, and there is evidence that she considered her marriage hitherto to have been a happy and successful one destroyed by the machinations of a third party. Roger Damory, Hugh Audley and William Montacute, and even Piers Gaveston, had never threatened her marriage or her position as queen and she tolerated them and their presence in her life, but Despenser was a different proposition. The rather later chronicler Ranulph Higden noted that as Despenser's power waxed, the queen's waned.[60] Why Edward allowed Hugh Despenser to come between himself and his wife, given that she had always been so loyal to him and that they had always shown each other affection and support, is a question which cannot be answered, but the collapse of the royal marriage was to have tragic consequences for all concerned.

In the autumn of 1322, Edward II led his last campaign in Scotland, which proved to be as disastrous and futile as the others. Once again he failed to engage Robert Bruce in battle, and achieved nothing worthwhile. Edward also suffered a sad personal loss at this time: his illegitimate son, Adam, died during the campaign, probably only in his early or mid-teens, and the king had him buried at Tynemouth Priory on 30 September 1322 with a silk cloth embroidered with gold thread laid over his body.[61] Adam, accompanied by his tutor Hugh Chastilloun, was probably serving his father as page or squire in Scotland, and Chastilloun was given £13 and 22*d* on four occasions during the summer and early autumn of 1322 to buy provisions and equipment for his student. Adam was openly acknowledged in the royal accounts as the 'bastard son of the lord king'.[62] He is very obscure; 1322 is the first and only time he has been found on record, and the identity of his mother is unknown. A letter written in the summer of that year, which says that 'all good qualities and honour are increasing' in the king's son, is very likely to be referring to Adam rather than to Edward II and Isabella's elder son, Edward of Windsor, or their younger son, John of Eltham (who were nine and six respectively in the summer of 1322).[63] There is no reason to suppose that Isabella was in any way hostile towards her husband's child, and she may even have attended his funeral, given that she was also in Tynemouth at the time. As Adam was born out of wedlock and was most probably the son of a lowborn mother, he was no possible threat to the birth right of her own children, and seemingly, as no references to him prior to 1322, when he was already a teenager, have yet been found, Edward had not had the boy raised at court close to the queen. Edward openly had male favourites, but proved rather more discreet about the existence of the child he had fathered with another woman. Given the absence of any documents naming Adam until shortly before his premature death, it may even be that Edward and Isabella did not learn of the existence of his son until the 1320s, though the records of the king's life and household are far from complete and it is impossible to know anything for sure about Adam's early life or to what extent Edward provided for him and his mother. The boy's name implies that his mother was the daughter or sister of a man named Adam, or that an Adam was his godfather. That he was named as Edward's son in the king's own household accounts demonstrates that Edward had openly acknowledged him as such, implying that he had had a relationship with the boy's mother long enough and serious enough that he could be certain he had fathered him. This sheds interesting light on the sexuality of a king often assumed in the twenty-first century to have disliked or even to have been incapable of intercourse with women. Even more light is shed on it, and on the king and queen's relationship, by a poem of 1327 called the 'Lament of Edward II', written shortly after Edward's deposition by one of the king's supporters, and perhaps even by the commission of Edward's son Edward III. In it, the poet has Edward declare his deep love for Isabella and his sorrow at losing her: 'God! How much I loved the fair one; but now the spark of true love is gone out, so that my joy is fled.' This may not, of course, represent his true feelings, but it does demonstrate that one of his contemporaries and followers saw nothing peculiar or implausible about him loving his wife and regretting that he had lost her.[64] Geoffrey of Paris, an eyewitness to the royal sojourn in France in 1313, also thought that Edward loved Isabella.

In the aftermath of Edward's failed campaign in Scotland, Robert Bruce led a counter-invasion of England, and on 2 October 1322 Edward summoned several men, including the earl of Carlisle (Andrew Harclay, victor of Boroughbridge) and the sheriff of Yorkshire, to bring horsemen and footmen to him at Blackhow Moor, between Thirsk and Helmsley in North Yorkshire.[65] Bruce and his army were then ravaging around the city of Carlisle, about 110 miles to the north-west, but marched remarkably fast towards Edward's location and almost took the king of England completely by surprise. By 13 October they were only fifteen miles from where he was staying at Rievaulx Abbey near Helmsley, and on the 14th his first cousin John of Brittany, earl of Richmond scrambled a force and met Bruce's army at the battle of Byland, close to Rievaulx. Bruce, unsurprisingly, prevailed, and took Richmond captive; Edward was forced to flee the fifty miles to Bridlington Abbey on the coast on horseback, and from there to safety behind the walls of York. The earl of Richmond remained a prisoner in Scotland for two years, until Edward was able to raise the large ransom demanded for his cousin: 14,000 marks.[66] The king was forced to leave his plate, treasure and the rest of his valuable possessions behind at Rievaulx Abbey, where they were captured by the appreciative Scots, who did, however, courteously return his privy seal to him.[67] Edward's flight after Bannockburn in 1314 had really been the only sensible thing he could have done, and he had at least fought bravely in the battle. Fleeing many dozens of miles inside the borders of his own kingdom was, however, a deep humiliation, for himself, for Isabella, and for his subjects; the *Flores* says contemptuously that he 'spurr[ed] on his horse, trembling and defenceless', and *Lanercost* calls him 'Ever chicken-hearted and luckless in war'.[68] Fleeing from and losing all his possessions to a Scottish army once might be considered unlucky, but to do so twice was ineptitude on a grand scale.

Edward's latest crushing setback at the hands of Robert Bruce, the brilliant enemy he could not even begin to match militarily, almost led to disaster for the queen. At the time of the battle of Byland, Isabella was staying at Tynemouth, eighty or ninety miles to the north of her husband's position and well behind the Scottish lines after Bruce's counter-invasion. According to a French chronicle which, with a charge Isabella levelled against Hugh Despenser the Younger at his trial four years later, is the only source that refers to the incident, the queen stood in danger from a possible attack and perhaps even capture by the Scots. Some of her household squires did their best to repair the fortifications of Tynemouth Priory where Isabella was staying, and commandeered a ship to take her to safety down the coast – itself a dangerous proposition, as the North Sea was rife with Flemish pirates. The French chronicle states that one of Isabella's damsels or ladies-in-waiting died during the escape, while another went into premature labour and also died somewhat later (claims which appear in no other source and cannot be verified).[69]

A furious Isabella later accused Hugh Despenser of 'falsely and treacherously counselling the king to leave my lady the queen in peril of her person' at Tynemouth.[70] Whatever the queen may have believed, it was in fact untrue that her husband abandoned her to danger without a thought: Edward's concern for her is apparent in the number of letters he rushed off at this time. Unable to ride all the way to Tynemouth and fetch her himself, he instead turned to men he trusted to help her, commanding Thomas Grey, constable of Norham Castle, to take Isabella under his protection. Should Scottish troops approach Tynemouth, Grey was to enlist the constables of all the castles in the north-east to come to her aid.[71] Edward also ordered the earls of Richmond and Atholl and his household steward Richard Damory (elder brother of the late Roger Damory and formerly the guardian of Isabella's son Edward of Windsor) to raise troops, who included some of Hugh Despenser's men, and go to help her. Isabella, making her feelings about her husband's chamberlain and favourite perfectly clear, refused to accept the presence of Despenser's soldiers, even though they would be commanded not by Despenser himself but by three men she had no reason to distrust, one of whom (John of Brittany, earl of Richmond) was her second cousin. Edward then sent Isabella's countryman Henri, lord of Sully and butler of France, then visiting England, to Tynemouth with his troops to protect her. Unfortunately, Sully was caught up in the chaos, and the Scots captured him, as well as the earl of Richmond, at the battle of Byland.[72]

Although several contemporary English chroniclers noted the 1319 plot of James Douglas to capture Isabella near York, not one of them, not even the well-informed author of the *Vita*, the deeply anti-Edward *Flores* or Adam Murimuth, a royal clerk who knew Isabella well, mentioned her supposed predicament in 1322. This seems to indicate that although it understandably loomed large in Isabella's mind for years, it was not considered of particular importance or interest to most of her contemporaries, and it seems likely that she exaggerated the danger she was in. Had the Scots captured Isabella, they would have demanded an enormous ransom, and it would have unthinkable for Edward II not to pay it. For Hugh Despenser, whose main interest in life was amassing vast amounts of money for himself and the king, this would have been anathema, and therefore it is hard to imagine that he would have wanted the Scots to capture the queen, as some modern commentators have suggested. One twenty-first-century writer has claimed that Hugh Despenser, father and son, 'decided once again to place the queen in danger' as though this is a certain fact, but fails to explain how the two men could have known what the movements of the Scots would be or how and why the two had conspired with Edward's enemies to capture Isabella or what their motivation was for this to happen, and his subsequent account of what happened at Tynemouth in the autumn of 1322 in fact makes it apparent that Isabella's alleged near-capture occurred by unfortunate chance, not design.[73] Despenser's own wife was attending the queen at this time, a fact missed or ignored by modern commentators who think the royal favourite deliberately placed Isabella in danger: Edward II wrote to Eleanor de Clare at Tynemouth on 13 September, and after he reached York in mid-October sent twenty pieces of sturgeon to his wife and thirteen to Eleanor.[74] Eleanor gave birth sometime in 1323, so may have been pregnant at this time, and it seems hard to imagine that Hugh Despenser would intentionally have placed his wife at risk from a Scottish army, however he might have felt about the queen. Pope John XXII commended Despenser in January 1324 for his 'good services, as related by Henry, lord of Sully', whom Edward had sent to Isabella's aid and who was captured at Byland on 14 October 1322.[75] Sully, who was in a good position to know what had really happened, would surely not have recommended Despenser to the pope had he held him in any way responsible for any ordeal suffered by the queen of England, and John XXII, who wrote frequently to both Edward and Isabella, never mentioned the incident. If the queen refused help from men she had no reason to distrust simply because some of Despenser's soldiers, though not Despenser himself, would be present, then the Tynemouth affair was to a large extent her own fault, but Isabella found it easier to lash out at Despenser than acknowledge her own responsibility for the deaths of her two attendants (assuming the French chronicle is accurate on this point). Her raising the issue against Despenser four years later demonstrates how livid she still was about it and how it had preyed on her mind, though simply because she blamed Despenser does not necessarily mean that he was indeed at fault. Relations between the king and queen worsened further in late 1322, presumably because Edward refused to share Isabella's belief in Despenser's culpability or to do anything about it. The king gave her messenger Jack Stillego 10s on 19 December 1322 for bringing him letters from her, but there is little evidence of further contact between the couple for the next few months, and equally little evidence of where Isabella was and what she was doing.[76] The two had always previously kept in frequent contact on the rare occasions they were apart – Isabella wrote to her husband three times when he was away from her for a mere four days in 1312, for example – and their lack of contact in 1322/23 is further evidence of the breakdown in their marriage. Four days after he received her letters and two days before Christmas, Edward informed sheriffs that Isabella was going on pilgrimage at 'diverse places within the realm' until the autumn of 1323. [77] It is not at all clear that she ever went, and, although perhaps she did, this may also have been Edward putting a politic face on her angry departure from him, or on the fact that he had sent her away.

It is obvious that Isabella loathed Hugh Despenser the Younger, and she later even claimed that her life was in danger from him, but did he rape or sexually assault her, as two writers of the twenty-first century have claimed? One of them cites a letter sent by Edward II to Isabella on 1 December 1325, when she was staying in France at the court of her brother Charles IV and refusing to return to him.[78] The long letter states that 'Hugh has always procured her [Isabella] all the honour with the king that he could; and no evil or villainy was done to her after her marriage by any abetment or procurement' (and here Edward reminded Isabella of 'words of reproof' he had occasionally addressed to her in private). The letter is both overly self-justifying and overly anxious to shield Despenser from any criticism, and almost certainly Edward was fooling himself and showing himself incapable of any insight into how he had allowed Despenser to come between him and his wife. The historian assumes, however, that Edward's defensive comment 'no evil or villainy was done to her' necessarily means that some evil or villainy certainly *was* done to her, which seems rather a stretch. He also cites part of another letter Edward sent to Isabella's brother Charles IV on the same day, wherein Edward explained that 'he could never perceive that Hugh privately or openly, in word or deed, or in countenance, did not behave himself in all points towards the queen as he ought to have done towards his lady'. The historian writes, 'It seems that Isabella had levelled allegations of a very sensitive nature' against Despenser, and that 'Edward is referring to some sexual misconduct, which Isabella found offensive and disgusting'.[79] He goes on to suggest that Edward had 'tried to pressure Isabella into accepting an open marriage in which de Spencer [*sic*] wished to play a part', and, peculiarly, that 'wife-swapping is not a phenomenon solely reserved for the twentieth or twenty-first centuries'. He further speculates, 'De Spencer's sexual harassment of her would also explain Isabella's conduct with [Roger] Mortimer. Because of de

Spencer's "intrusion", she may have regarded her marriage as null and void. If her husband insisted on playing the pander and allowing his favourite into her bed, why shouldn't Isabella choose for herself?' Such salacious conjecture appears out of place in a work of serious non-fiction, and is fantasy piled on fantasy not backed up by any evidence, only by a series of rhetorical questions asking, 'Did de Spencer … demand Isabella as well' as all the lands he was given after Boroughbridge? And, 'Did Edward II reciprocate?' in reference to the king's alleged sexual affair with Despenser's wife, Eleanor de Clare.

Another writer takes this sensationalist speculation a step further and accuses Despenser of possibly raping the queen, a word the first writer himself does not use.[80] She cites a letter sent by Isabella to the archbishop of Canterbury on 5 February 1326, in which the queen complained that Hugh Despenser *'nous voudrait deshonurer a son poair'*, 'Wished to dishonour us as much as he could.'[81] The writer proposes, with yet another rhetorical question, that this is 'suggestive of some serious sexual misconduct towards the Queen herself with the intention of humiliating and intimidating her. Had Hugh thrust himself into her marriage bed, with Edward's connivance, or even raped her? It is not beyond the bounds of possibility, considering his cruelty towards other women.' She also cites no evidence for this allegation except for Despenser's 'cruelty', meaning presumably his behaviour towards Elizabeth Comyn (whom he imprisoned temporarily in 1325) and his sister-in-law Elizabeth de Clare, among others. Though certainly deeply unpleasant and reprehensible, this was done with the aim of gaining control over some of the women's lands, and there is no mention of a sexual element. Illegal, thuggish methods of obtaining property do not automatically make a man a rapist; Despenser's greed for land does not automatically imply his desire for sexual access to the royal person of the queen.

Isabella herself explained in November 1326 what she meant by the 'dishonour' she had mentioned in her letter to the archbishop earlier that year, and how she felt that Hugh Despenser had harmed her: she accused him of persuading the king to take her lands away from her in 1324; of sending her to France in 1325 'meanly'; of persuading the king to abandon her in peril at Tynemouth in 1322; of sending money to the French court in 1326 to 'destroy' her and her son, the future king, and prevent them returning to England; of procuring discord between herself and Edward; of wrongly assuming her husband's royal power to himself; and, most seriously of all, of making it impossible for her to return to her husband and lord without endangering herself. This last point is the only one which might even come close to suggesting sexual assault; it seems that Isabella was afraid of Despenser to the extent that she felt she might be in danger of physical harm from him. There seems no real reason to suppose, however, that Hugh Despenser had any sexual interest in Isabella, whom he disliked and feared as heartily as she disliked and feared him. Turning the queen into a victim of sexual assault or rape seems more like an attempt to increase reader sympathy for Isabella using weak and flimsy 'evidence' and rhetorical questions, rather than a serious attempt at writing an accurate account of her life based on primary sources, and accusing someone of rape is a grave allegation, even after 700 years.

Edward II spent Christmas 1322 in York; it is not entirely clear where Isabella was. She was not with Edward on 19 December when he received her letters sent via a messenger, and by the second week of January, and perhaps before, she had returned to London without her husband. On 26 December 1322, however, Edward granted a safe conduct to Isabella's clerk William Boudon, who was going on pilgrimage to Santiago de Compostela in northern Spain 'to fulfil a vow made by Queen Isabella', and on the 23rd announced her own impending pilgrimage throughout England.[82] This might imply that the royal couple passed at least part of the festive season together. The eccentric king spent a few hours standing by a river watching ten men fishing and accepted a gift of two salmon from one of them, and paid two women for singing for him in his garden at the Franciscan friary in York on 26 December.[83] On 7 January 1323, at the royal manor of Cowick in Yorkshire, he paid four clerks for playing interludes for himself and Hugh Despenser the Younger. This would sound like a pleasant enough pastime, were it not for two points: Edward appeared to be treating Despenser as his consort rather than the absent Isabella, and at Christmas he had threatened his niece Elizabeth de Clare that she would hold no lands from him unless she capitulated to Despenser's demand to exchange her rich lordship of Usk for his of Gower. The *Scalacronica* comments on Despenser's vast influence over the king, and says that Edward 'after his example, did everything that wholly unfitted him for chivalry, delighting himself in avarice and in the delights of the flesh', perhaps a reference to Edward and Despenser having a sexual relationship (and the *Scalacronica* was written by the son of a knight who served in Despenser's retinue in the 1320s).[84] The *Flores Historiarum*, never exactly a fan of Edward, says that he 'removed from his side his noble consort and her sweet conjugal embraces', that he was 'condemned by God and men', and that he enjoyed his 'illicit bed, full of sin'.[85] Whether this means a sexual relationship with Despenser, an incestuous relationship with Eleanor de Clare, or something else, is not clear, but the marriage of Edward II and Isabella of France continued to deteriorate in 1323 and 1324.

1. The Basilica of Saint-Denis, Paris, the French royal mausoleum, 1861 lithograph. (Author's collection)

2. Caernarfon Castle, north Wales, where Edward II was born. (Courtesy of Peter Broster via Creative Commons)

3. Bust of Philip IV (1268–1314), Isabella's father, in Saint-Denis. (Courtesy of PHGCOM via Creative Commons)

4. The palace of Fontainebleau near Paris, where Isabella's father Philip IV died in 1314. (Courtesy of Nemanja Stijak via Creative Commons)

5. The basilica of Notre-Dame, Boulogne, France, where Isabella married Edward in January 1308. (Courtesy of Marc Ryckaert via Creative Commons)

6. Ruins of St Mary's Abbey, York, where Isabella and Edward spent much time, especially in 1319. (Courtesy of Kaly99 via Creative Commons)

7. Wallingford Castle, Oxfordshire, which belonged to Isabella. (Author's collection)

Opposite: 8. Westminster Abbey, where Isabella and Edward's coronation took place on 25 February 1308. (Courtesy of Elentari86 via Creative Commons)

9. Scarborough Castle, where Edward left Piers Gaveston in May 1312. (Courtesy of Kate Johnson via Creative Commons)

10. Tynemouth Priory, where Isabella stayed in 1312 and 1322, and where her husband's illegitimate son was buried. (Author's collection)

11. The Tower of London, where Isabella gave birth to her youngest child in 1321 and from where Roger Mortimer escaped in 1323. (Courtesy of Crux via Creative Commons)

12. Ludlow Castle, Shropshire, which belonged to Isabella's powerful favourite Roger Mortimer. (Courtesy of Darren Musgrove via Creative Commons)

13. Part of the ruins of Wigmore Castle, Herefordshire, seat of the Mortimers. (Author's collection)

14. The ruined gatehouse at Wigmore. (Author's collection)

15. Caerphilly Castle, South Wales, which held out against Isabella in 1326/27. (Courtesy of deadmanjones via Creative Content)

16. Leeds Castle, Kent, which held out against Isabella in 1321. (Courtesy of Adusha via Creative Commons)

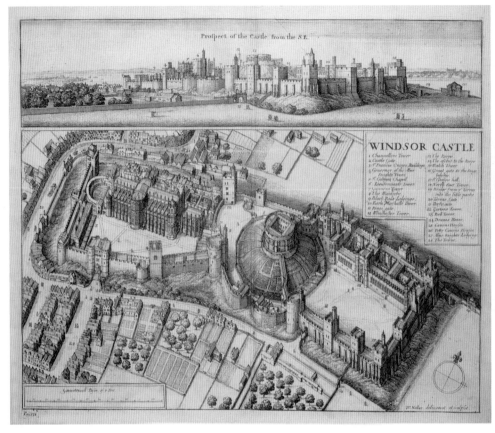

17. A seventeenth-century image of Windsor Castle, birthplace of Isabella's eldest child Edward III in 1312. (Author's collection)

18. Kenilworth Castle, where Edward II was forced to abdicate in January 1327. (Courtesy of Steve Taylor via Creative Commons)

19. Berkeley Castle, where Edward II was imprisoned and supposedly murdered in 1327. (Author's collection)

20. Berkeley Castle. (Author's collection)

22. The hermitage of Sant'Alberto di Butrio, Lombardy, Italy, where the Fieschi Letter of the 1330s says that Edward II went after escaping from Berkeley Castle. (Author's collection)

23. Sant'Alberto di Butrio. (Author's collection)

Opposite: 21. St Peter's Abbey, now Gloucester Cathedral, where Isabella buried her husband Edward II in December 1327. (Courtesy of Richard Gilin via Creative Commons)

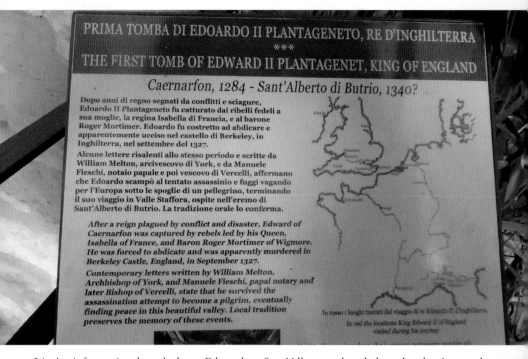

PRIMA TOMBA DI EDOARDO II PLANTAGENETO, RE D'INGHILTERRA

***

THE FIRST TOMB OF EDWARD II PLANTAGENET, KING OF ENGLAND

Caernarfon, 1284 - Sant'Alberto di Butrio, 1340?

Dopo anni di regno segnati da conflitti e sciagure, Edoardo II Plantageneto fu catturato dai ribelli fedeli a sua moglie, la regina Isabella di Francia, e al barone Roger Mortimer. Edoardo fu costretto ad abdicare e apparentemente ucciso nel castello di Berkeley, in Inghilterra, nel settembre del 1327.

Alcune lettere risalenti allo stesso periodo e scritte da William Melton, arcivescovo di York, e da Manuele Fieschi, notaio papale e poi vescovo di Vercelli, affermano che Edoardo scampò al tentato assassinio e fuggì vagando per l'Europa sotto le spoglie di un pellegrino, terminando il suo viaggio in Valle Staffora, ospite nell'eremo di Sant'Alberto di Butrio. La tradizione orale lo conferma.

After a reign plagued by conflict and disaster, Edward of Caernarfon was captured by rebels led by his Queen, Isabella of France, and Baron Roger Mortimer of Wigmore. He was forced to abdicate and was apparently murdered in Berkeley Castle, England, in September 1327.

Contemporary letters written by William Melton, Archbishop of York, and Manuele Fieschi, papal notary and later Bishop of Vercelli, state that he survived the assassination attempt to become a pilgrim, eventually finding peace in this beautiful valley. Local tradition preserves the memory of these events.

In rosso i luoghi toccati dal viaggio di re Edoardo II d'Inghilterra.

In red the locations King Edward II of England visited during his journey.

24. An information board about Edward at Sant'Alberto, placed there by the Auramala Project. (Author's collection)

25. An empty tomb at the hermitage of Sant'Alberto di Butrio, Lombardy, claimed to be Edward II's first tomb. (Author's collection)

26. Hertford Castle, where Isabella died in August 1358 and which has been considerably altered over the centuries. (Courtesy of Caitlin via Creative Commons)

27. Castle Rising, Norfolk, Isabella's favourite residence in the last years of her life. (Courtesy of William M. Connolley via Creative Commons)

28. The remains of the Greyfriars church in London, where Isabella was buried in November 1358. (Courtesy of Gryffindor via Creative Commons)

8

War with France
1323–1325

Isabella dined with her elder son and the heir to the throne, Edward
of Windsor, at the Tower of London in early February 1323. Now ten,
the boy was surely growing aware of his father's incompetence and
tyranny and his reliance on Hugh Despenser. The king himself was still
in Yorkshire with Despenser and remained there until the middle of
March. In the 1320s, Edward II seems to have been going out of his way
to make as many enemies as possible: as well as failing to reconcile the
many Contrariants languishing in prison or released, none too happily,
having been forced to acknowledge huge debts to the king, Edward
began a series of extraordinarily vindictive vendettas against several of
the English bishops. Most notably, these were Adam Orleton, bishop of
Hereford, whom he accused of supporting the Contrariants and especially
the Mortimers against himself in 1321/22; Henry Burghersh, bishop of
Lincoln, for no other reason than he was the nephew of the executed
but still loathed Bartholomew, Lord Badlesmere; and in 1323, the king
took great offence at the pope's appointment of John Stratford as bishop
of Winchester. Edward pettishly declared himself 'exceedingly incensed'
with Stratford and called him 'faithless and ungrateful'; he had been
hoping for Hugh Despenser's close ally Robert Baldock, archdeacon of
Middlesex, to be appointed to the bishopric.[1] Edward ordered Stratford
in November 1323 not to leave the country, forced him to acknowledge
a debt of £10,000 to him, and even began proceedings against him before
the King's Bench. He also allowed Hugh Despenser to extort £1,000
from the unfortunate bishop, which Despenser deposited with his Italian
bankers the Peruzzi.[2] Edward would conduct pointless vendettas against
other bishops as well, and also remained on cold terms with Thomas of
Lancaster's younger brother and heir Henry of Lancaster, his first cousin

and Isabella's uncle, even though Henry had played no role whatsoever in the Contrariant rebellion and had not had a close relationship with his brother (and even though Henry's late wife, Maud Chaworth, who died in 1321 or early 1322, was Despenser the Younger's half-sister). Edward's talent for antagonising men he should have been making every effort to keep on his side was to have tragic consequences for himself, and these men would form the core of Isabella's support when she later moved into a position of opposition to her husband.

On 17 February 1323, Isabella was again (or still) staying at the Tower of London with her niece-in-law Eleanor de Clare, with whom she had an apparently amicable and affectionate friendship for many years. The two women wrote almost identical letters on that day to the treasurer of England, asking that Roger Mortimer's wife, Joan Geneville, their 'dear and beloved cousin' who had been held under house arrest with eight servants since February 1322, received promptly the money allocated for her sustenance.[3] This has sometimes been seen as evidence of the queen's collusion with Joan's husband, Roger, with whom the queen began a relationship in about late 1325. Although it is possible that Mortimer smuggled a message to Isabella asking for her help, it is more likely that the queen was motivated by concern for a noblewoman who was her distant cousin. It is worth noting that Eleanor de Clare wrote almost exactly the same letter, and it is of course extremely unlikely that Eleanor was herself colluding with Mortimer. If Mortimer was in contact with the outside world – and later events were to prove that he was – he might have realised that asking Eleanor de Clare to help his wife might be more effective than asking the queen. There is absolutely no reason to suppose that Isabella saw Roger Mortimer at the Tower while she was staying there in early 1323: the prison cells were, of course, far away from the royal apartments where she lived, and had the queen attempted to see Mortimer for some reason, this would have been noticed and commented on. The idea that Isabella spent time with Mortimer in the Tower is based solely on knowledge of their later relationship, and on an error made by Agnes Strickland in the nineteenth century which later writers followed, that Mortimer was already imprisoned at the Tower when Isabella gave birth to her daughter Joan there in July 1321 (though how the queen was meant to indulge herself in a passionately sexual affair with him while giving birth or recovering from it was not explained). Besides, Isabella in 1321 was loyally supporting her husband against the Marcher lords, including Roger Mortimer. Several novels of the twentieth and twenty-first centuries which feature Isabella as a character have her sneaking off in 1322/23 to have sex with Mortimer in his cell: the queen of England manages to evade the notice her household of 200 people, the entire royal court and the large garrison of the Tower whenever she feels like it by the simple expedient of donning a hood, which, one assumes, must have been a Harry Potter-style invisibility cloak. Such absurdity hardly requires comment. There is precisely no evidence that Isabella was in contact with Roger Mortimer at this time or until years later, and no evidence that she yet sympathised with him or the dozens of other Contrariants also in prison.

In March 1323, Edward II executed the earl of Carlisle, Andrew Harclay, who – sick of the king's inability to protect his northern subjects from Scottish raids – had treasonously met Robert Bruce, king of Scots, and arranged with him that Edward would recognise him as king and that Edward would be granted the marriage of Robert's son and heir (though he didn't have one until March 1324).[4] Everything began going wrong for the king of England in 1323. Some weeks before the unfortunate Harclay suffered the full horrors of the traitor's death at Carlisle, two Contrariants almost managed to escape from captivity at Wallingford Castle: Maurice, Lord Berkeley, and Hugh Audley the Elder, father of Edward's former favourite of the same name, who himself did manage to escape from prison in 1325.[5] This was, or at least Edward believed that it was, the first part of a plot to release other Contrariants from captivity at Windsor Castle and the Tower of London (including the two Roger Mortimers), and he ordered the prisoners to be kept more securely.[6] Many of Edward's disgruntled subjects were making their support for the late Contrariants known: miracles were reported at Thomas of Lancaster's tomb in Pontefract and at the site in Bristol where the Contrariants Henry Wilington and Henry Montfort had been executed.[7]

Edward's nightmare came true on 1 August 1323, when the younger Roger Mortimer, lord of Wigmore, escaped from the Tower and fled to the Continent. With the aid of several prominent Londoners who sympathised with him, Mortimer procured sedatives to feed his guards in their wine – a few days later, the constable of the Tower was still seriously ill from the effects – and escaped over the walls to a waiting boat, which took him across the Channel.[8] It is just possible, though not very likely, that Mortimer was forced to flee because Edward was planning to execute him; although a couple of fourteenth-century chroniclers state this – one of them even claiming implausibly that Mortimer escaped the night before his execution – most of them do not, and there is nothing in any official government source to confirm the story. The tale in the *Flores* of Mortimer's flight is copied almost word for word from the Biblical account of St Peter's escape from Herod's prison.[9] Edward, over 200 miles away at Kirkham at Yorkshire, heard the news of the escape five days later, but although he ordered numerous men to pursue Mortimer and take him dead or alive, it was far too late. Mortimer made his way to Picardy and refuge with his kinsmen the

Fiennes brothers.[10] His wife, Joan Geneville, and most of their dozen children were left behind in England, at Edward's mercy; Joan remained under house arrest with her servants, and three of their eight daughters were sent to live at various convents in the spring of 1324 with a small sum of money allocated for their weekly expenses.[11] There is nothing except hindsight to suggest that Isabella was involved in Mortimer's escape and no evidence that she was anywhere near the Tower at the time.[12] The much later *Meaux* chronicle written in the 1390s says that Edward accused Isabella's uncle Charles of Valois of aiding Mortimer's escape.[13] Valois had been generally hostile towards England and the English ever since his brother Philip IV's war with Edward I in 1294, but as he and Edward II were negotiating for the possible marriages of several of their children in 1323/24, it doesn't seem terribly likely that Valois was directly aiding Edward's enemy at the time, and the story is probably either an invention or a misunderstanding based on Mortimer's later alliance with Valois's son-in-law the count of Hainault.[14]

Two dramatists writing 270 years later in the 1590s, Christopher Marlowe and Michael Drayton, were the first to suggest Isabella's involvement in Mortimer's escape.[15] One more contemporary French chronicle claims that Mortimer was imprisoned in the Tower because of suspicions in Edward II's mind regarding him and the queen, put there by Hugh Despenser, but this is clearly based solely on hindsight, and Mortimer and his uncle had committed ample crimes in 1321/22 which merited imprisonment.[16] Certainly it never occurred to Edward II (or indeed to any fourteenth-century English chronicler) that Isabella might be involved in Mortimer's escape, and given the extremely thorough investigation conducted afterwards it seems unlikely that she could have been implicated without this being discovered. The later chronicler Geoffrey le Baker accused Adam Orleton, bishop of Hereford, of complicity in Mortimer's escape, which Orleton's biographer also considers most improbable.[17] Baker did not believe Isabella to have been involved, though he did invent a conspiracy whereby Orleton, Bishop Henry Burghersh, Isabella, Roger Mortimer and Charles IV of France conceived a cunning plan to bring about Edward's downfall years before it happened, Mortimer's escape being the first step in this deep conspiracy. This story has often been repeated as fact, but it owes far more to Baker's imagination and many years' hindsight than to reality. Mortimer was a resourceful and courageous man, and it is far more probable that he planned his escape himself, working on the sympathy of his guards, including Gerald Alspaye, who fled with him. At some point Mortimer made his way to the court of Isabella's brother Charles IV; although it is sometimes claimed that Mortimer was received and honoured by Charles after his escape, if he was, this did not last long. In December 1323 he and other English exiles who had fled the country after the battle of Boroughbridge were 'forbidden to stay within the power of the king of France'.[18] The much later *Meaux* chronicle states that Roger Mortimer was held in great honour and favour among the nobles of France, not that he was welcomed with great honour there after his flight.[19] It has also been claimed that Charles IV might only have welcomed Mortimer at his court on his sister Isabella's recommendation, and that therefore Isabella must have had prior knowledge of the escape.[20] In and after 1323 other English exiles made their way to Charles IV's court too, so if Isabella asked her brother to receive Mortimer, presumably she asked him to receive her husband's other enemies as well. This seems improbable, and besides, Mortimer was a well-connected and highly born nobleman and an experienced soldier and administrator. Such men were welcome anywhere.

Isabella had joined Edward at Cowick by 10 June 1323 and may have spent the summer with him in Yorkshire, though once again her whereabouts are uncertain and she may have resumed her supposed pilgrimage. On or shortly before 17 August, Edward gave £2 to the minstrel of Hugues de Bouville, chamberlain of Isabella's brother Charles IV, who played before him and perhaps Isabella at Pickering, and on 15 August sent a gift of 'coursing dogs' to Charles.[21] Some months earlier the king had negotiated a deeply unpopular thirteen-year peace treaty with Robert Bruce and temporarily imprisoned his and Isabella's kinsman Henry, Lord Beaumont, for loudly disagreeing with it, and on 22 August granted forty of Bruce's envoys a safe conduct to come to him.[22] The endless conflict with Scotland was averted for the time being, but war with a much more powerful enemy was to come. Charles IV's accession to the throne of France in January 1322 meant that Edward II yet again owed homage for Gascony and Ponthieu to one of his wife's short-lived brothers. Charles waited politely until July 1323, then sent his brother-in-law amicable letters asking him to present himself at Amiens for this purpose between Candlemas (2 February) and Easter (15 April) 1324. Edward, predictably, made excuses, claiming that England was still in a state of turmoil and that he could not possibly leave.[23] Charles had probably expected this, but particularly unfortunate timing soon made the situation dangerous, and a sergeant-at-arms, a wooden stake and the lord of Montpezat were about to inadvertently start a war between England and France.

The trouble began in the small village of St-Sardos, between Bordeaux and Toulouse. The Benedictine abbey just outside the village was under the jurisdiction of the duke of Aquitaine – Edward II – but the mother house of Sarlat lay inside the kingdom of France, which had caused numerous problems and lawsuits in the past. Philip V had in 1318 granted permission for a *bastide*, a fortified town, to be built at St-Sardos, and on 15 October 1323 a French sergeant-at-arms drove a stake bearing the royal arms of France into the ground, to claim the land. This was a direct provocation to Edward, who could hardly be expected to tolerate a French fortress in the middle of his duchy. Raymond-Bernard, lord of nearby Montpezat, took matters into his own hands: he hanged the sergeant-at-arms from the stake he had just erected, and burned the village to the ground. News of this offence reached Charles IV on 1 November, but Edward himself did not learn of the event until three weeks later, just after his messengers had departed to proffer his excuses for delaying homage – most unfortunate timing. Annoyed as Charles IV certainly was with the situation, it did not immediately lead to a rupture between himself and Edward, and he wrote to his brother-in-law acknowledging his problems with Scotland and his other 'great business'. Addressing Edward as 'fair brother' and talking of 'the love which we have for you', Charles told him that he did not hold him responsible for the St-Sardos outrage and that he was willing to postpone the ceremony of homage until 1 July 1324. Edward, however, was angry with Charles, believing that he had welcomed Roger Mortimer and the other English exiles at his court, and wrote to him in November asking him to banish them from France, which he did.[24]

Edward and Isabella spent Christmas 1323 at Kenilworth, where the king gave £1 each to two minstrels of the bishop of Ely who performed for them. The couple travelled west and spent six days in mid-January 1324 as guests of Hugh Despenser the Younger at his Worcestershire castle of Hanley; this was probably an unpleasant experience for the queen, given her loathing of Despenser and her anger with him over what she saw as her abandonment at Tynemouth in the autumn of 1322. Edward turned forty in 1324, on the feast day of St Mark the Evangelist, 25 April – Roger Mortimer was born on the same day three years later – while Isabella had probably passed her twenty-eighth birthday in late 1323. Piers Gaveston was still on Edward's mind, and in June 1324 he sent his confessor to Langley Priory to keep the twelfth anniversary of Gaveston's death.[25]

In late March 1324, Isabella's sister-in-law Marie of Luxembourg, queen of France, died, at barely even twenty years old: while she and Charles IV were travelling back to Paris from Toulouse, they were involved in an accident, and Marie miscarried their child and died herself shortly afterwards. Charles turned thirty in June 1324 and was desperate for a son and heir, and so on 5 July that year married his third wife, his first cousin Joan of Evreux, one of the daughters of his father Philip IV's half-brother Louis, count of Evreux. She was about fourteen.[26] Edward's cousin Aymer de Valence, earl of Pembroke, whom the king sent to negotiate with Charles, died suddenly on 23 June before reaching Paris, when he collapsed suddenly after dinner and died in his servant's arms. Edward did not attend his funeral at Westminster Abbey (where Pembroke's tomb still exists) on 1 August – he was thirty miles away at Guildford in Surrey at the time – and allowed Hugh Despenser to harass Pembroke's widow Marie de Châtillon and his heirs, his nephew John Hastings and his nieces Joan and Elizabeth Comyn, over Pembroke's debts, lands and goods.[27]

On the day he married Joan of Evreux, 5 July 1324, Charles IV met Edward II's envoys at Annet-sur-Marne, near Paris, and abruptly informed them that because he had 'found no man' (*qil ne treove homme*) to pay him the homage due to him for Gascony and Ponthieu on the appointed date, he had taken his brother-in-law's lands into his own hands before the envoys' arrival.[28] Trouble had been brewing for a little while. In May 1324, Charles spoke rudely to Edward's envoys (Charles's own first cousin Edmund of Woodstock, earl of Kent, and Alexander Bicknor, archbishop of Dublin): they were 'reproved greatly for our simple-mindedness and folly, that we should undertake to talk to him or permit him to be addressed on behalf of you [Edward II] who are duke of Aquitaine, vassal and subject of the king of France, who is emperor of his realm and sovereign under God, of the wrongs done against his royal majesty.'[29] Although it was true that Edward, as duke of Aquitaine, was Charles's vassal for his French lands, when addressed to a fellow king this speech was provocative, and Edward must have seethed.

The king of France sent his and Isabella's uncle Charles of Valois into Gascony with an army in early August 1324, and suddenly Edward II and Charles IV were at war. Isabella found herself in a very awkward position, with her husband and her brother, her native land and her adopted country, at war with each other, and the little-known War of St-Sardos was to have a profound impact on her marriage, her financial situation, her position as queen and her well-being. With the lands he had inherited from his parents confiscated by his brother-in-law, and now a war declared between them, Edward ordered all French subjects in England to be arrested and their goods confiscated on 21 July 1324. The French complained that this seizure would be worth more than the annual revenues of Gascony.[30] Edward reached out to the Spanish kingdoms in a bid to find allies against France, and in 1324/25 betrothed three of his and Isabella's four children to members of the Spanish royal families. Eleanor of Woodstock, born in 1318, was betrothed to Alfonso XI of Castile, born in 1311; the heir to the English throne, Edward of Windsor, was betrothed to Alfonso's sister Leonor; and little Joan of the Tower was betrothed to the grandson of James II of Aragon, the future Peter IV, who was also a child and less than two years her senior.[31] A furious Charles IV described Edward's search for allies against him as a 'crime of *lèse-majesté*' against the crown of France.[32] Edward sent his half-brother the earl of Kent to Gascony as his lieutenant. Kent allowed himself to be boxed in at the castle of La Réole by his uncle Charles of Valois and was besieged there, and on 22 September 1324 signed a six-month truce with Valois.[33] The French captured parts of Gascony such as the Agenais, but its most important cities, Bordeaux and Bayonne, remained in English hands, as did numerous other towns.[34] Edward lost the support of several of his most important Gascon vassals during the War of St-Sardos, including the counts of Foix and Armagnac and the lord of Albret, all of whom took Charles IV's side. Albret's son Bérard, however, remained loyal to Edward and told him that seeing him would be the greatest joy he would ever have in his life, while Pierre Gros, prior of the Carmelites of Bordeaux, also remained loyal to Edward and was banished from France by Charles.[35] Another man exiled from France was Arnaud Caillau, a relative of Piers Gaveston (whose maternal aunt Miramonde de Marsan married Pierre Caillau of Bordeaux) and whom Edward described as 'good and loyal'.[36]

On 18 September 1324 came a great shock for Isabella. Edward confiscated her county of Cornwall and took it into his own hands, supposedly because it lay on the coast 'in the more remote parts of the realm' and might be vulnerable to a French invasion. Her husband also seized all her other lands and castles, though failed to explain how inland counties such as Oxfordshire and Wiltshire might be vulnerable to an invasion by Isabella's brother.[37] There was a precedent for Edward's actions, as he had briefly seized his stepmother Marguerite's lands in 1317, but they were soon returned to the dowager queen, and it is hard to escape the conclusion that in 1324 Edward was lashing out and punishing Isabella for a situation – the war with her brother – which was entirely beyond her control and which Edward himself could easily have avoided by paying homage to Charles IV when he was meant to. An incensed and deeply upset Isabella later blamed Hugh Despenser the Younger for persuading Edward to take her lands, though it is hard to be sure whether she really held him responsible or whether she was trying to avoid publicly blaming Edward at a time when he was still king and when Despenser and his father were being held accountable for the disasters of his reign.[38] As the king and as Isabella's husband, Edward must carry full responsibility for humiliating her by taking her property and for openly treating her as an enemy alien. In place of the income from her lands, he granted Isabella an allowance from the exchequer, said by some fourteenth-century chroniclers to be only £1 a day, though this is a gross underestimate. She was actually given 3,920 marks or £2,613 a year, a little over £7 a day – considerably lower than her pre-September 1324 income of £4,500 but hardly a 'fraction' of it as is sometimes claimed.[39] Sophia Menache points out that it is doubtful whether Isabella 'suffered a substantial economic setback' in 1324, and certainly she was not impoverished and she and her household could live on the amount: her uncle the earl of Lancaster had reduced Edward's income to £10 a day in 1314 for a household more than double the size of the queen's, and in 1305 Edward's father allowed him just over £5 a day for himself and all his servants.[40] Yet the loss was not only financial: it was proof that Isabella's husband no longer saw her as his loyal and supportive partner of more than a decade and a half, but as an enemy, no longer as his loving wife but merely Charles IV's sister, to be blamed and punished for Charles's actions. It must have been devastating for Isabella, who had done nothing wrong. Edward seizing her lands and, in doing so, implicitly making a public declaration that he no longer loved and trusted her, was almost certainly the thing which was soon to push her into opposition to him. Spitefully, Edward also refused to exempt Isabella's French servants and attendants (with the sole exception of her chaplain Peter Vernon) from the general order for the French living in England to be arrested – though he did permit some French people to remain at liberty – and they were either imprisoned or forced to return to their homeland.[41] What was going through Edward's mind when he decided to treat his queen in such an appalling and absurdly unfair way is hard to imagine. Edward could be vindictive to the point of cruelty towards people he loved who he thought, rightly or wrongly, had betrayed him, and somehow Isabella had come to reside in that category in his mind. Perhaps he suspected that she had sympathy for Roger Mortimer and the other Contrariants after all, or perhaps he was annoyed at her dislike and distrust of his beloved Despenser.

Two chronicles, *Lanercost* and *Flores*, claim that Edward's niece and Hugh Despenser's wife, Eleanor de Clare, was appointed as some kind of guardian over the queen in or about 1324, charged with monitoring her correspondence and carrying her seal.[42] The story may have some truth in it, though there is nothing to indicate hostility between the two women, who had spent much time together and apparently enjoyed an amicable relationship for many years. Even in 1326, after her refusal to return to England and to Edward, Isabella wrote letters to the justice John Stonor on behalf of Eleanor's chaplain John Sadington.[43] Eleanor had been Isabella's chief lady-in-waiting since at least 1311 and most probably since Isabella's arrival in England in 1308, and certainly wasn't foisted on her unwillingly in 1324. Supposedly, Isabella managed, despite Eleanor's constant presence, to smuggle a letter to her brother Charles IV claiming that Edward was being a 'gripple miser' to her, i.e. mean to her but generous to another, but as with her supposed letter of 1308 to her father complaining about Piers Gaveston this is an invention of many decades later by the chronicler Thomas Walsingham, who had no access to the queen's correspondence.

An extremely common idea nowadays about Isabella is that Edward II cruelly removed their three younger children, John of Eltham, Eleanor of Woodstock and Joan of the Tower, from her custody in September

1324 in order to humiliate and punish her even more. This story first appeared in the late 1970s and is pure modern invention, not mentioned or even hinted at in any fourteenth-century source, though in the last few years it has often been repeated as a certain 'fact'. The source given for the story is document E 403/201, now held in the National Archives in Kew, which is an issue roll of Edward II's wardrobe for the sixteenth year of his reign, 8 July 1322 to 7 July 1323, and which thus does not relate to events of September 1324. The section of the document cited for this popular theory (membranes 14 to 15) does not even exist.[44] It is true that Edward and Isabella's younger son, John of Eltham, was given into the care of Edward's niece Eleanor de Clare at some point, though the date when this happened cannot be established and it may only have lasted a few weeks. The two pieces of evidence that John was given into Eleanor's safekeeping are an undated membrane, now also in the National Archives, which bears the title 'Expenses in the household of Eleanor Despenser, who had the care of John of Eltham', and a single line in Edward II's chamber account of 1325/26 which states that Eleanor and John – who were first cousins, albeit with an age difference of almost a quarter of a century between them – had travelled to Kenilworth Castle in Warwickshire together in June 1326. Eleanor received £12 for their expenses.[45] In 1326, Isabella was staying in France by her own choice and thus could not have been looking after John and her daughters anyway, and there is nothing to suggest that the eight-year-old boy was ripped away from his mother in September 1324 and given into Eleanor de Clare's custody to inflict more emotional pain and punishment on the queen. The undated membrane of Eleanor's expenses might relate to 1326, or to the summer of 1320 when Edward and Isabella travelled to France and may have left their second son in the temporary care of the king's niece.[46] Modern historians often follow the story in *Lanercost* and *Flores* that Eleanor de Clare was also Isabella's guardian or even a kind of jailer in this period, but precisely how she was meant to be looking after Isabella's son somewhere where Isabella never or rarely saw him while also keeping close and constant watch over the queen is never explained.

At some point before 6 February 1325, Edward set up a household for his and Isabella's daughters, Eleanor and Joan, under the charge of Isabel, Lady Hastings, and her husband Ralph Monthermer, formerly earl of Gloucester, who was the widower of the king's sister Joan of Acre and who could thus consider himself the royal daughters' uncle. Isabel Hastings was Hugh Despenser the Younger's sister, but evidently a trustworthy, maternal type: when Edward II's niece Elizabeth de Clare attended his funeral some years later, she left her two young daughters, Isabella Verdon and Elizabeth Damory, in Isabel's custody, not allowing the machinations of Isabel's brother to deprive Elizabeth of her lands to colour her view of Isabel herself.[47] Eleanor of Woodstock and Joan of the Tower remained in Isabel Hastings' care until 19 January 1326, when Edward appointed Joan Jermy, sister of his half-brother Thomas, earl of Norfolk's wife Alice Hales, to be in charge of their household. The girls lived sometimes at Pleshey, Essex, and sometimes at Marlborough in Wiltshire, and one of them stayed for a while with the prioress of Ankerwick in Buckinghamshire sometime before May 1325.[48] All the people Edward II appointed to look after his and Isabella's three younger children in the 1320s were members of their extended family, and cannot be described as inappropriate choices: his niece, his niece's sister-in-law, his former brother-in-law (who was the father of four of his nieces and nephews) and his half-brother's sister-in-law.

There is no evidence at all to suggest that Isabella or anyone else thought that Edward had deprived her of her children, or that he had done anything out of the ordinary. In fact, he had not. In 1301, his father, Edward I, set up a household for his young sons Thomas and Edmund, then only babies (born in 1300 and 1301), who did not live with their mother, Queen Marguerite.[49] In the same year, Edward I ordered that his ten-year-old grandson, Gilbert de Clare, future earl of Gloucester, be sent to live in the household of his step-grandmother, Queen Marguerite, rather than remaining with his mother, Joan of Acre. Another grandchild of Edward I, Eleanor de Bohun, also lived with Queen Marguerite and later at Amesbury Priory at her uncle Edward II's expense, even though her parents, Elizabeth and Humphrey de Bohun, were both still alive.[50] In the summer of 1340, Edward II and Isabella's son Edward III set up a household for his and Queen Philippa's younger children, including twenty-month-old Lionel and John of Gaunt, then only about four months old, under the care of the Lady de la Mote. Isabella of France's daughter Eleanor of Woodstock lived in the household of her sister-in-law Queen Philippa after 1330, not in her mother's.[51] No modern writer has ever accused Edward I or Edward III of cruelty towards their wives (or daughters or mothers) for 'depriving' them of their children on these grounds, yet somehow Edward II is judged harshly for doing something entirely normal by the standards of fourteenth-century royalty. The idea that he cruelly and punitively took Isabella's children away from her had never been mentioned before the late 1970s but since then has made its way into just about every fictional and non-fictional book featuring Edward and Isabella. One self-published novel of 2010 even has Isabella's children being torn right out of her arms, for maximum pathos, after Isabella has spent much of the book unsubtly foreshadowing this event by declaring often that her children are all she has left and that she would be devastated to lose them. Equally ludicrously, Edward II in this novel is such an appalling parent that he struggles even to remember his children's names. Neither

Edward nor Isabella lived in the twenty-first century and it makes no sense to judge their lives by our norms; royal families of the Middle Ages were not modern nuclear families. As a medieval queen, Isabella was not expected to be the full-time primary carer of her children, and if she thought that Edward had taken them from her she would have raised the issue against Hugh Despenser in 1326, as she did with everything else Edward and Despenser had done which hurt and angered her. She did not, and neither she nor her brother Charles IV nor Pope John XXII nor any chronicler even hinted that they thought Edward had done anything wrong or unusual. There is, in fact, little surviving evidence which tells us about Isabella's relationship with her three younger children in the 1310s and 1320s or how much time she spent with them, other than an entry on the Patent Roll in May 1320 that she was being given the manor of High Peak 'to hold in aid of the expenses of' John of Eltham and Eleanor of Woodstock, and a statement by the mayor of London in early 1323 that 'the queen and her children were dwelling' in the city.[52]

Yet another myth invented about Isabella in the last few years is that she was asked to take an oath 'to live and die with the Despensers', and refused.[53] For the curious claim that the queen of England was asked to take an oath of loyalty to two of her social inferiors, the continuation of the annals of Sempringham Priory is cited. What it actually says is that Henry, Lord Beaumont, was imprisoned at Kenilworth Castle in Warwickshire in February 1326 for refusing to swear to the king and Hugh Despenser the Younger 'to be of their part to live and die', and that his sister Isabella Vescy was given temporary custody of his lands. The *French Chronicle of London* says that Beaumont and other magnates were imprisoned 'because they would not agree to do the bidding of Hugh Despenser'.[54] Queen Isabella is not even mentioned, and besides, she was in France in 1326 and therefore could not have been asked to take an oath to the Despensers. The charges against Despenser at his trial say that he committed Beaumont and unnamed others to prison for refusing to swear an oath to him, which cannot refer to the queen. Neither did Pope John XXII write to Hugh Despenser 'complaining at the harsh treatment of Edward's Queen'.[55] Only one of the pope's letters to Despenser, of the many dozens he sent him in the 1320s, even mentions Isabella: in March 1326, John suggested that Despenser should retire from court as 'his participation in the king's government is given by the queen as a reason for her being unable, without personal danger, to return to the king'. John XXII did not comment on the accuracy of the queen's belief but only repeated it neutrally, nor did he castigate Despenser for his 'harsh treatment' of her.[56]

Edward II spent Christmas 1324 at Nottingham, perhaps with Isabella, though once again her whereabouts are uncertain. If they were together, it would be the last festive season they ever spent together. On

13 January 1325, Piers Gaveston's daughter Joan, his only legitimate child and the king's great-niece, died at Amesbury Priory in Wiltshire, and in the spring of that year two of Edward's staunchest allies died as well: his and Hugh Despenser's brother-in-law Ralph Monthermer, and Robert Umfraville, earl of Angus. The country seethed with discontent and rebellion. Many Contrariants were still in prison, Hugh Despenser was all-powerful at court, and both he and Edward II were obsessed with gaining and keeping wealth and lands, whatever the cost to others. The *Vita* says that Edward amassed more money than any of his ancestors, and that his 'meanness is laid at Hugh's door, like the other evils that afflict the court. Hence, many conspired to kill him [Despenser], but the plot was discovered, some were captured and the others fled.'[57] This may be a reference to a plot by Roger Mortimer to kill the two Hugh Despensers and probably their allies Edmund Fitzalan, earl of Arundel and Robert Baldock, archdeacon of Middlesex: in mid-November 1323, Mortimer was said to have incited 'aliens to enter the kingdom and to murder the king's counsellors'.[58] Edward took to referring to his enemy as 'the Mortimer', as did the *French Chronicle of London* and the *Scalacronica*.[59]

The eccentric king spent a lot of time in early 1325 at a Westminster cottage of which he had taken possession in about 1320 and which he called *Borgoyne*, 'Burgundy'; it became one of his favourite residences. While there on 12 February 1325, perhaps with Isabella, Edward watched two of his squires perform some kind of act with fire for his entertainment, which went horribly wrong when both men burned themselves.[60] From mid-February to mid-March, the king lived at the Tower of London, with Isabella perhaps also present. It would be the last time they spent any time together, and in fact early March 1325, a little over seventeen years after their wedding, would be the last time they ever met, as far as we know.

On 9 March 1325, Isabella departed for her homeland of France from Dover, to try to work out a peace settlement between her brother Charles IV and her husband and end the War of St-Sardos. Edward remained at the Tower and was not at Dover to see her off. He claimed a few months later that Isabella had 'always behaved amicably' to Hugh Despenser the Younger, 'and he to her, in the king's presence, and particularly at her departure'. Edward also claimed that Isabella continued to send Despenser 'loving letters' and 'letters of as great and especial friendship as she might' for the next few months, which unfortunately no longer survive (assuming Edward was being truthful on this point).[61] Perhaps this show of friendliness represents Isabella's great relief at finally being able to escape from a man she feared. Edward also said that he had seen no evidence of Isabella's dislike of Despenser, saying, 'When she departed, towards no one was she more agreeable, myself excepted.' This has sometimes been seen as proof of the queen's brilliant deception of her husband and his favourite: that she managed over the years to manipulate them into believing that she could never be a threat to them so that they would agree to her going to France where she could work against them. This is certainly possible, but might also represent Edward's capacity for self-deception, which he demonstrated on other occasions to be considerable.[62]

The queen arrived at Wissant on the same day she sailed from Dover – 9 March. The chronicler Jean Froissart, who is often cited as a source for Edward II's reign, although he was not born until about 1337 – and whose account of the 1320s is inaccurate to the point of hilarity – claims that Isabella pretended to make a pilgrimage to Canterbury and secretly fled to her homeland from Winchelsea with her elder son, Edward of Windsor.[63] In fact, Isabella took with her a retinue of several dozen people, and, of course, went with Edward II's full knowledge and consent and without her son, who remained in England for another six months. She accused Hugh Despenser in 1326 of persuading Edward to send her to France 'meanly, against the dignity of her highness and her estate'.[64] This seems unjustified: Edward gave her £1,000 for her immediate expenses and authority to withdraw more money from the Italian bankers the Bardi in Paris as and when needed, and she received at least £3,674 from them. One of the people who went with her was her husband's French niece Joan of Bar, the estranged wife of John de Warenne, earl of Surrey, who was almost exactly the same age as she.[65] Isabella left her hunting dogs with Henry Eastry, prior of Canterbury, who later complained that they were eating him out of house and home.[66] That Isabella loathed Despenser seems to have been widely known, and she must have mentioned it to Eastry: he wrote to the archbishop of Canterbury to tell him that 'no real or personal calumnious charge should be instituted against our lord the king of England, or any people subject to him, as the letters recently sent to us by the lady queen of England most amply set at issue', adding that no one was liked by everybody and that some people were disliked through no malice or evil on their own part.[67] The perceptive Eastry had misgivings over Isabella's motives when she went to France in 1325, and told the archbishop of Canterbury before her departure that she should have her lands and French servants restored to her, presumably because Eastry thought that she would therefore have no reason to act against her husband.[68] This is almost certainly true.

Given that Isabella would not return from this trip to France for eighteen months, and when she did it would be at the head of an invasion force and with her husband's deadliest enemy, Roger Mortimer, at her side, it has often been debated who decided that she should leave England, and whether they had ulterior motives for doing so. It is often assumed that Isabella was already planning to meet Mortimer, perhaps that she was already in love with him and had been plotting with him against Edward since before his escape from the Tower in August 1323, and that she was desperate for some excuse to leave England and act against her husband. There is a notion that Charles IV of France conceived the idea of Isabella's 'escape' from England with the long-term aim of helping his sister, Roger Mortimer, the count of Hainault, other enemies of Edward's regime and sundry other European rulers to deprive Edward of his throne.[69] This idea of a vast years-long conspiracy against Edward II across much of northern Europe is imaginative but extremely implausible, and assumes that because something happened – Isabella eventually returned to England at the head of an invasion force – it must have been planned for a long time, rather than being something which came about organically and as a result of short-term decisions. It assumes Machiavellian levels of calculation and forethought in Isabella, Charles IV, Roger Mortimer and others as well as a remarkable ability on their part to communicate with fellow plotters in various countries without leaving a trace in any historical record, and also assumes that one king was willing to connive at the downfall of another, which would have set a very dangerous precedent. For all Charles IV and Edward II's hostility to each other in and after 1324, this seems quite a stretch, and the conspiracy against Edward is stated to have begun in 1323, a year before Charles and Edward went to war and before Charles had any possible motive to help an escaped English prisoner depose his brother-in-law. It is appealing to examine people's actions at a distant remove and see plots and cunning strategies and secret conspiracies underpinning everything they did, but it is far more likely that people simply muddled through, and made decisions and took actions which seemed best at any given time and were not necessarily part of a complicated and deliberate series of strategic steps taken by a large group of people over a number of years with the aim of bringing down the king of England. It is human nature to search for patterns and meanings, but it is not necessarily the case that the patterns are actually there.

So who did decide that Isabella should go to France in March 1325? The author of the *Brut* thought that the idea originated with the earl of Winchester, Hugh Despenser the Elder.[70] Geoffrey le Baker many years later turned the chaos of the end of Edward's reign into a coherent narrative and imposed a preconceived pattern and plan on it which never existed, and invented a conspiracy whereby Bishops Adam Orleton and Henry Burghersh worked on the queen in order to persuade her to bring down the Despensers. The Hainault chronicler thought that Edward II ordered the arrest of his wife and that she fled to Paris with Edward's half-brother the earl of Kent (in fact still in Gascony in 1325), while French chroniclers wrote that Isabella had been banished from Edward's kingdom and 'crowned the exiled queen, tortured by her cruel husband, with a martyr's halo'.[71] These romanticised and inaccurate accounts have been followed too slavishly by some later writers. It had been suggested in April 1324 that Isabella might intercede with her brother on Edward's behalf: an anonymous letter advised the queen of what she should say to a French knight returning to her brother, which included a reminder that her marriage had been arranged to ensure peace and love between France and England.[72] She had successfully travelled to France in 1314 to smooth out some difficulties relating to Gascony between Edward and her father, Philip IV, so it was hardly a wonder that her intervention between her husband and her natal family might once again be sought.

Charles IV's counsellors proposed at the beginning of 1325 that Isabella and her elder son should travel to France, the queen to negotiate for peace and Edward of Windsor to pay homage for Gascony and Ponthieu on his father's behalf. Although happy for Isabella, an adult and the French king's sister, to go, Edward's counsellors refused to allow young Edward to travel, understandably unwilling to send the twelve-year-old heir to the throne to an enemy country until peace had been established.[73] This suggestion has sometimes imaginatively been seen as evidence that Charles IV was planning a trap for Edward II at the instigation of Isabella and Roger Mortimer, who were hoping to get her son out of the country to use him as a hostage against his father. Pope John XXII, who called Isabella an 'angel of peace', wrote to her several times between April 1324 and January 1325 begging her to use her influence with her husband and her brother to bring about their reconciliation, and declared that the hope of peace would be 'greatly promoted' if she went to France, is in fact by far the most likely person to have suggested her journey.[74] Edward wrote in May 1325 that he had sent Isabella at the pope's urging, and as this was six months before she refused to return to him and before Edward realised his mistake, there is no reason to assume that he was not telling the truth.[75] John XXII in 1325/26 was endeavouring to remain neutral and to bring about a reconciliation between Edward and Charles, and later between Edward and Isabella.

Perhaps her French trip came about, at least in part, because of Isabella herself, though it is impossible to know whether as early as March 1325 she had ulterior motives for wishing to leave England. *Lanercost* thought a few years later that she had 'astutely contrived' to leave England with her son (though he stayed in England until September 1325). Whatever modern writers have imagined, it seems most improbable that she already had plans to invade England and force her husband's deposition, but it is possible that she wished to impose some conditions on Edward for her return: specifically, that he would send his chamberlain Hugh Despenser away from him, allow her to resume her normal married life with him, and return her confiscated lands and her French servants. The perceptive author of the *Vita Edwardi Secundi*, one of the king's clerks, wrote in 1325 that Isabella might not return 'until Hugh Despenser is wholly removed from the king's side', but it did not occur to him that she might be plotting against her husband.[76] As the *Vita* ends suddenly in late 1325, presumably because the author had died or become indisposed, it is the only chronicle written without the knowledge of Isabella's invasion of England in September 1326, and is therefore a very valuable source for what really happened in 1325, not coloured with the author's awareness of the queen's rebellion and Edward II's forced abdication. Whenever Isabella decided that overthrowing her husband was the correct course of action – and this may not have happened until as late as Christmas 1326, three months after her invasion – the king and queen of England would never see each other again, and in March 1325 Isabella took the first step along a path which would ensure her notoriety for 700 years.

9

The Queen and the Baron
1325–1326

Somewhat ironically, Edward II and his counsellors in March 1325 were afraid that Roger Mortimer and other English exiles on the Continent might hurt Isabella and her attendants on her way to her brother's court, 'which God forbid'.[1] In fact, the queen travelled perfectly safely. She arrived at Pontoise on 20 March 1325 and dined with the queen of France: her fifteen-year-old sister-in-law and first cousin Joan of Evreux, Charles IV's third wife, who may have been pregnant at this time with the first of the three daughters she would bear the king (the girl died in infancy). Isabella left for Poissy the following day, where she would meet her brother. On the 22nd and again on the 23rd she dined with her second cousin John of Brittany, earl of Richmond, released from captivity in Scotland, and the bishops of Norwich and Winchester, John Salmon and John Stratford.[2] Isabella sent a long and affectionate letter to her husband on 31 March, addressing him as 'my very sweet heart' (*mon tresdoutz coer*) five times. She told him that she had met her brother and found him very difficult to deal with, and declared that because the situation was so tense she was contemplating returning to England, but would remain in France unless Edward ordered her otherwise. The letter ended, 'My very sweet heart, may the Holy Spirit by his grace save and keep you always.'[3] Isabella, Charles and their advisers finally, on 30 May, thrashed out a settlement and sent it to Edward; he ratified it on 13 June 1325 and had his sheriffs proclaim a truce between the two kingdoms.[4] By its terms, he had to pay £60,000 for his duchy and another 50,000 marks as a war indemnity, surrender his French lands to Charles IV then receive them back with the exception of the Agenais, and perform homage for them at Beauvais on 29 August 1325.[5] The terms were catastrophic for Edward, though it was surely nothing more than he had expected, and this was not Isabella's fault: no one else could have done better.

Pope John XXII sent very strange letters to Charles IV and Isabella in July 1325, saying that Isabella had sent her steward John Launge to him 'about a story of a monk and an abbot and his nephews, which the king [Charles] is not to believe'.[6] Isabella returned to Paris on 1 April, where she visited various shrines in and around the city. On the 11th she dined with 'Lady Joan, queen of France', which probably means her brother Philip V's widow, Joan of Burgundy, rather than the present queen, Joan of Evreux, and she also dined twice with yet another queen of France, her brother Louis X's widow, Clemence of Hungary. Other dinner guests over the next few months included Louis, count of Clermont and later the first duke of Bourbon, a grandson of Saint Louis IX and her father's first cousin; the dowager countess of Foix, Joan of Artois, daughter of Edward II's cousin Blanche of Brittany, on four occasions; Blanche of Brittany's sister Marie, dowager countess of St Pol; Marie's daughter Mahaut de Châtillon, countess of Valois and Isabella's aunt by marriage; Elisabeth of Austria, duchess of Lorraine; and Othon or Otto Grandisson, an elderly knight of Savoy who had been a close personal friend of her husband's father, Edward I, and who was governor of the Channel Islands for life, who dined with Isabella four times. Isabella also met her uncle Charles of Valois, who would die two months later, on 16 October 1325, and the 'countess of Evreux', who was her thirteen-year-old niece, the future Queen Joan II of Navarre, only child of Louis X and his first, adulterous wife, Marguerite of Burgundy. Joan had married her cousin Philip of Evreux (brother of the queen Joan of Evreux) in 1318 when she was six.[7] There is no sign of any contact between Isabella and Roger Mortimer, or with any other of her husband's enemies on the Continent. Her stay in France for the first few months appears as conventional and ordinary as her last visit alone there in 1314, visiting shrines, giving alms, and dining with her family, members of the French nobility, bishops and abbots, and if she was in love with Mortimer and desperate to see him, it is not apparent.[8]

Two chronicles, *Lanercost* and *Annales Paulini*, claim that Edward II was trying to annul his marriage to Isabella in 1324 or 1325, and sent the Dominican friar Thomas Dunheved to Pope John XXII to achieve this.[9] Although this story is often repeated as though it is certainly true and a known fact with supporting evidence, Edward in fact sent Dunheved to the pope to register his complaints about Alexander Bicknor, archbishop of Dublin.[10] The only possible grounds for annulment would have been consanguinity, as Edward and Isabella were second cousins once removed, but they had received a dispensation for this from the pope. Divorce in the modern sense was impossible and there had to be a pre-existing impediment for an annulment to be granted, and Edward of course knew that he did not have one. The lack of a pre-existing impediment was the reason why the marriages of Isabella's brothers Louis and Charles had not been annulled in 1314 despite the adultery of their wives, and why Edward II's nephew-in-law the earl of Surrey, casting about for any excuse to rid himself of his wife Joan of Bar so that he could marry his latest mistress, pretended to have had an affair with Joan's aunt Mary the nun before he married Joan. He hoped this would persuade the pope to grant him an annulment on the grounds that his marriage had been incestuous – a desperate ploy which failed. When the friar Thomas Dunheved wrote to Edward in 1325, he did not mention an annulment, and no trace of any attempt on Edward's part to annul his marriage to Isabella has ever been discovered in the Vatican archives. The *Lanercost* chronicle, written in a priory near the Scottish border twenty or so years later, is a very useful source for events in the north of England and Scotland but not for the English court, and the annals of St Paul's are reporting a rumour the writer had heard (*ut dicebatur*, 'it is said') rather than stating a fact. When examining whether stories told by medieval chroniclers are likely to be true, it is often equally important to note who does not mention the story as well as who does. Neither Edward's clerk who wrote the *Vita Edwardi Secundi*, nor the monk who wrote the Westminster chronicle *Flores Historiarum* and who was viciously hostile to Edward and supportive of Isabella, nor the royal clerk and chronicler Adam Murimuth who visited the papal court in 1324, mention or even hint at a possible annulment of the royal marriage. Nor is Edward remotely likely to have contemplated annulling his marriage to Isabella while sending her as an envoy to her brother.[11] Edward simply had no grounds whatsoever for an annulment, and even if he had done so successfully, it would have made their four children illegitimate: there was no way of ending a marriage except by death, and an annulment would mean that it had never officially taken place in the first place, so their children would have been born outside wedlock. He was negotiating with the royal families of Spain at this time for the future marriages of three of the children, and it is basically impossible that he would have risked making them illegitimate. The story can be dismissed as a baseless rumour, one of many which flew around near the end of Edward's reign, such as the false statements in various chronicles that Edward had it publicly proclaimed in 1326 that his wife and his son were his enemies, that he would arrest anyone who brought their letters into England, and that 'the queen of England might not be called queen'.[12] Although Edward did pointedly refer to Isabella in one letter as 'the king's wife' after her invasion, he certainly never ordered anyone else not to call her queen, and his own chamber account continued to name her as *ma dame la roine*, 'my lady the queen', even after the invasion.[13]

In September 1325, Edward II made one of the greatest mistakes of his life when he sent his and Isabella's twelve-year-old son, Edward of Windsor, earl of Chester to France. According to the terms of the treaty with Charles IV, the king still had to pay homage at Beauvais on 29 August. For many reasons, Edward was deeply reluctant to go; he had backed himself into a corner where every option available to him was full of possible danger. He was afraid of being attacked and perhaps taken captive on the Continent by Roger Mortimer and the other English exiles; he was afraid that he might be indicted in the French court for the 1322 execution of Thomas of Lancaster, Charles IV's uncle; he was afraid that rebellion might break out in a deeply discontented England in his absence; he was afraid that Hugh Despenser the Younger and his father the earl of Winchester would be hurt or even assassinated in his absence, and he could not take the Despensers with him, as they had been banished from the kingdom of France and it was said they would be tortured if they set foot there.[14] Edward could not travel to France with his beloved Despenser and he could not travel without him. He could not avoid paying homage without losing Gascony and Ponthieu, and the *Vita* comments that no one dared advise Edward not to go to France for fear of later being accused of treason by the king or his son and successor.[15] The only other choice which remained was to make his and Isabella's son Edward of Windsor duke of Aquitaine and count of Ponthieu in his place and send him to France to pay homage to Charles IV instead. This plan also had serious drawbacks: Edward would lose control of his French lands and their income and his son might also be seized and held hostage as he himself might, either by Roger Mortimer and his allies or by Charles IV, a man with whom Edward had only very recently been at war and one he did not trust an inch. Perhaps Edward also suspected that Isabella might use their son as a weapon against him, as she did in actuality, and he claimed later that he had asked her to return to England before their son performed homage to Charles (though if he did, the letters do not survive).[16]

Although some modern writers have claimed that Edward II was utterly oblivious to the dangers of sending his son to France and stupidly fell into a trap set for him by Charles, Isabella and Mortimer, the king's indecisiveness as to the best course of action in the late summer of 1325 is painfully apparent. If he had truly been unaware of the consequences, he would have had sent his son to France without a second thought, but he changed his mind between travelling himself and sending his son on an almost daily basis.[17] One day he would declare that he was going to France himself, make preparations for ships to carry him and his attendants, and appoint officials to take care of the kingdom while he was away; the next day he would claim that he was ill and was thus sending his son instead; the next, change his mind again and appoint his son keeper of the realm while he was away in France; and so it went on for the second half of August and early September 1325. On 2 September, Edward made his son count of Ponthieu, but, still agonising over what to do, continued to issue safe conducts over the next few days for his own retinue to accompany himself to France, and waited until the 10th before making his son duke of Aquitaine.[18] As to whether Isabella was hoping that her husband would send their son to her so that she could use him against Edward, or whether she wished for her husband himself to come so that she could see him without Hugh Despenser's constant presence and persuade him to treat her once again as his honoured wife and queen, we cannot know.

Edward II did his best to amuse himself during this period of stress. As fond of the company of his common subjects as ever, he travelled around Kent with a group of fishermen and a group of carpenters, and spent time with two old friends, a Thames fisherman named Colle Herron whom he had last seen some years before at Hadleigh in Essex, and William, abbot of Langdon. He still enjoyed the outdoors and physical exercise, and paid twenty-two men for playing a ball game for his entertainment at Langdon Abbey on 25 August. A few months later, the king himself took part in a ball game at Saltwood Castle in Kent with some of his household knights. The game is not specified on either occasion but may have been some kind of football or even cricket.[19] Edward and Isabella's second son, John of Eltham, who had just turned nine, was with the king and his elder brother, Edward of Windsor, in Kent in late August 1325.[20] Edward II finally made up his mind to send his elder son to France in his place when, according to several chroniclers including Adam Murimuth, who was with the king at the time, Hugh Despenser the Younger persuaded him that he would be killed in his absence.[21] Given the ultimate result of this choice – Edward's being forced to abdicate his throne to his son – it seems an incredibly foolish decision, but all the options open to the king in the early autumn of 1325 were equally dangerous, and if he had gone to France himself and been attacked by Mortimer and the others, historians would be asking why he decided to travel himself when he could have sent his son instead. No one in September 1325 could possibly have guessed that Edward's decision would soon result in the first forced abdication of a king in English history.

Edward of Windsor, who would turn thirteen on 13 November 1325, sailed from Dover on 12 September. With him went, among many others, his parents' kinsman Henry, Lord Beaumont, and Walter Stapeldon, bishop of Exeter, a man whom Isabella hated for his support of the Despensers. Young Edward was reunited with his mother for the first time in six months, and in her presence performed homage to his uncle Charles IV at Vincennes on 24 September, having missed the official deadline set for his father (29 August) by some weeks. Isabella and presumably her son dined that day with Charles.[22]

At some point in the autumn or early winter of 1325, Isabella made the momentous decision not to return to Edward. She publicly declared, 'I feel that marriage is a joining together of man and woman, maintaining the undivided habit of life, and that someone has come between my husband and myself trying to break this bond; I protest that I will not return until this intruder is removed, but discarding my marriage garment, shall assume the robes of widowhood and mourning until I am avenged of this Pharisee,' by whom she meant Hugh Despenser. The *French Chronicle of London* confirms that Isabella took to wearing widow's weeds 'as a lady in mourning who had lost her lord'.[23] Charles IV, 'not wishing to seem to detain her said "The queen has come of her own will, and may freely return if she so wishes. But if she prefers to remain in these parts, she is my sister, and I refuse to expel her."'[24]

Isabella's speech has usually been interpreted as open defiance of Edward and a declaration of rebellion against him, but she did not – either at this time or later – say a word against him personally. Her speech has rarely if ever been taken to mean what it actually says: that the queen was sincerely mourning for the breakdown of her marriage and felt as though she had lost her husband, and that she hated Despenser so viciously for intruding between herself and Edward that she wished to 'avenge' herself on him. The real meaning of Isabella's words has almost always been overlooked because of the frequent but wrong assumption that her relationship with Edward had been nothing but an unhappy disaster since 1308 and that she was already in love with Roger Mortimer and despised Edward, which she certainly did not. There are simply no grounds for assuming that Isabella felt 'profound revulsion' for her husband in 1325 or any other time, as one writer has claimed, and no reason to think that she shared the negative opinion of many writers in the last 700 years towards his sexuality.[25] Her words indicate her sorrow that she felt she had lost Edward, which would not have been the case had she thought their marriage was not a happy one or had she felt the hatred, contempt or indifference towards him that some writers think she did. She was not defying her husband or setting out her opposition to him and declaring her love for Roger Mortimer, but setting Edward an ultimatum: send Despenser away so that she could return to him and they could resume their formerly loving and successful married life together, and she could resume her rightful position as queen with the return of her lands and her servants. Isabella herself said, 'I will not return unless this intruder is removed,' and there seems no real reason to think that at this point she did not genuinely intend to go back to Edward if he sent Despenser away from him. He had learnt to live without Gaveston, Damory, Audley and Montacute, and perhaps she thought Despenser would be no different. Tragically, Edward, who was in some way highly dependent on Hugh Despenser – politically or emotionally or both – refused, which left Isabella with no choice but to stay in France and act on her threat. Edward had heard of her ultimatum by mid-November 1325, and reacted furiously: he cut off Isabella's income, and, short of funds, she was forced to borrow 1,000 Paris *livres* from Charles IV on 31 December. This was less than a month's income for the queen, even on the reduced amount imposed on her in September 1324, and was a loan not a gift, and so was hardly a sign of her brother's great favour towards her as it has often been interpreted. Charles's rather grudging remark, 'She is my sister, and I will not expel her,' certainly demonstrates that he wished to protect Isabella from any harm and was willing to let her stay in France if she wished, but is hardly evidence that he was throwing his weight behind her and had been supporting her behind the scenes to secure her son's presence in France and ultimately to rebel against her husband, as has been claimed.[26]

Isabella sent an irate letter on 8 December to Walter Stapeldon, bishop of Exeter, who had accompanied her son to France and who fled back to England, apparently in the belief that some at the French court meant him harm. He had been authorised to pay Isabella's expenses for her return to England, but left before he gave her the money, thus forcing her into a decision.[27] The queen accused Stapeldon of dishonouring herself, Edward II and Charles IV and of being loyal only to the Despensers. The unfortunate bishop was to suffer a tragic fate some months later for his alliance with the Despensers and the queen's anger with him, which may have been justified: the *Vita* thought that Edward confiscated her lands in 1324 on Stapeldon's advice as well as Hugh Despenser's.[28] Isabella could no longer afford to pay her servants, and many of them returned to England from late November 1325 onwards, including her usher John Dene, her cook John de la Marche, her huntsman Thomas Martel, her carter Henry Pletour, the marshals of her hall Robert Sendal and Geoffrey Mildenhale, and several clerks and squires. Edward II gave them money for their expenses on their return. Peter Eketon, a sergeant-at-arms who had accompanied Edward of Windsor to France on 12 September, was among the first to return, on or before 26 November, and the young duke of Aquitaine's Dominican confessor had arrived in England by the beginning of 1326. Another of the queen's cooks, Will Balsham, also left her service, and in July 1326 made a meal for Edward II and his niece Eleanor de Clare when the two 'ate privately' in the park of Windsor Castle.[29] Edward, though he paid the expenses of Isabella's returning servants, resisted for as long as possible the notion that his wife was serious about not coming back to him and continued to renew letters of protection for the members of her retinue still in France with her as late as 26 January 1326.[30]

Yet Edward refused to listen to Isabella or take her seriously. In a session of parliament which began at Westminster on 18 November 1325 – the last parliament of Edward II's reign – the king demonstrated that his priority remained Hugh Despenser, and claimed that the favourite was 'much cast down' by Isabella's hostility towards him. His refusal even to consider her point of view and his putting Despenser's interests and feelings above hers can only have hurt her even more, especially when Edward persuaded all the English bishops to write a letter to her asserting that Despenser had 'solemnly demonstrated his innocence before all'. Edward was convinced, or at least was feigning conviction, that Isabella was simply fabricating her loathing of Despenser and 'has been led into this error at the suggestion of someone, and he is in truth wicked and hostile whoever he may be'.[31] This is probably a reference to their mutual cousin John of Brittany, earl of Richmond.

On 1 December 1325, Edward sent a letter to Isabella, the last he would ever write to her. He addressed her abruptly as 'Lady', a style which makes his anger with her apparent. The letter began, 'Lady, oftentimes we have summoned you to us, both before the homage and after, because of the great desire that we have for you to be near us and the great damage of heart caused by your so very long absence,' and went on to say that Isabella was likely to fall into great mischief and should return to him immediately, making no more excuses.[32] Any second thoughts which may have formed in Isabella's mind on reading these words were surely dispersed by the rest of the letter, when Edward spent many lines once again defending and excusing Hugh Despenser's behaviour. He also ordered Isabella to permit the return of 'our very dear son Edward' to him, 'because we have a very great desire to see him and talk to him'. Edward II sent a very similar letter on the same day to Charles IV and various French bishops and noblemen, including the dukes of Brittany and Burgundy, in which he showed himself anxious above all else to defend Despenser. How Edward felt about Isabella refusing to come back to him is unknown; perhaps he regretted that he had let things deteriorate so far, or perhaps his rage and self-righteousness blinded him to what he had done.

In the evening of 2 December, the day after he wrote to Isabella, Edward travelled along the river Thames from Westminster – apparently rowing himself, with eight attendants following behind in another boat – to visit his niece Eleanor de Clare, who was then staying at his palace of Sheen. He gave her a large gift of 100 marks, and the following day she sent him a present of a robe. A few days after this visit, Edward made an offering of 30s to the Virgin Mary to give thanks that God had granted Eleanor a speedy delivery of her latest child (not named but perhaps Elizabeth, future Lady Berkeley, the youngest of the Despensers' many children).[33] Hugh Despenser himself, meanwhile, was in south Wales, where the king kept in frequent touch with him. In November 1325, Edward received news from one of his servants that Despenser had been killed, and hastily sent men to Wales to find out what had happened; he rewarded them with ten marks each on learning that Despenser was in fact perfectly well.[34] Edward's visiting his niece Eleanor shortly before she gave birth, giving her a hugely generous gift then shortly afterwards giving thanks for the prompt delivery of her child, does all perhaps rather add fuel to the fire of the Flemish chronicler's statement that he was involved in some kind of relationship with her beyond that of uncle and niece. In October 1325 Eleanor stayed at his palace of Sheen at a time when Edward himself was also there; the king spent 33d on caged larks as a gift for her in June 1325, and on 9 October that year bought her forty-seven caged goldfinches; at New Year 1326 Eleanor sent him a gift of a palfrey horse with all equipment; and in March 1326 Edward gave her a silver goblet when they were together at Kenilworth.[35] Edward and Eleanor spent much of June and July 1326 together, sometimes sailing up and down the Thames in the king's barge, and dined privately in the park of Windsor Castle. Eleanor is the only other woman besides Isabella to be called by the honorific *ma dame*, 'my lady', in Edward's chamber account of 1325/26; her cousin the countess of Surrey, also the king's niece, and Edward's sister-in-law the countess of Norfolk are not so named. Sometimes in the many dozens of entries in the chamber account in which Eleanor appears, she is called simply *ma dame* with no other identification necessary, whereas in Edward's Household Ordinance of 1318 *ma dame* alone had referred to the queen. It would appear from the chamber account that Eleanor, rather than her husband Hugh Despenser, was the person closest to and most favoured by Edward in the last months of his reign. For all his fear that his life would be in danger if Edward travelled to France in September 1325, Despenser spent most of the following few months away from the king.

Isabella must have received news while in France in late 1325 or early 1326 of the death of her former sister-in-law Blanche of Burgundy, who had been kept in prison for adultery since 1314, and on 16 December 1325 her uncle Charles, count of Valois died at the age of fifty-five. His heir was his eldest son, Philip, born in 1293, who later succeeded Charles IV as Philip VI, king of France; the Valois dynasty would rule the kingdom until 1589. Charles of Valois's daughter Joan, countess of Hainault and her daughter Philippa of Hainault visited the French court between 1 December 1325 and 19 January 1326.[36] This may have been the first time that thirteen-year-old Edward of Windsor met his second cousin and future wife, Philippa, then about eleven. Philippa's father, William, count of Hainault and Holland, had been in negotiations with Edward II some years earlier regarding the possible marriage of

Edward of Windsor and the count's eldest daughter, Margaret, but the plans foundered and Margaret married Louis of Bavaria, future Holy Roman Emperor, in 1324. William now held a grievance against Edward for his failure to do justice to the count's men who had been robbed in England, and although Edward offered safe conducts for the count's envoys to come and 'treat with the king or his deputies touching damages on both sides' in September and November 1325 and again in 1326, as 'it is not fitting that war and anger should arise between the king and the count', it was too late, and William and his wife Joan of Valois, Isabella's first cousin, threw in their lot with Isabella in late 1325.[37] Presumably Isabella and Joan discussed the marriage of Edward of Windsor and Philippa of Hainault in December 1325: on 1 January 1326, Edward II sent a letter to his kinswoman Maria Diaz de Haro, lady of Biscay and one of the regents of Castile for the underage Alfonso XI, assuring her that his and Isabella's son – officially betrothed to Alfonso's sister Leonor – was not marrying into France (in October he had asked the pope to grant dispensations for Edward of Windsor and Eleanor of Woodstock to marry Leonor and Alfonso).[38] Just two days later, his certainty was given the lie by his pleas to the pope not to grant a dispensation for his son's marriage to any member of the French royal family without his consent. John XXII respected this wish and did not grant the dispensation until late August 1327, seven months after Edward's deposition.[39] For rumours of Edward of Windsor's possible betrothal to someone other than Leonor to have travelled from France to Castile and then to England by 1 January 1326 indicates that it must have taken place at least some weeks earlier. Edward II well knew the dangers of his son marrying while away from his control: he ordered Edward of Windsor both on his departure to France on 12 September 1325 and in subsequent letters not to marry 'without the king's assent and command'.[40] Walter Reynolds, archbishop of Canterbury, sent the king a letter on 2 January 1326 telling him that Charles IV had written to the count of Hainault to begin negotiations for the marriage of Edward of Windsor and one of the count's daughters, and also that Charles had asked for his aid regarding an invasion of England.[41] Reynolds informed Edward some weeks later that a French invasion could be expected imminently, but although Edward himself evidently believed that Charles would indeed invade England on Isabella's behalf, this was highly unlikely; the French king may well have wanted, out of fraternal affection, to protect Isabella, but this did not extend to invading a sovereign country on her behalf.[42] Despite his anguish over his wife and son, Edward II found time to co-found Oriel College at the University of Oxford with his almoner Adam Brome on 21 January 1326.

One of Isabella's first important allies in France was her kinsman and Edward's, John of Brittany, earl of Richmond, who had been loyal to the king for almost his entire reign but who evidently had grown sick, like so many others, of the excessive and malign influence of Hugh Despenser and his father, Hugh Despenser the Elder, earl of Winchester. Edward seized Richmond's lands in March 1326.[43] Isabella also gained another vital ally, Edward's half-brother and her own first cousin Edmund of Woodstock, earl of Kent, who had been in Gascony and who joined her in Paris sometime in 1326. Kent married Margaret Wake around the middle of December 1325.[44] This has sometimes been thought to represent Kent making a public alliance with Roger Mortimer, who was Margaret's first cousin, but it is much more likely to been a love or lust match: John XXII had given Kent permission to marry a woman to whom he was related in the third or fourth degree on 6 October 1325, which is far too early for Kent to have made a public alliance with a man who then was merely a disgraced traitor and exile.[45] Margaret, although a descendant of Kent's great-grandfather King John via one of John's illegitimate children, came only from a minor baronial family and thus was not a great match for a man who was the son and brother of kings. The couple would, however, become the grandparents of Richard II (b. 1367) via their daughter Joan of Kent, who was born in 1326 or 1327.[46] Edward II heard by March 1326 that his half-brother had joined Isabella and confiscated Kent's lands, though Kent continued to write to the king assuring him that he was not acting treasonably, and it does seem from the earl's later actions that in 1325/26 he sought the downfall of the Despensers, not Edward.[47]

A third important ally of the queen in Paris was William Airmyn, the new bishop of Norwich, yet another bishop against whom Edward II had begun a vendetta. Edward summoned Airmyn twice to appear before King's Bench on a charge of maliciously and treacherously agreeing that the king of France should continue to hold some of Edward's inheritance, even ordering the arrest of his two brothers when Airmyn failed to appear. Persecuted by the wrathful king, Airmyn fled to France and Isabella sometime between March and June 1326.[48] Thus Edward lost the support of another able man who would have made a very useful ally, who joined Isabella instead. Although several chroniclers say that the pope granted Airmyn the bishopric of Norwich at Isabella's request, it is clear from John XXII's letters that he thought he would be pleasing Edward, not the queen, by promoting Airmyn, given that the king had made efforts six months earlier to secure the bishopric of Carlisle for him, and although Isabella did write to John XXII on Airmyn's behalf, the pope told her that her letters arrived too late to have any effect on his decision.[49] Isabella also had, and probably knew that she had, other undeclared allies in England: her uncle Henry of Lancaster; her brother-in-law Thomas of Brotherton, earl of Norfolk; Adam Orleton, bishop of Hereford; and John Stratford, bishop of Winchester.

Sometime before 8 February 1326, when Edward had come to hear of it and declared in a public proclamation that Isabella 'is adopting the counsel of the Mortimer, the king's notorious enemy and rebel', the queen of England began some kind of relationship with Roger Mortimer.[50] She had known him since 1308, when she was twelve: he attended her wedding in Boulogne, and a month later was one of the four men who carried the royal robes during her coronation procession. How she felt about him before 1325, or if they had ever had any personal contact, is unknown. Their political aims in early 1326 coincided: they both detested Hugh Despenser the Younger (the Despensers and the Mortimers had been feuding since the 1260s when they were on opposite sides of the baronial conflicts of that decade) and desired his removal from power and preferably his death, and they both wanted their lands and their political influence back. As long as Despenser ruled over Edward II, Mortimer would never see his family and his homeland again, and, still only in his late thirties, was destined to remain an impoverished, homeless exile. The exact nature of Isabella and Roger Mortimer's relationship is uncertain, and it is possible or even probable that, at least at the start, it was a hard-headed political alliance, though it may have developed into something more later on. Mortimer's feelings for the queen are impossible to determine. Given the enormous benefits which accrued to him from becoming the queen's favourite – he ruled England through Isabella and Edward III from early 1327 to October 1330, granted himself an earldom and became at least as wealthy as Hugh Despenser had been – it seems overly convenient that he just happened to fall in love with her, just as one would doubt that Despenser genuinely happened to fall in love with Edward II in the late 1310s. Without Isabella and her son, Mortimer had no chance of removing Despenser from power or of getting his lands, position and family back, and it therefore seems unlikely that he began a relationship with her solely, or even primarily, because of love or lust.

Fourteenth-century chroniclers were also uncertain as to the real nature of Isabella and Mortimer's relationship, which rather disproves the common modern notion that Isabella openly took him as her lover and that the two flaunted their affair and lived in flagrant adultery (they did not). Both of them were married to others – Roger Mortimer had wed Joan Geneville when he was only fourteen in 1301 and would remain married to her until his death in 1330 – and as Isabella was the queen and would have been committing treason against her husband as well as a huge sin in the eyes of the Church, it is understandable that they would have wanted to keep their relations secret, and not have publicly flaunted their affair. The extreme reticence of the chroniclers and the fact that the many enemies Isabella and Mortimer made during their regency of 1327 to 1330 never used adultery or sexual impropriety as an accusation against them – when they used everything else – suggests that if they were indeed lovers, they were very discreet and no one was sure what was going on. There is no more certain evidence that they were lovers than there is that Edward II and Piers Gaveston or Hugh Despenser were, so it seems a little odd that in the twenty-first century Mortimer is inevitably called Isabella's 'lover' while Gaveston and Despenser are usually called Edward's favourites but seldom his 'lovers'. Isabella and Mortimer may at some point have had a sexual relationship, but there is no source which states that they were in love, let alone involved in the great love affair so beloved of much later writers.[51] Christopher Marlowe's play about Edward II, written around 1592, detailing his downfall and murder has had a far greater impact on our assumptions and opinions about Isabella and Mortimer's relationship than any fourteenth-century evidence.

Adam Murimuth, a royal clerk who knew Isabella and Mortimer well, wrote that they had an 'excessive familiarity', a comment reminiscent of various chroniclers' remarks about Edward's relationship with Gaveston.[52] *Lanercost* says that at the time of Mortimer's downfall in October 1330 'there was a liaison suspected between him and the lady queen-mother, as according to public report' – in short, the writer was merely reporting a rumour – and Geoffrey le Baker's scurrilous and generally unreliable *Vita et Mors Edwardi Secundi* (The Life and Death of Edward II) of the 1350s says that Isabella was 'in the illicit embraces' of Mortimer.[53] Although they were both fertile, their supposedly passionately sexual five-year affair produced no children. Many decades later Jean Froissart claimed that Isabella was pregnant at the time of Mortimer's downfall, but he is hopelessly untrustworthy for this time period and there is nothing to confirm his story (or the story one sometimes reads nowadays that Isabella secretly gave birth to a child who was smuggled out of court by one of her allies). One chronicle refers to Mortimer as Isabella's *amasius*, 'lover', though three other chronicles use the same word to describe Piers Gaveston's relationship to Edward II, and this has never been taken as definitive proof of physical relations between the two men, let alone that Gaveston must have been in love with Edward.[54] The *Scalacronica* of around 1360 describes Mortimer only as 'chief of her [Isabella's] council'. The *French Chronicle of London* does not mention Mortimer with Isabella in any context until September 1326, when it talks of Isabella, her son, 'the Mortimer' and other great lords arriving with an invasion force in Suffolk. It also mentions 'Lady Isabella the queen, the king's mother, and Sir Roger Mortimer and others of their faction' taking part in the negotiations regarding the marriage of her daughter Joan of the Tower into Scotland in 1328, and that is all it has to say on the matter of the queen and her supposed lover. The *Brut* says that Isabella allied herself with 'the knights that were exiled out of England' because of the king's quarrel with Thomas of Lancaster in 1322, 'that is to say, Sir Roger Mortimer of Wigmore, Sir William Trussell, Sir John Cromwell, and many other great knights'.[55] A rumour in the 1340s of a 'liaison', a remark in the 1350s of 'illicit embraces' and one unsubstantiated claim by a man born in about 1337 that Isabella was pregnant five years after the commencement of her association with Mortimer seem a remarkably thin basis for the frequent assumption that the two had an all-consuming love affair and publicly flaunted their sexual and romantic relationship. It is of course not impossible that they did fall in love or lust, but we have no way of knowing this for sure, and there are no letters and of course no diaries where the two reveal their feelings. The idea that Isabella, having been unsatisfactorily married for many years to a gay man unable and unwilling to fulfil her desires, fell deeply in love with an unequivocally heterosexual, virile and manly man who was her husband's exact opposite is a popular modern narrative, but that does not necessarily make it true. We should remember how very little we really know, or ever can know, about the nature of Isabella and Mortimer's association or about their personal feelings.

Whatever happened between the two, allying with her husband's greatest enemy was a sign that Isabella was deadly serious about her aim of removing Hugh Despenser from Edward's side, and taking revenge on Despenser. Her later behaviour, when she and Mortimer ruled England for several years during the minority of her son Edward III, suggests that she had become dependent on Mortimer in some way, perhaps in much the same way as her husband had been dependent on Despenser. Edward II said in letters to Charles IV and his son Edward of Windsor in March 1326 that Isabella 'keeps his [Mortimer's] company within and without house', usually assumed to be a euphemistic reference to adultery. This phrase, however, occurs in the context of Edward's complaining about Isabella's retention of Mortimer and 'others of his faction', i.e. the English exiles on the Continent such as William Trussell, John Cromwell and John Maltravers, as members of her council and her affinity.[56] Many of Edward and Hugh Despenser's letters of 1323 to 1326 talk of 'Roger Mortimer and the other exiles' in the same fashion; they saw Mortimer as the leader of the exiled Contrariants and the greatest threat to them, and he is either the only one named or the first one named in a list.[57]

It is at least possible that at first, and perhaps for some considerable time, Isabella, and perhaps even Mortimer and some of his allies, did not desire Edward II's forced removal from his throne. Something so drastic had never been done in England before, and they cannot have known whether it would even be possible, legally or otherwise, or how many people would be willing to follow them so far. For all the intense dissatisfaction of many of the king's most important magnates with him and the empty threats of deposition made against him several times throughout his reign, they may well balk at his removal from the throne if and when it really came to that moment. Isabella, a staunch royalist, might also have balked at the idea initially. She owed Edward her loyalty and obedience not only as her king but as her husband, and rebellion against him, for all her anger at what he and Despenser had done, must have been difficult for her. For a long time, until well past their invasion of England, Isabella, Mortimer and their allies claimed that they only sought the removal of the Despensers from the king's side and not the downfall of the king himself, and although this may have been simply how they presented their aims in public while Edward still sat on the throne, it is not impossible that it was true. It may be that the original intention was to separate Hugh Despenser and his father, the earl of Winchester, from the king and kill them, then force Edward to grant the rebels a pardon for the deaths of the Despensers and for Mortimer and his allies' original crimes during the Contrariant rebellion of 1321/22 and restore their lands to them. The king had been made to pardon Piers Gaveston's killers in 1313 and the numerous men who had sacked the Despensers' lands and exiled them in 1321, so there were precedents for forcing him to do so a third time. The chaotic events of 1326/27 have always been interpreted with decades or centuries of hindsight and knowledge of Edward II's catastrophic downfall, and it has generally been assumed that Isabella, Roger Mortimer and his allies and even Charles IV must have plotted for years to destroy the king. This is not necessarily the case, especially as Isabella's presumed desire to overthrow her husband is predicated on the supposition that she had long hated him, which she had not. At some point, perhaps not until as late as Christmas 1326 when it had become apparent to all that Edward II could not continue to reign as king of England, the queen and her allies decided that Edward must be replaced by his son Edward of Windsor.

Edward of Windsor, the teenaged heir to the English throne, was key to the events of 1326. He hated the Despensers as much as anyone, and for all his youth, his at least passive involvement in a campaign by the surviving Contrariants against the Despensers was necessary. Edward II's greatest error in 1325 was not to send his son to France, but to send him unmarried (as the king himself recognised). Had the boy already had a wife, his value as a hostage would have been severely limited, as without the financial and military support provided by the father of young Edward's fiancée, the exiles would not have been able to raise enough ships and troops for an invasion of England; if this had been possible, they would have struck against the Despensers long before 1326. Roger Mortimer and the other English exiles, men such as John Maltravers and William Trussell who had fled from England after Boroughbridge and who were with Mortimer on the Continent, had been searching for allies who could help them achieve an invasion of England and bring down the Despensers since 1323. The exiles, understandably, wanted nothing more than to return to their homeland and their families and be restored to their lands and income, but this was never going to happen while Edward II was king of England and while Hugh Despenser dominated him. Edward was only forty-one in 1325, and his father had lived to be sixty-eight; the exiles would be old men before they saw England again, if they ever did. It is most unlikely that they had spent the time since the battle of Boroughbridge in March 1322 witlessly twiddling their thumbs until Isabella brilliantly and single-handedly rescued them by devising the strategy of arranging her son's marriage to pay for their invasion. The exiles had no chance of putting the plan into action without the queen, as they could not possibly approach Edward of Windsor and ask him to betray his father by marrying a bride of their choice, so that they could pay for ships and soldiers and bring down his father's favourites and even the king himself. The exiles had probably never even met the boy, except perhaps on ceremonial occasions at court before 1322, but this does not preclude the possibility or probability that some kind of plan was already in place, and that Isabella fell in with it but did not initiate it. The count of Hainault, although annoyed with Edward II over his failure to do justice to the count's subjects, was not nearly so hostile to him that he would be willing to fund an invasion of England without a substantial vested interest in the outcome. The betrothal of Edward II and Isabella's son to one of William's daughters provided this: she would be queen of England, the next king would be William's grandson, and he could look forward to decades of peaceful relations and lucrative trade connections with a rich and powerful kingdom. There was nothing else Mortimer and his allies could have offered the count to secure his help. For the exiles to plot the marriage of Edward's son without the king's consent was a long-term strategy with a very high possibility of failure, but since Edward had imprisoned and exiled them, they had little else to do but wait and plot their revenge and methods whereby they could return to England, by any means necessary. Mortimer and the exiles had no possible access to Edward II's son except through the boy's mother, and Mortimer's association with Isabella thus appears calculating rather than romantic.

In refusing to return to Edward II, Isabella herself could cause embarrassment but do him little harm, but she had a vital weapon in her grasp: her son, the heir to the throne, whom she kept with her in France. Whether her son remained with her and her allies of his own free will or whether he would have preferred to return to his father is impossible to say; Isabella was not about to let the future king of England, the most important chess piece on the board, slip out of her control, and probably he was little more than a prisoner.[58] Edward of

Windsor was only thirteen in 1326 and not operating under his own agency. A letter supposedly written by the boy to his father sometime before 18 March 1326, talking about his mother's 'very great anxiety of heart' and his unwillingness to leave her and return to England because of it, sounds far more likely to have been the work of Isabella herself.[59] In using her thirteen-year-old son as a weapon against her husband in this way, Isabella was forcing the boy to choose between his parents, and whichever he chose – or was forced to choose – he would lose the other parent. Either he could stay with his mother, disobey and commit treason against his father, enter into a betrothal with a daughter of the count of Hainault without his father's consent, associate himself with Edward II's greatest enemy, Roger Mortimer, and take part in an invasion of his kingdom, or he could return to his father and see his mother either forced to remain in France and be dependent on her brother's charity or return to England and probably be imprisoned in a convent or a castle by the furious king. However canny Isabella's actions may have been politically, they can only have caused intense emotional strain on her thirteen-year-old son.

On 5 February 1326, three days before Edward II's proclamation that she was 'adopting the counsel of the Mortimer', Isabella wrote a letter to Walter Reynolds, archbishop of Canterbury. She told him that Hugh Despenser the Younger 'wished to dishonour us as much as he could' and that she had hidden her dislike of him for a long time in order to escape danger. She explicitly stated later in the letter that she meant danger to her own life, this being the reason why she did not dare to return to 'the company of our said lord', i.e. Edward. Isabella wrote that her inability to return to her husband without putting herself in mortal peril caused her such serious distress that she could write no more of it. The queen also told the archbishop that she wished above all else, after God and the salvation of her soul, to return to Edward's company and to live and die there, and called her husband 'our very dear and very sweet lord and friend' (*nostre treschier et tresdouche seignur et amy*).[60] There is no real reason to suppose that Isabella was lying, and the description of Edward II as her 'very dear and very sweet lord and friend' is most unconventional – the conventional way to refer to one's husband was merely 'our very dear lord' – and speaks to her strong feelings for him. When this letter has been cited in books about Isabella, it is usually assumed that she was not telling the truth but merely keeping up appearances, that of course she had to say such things about her husband and king in public; yet nothing forced her to write a private letter to the archbishop of Canterbury explaining how she felt. Furthermore, the assumption that she was lying is based on more assumptions that she was deeply in love or lust with Roger Mortimer and involved in an intense physical relationship with him, and that she hated and felt repulsed by Edward and therefore could not possibly have desired a reconciliation with him. We do not know that Isabella was in love and sleeping with Mortimer in February/March 1326 and, besides her husband's statement that she was adopting his and his allies' counsel 'within and without house', there is no evidence to indicate that she was. Later writers have been too keen to assign different meanings to Isabella's speech and letter of late 1325 – the ones they think she really meant or should have said rather than the ones she actually did send or say. We should do her the courtesy of reading to her words, which strongly imply not hatred or disgust for her husband, defiance of him and love for Roger Mortimer but bafflement and hurt that Edward had allowed Despenser to come between them and ruin a marriage in which she had been content.

In late 1325, Isabella declared that she would return to Edward if Hugh Despenser were removed from his side; in early 1326 she stated again that she wished to return to Edward but dared not because of her physical fear of Despenser, and that being unable to be in her husband's presence caused her great distress; and sometime before mid-June 1326 she told Roger Mortimer that she wanted to go back to Edward. A furious Mortimer told her that if she did so, he would kill her, with a knife or in some other way, 'and by his [Mortimer's] other subtle scheming, he caused the said queen not to come to her said lord'.[61] It is not clear from the wording of the Rochester chronicle and the records of parliament in November 1330 (where this incident is recorded) whether the 'he' who would kill Isabella means Edward II or Roger Mortimer himself.[62] If Isabella returned to Edward, she would take her son the future king with her, and Mortimer would lose his only weapon and his chance to return to his homeland, his family and his lands. Most probably, he would never again have the opportunity and would remain a destitute exile on the Continent for the rest of his life. It is hardly a wonder that he raged at the prospect, which is far more likely to have been his motive for threatening Isabella that either he or her husband would stab her to death than sexual jealousy, as sometimes surmised.[63] Even now, months after she had discussed the marriage of her son into Hainault and must therefore have been planning some kind of action against the Despensers and by extension Edward himself, Isabella was still hoping for reconciliation with her husband, at least sometimes. He, however, still would not remove Hugh Despenser from his side, not even in the face of Isabella's pleas. Perhaps he received news of her letter to the archbishop at the same time as the news that she was consorting with his greatest enemy; his proclamation was issued three days after she wrote the letter, and perhaps he was too angry with her to try to build bridges.

On 15 February 1326, Pope John XXII wrote to both Isabella and

Edward to say that he had 'heard with grief of the dissension' between them and was sending two envoys, the archbishop of Vienne and the bishop of Orange, to them both to 'interpose and remove' the dissension and remove any obstacles which hindered their reconciliation. John also wrote to Despenser the Younger suggesting that he retire from court as his participation in Edward's government had been given by Isabella as a reason for her inability to return to her husband.[64] Henry Eastry, the perceptive prior of Canterbury who was rather reluctantly taking care of Isabella's hunting dogs, believed that the two envoys persuaded Isabella to return on condition that Hugh Despenser and his father the earl of Winchester retired from court, and, correctly identifying Isabella's main priority, that the queen was fully restored to her estates.[65] It is extremely likely that Isabella's main motive in 1326 was to regain her lands and income and her political influence, which she had lost to Hugh Despenser. Until 1322 she had been a highly effective and frequent intercessor with her husband and had successfully intervened with Edward on several occasions, most notably when she persuaded him to abandon his own candidate and support hers in a bishop's election. Some modern writers have claimed that one of her chief motives was to liberate her husband's subjects from tyranny and oppression, but as she and Mortimer themselves imprisoned women and children, took lands belonging to other people and behaved in ways indistinguishable from their predecessors, this is most unlikely to have been the case.[66] Perhaps Isabella loved Edward as her husband but realised – as she could hardly fail to do – that his kingship was a disaster, and threatened her son's inheritance. Edward II was, in effect, two people: a man, and a king. Isabella's rebellion against the king does not necessarily mean that she hated the man, her husband.

Edward II sent long letters to his son Edward of Windsor and his brother-in-law Charles IV on 18 March 1326, though not, revealingly, to Isabella herself.[67] The king addressed Edward of Windsor as *Beaufuitz*, 'fair son', half a dozen times throughout the letter (Isabella herself also called him 'fair son'), said that 'we have loved and cherished her', i.e. Isabella, and complained that not only had she made Roger Mortimer her own counsellor but had delivered the king's son into the company of 'the Mortimer, the king's traitor and enemy', as well. There is no hint in either letter of an adulterous relationship between Isabella and Mortimer, only that she had made him her adviser. Edward once again indulged himself, in both letters, in long and tedious justifications and excuses for Hugh Despenser, and ordered his son to come home to England with all haste. Meanwhile, rumours had come to the pope's ear that Edward had publicly declared his wife and son to be his enemies and exiled them from his realm, and intended to harm them. Edward wrote to John XXII indignantly refuting this, and his surviving proclamations make clear that although in 1326 he named Isabella's allies as 'the king's enemies', he specifically excluded Isabella herself, his son Edward of Windsor and his half-brother the earl of Kent, even after the invasion, from being named as such.[68]

On 11 May 1326, Isabella's sister-in-law Joan of Evreux was crowned queen of France at Sainte Chapelle in Paris, twenty-two months after her wedding to Charles IV. Joan must have been pregnant at the time, as her second daughter, Marie, was born towards the end of the year; the girl was perhaps named after Charles IV and Isabella's step-grandmother Marie of Brabant, or after Charles' former wife Marie of Luxembourg. Marie outlived her father but died in 1341 in her teens and unmarried, and her sister, Charles and Joan of Evreux's child born probably in late 1325 whose name is uncertain, was still alive at Queen Joan's coronation but died around the time that Marie was born. Isabella appeared first on the list of ladies attending Joan's coronation, even before Joan herself, and was attended by a 'Madame Sezile'. *Madame la Royne d'Angleterre* wore nine panels of vermilion velvet and a robe of eleven panels of blood-red velvet (which sounds very warm for the time of year).[69] Also present were Edward II's first cousin Blanche of Brittany; the duchess of Burgundy, who was Isabella's eighteen-year-old niece Joan of France, eldest daughter of Philip V; and the duchess of Brabant, Edward II's niece-in-law and Joan of Evreux's elder sister Marie of Evreux. Isabella's son Edward of Windsor and Roger Mortimer were not officially invited to the coronation, perhaps out of respect for the king of England, but went anyway, and Mortimer carried the boy's train. A few weeks later, Edward II complained vociferously about this to Charles IV.[70] Shortly after Queen Joan's coronation, the king of England attended the wedding of Hugh Despenser's niece Margaret Hastings at Marlborough in Wiltshire, where he must have spent time with his and Isabella's daughters, eight-year-old Eleanor and five-year-old Joan, who were living there under the care of his sister-in-law the countess of Norfolk's sister Joan Jermy. In late July the royal daughters were still at Marlborough, where Edward sent them letters.[71]

In late May and early June 1326, Edward II travelled to Kent to meet the pope's envoys, the archbishop of Vienne and the bishop of Orange, who were attempting to bring about his and Isabella's reconciliation. Hugh Despenser refuted the accusations the queen had made against him, and Edward refused once again to expel him from his company. The king wrote to the pope afterwards, complaining how his son and heir was being detained in France and that Isabella was forcing the boy to associate with Roger Mortimer, his mortal enemy. Edward declared that he had sent Isabella to France at John XXII's suggestion and 'in all the sweetness of true love' (*in omni dulcedine veri amoris*). He referred to Isabella in the letter as 'the queen of England, our wife' rather than 'our very dear consort' or 'our dear consort, our very dear lady' as he had done throughout his reign, his use of language once again pointing to his anger with Isabella.[72] Something of the fevered atmosphere of 1326 is apparent in two of the pope's letters, where he assured Isabella that Edward's envoy William Weston had not only said nothing against her honour but had proved himself a 'zealous defender' of it, and told Hugh Despenser that the earl of Kent's messenger had not 'said any ill' of him.[73] In mid-June, Edward and Despenser met Hamo Hethe, bishop of Rochester and one of the few important men in England kindly disposed towards Despenser, while riding through Kent. Despenser informed the bishop that the papal envoys had sought guarantees for the safe return of Isabella, her son and the earl of Kent, and pointed out that no such guarantees were necessary as they could return to England in safety at any time. He also told Hethe that Roger Mortimer had threatened to kill Isabella (or told her that Edward would kill her) if she returned to England. Edward asked the bishop if it were true that a queen of England who had defied her husband had been deposed of her royal dignity, perhaps an indication that he was by now considering an annulment of their marriage, though if he was, he took it no further. Hethe told Edward sharply that whoever had told him this story deserved little thanks, a rebuke Edward took with surprisingly good grace.[74]

Edward II wrote to his son Edward of Windsor again on 19 June 1326, the last contact between father and son; his anguish is very apparent, especially as his son had told him untruthfully that Mortimer was not an adherent of himself or his mother, 'whereby the king considers himself very evilly paid'. Edward wrote that his son had not behaved as a good son should by obeying his father's commands, threatened him with forfeiture of all lands and goods if he did not return, and ordered him again not to marry. He ended the letter by writing that if his son was 'contrary and disobedient hereafter to his will ... he will ordain in such wise that Edward [of Windsor] will feel it all the days of his life, and that all other sons shall take example thereby of disobeying their lords and fathers'. As it turned out some months later, this was an empty threat, but it must have pained the young duke of Aquitaine, whose mother had committed him to her plan of action whether he wanted to or not, to read such harsh angry words from his father. Edward II also complained to Charles IV in a letter written the same day about his son's forced adherence to Mortimer 'and our other enemies over there' by Isabella, and wrote that 'your sister, our wife' had shamefully withdrawn herself from him.[75] Charles, in fact, seems to have become unhappy with his sister's prolonged sojourn in France, and thus at some uncertain date in the summer of 1326, after 10 June and before 3 August, Isabella left the French court and went to Hainault (though her husband, evidently unaware of her whereabouts, thought that she was still in France on 4 September).[76] It is not entirely clear whether she left her brother's kingdom of her own accord or whether she felt compelled to, though a few months later she and her allies accused Hugh Despenser of sending 'over the sea a large sum of money to certain evil men, your [Despenser's] adherents, to destroy my lady and her son, the rightful heir of the kingdom'.[77] Presumably Isabella meant that she had begun to fear for her safety in France, and the *Brut* says that Despenser sent masses of silver to the French court as a bribe to send her back, but that his envoy was captured and Isabella herself seized the money.[78] On 10 June while still in Paris, the queen was already planning the invasion of her husband's kingdom: she pledged the revenues of their county of Ponthieu to William, count of Hainault to cover the cost of ships and supplies, giving Charles IV as her ultimate guarantor in case of default, though it is not clear whether the French king consented to this or even knew of it.[79] The *Flores Historiarum* claims that Charles IV and the entire nobility of France had promised to help Isabella's invasion of England: a ludicrous statement.[80] Precisely when and why Isabella left France is uncertain; colourful stories by various chroniclers that she departed in the dead of night after being warned by her and Edward II's kinsman Robert of Artois (son of Blanche of Brittany) that her brother was about to have her arrested and returned to England, and that William of Hainault's brother John of Beaumont met her on her arrival in Hainault and romantically agreed to do everything he could to restore her to England, are implausible. Roger Mortimer and presumably the other English exiles were in Hainault by the end of July 1326, gathering ships and supplies in the queen's name, to be ready at Dordrecht by 1 September.[81]

On 27 August 1326, Isabella's son Edward of Windsor was betrothed to Philippa, daughter of William, count of Hainault and Joan of Valois, and then about twelve years old. Joan's brother Philip of Valois was now head of the family since the death of their father, Charles, in December 1325, and heir apparent to the throne of France until Charles IV fathered a son. There was a chance that Isabella might try to claim the throne for her son, who was, apart from his younger brother, John of Eltham, Philip IV's only surviving grandson. The Valois family therefore had an interest in allying with Isabella so that she would renounce her son's claim to the French throne, as in fact she did.[82] The young duke of Aquitaine, still only thirteen, bound himself to marry Philippa of Hainault within two years, and Roger Mortimer and Edward II's half-brother Edmund of Woodstock, earl of Kent stood as guarantors to the contract. Edward of Windsor was still officially betrothed to Alfonso XI of Castile's sister Leonor, and as he was under age and his legal guardian, his father Edward II, had not consented to his engagement to Philippa and indeed stood in firm opposition to it, the legality of the process was extremely dubious.[83] Philippa of Hainault and Edward III went on to have a long, happy and extremely fruitful marriage, and seemingly they got on well right from the start: Philippa was later to claim to the chronicler Jean Froissart that Edward of Windsor liked her best of all her sisters and chose her as his bride.[84] In fact she was the eldest unmarried sister (her sisters Margaret and Joan had married Louis of Bavaria and William of Jülich respectively in 1324) and therefore next in line to marry. Her betrothal in 1326 had everything to do with power politics at the highest level and nothing to do with the whims of adolescents, being the means by which her future mother-in-law and a group of exiles could invade a sovereign nation with ships and mercenaries – surely the least romantic start to a marriage imaginable, whatever Philippa might have convinced herself of later. Had something untoward happened to Philippa before her marriage to Edward could take place, it would have gone ahead with the next sister instead.

In England, Edward II was pretending that Charles IV was detaining his son against the boy's will, and when on 6 September the king of England asked for the prayers of the Dominican friars of Oxford on behalf of himself and his realm (as he often did), Isabella and Edward of Windsor were, for the first time, not included.[85] Sometime in August Edward attacked Normandy with a force of about 140 ships, possibly in an attempt to seize his son, said in 1327 to have been 'in those parts', though the king said that his intention was 'to restrain the malice of the men of the king of France in case they wish to enter the realm'. The force was repulsed with heavy losses, precisely the last thing that Edward needed with his wife's invasion imminent.[86] Everything went wrong for Edward II in the summer of 1326: as well as growing tension with Scotland and the impending invasion of England, the situation with France deteriorated again. In late June, Edward set out his claims to be 'guardian and administrator of Gascony' in Edward of Windsor's name, in an attempt to limit the damage caused by the loss of his son. Charles IV, claiming for his part to be protecting his nephew's rights in the duchy, began reoccupying the areas of Gascony from which he had been in the process of withdrawing, and Edward would end his reign at war with France once more. He asked the citizens of Bayonne on 6 July to 'annoy and injure' all Charles IV's subjects and once more ordered the arrest of all French people in England, though also claiming at the same time that he was eager for peace with France. Still fearing an invasion from that country, he ordered all monks who were citizens of France and who lived near the coast to be moved inland.[87]

Isabella was in Dordrecht with Count William of Hainault on 7 September.[88] With her were Roger Mortimer, probably the earls of Kent and Richmond, and other English exiles who had fled the country in or after 1322, including John Maltravers, John Cromwell (who was a former steward of Edward II's household) and William Trussell. Henry, Lord Beaumont, was not with her, however, as often stated: he had returned to England after witnessing Edward of Windsor's homage to Charles IV in September 1325 and was imprisoned at Warwick Castle in the late summer of 1326.[89] John of Beaumont, Count William of Hainault's brother, had raised an army of 700 mercenaries in Hainault and Germany, and Isabella and her allies had ninety-five ships with around 1,000 to 1,500 men in total.[90] The long-awaited invasion of England, the first since Isabella's great-great-grandfather the future Louis VIII of France had attempted to wrest the English throne from Edward II's great-grandfather King John 110 years previously, was about to begin.

10

Invading England and Deposing a King

1326–1327

On 21 or 22 September 1326, Isabella's little invasion force left Dordrecht, and they landed at Orwell in Suffolk around midday on the 24th, after a long and probably most uncomfortable sea journey. According to the Flemish chronicler Jean le Bel, who was with the queen, when they arrived they had no idea where they were.[1] Edward II and Hugh Despenser the Younger had anticipated as far back as October 1324 that Roger Mortimer and the other English exiles might land in Suffolk or Norfolk with the aid of the count of Hainault and Charles IV's brother-in-law the king of Bohemia, though their prescience did them no good whatsoever.[2] The site where Isabella landed lay on or near the lands of Edward's half-brother Thomas of Brotherton, earl of Norfolk, who went to join Isabella and his brother the earl of Kent, despite having been appointed to defend the counties of Norfolk, Suffolk, Essex and Hertfordshire against the invaders. The bishops of Hereford, Lincoln, Ely and probably Norwich, and the archbishop of Dublin, also soon joined the queen.[3] Edward II, in the Tower of London with the Despensers, the earl of Arundel, his niece Eleanor de Clare and his and Isabella's second son, John of Eltham, heard the news of the invasion force's arrival three days later on the 27th; the news was brought to him by the crew of the ship in which Isabella herself had travelled, which was captured by some of the king's men after she disembarked at Orwell, and sailed to London. It may therefore be that Isabella herself came close to capture on arrival.[4]

The destruction of Edward's fleet in Normandy some weeks before and the alacrity with which the earl of Norfolk joined the rebels ensured that the small invading force, which could easily have been destroyed on arrival, progressed with no resistance. Isabella and her allies headed west in triumph and, perhaps, amazement at the absolute lack of resistance or hostility: most of Edward's men either fled from them or joined them. According to the *French Chronicle of London*, 'The mariners of England were not minded to prevent their coming, by reason of the great anger they entertained against Sir Hugh le Despenser', and the Lichfield chronicler says that the people of the whole region of East Anglia joined the queen.[5] Five days after the landing, Isabella and the others arrived at the town of Bury St Edmunds, where she helped herself to – or 'caused to be taken for his [her son Edward of Windsor's] affairs' as she euphemistically glossed the theft – £800 which Hervey Staunton, chief justice of the court of Common Pleas and an ally of Edward II, had stored at the abbey, to pay her soldiers. Staunton died a year later without recovering the money.[6] The Lichfield chronicler claims that Isabella and her son paid for food and necessities for themselves and their soldiers wherever they went rather than plundering the countryside, though in fact they did pillage from Despenser manors, and according to a contemporary petition, Isabella declared that her followers could plunder what they wished from the lands of her enemies, with one quarter of anything taken to be given to her personally and another quarter to Roger Mortimer. £1,800 belonging to Hugh Despenser the Elder was stolen from Leicester Abbey and never seen again; in Gloucestershire goods of the value of £800 were taken from the younger Despenser; and Edward II's half-brothers, the earls of Kent and Norfolk, later received a pardon for looting the property of the Despensers and their ally the earl of Arundel on twenty-three estates across the country.[7] On 9 October Isabella placed a reward of £2,000 on the head of Hugh Despenser the Younger as a response to the king's declaring on 28 September that Roger Mortimer and others 'have entered the realm in force, and have brought with them alien strangers for the purpose of taking the royal power from the king', and offering a ransom of £1,000 on Mortimer's head.[8]

As early as 28 September, the day after he learned of the force's arrival, Edward II must have realised how little support he had and pardoned all felons in prison, excepting any adherents of Roger Mortimer, if they would join him.[9] On this day, he ordered men in Kent, Oxfordshire, Berkshire and Buckinghamshire to raise hundreds of footmen to 'repel the invaders' and 'take them alive or dead'. The order was repeated to his Welsh allies Rhys ap Gruffydd and Gruffydd Llywd, while Sir Robert Wateville was ordered to raise footmen in six counties and 'do what harm he can to [the rebels] except to the queen, the king's son and the earl of Kent'.[10] Wateville soon joined Isabella instead, which must have been painful for Edward, who had shown Wateville considerable kindness and generosity in 1325/26 and attended his wedding to Despenser the

Younger's niece Margaret Hastings earlier that year. But Wateville, like many others, realised which way the wind was blowing. The defection of Edward's half-brother Norfolk, who immediately joined Isabella and the King's other half-brother Kent, must have been a bitter blow to Edward; an even worse one was soon to come, when his cousin Henry of Lancaster declared for the rebels, joined his niece Isabella at Dunstable on 9 or 10 October, and seized money and goods belonging to Hugh Despenser the Elder, earl of Winchester.[11] Henry of Lancaster had rightful cause to be furious with the king, who had unjustly kept in his own hands the bulk of the vast inheritance Henry should have received from his brother Thomas in 1322, and only allowed Henry the earldom of Leicester. Defiantly, Henry began styling himself 'earl of Lancaster' and took the northern lords with him to Isabella's cause, including his son-in-law Thomas Wake, formerly Isabella's ward (whose sister Margaret was married to the earl of Kent and who was Roger Mortimer's first cousin) and Henry, Lord Percy. Edmund Fitzalan, earl of Arundel remained loyal to the king, and apparently so did Arundel's brother-in-law John de Warenne, earl of Surrey, at least for the time being, but the grand coalition of the queen, the Contrariants, Henry of Lancaster, at least three or four bishops and the archbishop of Dublin, the northern lords and the king's half-brothers was unassailable. Edward heard the bad news of Lancaster's defection on 10 October and seized Henry's lands, sending his teenaged great-nephew, Hugh Despenser's eldest son, Hugh or Huchon, to take possession of them.[12] Some people, though, still hedged their bets: Edward's niece Elizabeth de Clare, whom he had temporarily imprisoned in 1322 and allowed Hugh Despenser to persecute, cautiously made sure to keep in touch via letters and messengers with both the king and queen, and on 15 October paid a man sent to 'report rumours from the king's court' to her.[13]

Edward left London on 2 October 1326 and headed towards Wales, leaving his beloved niece Eleanor de Clare – the last time he or Hugh Despenser would see her – in charge of the Tower. His and Isabella's ten-year-old younger son, John of Eltham, also remained there in nominal charge of the city. Although it appears that Edward was fleeing his capital, unwilling to be trapped in a city usually hostile to him (as he had been in 1321 when the Marcher lords and their armies surrounded it), a plan drawn up some months before for the defence of the realm declared that 'our lord the king himself will make his way towards the March of Wales to rouse the good and loyal men of that land and will punish the traitors', so apparently he was sticking to a previously arranged plan.[14] Edward wrote from Acton on 3 October that he had heard his wife was writing to all the cities and commonalties of the realm, and ordered them not to open the letters but to arrest the bearer and send him to the king. No one was to favour 'the king's wife or his son Edward or anyone in their company so long as they behave as they do now', and all others in their company were to be treated as the king's enemies.[15] Even at this desperate stage, however, Edward still refused to name his wife and his son in public as his enemies. Isabella, meanwhile, was spitefully ransacking the manor of Baldock in Hertfordshire, apparently for no other reason than it belonged to Thomas Catel, brother of the detested Robert Baldock, chancellor of England and ally of Hugh Despenser.[16]

Isabella, daughter of the master propagandist Philip IV, well knew the benefits of public relations, far better than Edward did. She and her allies pretended that they had two cardinals with them, carrying a papal bull absolving all Englishmen from their oath of allegiance to Edward II and threatening to excommunicate anyone who raised arms against the invasion force.[17] Few men wished to fight against their future king, even on behalf of his father, the present one, especially as the invasion force marched under the royal banner. At Wallingford near Oxford on 15 October, a proclamation was read out in the name of the queen, her son the duke of Aquitaine, and her brother-in-law the earl of Kent, in which Hugh Despenser the Younger was accused of damaging the realm and Church, sending great men to their deaths, being a tyrant, and usurping royal power. Edward II himself incurred no criticism and was never, at this time or later, said to be a tyrant, but was presented instead as the victim of an evil counsellor, whom Isabella and her allies had come to destroy in order to end the oppressions suffered by the people of England.[18] They were still claiming publicly that their only quarrel was with Despenser, not with the king himself.

Shortly afterwards, the bishop of Hereford, Adam Orleton – who had been persecuted by Edward II because of his alleged support of the Mortimers in 1322 and who travelled to meet Isabella soon after her arrival – publicly accused either Edward II or, more probably, Hugh Despenser the Younger of being a sodomite. Orleton preached a sermon from Genesis: 'I shall put enmity between you and the woman, and thy seed and hers, and she shall bruise your head.' Orleton was to claim in 1334 that he had certainly been referring to Hugh Despenser, not Edward, and that no one sane could possibly interpret his sermon as referring to the king (though some people evidently did, as he was charged with having maliciously attacked Edward and Isabella's relationship and causing animosity between them).[19]

The city of London exploded into chaos. The city tended to be politically volatile and anti-royalist, or rather anti-authority; Isabella and Roger Mortimer would find out for themselves two years later that the affections of the Londoners were fickle, but for the moment the city stood on their side. The mayor Hamo de Chigwell had been one of the men who sentenced Roger Mortimer to death in 1322, so had every reason to feel trepidation at Mortimer's return, and indeed he was replaced as mayor by Mortimer's adherent Richard de Béthune soon afterwards and saved his life only by swearing to support Isabella.[20] Eleanor de Clare, meanwhile, soon had little choice but to surrender the Tower to the mob, and according to the Flemish chronicler who thought she was having an affair with her uncle Edward, she was afterwards imprisoned there in case she might be pregnant by the king. Prisoners held in the Tower, including two of Roger Mortimer's sons, Thomas, Lord Berkeley, and the late Bartholomew Badlesmere's nephew Sir Bartholomew Burghersh – whose brother Henry, bishop of Lincoln, was with Isabella – were freed.[21] An emergency convocation of the archbishop of Canterbury and the bishops of London, Rochester, Winchester, Exeter and Worcester held at Lambeth on 13 and 14 October decided to send two envoys to the queen. The following day, tragedy struck when Walter Stapeldon, bishop of Exeter, former treasurer of England, founder of Exeter College at Oxford in 1314 and ally of Edward II, a man whom Isabella hated, was pursued by an angry crowd and beheaded with a bread knife in Cheapside while trying to reach sanctuary inside St Paul's. The doors of his house were burned down, his jewels and silver stolen, and many of his books destroyed.[22] Two of Stapeldon's squires were killed with him. His head was sent to the queen at Gloucester and she received it with pleasure as an offering to Diana, the goddess of hunting, according to chronicler Geoffrey le Baker (who detested Isabella, so this statement may not be accurate). The bishop of London Stephen Gravesend was lucky to escape the same fate, and Edward's remaining allies in London thought it prudent to leave the city: Geoffrey le Scrope, chief justice of King's Bench, escaped across the Thames on a horse belonging to Archbishop Reynolds; Reynolds commandeered the horses of the bishop of Rochester Hamo Hethe; and Hethe himself fled on foot.[23] The community of Dominican friars, who had long been staunch supporters of the king, also thought it safest to leave the city.[24] Isabella herself, however, decided for now – wisely – to avoid the city, though sent letters to the citizens on two occasions. Having received no answer to her first one, supposedly because the Londoners were afraid of the king, her second asked them to arrest Hugh Despenser if at all possible, 'by the faith which you owe to our lord the king and to us'.[25]

Edward sent out spies to report to him on Isabella's movements, the first payment for this appearing on 11 October: 20s to one Thomas Geyton for 'news of the coming of my lady the queen'. On 17 October the king paid his chamber valet Richard Mereworth another 20s for observing Isabella's entry into Gloucester.[26] Edward, the two Hugh Despensers, the earl of Arundel and Robert Baldock, archdeacon of Middlesex and chancellor of England, travelled west towards south Wales where Despenser held most of his lands, pursued at some distance by Isabella and her allies. The king had a considerable amount of money with him – £29,000 – with which to pay his soldiers, but most of them refused to go against Isabella and her son. The speedy success of the invasion took everyone by surprise, not least those who were leading it, and it soon became clear that Edward II's position was becoming increasingly untenable. On 20 October, Edward, Hugh Despenser the Younger and Despenser's confessor Richard Bliton tried to sail from Chepstow in south Wales, presumably intending to reach Despenser's island of Lundy in the Bristol Channel and ultimately Ireland, from where Edward may have hoped to launch a counter-invasion of his kingdom. Even the wind was against the king of England, however: five days later they were forced to put in at Cardiff again, having got nowhere. The king's unsuccessful sea journey allowed Isabella and her allies to claim that he had left the kingdom, and therefore they appointed her son keeper of the realm on 20 October.[27] Edward of Windsor turned fourteen on 13 November.

Edward left the city of Bristol in the hands of Hugh Despenser the Elder, earl of Winchester. Isabella arrived there on 18 October, and the city fell on the 26th. Winchester was given a mock trial at which he was not allowed to speak, on the grounds that he and his son had not allowed Thomas of Lancaster to speak at his own trial in Pontefract Castle in March 1326 (Edward II's half-brother the earl of Kent, one of the men sitting in judgement on Winchester, had also been among those who condemned Thomas of Lancaster to death, though no one commented on the hypocrisy). Winchester, who was born in 1261 and who was thus sixty-five in 1326 – not ninety, as later claimed by Jean Froissart – was condemned to death by Sir William Trussell, and the sentence was carried out immediately: he was hanged while still wearing his armour, and his body, horribly, fed to dogs, with the exception of his head, which was carried on a spear to the city of Winchester and publicly displayed there.[28] Isabella was certainly present during Winchester's trial, and a chronicler of Bury St Edmunds, 200 miles from Bristol on the other side of the country, claimed that she pleaded for the elderly earl's life to be spared.[29] This seems extremely unlikely. Jean le Bel, the Flemish chronicler present during her invasion and campaign, does not mention that she did this, and her social inferiors – who included all of her allies and associates with the exception of her son – would hardly have dared to override her wishes in public. Neither does her subsequent treatment of Hugh Despenser the Younger's children suggest that she had any mercy in her heart towards the Despensers, and the rather later Lancastrian chronicler Henry Knighton says that she and her allies intended to eradicate the entire family (though this is an exaggeration).[30] Froissart also claims that Isabella was joyfully reunited with her daughters, Eleanor of Woodstock and Joan of the Tower, at Bristol, apparently under the impression that the girls were under the care of the earl of Winchester or his daughter Isabel Hastings, but in fact they had been living at Marlborough with the earl of Norfolk's sister-in-law Joan Jermy since January 1326. Exactly when Isabella saw her daughters again for the first time in more than eighteen months is uncertain. Evidently worried about her ten-year-old son, John of Eltham, in volatile and violent London, she sent a group of eight men-at-arms to bring him to her in late October.[31]

Isabella spent most of November 1326 in Hereford, staying at least sometimes at the palace of Adam Orleton, bishop of Hereford. On 17 November, the king's ally Edmund Fitzalan, earl of Arundel was executed in the city on the orders of Roger Mortimer, or rather murdered, as there is no evidence that he had a trial and Mortimer had no authority to conduct one anyway. The *Lanercost* chronicler says the earl 'was condemned to death in secret, as it were', and an entry on the Fine Roll three months later states that he was 'hanged for seditions and felonies' (a self-serving and inaccurate justification by his killers; Arundel was not in fact hanged).[32] Isabella may have attended the execution. Arundel had been captured by John Charlton, Edward II's chamberlain until 1318, who had joined the Contrariant rebellion in 1321/22 and whose son and heir was married to one of Mortimer's eight daughters. Arundel's career followed a strange trajectory: present at Piers Gaveston's death in 1312, now killed for his staunch support of Edward II and because his cousin Roger Mortimer despised him with a 'perfect hatred'.[33] The two men had been on opposing sides of the Contrariant rebellion, were rivals for land and influence in Wales, and of course Arundel had been a long-term adherent of the king and Despenser and married his son and heir, Richard, to Despenser's daughter Isabella. With Arundel were John Daniel, younger brother of a landowner in Derbyshire and Herefordshire named Richard Daniel, and Robert de Micheldever, who was merely a squire of Edward II's chamber. There is no evidence that these two were Arundel's 'henchmen' or associated with him in particular; more likely, they were merely in the wrong place at the wrong time, perhaps sent by the king to help the earl raise troops in the Marches.[34] Neither of the two men was accused of any crime, let alone convicted, but they were both beheaded anyway. If Isabella protested at Roger Mortimer's murder of these three men it is not recorded, and chronicler Adam Murimuth says that at the time of their deaths she followed Mortimer's counsel in all things. The earl of Arundel was beheaded by a 'worthless wretch', who needed at least seventeen and perhaps twenty-two strokes of the axe to sever the unfortunate man's head.[35] It seems likely that Mortimer ordered a blunt blade to be used and chose a man who was not an experienced executioner, presumably in order to cause Arundel as much suffering as possible.

The day before the earl of Arundel's death, on 16 November 1326,

Edward II and Hugh Despenser the Younger were captured in south Wales. They had been wandering hopelessly around south Wales, having abandoned the safety of Despenser's great stronghold of Caerphilly two weeks previously, for reasons which seem inexplicable, and left the castle in the hands of Despenser's seventeen or eighteen-year-old eldest son, Hugh (called Huchon). Sometime in November or December 1326, Isabella and Roger Mortimer sent their ally William la Zouche – who had fought for Edward's army at the battle of Boroughbridge in March 1322 – to besiege Huchon Despenser at Caerphilly and to take possession of the many precious goods and barrels full of money which Edward II had left there. Determined to execute the third Hugh Despenser, Isabella offered the castle garrison numerous free pardons if they would surrender, but they refused to give the young man up.[36] Finally, in March 1327, Isabella realised the futility of continuing the siege, and agreed not to execute Huchon Despenser, who remained in prison until she fell from power some years later. When the Caerphilly garrison surrendered, she took possession of her husband's remaining money – £14,000 contained in twenty-seven barrels – and the goods he had left in the castle. These included, rather charmingly, a red retiring robe with saffron stripes and embroidered with bears, and a black cap lined with red velvet decorated with butterflies made of pearls.[37] Isabella also helped herself to the money, goods and jewels of the late earl of Arundel and of Hugh Despenser the Younger which they had stored at the cathedral church of Chichester and the Tower of London respectively. Arundel's goods included £524 in six canvas sacks, a silver salt cellar 'enamelled all over', a silver-gilt enamelled cup with matching basin, and seven partly broken cups. Despenser's included about two dozen gold cups, some of them with matching ewers (pitchers or jugs).[38] Edward II's great seal, £6,000 and some of the chancery rolls were later found at Neath and Swansea by Henry of Lancaster and taken to Isabella.[39]

The *Annales Paulini* say dramatically that Edward II and Despenser the Younger were captured during a terrific storm, at or near Llantrisant. Edward had appointed five men to send to 'Queen Isabel, Edward his firstborn son, and some others in their company, on diverse affairs affecting the realm' on 10 November, including his teenaged nephew Edward de Bohun (whose father the earl of Hereford was killed at Boroughbridge in 1322) and his squires John Harsik and Oliver de Bordeaux.[40] It is not clear if they ever went, and even if they did, they would have achieved nothing; Isabella held the upper hand and had no reason to negotiate with her husband. How she felt at this point – triumphant, relieved, bewildered, savage – is a matter for conjecture. Edward's household and most of his allies were deserting him, or were overtaken by the speed of events and never reached him. The account of his chamber was kept for the last time on 31 October 1326, and the last payment out of it was made to five carpenters and twenty-four of the king's valets, including two women, who had stayed with him. Some of them remained at Caerphilly Castle when the king left at the beginning of November and were among the garrison pardoned there with Huchon Despenser in March 1327 for holding out against Isabella.[41] At some point the king's nephew-in-law John de Warenne, earl of Surrey went over to Isabella's side, perhaps on hearing of the slow and brutal death of his sister Alice's husband the earl of Arundel. He joined the queen sometime before 8 December 1326, when some of Arundel's lands and goods were granted to him.[42] Robert Bruce's nephew Donald, earl of Mar returned to his native Scotland around the time of the fall of Bristol in late October, probably intending to try to aid Edward II in some way from a distance (he was still trying to help Edward in the summer of 1327 and even years after his supposed death). With Edward and Despenser when they were captured were two knights called Thomas Wyther and John Bek, formerly adherents of Thomas of Lancaster; Robert Holden, controller of the king's wardrobe; a sergeant-at-arms called Simon of Reading; Robert Baldock, chancellor of England; a valet named John le Blount; and a clerk named John Smale.[43] The men were captured by Isabella's uncle Henry of Lancaster, William la Zouche – who would kidnap and marry Despenser's widow and Edward's niece Eleanor de Clare in 1329 – and two sons of the Welsh nobleman Llywelyn Bren, whom Despenser had had grotesquely executed in Cardiff in 1318.[44] Most of the men were released. Edward II, still the king though in practice his reign ended at that moment, was given into the custody of his cousin Lancaster and treated with courtesy and respect. At Henry of Lancaster's castle of Monmouth, Edward was forced to give up his great seal to Adam Orleton, bishop of Hereford, whom he loathed. Still grappling with the legal niceties of an entirely unprecedented situation, Isabella and her allies had this recorded in a memorandum on the Close Roll, most implausibly, as the king deliberating for a while then announcing that 'it pleased him to send his great seal to his consort and his son' and that he was thinking of his subjects' well-being.[45] For several weeks, writs continued to be recorded in the chancery rolls as though they came from Edward II himself, at the location where the captive king happened to be at the time, though were carefully recorded as being issued 'by the queen and the king's first-born son' or 'by the king on the information of the queen'.[46] Meanwhile, Hugh Despenser, Robert Baldock and Simon of Reading were taken to Isabella at Hereford and treated with every indignity possible by their triumphant enemies.

Robert Baldock, who as a cleric could not be executed, was given into the custody of Bishop Adam Orleton, who imprisoned him in his London house. Some months later a mob broke into the house and dragged Baldock off to the notorious prison of Newgate, where the unfortunate man died in torment.[47] Simon of Reading, like Robert de Micheldever and John Daniel, was given no trial but was sentenced to death anyway and hanged on a vague accusation of insulting Isabella, even though 'insulting the queen' was not in fact a capital offence in England in 1326.[48] The real reasons behind Reading's death are mysterious: although he has been described in modern times as a close personal friend of Hugh Despenser or as his marshal, he was not, but merely a sergeant-at-arms in Edward II's household.[49] And the greatest prize was on its way. Isabella, a year before, had promised that she would seek revenge on Hugh Despenser for coming between her husband and herself. She did exactly that. On his way from Llantrisant to Hereford, Despenser was tied to a mean little horse and a 'chaplet of sharp nettles' was placed on his head, while Simon of Reading was made to go before him carrying Despenser's coat of arms reversed. Two squires blew in their ears with great bugle horns, and 'more than a thousand and one' people also blew horns, presumably meaning members of the public watching and rejoicing at the downfall of the hated royal favourite. Biblical verses were written or carved into Despenser's arms, shoulders and chest, including 'Why do you boast in evil?' from Psalm 52. Four years almost to the day later, the same verse would be read out to Roger Mortimer as he went to his own execution. There was much discussion as to where Despenser would be put on trial and killed: Isabella favoured London, presumably to ensure the maximum number of spectators. Despenser, however, refused all food and drink so that 'he was dead almost for fasting', and thus it was decided to judge him in Hereford on 24 November so he would not die by his own will and cheat the queen of her revenge.[50]

Before he died, Despenser was given a mock trial during which William Trussell, who had also presided over Despenser the Elder's mock trial and who had been with Roger Mortimer and the other exiles on the Continent, read out before Isabella, her allies and many others, a long list of charges against him in French.[51] Some of the charges are true or partly true, some are perfectly ludicrous, and most of them pile all the blame for Edward II's failed reign on Despenser's head. He was accused of, among other things, sole responsibility, with his father, for Thomas of Lancaster's death, the earl of Kent's attendance at Lancaster's trial still escaping the notice of chroniclers; murdering, executing and imprisoning many magnates; piracy (correctly); leaving the queen 'in peril of her person' at Tynemouth in 1322 (this was still clearly preying on Isabella's mind); destroying the privileges of Holy Church, robbing prelates and plundering the Church 'as a false Christian'; forcing the king to ride against the Contrariants in 1322; persuading Edward to give the earldom of Winchester to his father; trying to bribe people at the French court to kill the queen; and most curiously of all, of breaking the limbs of one Lady Baret until she was 'forever more driven mad and lost', seemingly sheer invention or at the very least gross exaggeration.

The verdict was never in doubt: Sir Hugh Despenser, lord of Glamorgan and the king's chamberlain, then probably in his late thirties, was sentenced to be hanged, drawn and quartered. Trussell ended the sentence by declaring, 'Withdraw, you traitor, tyrant, renegade; go to take your own justice, traitor, evil man, criminal!' Despenser was tied to a hurdle and dragged by four horses through the streets to Hereford castle, his own, where a gallows fifty feet high had been erected especially. A noose was thrown around his neck and he was hauled up and partially strangled, then lowered onto a ladder, where according to le Bel and Froissart his penis and testicles were cut off 'because he was a heretic and a sodomite, even, it was said, with the king, and this was why the king had driven away the queen', though this was not part of his sentence. He was eviscerated and his heart was cut out and thrown onto a fire 'because he was a false-hearted traitor'. At last he was beheaded. Simon of Reading, the obscure sergeant-at-arms, was hanged below him; Isabella may have believed that Reading had insulted her in some way, though she didn't give him a trial to prove the accusation, and it is doubtful whether many of the spectators cheering Despenser's death had the faintest idea who he was. Despenser's head was taken to London and, to great jubilation and the sound of trumpets, placed on London Bridge, and the four quarters of his body were sent to Carlisle, York, Bristol and Dover. They remained there for four years until Edward III, shortly after he took over the governance of the kingdom, allowed them to be buried; Despenser's tomb still exists at Tewkesbury Abbey in Gloucestershire.[52] Henry of Lancaster attended Despenser's trial and execution, and it is not entirely clear where Edward II was at this time, as he was in Lancaster's custody and thus may also have been present in Hereford. One hopes that he was not forced to see Despenser's execution; for all his and Despenser's misdeeds, making him watch the drawn out and atrocious death of a man he loved dearly would have been cruel. If Edward and Isabella met or saw each other in or near Hereford in November 1326, for the first time since Isabella had departed for France in early March 1325, it is not recorded, either in the chancery rolls or in any chronicle, and it seems probable that they did not in fact meet.

Despenser's eldest son, Huchon, held out against the queen at Caerphilly Castle for several more months and then remained in prison at Bristol Castle until 1331. Despenser's widow, Eleanor de Clare, was apparently imprisoned at the Tower of London after she surrendered it on 17 November 1326, her three younger sons presumably with her. The eldest Despenser daughter, Isabella, who was about fourteen, was already married to the late earl of Arundel's son Richard and the youngest, Elizabeth, was a baby or perhaps still *in utero*, but the middle three Despenser daughters, Joan, Eleanor and Margaret, were to suffer an unenviable fate as a result of Queen Isabella's hatred of their father. On 1 January 1327, the three girls, who were about ten, seven and three or four, were forcibly veiled as nuns in three different convents on Isabella's orders. Evidently she believed the matter to be extremely pressing: the children were to be 'admitted and veiled without delay'.[53] It is hard to discern a motive for Isabella's actions except a desire to hurt the Despenser family; it has been suggested that she wished to prevent anyone claiming the Despenser lands through the girls via marriage, which seems very unlikely, as the Despenser lands were forfeit to the Crown and the huge de Clare inheritance belonged to their mother. As the girls had four brothers, their chances of inheriting their parents' lands were remote in any case.[54] In 1324, Roger Mortimer's three eldest daughters, Margaret, Joan and Isabella, had been sent to live in various convents by Edward II, though they were not veiled as nuns and were released on their father's return to England. Isabella's fury with Hugh Despenser the Younger, which she took out on some of his children as well, indicates the depth of her feeling for Edward and their marriage. If Despenser had intruded into a marriage which had always been a disaster, or took from her a husband she despised and felt nothing for, she would hardly have been so furious and bitter, and so desperate to avenge herself on Despenser. She wanted to destroy him and his family utterly. This was not the last of Isabella's rather severe actions towards children in 1327: later that year, she imprisoned eighteen young boys as hostages in Chester Castle, at the townspeople's own expense, because the people of the town had been 'disobedient and ill-behaved' towards her son. The citizens begged for the children's release; Isabella allowed for six of them to be imprisoned for one week, another six for the next week and the remaining six for the third week.[55]

The captive Edward II had arrived at Kenilworth Castle in Warwickshire, recently restored to his cousin Henry of Lancaster, by 5 December 1326, and spent what must have been a bleak and lonely Christmas there. We have no way of knowing how he felt at this time, but he must have been grieving for Despenser and bewildered and horrified at his rapid downfall. Isabella herself spent Christmas at Wallingford, which had once belonged to Piers Gaveston, with her allies including Roger Mortimer and her two sons, Edward of Windsor and John of Eltham. Many people were uneasy about the queen's failure to return to her husband, not least Pope John XXII: he continued writing to Isabella in 1327 begging her to return to her husband, and also asked Charles IV to use his influence to bring about a reconciliation between the couple.[56] But Isabella could hardly return to Edward, as this would render the whole invasion and its aftermath pointless. As she had invaded his kingdom and done numerous things for which she knew Edward would never forgive her, not least the hideous executions of the Despensers and the earl of Arundel, a resumption of their marriage had become near impossible. Isabella needed a good excuse to absolve herself in the eyes of the Church for her failure to become Edward's wife again in more than just name, and her ally Adam Orleton, bishop of Hereford, provided one: he claimed that Edward carried a knife in his hose with which to hurt Isabella, and if he had no other weapon would 'crush her with his teeth'. This claim, however, came at a time when John XXII and other men were wondering out loud when Isabella would return to Edward, and there is no real reason to suppose that Edward had ever been or wished to be physically abusive to Isabella. According to the *Brut* chronicle, Edward was informed after his deposition that people suspected him of wanting to strangle his wife and son Edward of Windsor to death. He responded emotionally, 'God knows, I thought it never, and now I would that I were dead! So would God that I were! For then were all my sorrow passed.'[57]

At the council meeting in Wallingford over Christmas 1326, Edward's fate dominated proceedings, though even at this late date it was unclear what should happen to him. The extraordinarily fast success of the invasion had taken everyone by surprise, and now Isabella and the bishops and magnates with her had to decide what was to be done next. No king of England had ever been removed from his throne before, but eventually it was decided that the succession to the throne would be speeded up, as it were: Edward II would be made to abdicate to his and Isabella's fourteen-year-old son, Edward of Windsor. There was no possible precedent for such an act, and the queen and her allies had to step their way delicately through a morass of illegal acts and discuss how such a thing might best be achieved. Some council members present (their identity is unclear) called for the king to be executed, though this suggestion was rejected and it is not true, as one modern historian has claimed, that these calls for the king's death were 'prompted by Isabella'. Demanding in front of many of the bishops and magnates of England that her own husband and lord should be killed, or even whispering behind the scenes to others to put forward this point of view on her behalf, would have made her look monstrous, and she would have known it. There is no reason to suppose that Isabella, despite her rebellion against her husband, wished him any physical harm or 'had murder in her heart' towards him, or that he became a 'non-person' to her.[58] She continued to send him letters and gifts in 1327, and in April 1327 told a council meeting that she was ready and willing to visit him (the council forbade it).[59] Whatever Edward had done, he was of royal birth and ancestry as much as Isabella herself was, and it was thus decided that he would be kept for the rest of his life in captivity as honourable and comfortable as possible, as befitted his status as a royal and as the new king of England's father.

Isabella arrived in London on 4 January 1327, the first time she had set foot in the capital for nearly two years.[60] Walter Reynolds, archbishop of Canterbury, had come over to her side now, though the other English archbishop, William Melton of York, maintained his staunch support for Edward II. On 10 and 11 January 1327, the queen restored to herself the county of Cornwall and all the lands in fifteen counties which Edward had confiscated from her in September 1324.[61] Some weeks later on the day of her son's coronation, she awarded herself the highest income which anyone in England, excepting the kings, earned during the whole of the Middle Ages: 20,000 marks, or £13,333 a year, 20 per cent more than her fabulously wealthy uncle Thomas of Lancaster had earned from five earldoms and triple her pre-September 1324 income of £4,500. It amounted to a third of the entire annual royal revenue.[62] She also awarded herself cash grants of £31,843 between December 1326 and January 1327, supposedly to pay her debts abroad – which had in fact already been paid – and appropriated much of the inheritance which belonged to her uncle Henry of Lancaster and to which she had not a vestige of a right.[63] Perhaps she felt it was nothing less than she was owed after being deprived of her full income in September 1324 and after leading the invasion which allowed her allies to be restored to their lands and incomes, but the amounts of money were excessive. Isabella also took control of her husband's treasury, which thanks to his and Hugh Despenser's despotism and greed contained £60,000. This already large amount was soon swollen by the forfeiture of the Despensers and the earl of Arundel to almost £80,000.[64] By the time of Isabella's downfall in October 1330, a derisory £41 was left of this vast sum – and that does not even include the numerous loans Isabella and Roger Mortimer borrowed from the Italian banking firm the Bardi.[65] Her allies such as Thomas Wake (formerly her ward), William la Zouche, William Trussell and her uncle Henry of Lancaster received lands and wardships in early 1327 and were granted favours, and the lands which had belonged to the Despensers were parcelled out among the queen's followers. Thomas Wake was appointed keeper of the Tower of London, and William Trussell the royal escheator in the south of England.[66] Isabella wisely showed herself capable of mercy and forgiveness as well: long-term adherents of the Despensers such as Sir Ingelram Berenger and Sir Ralph Camoys (Hugh the Younger's brother-in-law) were officially pardoned and remained at liberty and in full possession of their lands and goods.[67] The queen also took the opportunity to reward members of her household for good service to her, presumably for staying with her in France, including her steward Robert Staunton and her valets Geoffrey of Cornwall and John Giffard. The men received gifts of money or were appointed as custodians of various royal parks and forests and of lands temporarily in the king's hands.[68] Roger Mortimer was appointed justice of Wales on 20 February 1327 – he was later appointed or appointed himself to this office for life – and was officially pardoned for breaking prison in the Tower the next day, while all the fines Edward II had imposed on the Contrariant faction in 1322 were cancelled.[69] In February 1327, Mortimer was also granted the valuable wardship of the heir to the earldom of Warwick and the marriage of the future earl of Pembroke, Thomas Beauchamp and Laurence Hastings, whom he married to his daughters Katherine and Agnes.[70]

Parliament opened on 7 January 1327, deliberately held in London because the city was hostile to the king (as London often was towards royalty in the thirteenth and early fourteenth centuries). Edward II was deposed in this parliament, or by this parliament, though as he himself had not summoned it, it was technically an illegal gathering. Chroniclers, uncertain as to whether it was really a parliament or not, referred to it as having been summoned by the queen, or by the queen and her son.[71] The roll of this parliament no longer exists, perhaps because Edward and Isabella's great-grandson Richard II had it destroyed after it was used to threaten his own position in 1386, though the records of most of the parliaments of Edward II's reign also no longer exist and it may simply be unfortunate chance that the January 1327 one is among them.[72] The *Pipewell Chronicle* says that at this parliament 'it was further ordained that our lady the queen, for the great anxiety and anguish she had suffered as well this side [of the Channel] as overseas, should stay queen all her life'.[73] If this is true, it means only that Isabella would be allowed to keep the title of queen, which she no longer had an automatic right to, given that her husband would no longer be king. It did not mean that parliament granted her the right to rule all her life, as has sometimes been stated; parliament would never have done such a thing. The right to rule was vested in Isabella's son and, during his minority, the regency council, never in Isabella herself.

It is unlikely that Isabella and Roger Mortimer themselves planned and managed the process of Edward's deposition; it was a cleverly stage-managed affair which bears all the hallmarks of having been carried out by a cool, competent and subtle brain, surely Adam Orleton, bishop of Hereford, or John Stratford, bishop of Winchester (and a few years later, archbishop of Canterbury), or both of them. Isabella and Mortimer's subsequent behaviour during their next few years in power hardly demonstrates that they had the ability to undertake an unprecedented and revolutionary act of this magnitude. Within less than two years, they had lost the support of all the men who played an important role in the deposition – John Stratford, Thomas Wake, William Trussell and even

Adam Orleton – political ineptitude on a greater scale than even Edward II and the Despensers had managed. At first, support for Edward's deposition, even at this late date, was muted. Thomas Wake, Mortimer's first cousin and Henry of Lancaster's son-in-law, and some of his men were planted in the crowd to cheer and shout at appropriate intervals to make it appear that the assembly consented unanimously when Mortimer announced on 13 January that the magnates no longer wished to have Edward II as king. It was only then that much enthusiasm was shown for deposing him. Adam Orleton, John Stratford and the archbishop of Canterbury Walter Reynolds, formerly an ally of Edward II's who had recently joined the cause, gave speeches in favour of deposing the king and replacing him with his son. Orleton announced that 'a foolish king shall ruin his people' and 'dwelt weightily upon the folly and unwisdom of the king, and upon his childish doings [if indeed they deserved to be spoken of as childish] and upon the multiple and manifold disasters that had befallen England in his time'.[74] For three days, a ceremony of oath-taking to Isabella and her son took place in the Guildhall, with Roger Mortimer's name heading the list. With no doubt whatsoever that the process would be successful, on 13 January Mortimer ordered robes for his sons to wear when they were knighted during the new king's coronation.[75]

The events of January 1327 have been described as 'an attempt by what was a relatively small group of enemies of Edward II, most of its leaders motivated by personal grudges against him, to give an aura of legality to acts which were unprecedented and therefore illegal. The fiction was that Edward II was deposed by the will of the English people, but now a precedent had been set, and the same fiction could be used again.' There was no rule in English law providing any procedure for deposing a king on the grounds of his unworthiness or lack of suitability for the role he had been born into.[76] It is unlikely that the revolutionaries had any coherent ideas of what should be done with a deposed king, or that they truly appreciated the significance of their actions: they set a precedent which would be followed again and again down the centuries of English history, including with Isabella and Edward's great-grandson Richard II in 1399.[77]

It seems highly unlikely that Isabella, Mortimer, Adam Orleton and John Stratford would have allowed Edward II to appear at parliament; some sources claim they sent a delegation to Kenilworth to ask him to attend, but he refused, which was reported to parliament when the delegates returned to London on 12 January. Appearing at parliament might have allowed the king to arouse sympathy and to remind his subjects of the oath of loyalty they had sworn to him.[78] Even now, it was not entirely obvious that Edward II's deposition was confirmed and done, and it was probably only when Edward's refusal to attend parliament – whether real or pretended – was reported to the participants that the possibility of replacing him with his son began to be seriously considered.[79] Neither was it clear whether Edward and Isabella's son Edward of Windsor would accept the throne or balk. Indeed, according to the later chronicler Thomas Walsingham – not, admittedly, a particularly reliable source for events of the 1320s – the fourteen-year-old refused to accept his father's throne until he knew for certain that Edward II was abdicating voluntarily.[80] Delegates did visit the king at Kenilworth, but there was not enough time for them to leave on 7 January and return on the 12th as some sources state (a round trip of almost 200 miles in five days was impossible in the depths of winter). Only four men had the courage to speak out for Edward, at least that we know of: the bishops Hamo Hethe of Rochester, John Ros of Carlisle and Stephen Gravesend of London, and William Melton, archbishop of York. In such an atmosphere, it would not be surprising if few men dared to speak out for Edward, assuming they didn't; the only chronicler who mentions that anyone at all defended Edward is William Dene, the Rochester chronicler, a close associate of Hamo Hethe. Every other chronicler writes as though the deposition passed without a single word of protest, which, as Claire Valente has pointed out, is a sign of a cover up.[81] In the same way that Edward II's contrite reaction to events of January 1327 as recorded by every contemporary chronicler only reflects the official story that was allowed to come out, it was not in the interests of Isabella, Orleton and their allies to make it known that some people had protested.

When a deputation from parliament travelled (again) to Kenilworth and met Edward II, who according to several chroniclers was dressed all in black and half fainting, William Trussell was their main spokesperson and officially renounced the kingdom's allegiance to Edward. Other men present were Edward's nephew-in-law John de Warenne, earl of Surrey, Adam Orleton, and a number of Franciscan friars, Isabella's favourite order. Edward's last household steward, Sir Thomas Blount, ceremonially broke his staff of office on 21 January 1327, and the turbulent and disastrous reign of King Edward II was over. The reign of his and Isabella's fourteen-year-old son, Edward III, officially began on 25 January.

Various chroniclers depict Edward II as swooning, penitent and acquiescent, begging his subjects' forgiveness for the numerous trespasses he had committed against them in the nineteen and a half years of his reign; the *Flores* rather movingly has him acknowledging his faults and errors but declaring, 'I could not be other than I am.'[82] As with most other chronicles of the day, the *Flores* then states that Edward announced, 'I am pleased that my son who has been thus accepted by all the people should succeed me on the throne.' Edward's real attitude to his deposition, or forced abdication, are in fact not entirely clear; we can only know what chroniclers of the day recorded, and they only had access to the official story. His opponents had already shown themselves adept at using propaganda against him, and had good reasons to concoct a subservient and pious reaction on his part.[83] They had already made up a story that Edward gave his wife and son his great seal voluntarily, and even with pleasure, in November 1326, thinking on the state of his realm and deciding to do what was best for his subjects. Publicly, Edward II's deposition, or forced abdication, was presented as the king deciding entirely of his own free will to give up his throne to his son, and his subjects accepting this. The later chronicler Geoffrey le Baker claims that Edward was threatened that if he did not consent to abdicate his throne to his son, his children would be passed over and a person of non-royal blood chosen as king instead, which has usually been interpreted to mean Roger Mortimer, though Baker does not say this. The story is extremely doubtful: no one would have accepted Mortimer as their king in place of Edward of Windsor and, after him, John of Eltham, not least Edward II's half-brothers the earls of Norfolk and Kent, or indeed Isabella herself. A list of the king's manifold failings was issued, though they were not officially published until Adam Orleton produced them in 1334 when accused of having acted against the king in 1326/27. The articles included claims that Edward had lost Scotland and lands in France; that he 'gave himself up always to improper occupations, neglecting the business of his realm'; that he had persecuted noblemen and churchmen; and that he was 'incorrigible without hope of amendment'. He was also accused of cruelty and pride and of listening to bad counsel, though not of being a tyrant. Although the overall picture of an incompetent, uninterested ruler is undeniable, the charges were generally weak and in some cases entirely false, such as the one that Edward had been left Scotland 'in good peace' by his father, who had in fact died on the way to a military campaign there in July 1307. The hypocrisy of the charges of losing Scotland and Gascony is demonstrated by a secret treaty Isabella and Mortimer had already made with Robert Bruce earlier in 1326 (at least, according to the later Lancastrian chronicler Henry Knighton) that they would recognise him as king of Scots, and Scotland as an independent kingdom, if he agreed not to invade England at the same time as their own invasion and thus prejudice their chances of success.[84] Little more than a year after Edward II's deposition, Isabella or other persons ruling England in Edward III's name signed a treaty with Robert Bruce giving up all English claims to Scotland. In the last few months of Edward II's reign, his steward of Gascony had raised an army of Gascon and Spanish mercenaries and regained Saintonge and the Agenais from the French.[85] Isabella, however, handed these lands back to Charles IV in March 1327 when she signed a humiliatingly one-sided treaty with him, also agreeing – astonishingly – to give up the whole of Gascony to France, with the exception of a narrow coastal strip between Bordeaux and Bayonne, and to pay her brother 50,000 marks in reparation in addition to the £15,000 agreed in 1325.[86] For all Edward II's incompetence, it is hard to agree that it was he who 'lost' Scotland and Gascony; his enemies accused him of such, then within fifteen months oversaw the tearing apart of his and his son's inheritance.

Edward's deposition in January 1327 was not inevitable, though so many centuries later it is hard to imagine how it (and indeed, historical events in general) could have happened in any other way than it did. If Roger Mortimer – probably the only man with the ability, energy and willingness to plan and lead the invasion – had not escaped from the Tower in 1323, if Isabella had been a different kind of person, if Edward had not confiscated her lands in 1324 and given her a reason to act against him, if Edward had made more of an effort to maintain amicable relations with his cousin Henry of Lancaster and the bishops of Hereford and Winchester, and so on, his deposition may well never have come about. He and the Despensers were extremely unpopular, but by 1326 Edward had filled the empty treasury he had inherited from his father in 1307; even his war with France in the 1320s was not a complete disaster and was hardly an infrequent occurrence between the two kingdoms: his father and Charles IV and Isabella's father had also gone to war in the 1290s, and the war of St-Sardos was merely one part of a long-running problem between England and France which later exploded into the Hundred Years War.[87] Even in early 1327, Edward II still had supporters in parliament, and events of later that year were to show that there were still, despite intense dissatisfaction with his rule in many quarters, plenty of men who wished to see him restored to the throne. At the January 1327 parliament, enthusiasm for Edward's deposition was muted and support for it was far from unanimous – many barons probably only accepted it with reluctance, something the king's rapid downfall has tended to obscure.[88]

And so Isabella of France, still only in her early thirties, became the mother of the king of England. Her son would reign for fifty years, start the Hundred Years War against France, live through the first terrible outbreak of the Black Death, win famous military victories against France, and die at the age of sixty-four with his mistress Alice Perrers allegedly stripping the rings from his fingers as he lay helpless and dying. In 1327, however, all of that lay far in the future, and Edward III's coronation took place at Westminster Abbey on Sunday 1 February 1327. According to the much later, gossipy and unreliable chronicler Thomas Walsingham, Isabella cried during her son's coronation and maintained the bearing of a sorrowful widow, but he says that this was mere pretence. That Isabella wept is certainly possible but is not confirmed by any other source, and other evidence indicates that she was absent from her son's coronation, spending three days at her Kent palace of Eltham.[89] Roger Mortimer's name appears first on the list of magnates attending the coronation, behind the five earls (Edward II's half-brothers Norfolk and Kent, his cousin Lancaster, his nephew-in-law Surrey and his nephew Hereford) and nine bishops who attended and John of Beaumont, brother of William, count of Hainault.[90] Beaumont was extraordinarily well-rewarded for aiding Isabella before, during and after her invasion: he received over £32,000 between 11 May 1327 and 1 March 1328.[91]

The young king was knighted either by his great-uncle Henry of Lancaster or by John of Beaumont, as were his cousins John and Edward de Bohun (John was the earl of Hereford) and three of Roger Mortimer's sons, whom their father had had dressed as earls for the occasion.[92] The ceremony, arranged as rapidly as possible to help legitimise the young king's occupation of the throne, cost thousands of pounds, and during the banquet afterwards Westminster Hall must have looked magnificent: violet, red and grey coverings adorned the royal dais, and Edward III sat on a throne with samite cushions and gold silk curtains.[93] The new king had two fleur-de-lis engraved on his new great seal, in Isabella's honour (Edward II had always used the castles of Castile on his seal, in honour of his own mother, Eleanor of Castile).[94]

Isabella of France had led a successful invasion of her husband's kingdom, and taken part in a process which saw an English king deposed for the first time. Now the really hard work began, and like many people before and since, Isabella was to learn that being in opposition and criticising the government is a far easier matter than governing yourself. Before that, however, there remained the thorny problem of what precisely should happen to her husband. The endless drama of Edward II's life was far from over.

11

Captivity and Death
of a King
1327

Sir Edward of Caernarfon, formerly King Edward II of England, spent the first few months of 1327 in honourable confinement at Kenilworth Castle in Warwickshire, in the custody of his cousin Henry, earl of Lancaster, who treated him with respect and honour. Edward's state of mind remains unknown to us, and little evidence exists to tell us what his life at Kenilworth was like, though we know his son the new king sent him two tuns of wine.[1] Outside the castle, however, the former king's supporters were mobilising. Little is known about the event, but it seems that sometime in about March 1327 a group of Edward's friends tried to free him from Kenilworth. They failed – Kenilworth was one of the most fortified strongholds in the country – but their attempt was probably one of the factors which persuaded Roger Mortimer and perhaps Isabella that the former king – Isabella husband – must be removed from the earl of Lancaster's custody. Another factor was that they did not trust her uncle: they had needed his support after their invasion and been grateful for it, but now they feared his enormous influence. With his vast income and lands and his large number of followers, Henry of Lancaster would always be far too powerful to ignore, and Mortimer and Isabella had seen first-hand how his brother Thomas of Lancaster had done more than anyone to ruin Edward II's reign. Henry's custody of the former king was a danger to them. The legality of the parliament which deposed Edward was uncertain, and there remained the possibility that Edward might be able to overturn it and restore himself to the throne, if he attracted enough support. Lancaster's custody of Edward gave him leverage over Mortimer and Isabella, as he would always have the chance to hold Edward's possible return to the throne over their heads if they annoyed him, which they foolishly seemed to go out of their way to do (such as their decision to release Sir Robert Holland from prison, a man who had been a close friend and adherent of Thomas of Lancaster but who betrayed him in 1322). Lancaster wielded little if any power in the government.

To protect themselves, Mortimer and Isabella had the former king removed from Lancaster's custody and given to men whom the pair could trust. The men they selected as Edward's new guardians were Mortimer's son-in-law Thomas, Lord Berkeley, and Berkeley's brother-in-law Sir John Maltravers, neither of whom had any reason to love Edward of Caernarfon. Berkeley, now probably in his early thirties and married to Mortimer's eldest daughter, Margaret, since 1320, had spent four and a half years in prison and seen his lands given to Hugh Despenser and plundered, while his father died in prison in 1326. Maltravers was about thirty-seven, had been knighted in May 1306 alongside the future Edward II and Roger Mortimer himself, and was a long-term adherent of the Berkeleys and Mortimer. He had spent years in exile on the Continent with Mortimer, although his father of the same name stayed in England and remained loyal to Edward II.

On 3 April 1327, custody of the former king of England was transferred to Berkeley and Maltravers, who were appointed as Edward's guardians with joint and equal responsibility for his safety.[2] The chronicler Henry Knighton suggested a few decades later that the earl of Lancaster gave up custody of Edward voluntarily, but it is most unlikely that he would willingly have surrendered such a powerful political weapon. Although an indenture was drawn up on 21 March, the fact that Roger Mortimer waited near Kenilworth with an armed force during Edward's transfer from Lancaster to Berkeley and Maltravers is telling, and the following year Lancaster accused Mortimer of taking Edward from him by force.[3] It seems probable that Lancaster had been coerced, tricked or manipulated into giving up custody of the former king. To what extent Isabella herself was responsible for her husband's transfer into the hands of Berkeley and Maltravers, and for the probable deception of her uncle Lancaster, is uncertain. That same month she and her son the king attended a meeting of the royal council in Stamford, at which the thorny issue of Isabella's failing to honour her marriage vows and return to Edward (obviously, completely out of the question) was once again raised by concerned churchmen.[4]

With a large armed escort, Thomas Berkeley and John Maltravers left Kenilworth on 3 April 1327, and took Edward the fifty-five miles to Berkeley's castle in the Gloucestershire village of Berkeley. Edward and his escort spent the night of 4/5 April at the Augustinian priory of Llanthony Secunda near Gloucester, and arrived at Berkeley Castle by 6 April at the latest, most probably the 5th, two or three days after they had left Kenilworth.[5] It is impossible for Berkeley and Maltravers to have taken Edward to Corfe Castle first, then to Berkeley via Bristol as the later chronicler Geoffrey le Baker claimed: Corfe is about sixty-five miles south of Berkeley, and it is logistically impossible for them to have made this journey in two or three days.

Geoffrey le Baker gives a highly colourful and highly improbable account of Edward's journey to Berkeley, claiming that his captors tormented him by crowning him with hay, forcing him to shave with cold ditchwater and eat poisoned food, clothing him in rags despite the cold, not allowing him to sleep despite his exhaustion, jeering at him and trying to make him believe that he was mad. Baker's account of Edward's imprisonment at Berkeley in 1327 is well-known: he claims that Edward was kept in a cell near a deep pit containing rotting animal corpses, his jailers hoping that the stench and the contagion would kill him.[6] It is impossible to take Baker's allegations seriously. (Unfortunately, many writers on the subject *have* taken them seriously, and they are often repeated as certain fact to this day, not least by the guides at Berkeley Castle itself.) Baker was not writing history, but hagiography; by the middle of the fourteenth century when he wrote his chronicle, the popular campaign to have Edward canonised as a saint was well underway, and Baker's intention was to portray him as a Christ-like figure nobly and patiently suffering the torments of lesser men, the 'satraps of Satan' as he memorably called them.[7] Accepting Baker's account of Edward's journey to Berkeley and torment while being imprisoned there as historical truth is akin to accepting Thomas More's and Shakespeare's portrayals of Richard III as the hunchbacked and murderous epitome of evil as historical truth. Baker is keen to blame Isabella, whom he calls 'Jezebel' and 'the iron virago', for Edward's supposed torments, yet there is nothing in the queen's character or behaviour to suggest that she would have allowed her royal husband to be subjected to such inhuman treatment. And although Edward III was only fourteen, he would grow up and one day take over the governance of his kingdom, and would not take kindly to allegations that his father's custodians had abused and tormented him. In later years, Edward III neither accused Thomas Berkeley and John Maltravers of mistreating his father, nor Roger Mortimer of ordering the torment, as he surely would have done had Baker's stories had any substance in fact. At some unknown date in 1327, Thomas Berkeley appointed Thomas Gurney, a knight of Somerset, to share custody of Edward of Caernarfon with himself and John Maltravers.

All the available evidence suggests that Edward was in fact well-treated on his journey to Berkeley and during his incarceration there. An entry on the Close Roll refers to the expenses of himself and his household, meaning that he had servants attending him, and Berkeley Castle records show that his custodians bought wine, cheese, capons, beef and eggs for him, and wax for his candles.[8] That Edward's guardians bought expensive wax, not the much cheaper tallow, is indirect proof that he was well-treated, and they would hardly have provided wax candles had they been intending to kill him by incarcerating him near a pit containing animal corpses, as Baker claims. Although we cannot prove conclusively that Edward received the food bought for him, there is no reason to assume that he didn't and that it went to other people, as one modern historian has suggested.[9] The payments for food, wine and wax appear in Lord Berkeley's own household accounts; they were not presented to the exchequer as proof that the former king was being fed properly, and there was no reason for Berkeley to falsify his own accounts and pretend he was buying food for Edward and giving it to him if he were not. For Edward's upkeep, Berkeley and Maltravers received an enormous £5 for 'every day they were in the said king's company', a sum that would have fed most people for years, and on 15 May 1327 they were given £500 for Edward's expenses.[10] Adam Murimuth says that although Thomas Berkeley welcomed Edward kindly and treated him well, John Maltravers behaved with 'much harshness' towards him. This may be true, though as Murimuth believed, wrongly, that Maltravers was one of Edward's murderers, his testimony on this point is rather suspect. He also states that Berkeley and Maltravers switched custody of Edward, each man taking responsibility for a month, which may also be true but is uncorroborated by other sources.[11] Jean Froissart, who visited Berkeley Castle forty years later with Hugh Despenser the Younger's grandson Edward Despenser, says that Lord Berkeley 'was urged to take good care of him [Edward], with orders to give him all honourable service and attention and to place court officials round him who were familiar with their duties, but never to allow him to leave the castle precincts'.[12] Although Froissart is an unreliable source for Edward's reign and its aftermath, this account is borne out by other evidence. An anonymous fourteenth-century chronicle claims that carpenters working on the castle heard Edward moaning and groaning, which may indicate that he was being mistreated, but is far more likely to mean only that Edward, a highly emotional man at the best of times, was feeling the depths of despair at this, the worst of times.[13] After all, he had lost his throne, his wife and family, his beloved Hugh Despenser and his freedom, so it would hardly be surprising if he suffered from depression and loneliness.

Isabella kept in touch with Edward at Berkeley, sending him affectionate letters enquiring after his health and comfort, and gifts of fine clothes, linen, delicacies and little luxuries. She also claimed that she wished to visit him but that the 'community of the realm' would not permit it, according to the royal clerk and chronicler Adam Murimuth.[14]

This is probably a reference to the Stamford council meeting of April 1327, when a reason had to be found for Isabella's failure to return to Edward and live with him as husband and wife. For all the impossibility of continuing their marriage, her letters and gifts imply that she still had feelings for him, whatever those feelings might have been. After all, there was no reason for her to write to Edward and send him gifts unless she wanted to: he was imprisoned and powerless, and she had no incentive to try to manipulate him. Geoffrey le Baker claims that Edward begged Isabella in tears to allow him to see his children, but she, 'whose heart was harder than stone ... that woman of iron', refused; however, Baker's hatred of Isabella and attempts to portray Edward as a long-suffering saint make his testimony completely unreliable. Even if the story is true, this does not automatically mean that Isabella acted out of cruelty and malice towards her husband, but perhaps out of a desire to spare their children the distress of seeing their once-powerful father cast so low and in captivity. There is no evidence that any of the former-king's family, such as his half-brothers Norfolk and Kent, visited him at Berkeley Castle, though this does not necessarily indicate lack of concern or affection: visiting Edward when they had taken part in his downfall and in the execution of the Despensers would have been most awkward. Later events were to demonstrate that Kent, at least, regretted what had happened to Edward.

The plot to remove Edward of Caernarfon from Kenilworth in March had failed, but the fierce and fanatical supporters of the former king were undeterred. Their leader was Thomas Dunheved, a Dominican friar (the Dominicans were always strong supporters of Edward II) whom the king sent to Avignon to complain about the archbishop of Dublin in 1325, and whom two chroniclers wrongly said had been sent to the pope to secure an annulment of Edward and Isabella's marriage. Thomas was aided by his brother Stephen Dunheved, formerly lord of the manor of Dunchurch in Warwickshire, who had fled the country after committing an unspecified felony, been pardoned by Edward II and joined his household in 1322, at least temporarily.[15] The Dunheved brothers travelled through England, seeking allies in their plan to free the former king from captivity and, one assumes, try to restore him to the throne.[16] Some members of Edward II's household joined them, including three of his sergeants-at-arms: Roger atte Watre, John le Botiler and Thomas de la Haye.[17] Two former adherents of the Despensers, a knight called Edmund Gascelyn and the under-sheriff of Buckinghamshire, Peter de la Rokele – grandfather of William Langland, one of the great English poets of the Middle Ages – also joined, and the group had a strong clerical element: Robert Shulton, a Cistercian monk of Hailes Abbey in Gloucestershire; Henry de Rihale and John de Stoke, Dominican friars of Warwick; William atte Hull and his uncle Michael, a canon of Llanthony Secunda Priory in Gloucester; two parsons, both named William Aylmer; and John, a monk from the Cistercian abbey of Newminster in distant Northumberland.

Roger Mortimer and Isabella got wind of the Dunheveds' plans, and as the fact that they were trying to free Edward of Caernarfon was too sensitive to commit to writing ordered the known members of the group to be arrested on other charges, such as theft, breaking and entering, extortion and assault. The Patent Roll of March to July 1327 is full of entries accusing Dunheved adherents of these crimes, as the important thing was to arrest and imprison them at all costs: the thought of the former king of England wandering around freely in the company of men who were determined that he be free and perhaps even restored to the throne was too awful to contemplate.[18] And the Dunheved group were not alone in plotting to restore Edward. His old friend Donald, earl of Mar, Robert Bruce's nephew who had spent most of his life in England after being captured by Edward I as a child in 1306, 'had returned to Scotland after the capture of the king, hoping to rescue him from captivity and restore him to his kingdom, as formerly, by the help of the Scots and of certain adherents whom the deposed king still had in England'.[19] Although Mar was in the north of England in the summer of 1327, leading one of the three columns of his uncle Robert Bruce's army against the new regime, his adherents gathered in the south-west of England and the Marches 'to do and procure the doing of what evils they can against the king [Edward III] and his subjects' – that is, stirring up trouble on Edward of Caernarfon's behalf.[20] Isabella and Mortimer ordered the arrest of two of Mar's supporters in Staffordshire in August 1327, merely for sending letters to him.[21] On 14 July, they ordered the justice of Chester – Richard Damory, elder brother of Edward of Caernarfon's late favourite Roger Damory and guardian of Edward of Windsor before he became king – to keep Richard le Brun, former mayor of the town, 'safely in the king's [Edward III's] prison' for adherence to Donald of Mar. It is probably not a coincidence that the Dunheved brothers were in the town in June: Richard Damory was ordered to arrest and imprison Thomas and Stephen Dunheved and 'other malefactors who have assembled within the city of Chester and parts adjacent and perpetrated homicides and other crimes'.[22] It was perhaps in connection with the Dunheveds' presence in Chester that Isabella ordered the imprisonment of eighteen children as 'boy-hostages' for the townspeople's good behaviour.[23]

In the summer of 1327, Robert Bruce decided that the opportunity to take advantage of the political chaos in England was too good to resist. Although Isabella and Mortimer sent envoys on 23 April to negotiate a peace with him, the Scots launched an attack on England on 15 June, with Bruce's nephew Donald of Mar and his friends Thomas

Randolph and James Douglas leading the three columns.[24] With Edward of Caernarfon's greatest enemy, Roger Mortimer, safely out of the way hundreds of miles to the north, the Dunheved group could go ahead with their plan to liberate Edward. Probably in mid- to late June, they launched an attack on Berkeley Castle. The truly astonishing thing is that the Dunheveds achieved their goal. However they achieved it, somehow the men got in, seized Edward, plundered the castle – for food, weapons, carts and horses – and fled into the Gloucestershire countryside. Lord Berkeley wrote a letter on 27 July 1327 to John Hothum, chancellor of England: 'I recently certified you by letter of the names of some people indicted before me in the county of Gloucestershire ... for having seized [*ravi*] the father of our lord the king out of our keeping.'[25] Berkeley asked for special powers to arrest the surviving members of the group, which were granted five days later, deeming the men guilty of 'coming with an armed force to Berkeley Castle to plunder it, and refusing to join the king in his expedition against the Scots' (the latter was a false charge and the seizure of Edward of Caernarfon was carefully omitted).[26] Berkeley also informed Hothum that another plot to free Edward existed in Buckinghamshire and adjacent counties, and that two 'great leaders' of this conspiracy, Dominican friars named John Redmere and John Norton, had been imprisoned on this account in Dunstable, Bedfordshire. This information is confirmed by a petition from the two men and various entries in the chancery rolls stating that they were sent from Dunstable to Newgate prison in London.[27] Members of the Dunheved group scattered: one of the two men called William Aylmer was captured in Oxford and the Dunheved brothers, Thomas and Stephen, in Warwickshire and London respectively. Thomas Dunheved was taken to Isabella and died in captivity at Pontefract Castle in Yorkshire some time later, having made an unsuccessful attempt to escape; Stephen was imprisoned at Newgate prison in London and escaped in the summer of 1329, his role in Isabella and Edward of Caernarfon's life not yet over.[28] The *Annales Paulini* even claim that 'certain magnates' supported the Dunheveds' plot to free Edward, though their identity is unknown.[29]

Most of the Dunheved gang were either dead, in prison, or in hiding on the continent or in England by the autumn of 1327. However, Edward of Caernarfon still had supporters determined to free him, and in early September they hatched yet another plot. The leader of this latest attempt was Rhys ap Gruffudd, formerly a squire of Edward's chamber, whom Edward had appointed as an envoy to Isabella in November 1326. Possibly, Donald of Mar also aided this latest attempt in person. Sir Gruffudd Llwyd, who had aided Edward during the Marcher campaign in 1322, also joined. The plot failed when it was betrayed to William Shalford, Roger Mortimer's deputy justice of Wales, on 7 September.[30] Roger Mortimer, as it happened, was in Wales at the time, and by 26 October had imprisoned thirteen conspirators at Caernarfon Castle, Edward II's birthplace.[31]

This latest plot to free Edward of Caernarfon, the third or fourth of 1327, convinced some men that he was too dangerous to be allowed to live. One of them, according to the 1331 testimony of the Welshman Hywel ap Gruffudd (one of Rhys ap Gruffudd's co-conspirators of 1327), was Roger Mortimer's deputy justice of Wales, William Shalford. Supposedly, Shalford, while on the north Wales island of Anglesey, sent a letter on 14 September 1327 to Mortimer, who was then at Abergavenny in south Wales. Hywel ap Gruffudd accused Shalford of complicity in the death of Edward II, and his testimony against Shalford runs as follows:

> Rhys ap Gruffudd and others of his faction had assembled their power in South Wales and in North Wales, with the agreement of certain great lords of England, in order to forcibly deliver the said Lord Edward, father of our lord the king, who was then detained in a castle at Berkeley. And he [Shalford] also made clear in that letter that if the Lord Edward [II] was freed, that Lord Roger Mortimer and all his people would die a terrible death by force and be utterly destroyed. On account of which the said William Shalford, like the traitor he is, counselled the said Roger that he ordain such a remedy in such a way that no one in England or Wales would think of effecting such deliverance.[32]

Again, we learn that 'certain great lords' supported Rhys' plot. In response to Shalford's letter, Mortimer allegedly sent a messenger, William Ockley, to Berkeley Castle to show Shalford's letter to Edward's custodians Thomas Berkeley and John Maltravers, and 'charged him to tell them to take counsel on the points contained in the letter and to quickly remedy the situation in order to avoid great peril'. Ockley, or Ockle or Ogle, a man-at-arms and a rather obscure figure, was convicted of the murder of Edward II in November 1330. He seems to have come from Ireland, or at least to have had connections there.[33] Ockley is presumably to be identified with the 'William de Okleye' who accompanied Roger Mortimer's wife, Joan Geneville, during her imprisonment in March 1322, and was thus a long-term Mortimer adherent.[34]

Edward of Caernarfon is usually said to have been murdered at Berkeley Castle on Monday 21 September 1327, the feast day of St Matthew the Evangelist. Coincidentally or not, both he and Roger Mortimer were born on 25 April, the feast day of St Mark the Evangelist, so perhaps 21 September as the day of another evangelist was deemed to be a fitting day for him to die. It was also the first anniversary of the departure of Isabella's invasion force from Dordrecht.[35] News was taken

to Edward III, not yet fifteen, and Isabella at Lincoln by Sir Thomas
Gurney, and the young king told his cousin John de Bohun, earl of
Hereford on the 24th that he had heard the news on the night of 23/24
September (Gurney must have ridden extremely fast to cover the 150
miles from Berkeley to Lincoln in 48 hours or less).[36] A few days later, it
was announced to parliament that Edward II had died of natural causes
– it is hard to imagine that anyone believed this – while the parliament of
November 1330, the first after Edward III took charge of his kingdom,
gave the cause of Edward's death as murder for the first time. This later
parliament convicted Thomas Gurney and William Ockley of the deed
and sentenced them to death in absentia, but the parliamentary rolls say
only that they 'falsely and treacherously murdered him'.[37] One of the
many charges against Roger Mortimer at this parliament was also that
he had had Edward murdered. The method of the alleged murder was
never stated. None of the killers or anyone else involved with it ever
spoke publicly about it, and no official government source ever stated
the method, which leaves only the reports of contemporary and later
chroniclers – and none of them knew the cause of death for certain. It is
often assumed that Roger Mortimer, and perhaps Isabella as well, had
Edward murdered to safeguard themselves and their political position;
Edward freed and restored to his throne, presuming this would have
been possible, would surely have avenged himself on them, inflicting the
full horrors of the traitor's death on Mortimer and imprisoning Isabella.
This assumption may well be true, but is only an assumption.

Fourteenth-century chronicles give a wide variety of causes of Edward's
death and the date as either 20, 21 or 22 September (Isabella and her son
Edward III kept the anniversary as the 21st).[38] The *Annales Paulini* say
only that Edward died at Berkeley without further details, the *Anonimalle*
(whose author knew about the Dunheveds' plot to free Edward) says he
died of an illness, and several continuations of the French *Brut* claim he
died *de grant dolour*, 'of great sorrow' or 'pain'.[39] Adam Murimuth in
the 1330s thought at first that Edward had been killed 'by a trick' or
'as a precaution' (*per cautelam occisus*) and later wrote that the former
king had been suffocated, and the Bridlington chronicler wrote that he
did not believe the rumours which were current regarding Edward's
death – presumably a reference to the infamous 'red-hot poker' story.[40]
Lanercost in the 1340s says unhelpfully that Edward died 'either by a
natural death or by the violence of others', while the *Scalacronica* of the
early 1360s says, rather movingly, that Edward died 'by what manner
was not known, but God knows it'.[41] The Wigmore chronicler was sure
that Edward died of natural causes; the Lichfield chronicler says he was
strangled; the Peterborough chronicler writes that he was well in the
evening but dead by morning; the *French Chronicle of London* says he
was 'vilely murdered' but doesn't specify how.[42]

Chroniclers who give the notorious 'red-hot poker' story include Ranulph Higden's *Polychronicon* of around 1350 and the English *Brut*, which has Thomas Gurney and John Maltravers (wrongly: Maltravers was never accused or convicted of any complicity in Edward's murder) coming into Edward's chamber as he slept. It says that they laid a table on his stomach and took 'a horn, and put it into his fundament as deep as they might, and took a spit of copper burning, and put it through the horn into his body, and oftentimes rolled therewith his bowels, and so they killed their lord, that nothing was perceived'.[43] The account of Geoffrey le Baker in the 1350s is also well known:

These cruel bullies, seeing that death by foetid odour would not overcome so vigorous a man, during the night of 22 [*sic*] September, suddenly seized hold of him as he lay on his bed. With the aid of enormous pillows and a weight heavier than that of fifteen substantial men they pressed down upon him until he was suffocated. With a plumber's red-hot iron, inserted through a horn leading to the inmost parts of the bowel, they burned out the respiratory organs beyond the intestines, taking care that no wound should be discernible on the royal body where such might be looked for by some friend of justice.[44]

The utterly ludicrous scenario presented here – why would Edward's murderers bother with a red-hot iron when they had no fewer than fifteen 'substantial men' and enormous pillows and could simply have had him suffocated? – has not prevented the account being repeated as 'fact' from the late fourteenth century until the present day. Edward's death by red-hot poker is often assumed to have been his just punishment for (presumably) being the passive partner in sexual acts with men, or to have been a way of killing him without leaving a mark on the body so that his death could be presented as natural, but there is no good reason to accept this fantastically lurid and revolting story. Those who invented it and repeated it were distant in place and time from Berkeley Castle, and the wide variation of causes of death given in fourteenth-century chronicles – most of which do not mention a poker – indicate that no chroniclers knew what had really happened and were either making up stories or repeating rumours they had heard. It is virtually certain that the red-hot poker tale of Edward's demise can be dismissed as a myth, and there is also compelling evidence that Edward II did not die at Berkeley Castle in 1327 at all.

Assuming for the moment that he did, his body remained at the castle for another month, until 20 October, where it was guarded by one man, a royal sergeant-at-arms named William Beaukaire. He was a Frenchman who, curiously, had been one of the garrison who held out against Isabella at Caerphilly Castle some months earlier with Hugh

Despenser the Younger's son Huchon, some of Edward II's household and several of the men who later joined the Dunheved brothers in their attack on Berkeley Castle to free Edward. Why one of the former king's and Despenser's adherents, of all people, should have been sent to Berkeley Castle to guard Edward's body after death is unclear. The royal clerk Adam Murimuth, the only chronicler in the south-west of England in September 1327 (albeit 100 miles away in Exeter) says that a group of knights, abbots and burgesses from the local area observed the former king's body by invitation and *superficialiter*, 'superficially'.[45] This statement raises more questions than it answers. Murimuth does not specify how many men saw Edward II's body, whether they attended in one group or individually, whether they saw the body at Berkeley Castle or later after it had been moved to Gloucester, who invited them, or even what the purpose of the visit was: to make sure that Edward really was dead, or simply as a kind of ritual to mark the passing of the king's father? Edward III himself did not send men to view the body, and – a key point – started disseminating news of his father's death immediately, before he could possibly have verified that the news he had received from Thomas, Lord Berkeley, sent via Thomas Gurney was accurate. Neither, as far as we know, did any of Edward of Caernarfon's other family such as Isabella, his half-brothers the earls of Norfolk and Kent, or his cousin the earl of Lancaster see his body before burial. The body was embalmed, presumably reasonably soon after death in order to prevent decay, by a local wise woman; the heart was removed and sent to Isabella in a silver casket, a payment for which appears in Lord Berkeley's household accounts. Royal burials of the early fourteenth century involved covering the entire body, including the face, with cerecloth, that is wax-impregnated cloth.[46]

Isabella's reaction to her husband's sudden death is unrecorded; was she shocked, relieved, grieving, triumphant? We cannot know. There is, however, no reason to think that she had wished for her husband's death or that she played any role in it or was 'secretly delighted' to hear of it.[47] Roger Mortimer was in Wales in September 1327 when he received news of the latest plot to free Edward and responded by sending William Ockley to Berkeley Castle. Isabella was far away in Lincoln and could not have heard of the Welsh plot, or of the sending of Ockley, before her husband's death. Her dire posthumous reputation as a 'she-wolf' rests mostly on the assumption that she was involved in Edward II's death in some way, or at least stood by without protesting while it happened and continued her sexual relationship with Roger Mortimer for three more years, knowing or suspecting that he had had her husband killed. Although she and Mortimer did continue their association until his arrest in October 1330 and the queen never denounced him for murdering Edward or anything else, there are no real grounds for assuming that Isabella was in love with Mortimer or having physical relations with him.

Isabella and her fifteen-year-old son attended the former king's funeral at St Peter's Abbey in Gloucester, now Gloucester Cathedral, on 20 December 1327. For two months the body had lain in state at the abbey, watched over by a number of men, including the sergeant-at-arms William Beaukaire and the Dominican bishop of Llandaff, John Eaglescliff, and with the face still covered. It lay in a coffin topped by a wooden image or effigy in Edward's likeness, which was dressed in his coronation robes and a copper gilt crown. This was the first royal funeral in the history of western Europe where a wooden effigy is known to have been used.[48] The hearse on which the coffin and body lay had four gilded lions and standing figures of the four evangelists, and 800 gold leaves were bought to gild a leopard decorating the cover over Edward's body. Oak barriers were placed around the hearse to keep visitors away.[49] The funeral cost over £350, though otherwise little is known about it, even who attended.[50] Edward II's niece Elizabeth de Clare (who left her two young daughters, Isabella Verdon and Elizabeth Damory, in the care of Hugh Despenser the Younger's sister Isabel Hastings while she travelled to Gloucester) and his half-brother Edmund of Woodstock, earl of Kent were certainly present, and presumably much of the English nobility and episcopate as well, assuming they had been able to make the journey to distant Gloucester in the dead of winter. Roger Mortimer attended and had himself a new black robe made for the occasion. Less than three years later, he would be forced to wear this tunic as he was dragged to his execution. It is interesting to note that after the funeral, Isabella had the woman who had embalmed Edward's body brought to her for questioning at her son the king's command, though what questions the queen asked her and why are unknown. Perhaps she was perturbed or distressed at Edward's sudden death and wanted to ask about it, or perhaps she was in some way trying to ensure the woman's silence. The royal clerk Hugh Glanvill, who took the woman (her name is not recorded) to the queen, apparently tried to cover up the fact in his accounts, which seems to indicate that Isabella and her son, for whatever reason, wanted her interview of the woman to remain private.[51]

Edward II was dead and Isabella of France was a widow. Or so it appeared. But in Edward's turbulent life, nothing could ever be that simple.

12

Regency and Rebellion
1327–1328

From his accession in January 1327 until he took over the governance of his own realm shortly before he turned eighteen in October 1330, Edward III was underage and thus not in command of his government and kingdom. Unfortunately, it is basically impossible to determine from the surviving documentation how much of a role Isabella played, or did not play, in governing England and Wales during her son's minority. Almost every writ and letter extant in the chancery rolls from 1327 to 1330 was issued in the name of Edward III, and although it is apparent that the young king was not, in fact, governing his own kingdom, it is extremely difficult to say who was. Historians have almost always assumed that Isabella and Roger Mortimer were mostly in control and behind every action taken by the government between 1327 and 1330, which is likely to be true or mostly true, though is still only an assumption.[1] If they did control the government, it is also impossible to determine if they were acting together, or if Isabella mostly ruled alone with Mortimer and perhaps others as her advisers, or if Mortimer used his personal association with the king's mother to take control most or all of the time with Isabella more in the background. The debate marches on across the pages of books, articles and dissertations, but unfortunately we cannot come to a firm conclusion. In November 1330, Edward III certainly thought that Roger Mortimer had usurped much of his royal power: of the fourteen charges he raised against his mother's favourite during Mortimer's trial, eight of them accused him of taking, using and abusing royal power to which he was not entitled, and another stated that he had ordered the king's subjects to obey his commands rather than the king's. The *Scalacronica*, which was written much later but whose author is generally well-informed (his father fought for Edward II at Bannockburn and served in the retinue of Hugh Despenser the Younger), says that 'the queen, with advice of the earl of March [i.e. Mortimer] had everything in her governance', and that Edward III's growing independence in 1329/30 annoyed Mortimer, 'by whose direction the queen acted in everything'.[2]

A regency council was appointed to rule for the underage king, though little is known about it: one of the few direct contemporary references to it survives in the records of parliament held after Isabella's downfall in 1330, when it was stated that four bishops, four earls and six barons would remain close to Edward III to advise him. There was no one single regent and it is not entirely clear who sat on the council, and whether it changed from time to time or was a fixed group of people. The Flemish chronicler Jean le Bel thought that Isabella, Roger Mortimer and Edward II's half-brother Edmund of Woodstock, earl of Kent were the leaders of the young king's council, which is certainly possible though uncorroborated by other sources.[3] The itineraries of both Edward III and Isabella are difficult to establish in the late 1320s, and consequently it is also difficult to ascertain how much personal contact Isabella had with her son and whether she had access to his great and privy seals, which she would have needed to issue writs in his name.[4] In short, it is frustratingly hard to come to any firm conclusions about Isabella's rule during her son's minority and how much power she was really wielding or allowing Roger Mortimer to wield. It seems probable, however, that she exercised influence in much the same way as she had during her husband's reign, by interceding with her son and with the chancellor of England.[5] Some entries on the Patent Roll in the late 1320s reveal men being appointed to certain offices 'during the pleasure of the king and Queen Isabella', and numerous others refer to pardons and favours being handed out at her request and to grants of land and offices being made to her followers and members of her household.[6]

Fourteenth-century chroniclers often assumed that the queen and Roger Mortimer were indeed ruling the country, and were mostly scathing about them. It is easy to gain the impression from their contemporaries that although Isabella and Mortimer had led a brilliantly successful and popular invasion, they had little idea how to rule the kingdom, and that neither of them had a great deal of political judgement or acuity or much ability beyond enriching themselves as much as possible. The *Scalacronica*, whose author describes Mortimer merely as an important member of the queen's faction, not as her lover, says that 'Queen Isabella and Mortimer governed all England in such fashion as to displease many of the nobles of the realm', and that they subjected Edward III to 'bad, indolent and negligent counsel' in all things.[7] The *French Chronicle of London* comments, 'The queen, Lady Isabel, and Sir Roger Mortimer assumed to themselves royal power over many of the magnates of

England and of Wales, and retained the treasures of the land themselves, and kept the young king wholly in subjection to themselves.' It further states that Edward III realised he had unwise counsel and that his realm was at the point of being lost, and the people too.[8] The *Brut* says that the regency council 'was soon undone, and there was much loss and harm to all England; for the king and all the lords that should govern him were governed and ruled after [i.e. by] the king's mother Dame Isabel and by Sir Roger the Mortimer … and they took unto them castles, towns, lands and rents, in great harm and loss unto the Crown, and of the king's state also, out of measure'. The chronicler also says that because of Isabella and Mortimer's counsel 'many harms, shames and reproofs have fallen unto the king' and criticises the way they wasted Edward II's treasure 'without the will of King Edward his son, in destruction of him and his folk'. Within a very short time, Isabella forfeited all her popularity of 1326: 'The community of England began to hate Isabel the queen, that so much loved her when she came to pursue the false traitors the Despensers from France,' the *Brut* laments.[9]

It is worth noting that these chroniclers criticised Isabella for ruling her son's kingdom badly and bankrupting it and for giving him harmful and self-interested advice, and not for her supposed sexual immorality and affair with Roger Mortimer, which they barely (if at all) mention. Although it is often claimed in modern writing that fourteenth-century chroniclers vilified Isabella because she was a woman in a man's world, with the possible exception of Geoffrey le Baker they did not. Neither did they paint her as sexually voracious or immoral. The treasury was indeed overflowing with money at the end of Edward II's reign but empty when Edward III took over four years later; Isabella did grant herself an excessively large income while deliberately keeping her son and daughter-in-law short of money; the chroniclers' criticisms of her and Mortimer were not unreasonable and had also been made of their predecessors. Isabella and Mortimer repeated all the mistakes of Edward II and the Despensers, and added a few more. Their policies were mostly short-sighted and self-serving, with little purpose beyond their own enrichment and determination to cling on to power as long as possible. By 1330, most of their allies had turned from them in disgust; having rid the country of a greedy tyranny, they found they had merely replaced it with a worse one. Isabella became as dependent on her own favourite as Edward II had been on his, with the same result: Mortimer came to hold great influence, to the exclusion of the men whose birth and position gave them the right to govern England during Edward III's minority, and abused his power to benefit himself, as Despenser had done before him. Isabella was more like her husband than perhaps she knew, in her inability or unwillingness to separate her private self from her political role. Instead of the king and his permitting a ruthless, greedy Marcher lord to rule the kingdom and the treasury, Edward III's subjects now had to suffer the queen and her permitting a ruthless greedy Marcher lord to rule the kingdom and the treasury – hardly a great improvement.

Eight days before Edward II's supposed death on 21 September 1327, Mortimer received all the lands in Shropshire, Wales and the March of his murdered cousin the earl of Arundel, though the late earl's Sussex lands and castles passed to Edward III's uncle Edmund of Woodstock, earl of Kent.[10] On 12 June 1327 came one of the richest prizes of all: Mortimer was given custody of the great south Wales lordship of Glamorgan, which belonged by right to Edward II's niece and Hugh Despenser the Younger's widow Eleanor de Clare as her share of the large inheritance of her brother the earl of Gloucester.[11] Eleanor was still alive, and had to wait till her cousin Edward III took over control of the kingdom to get her lands back. Mortimer also received or awarded himself the great gift of the rich north Wales lordship of Denbigh, which belonged by right to Isabella's aunt by marriage Alice Lacy, countess of Lincoln and formerly the wife of Thomas of Lancaster. Hugh Despenser the Elder had deprived Alice of her lordship with Edward II's connivance. Rather than giving it back to her, Isabella allowed Mortimer to take it. Mortimer thus granted himself the lands of two vulnerable women, and gave notice that the regime which had succeeded that of the Despensers was no better or fairer than theirs had been. He spent vast sums of money that did not rightfully belong to him on his Shropshire castle of Ludlow, part of his wife, Joan Geneville's inheritance, and, not unreasonably, used his position as the dowager queen's favourite to benefit his children. He arranged the marriage of his daughter Beatrice to young Edward, son and heir of Thomas of Brotherton, earl of Norfolk, elder of the two half-brothers of Edward II (Edward of Norfolk died as a child in the early 1330s). Mortimer also secured the marriage of Marie de Châtillon, widow of Aymer de Valence and dowager countess of Pembroke, for his son Roger, which did not work out as the younger Roger died in 1328.[12] In the late 1320s Mortimer attended the weddings of his daughters Agnes and Katherine to the nine-year-old Laurence Hastings, future earl of Pembroke, and the fourteen-year-old Thomas Beauchamp, earl of Warwick. Thirty-nine-year-old Mortimer's heir was born in 1328: his namesake Roger Mortimer, child of his eldest son and heir, Edmund, and Elizabeth, one of the daughters of Bartholomew Badlesmere who had been executed by Edward II in 1322. 1328 was not, however, an unqualified success for the royal favourite, as two of his four sons died.[13] His eldest son, Edmund, also barely outlived him and died still in his twenties. Mortimer and his wife, Joan Geneville, presumably were somewhat estranged in the late 1320s. She had been freed from the house arrest under which she had been living since 1322 after her husband's return to England, though what she thought of his association with Isabella is unknown. Joan is often presented in fiction – and sometimes even in non-fiction – as a sexless matron whose husband understandably much preferred the beautiful, glamorous queen, though in reality she and Mortimer seem to have had a good marriage; they had four sons and eight daughters and spent a lot of time together. Joan Mortimer née Geneville's whereabouts during her husband's years of power are uncertain, except that in 1327 she was at Ludlow in Shropshire when her son-in-law Thomas, Lord Berkeley, sent her a gift of pears.[14]

Robert Bruce, the aging king of Scotland, decided that the political chaos in the southern kingdom in the aftermath of Edward II's deposition was too good an opportunity to resist, and invaded the north of England in June 1327 with his nephew Donald of Mar (also involved in trying to aid Edward of Caernarfon at Berkeley Castle) and his loyal long-term associates James Douglas (who had plotted to capture Isabella in Yorkshire in 1319) and Thomas Randolph leading his armies. The English response to the invasion was led by Roger Mortimer, though nominally Edward II's half-brothers, the earls of Norfolk and Kent, and cousin the earl of Lancaster were in charge.[15] The campaign ended up as much of a complete disaster as any of Edward II's had been, and almost led to the capture of Edward III, who burst into tears of rage and humiliation. In the spring of 1328, therefore, a group of persons acting on behalf of the English government, whose identities are uncertain but who probably included Isabella, signed a peace treaty with Robert Bruce which acknowledged him as king of Scotland and gave up all English claims to overlordship of his realm. Bruce then was near the end of his life – he would die on 7 June 1329 at the age of fifty-five – and finally, twenty-two years after the start of his reign, saw himself recognised as rightful king by his powerful southern neighbour. Although it was known officially as the Treaty of Northampton and as the Treaty of Edinburgh in Scotland, the disgruntled English preferred to call the settlement the 'Shameful Peace'. Edward III himself, forced to ratify it on 4 May 1328, repudiated it years later when he was in a position to do so. As Lisa Benz St John has pointed out, Isabella's name does not appear in a single source relating to the treaty itself or in the negotiations leading up to it, and therefore it is impossible to know what role she played in it.[16] Chroniclers generally assumed, most probably accurately, that she was primarily responsible for the 'Shameful Peace', but as with all the other actions of the English government between 1327 and 1330, it is extremely difficult to prove this conclusively. Robert Bruce agreed to pay the princely sum of 20,000 marks to the English treasury, presumably intended as compensation for the people of the north of England for the devastation caused to their lands and possessions by years of Scottish incursions. Edward III later accused Roger Mortimer of keeping the entire amount himself, though in fact it is unclear how much of the promised money ever materialised.[17] To seal the alliance, Isabella's youngest child, Joan of the Tower, whose marriage to the future Peter IV of Aragon Edward II had arranged in 1325, was betrothed to Robert Bruce and Elizabeth de Burgh's son and heir, David, and the wedding took place almost immediately on 17 July 1328. Joan had just turned seven, born on 5 July 1321, and David was only four, born on 5 March 1324. Joan presumably was chosen in preference to her older sister, Eleanor, who turned ten in June 1328, because she was closer to David's age. Less than a year later, Robert Bruce died, and Joan's five-year-old husband succeeded as David II of Scotland. Their marriage of thirty-four years proved unhappy and childless.

Meanwhile, Isabella's eldest child, Edward III, had married Philippa of Hainault in York on 25 or 26 January 1328, when he was fifteen and she perhaps thirteen or fourteen. The ceremony was conducted by William Melton, archbishop of York, who had spoken out for Edward II at the London parliament a year before but who thereafter showed the same loyalty to the young king as he had shown to his father. Whether by accident or design, Edward III and Philippa married on or almost on his parents' twentieth wedding anniversary, Edward II and Isabella having married in Boulogne on 25 January 1308. Philippa, humiliatingly, would not be crowned as queen of England until more than two years later on 18 February 1330, when she was five months pregnant with her first child, almost certainly because Isabella wished to remain the only queen in the country. Neither would the young queen be granted any lands until two years after her marriage, although on 15 May 1328 Edward III (or Isabella, or whoever else was acting on his behalf) promised to assign lands for her dowry within a year. The month of her coronation, Philippa was finally given lands of her own, the lordship of Glamorgan, which belonged by right to her husband's first cousin Eleanor de Clare and which was returned to Eleanor after Isabella's downfall.[18] Glamorgan was a rich lordship, but the income Philippa derived from it still fell far short of the £3,000 she had been promised as her dower at the time of her betrothal. She was not even granted her own independent household until at least a year after her wedding.[19] Isabella treated her new daughter-in-law, it has to be said, shabbily.

On 1 February 1328, a few days after Edward III's wedding, the last of Isabella's short-lived brothers, Charles IV of France, died. He was not even thirty-four. He left his widow, Joan of Evreux, pregnant; his cousin Philip of Valois, who was his next male heir and who was appointed regent after Charles's death, was forced to endure an anxious wait to see if he would become king. Exactly two months after her husband's death, Queen Joan gave birth to his posthumous daughter, Blanche, Charles IV's only child who lived into adulthood. None of Isabella's three brothers thus left any sons, the Capetian dynasty came to an end, and Philip of Valois became Philip VI and founded the dynasty which would rule France until 1589. Charles IV and Isabella's sixteen-year-old niece, Louis X's only surviving child, succeeded as Queen Joan II of Navarre in her own right in 1328, as Philip VI was not a descendant of Joan I and thus had no claim to that kingdom. Joan II and her husband and cousin, Philip, count of Evreux, were crowned king and queen of Navarre at Pamplona a few months later. Two of Isabella's sisters-in-law, dowager queens of France, both passed away not long after Charles IV, both of them still young women: Louis X's widow, Clemence of Hungary, in October 1328, and Philip V's widow, Joan of Burgundy, in January 1330. Meanwhile, Isabella urged her son Edward III to claim his rights to the throne of France. On 16 May 1328, an embassy, one of whom was Adam Orleton, was sent to Paris to register Edward's claim.[20]

At the parliament held at Salisbury in October 1328, Isabella's second son, John of Eltham, now twelve, was granted the title of earl of Cornwall. This had formerly belonged to Piers Gaveston, and apparently Edward II had been reluctant to grant the title to anyone else, even his own son. John's elevation to an earldom, given that he was son and brother of kings and heir to the English throne until Edward III and Queen Philippa had a child, was entirely uncontroversial. The same could not be said of the other appointment made at this parliament: Roger Mortimer was made, or made himself, earl of March, a grandiose and unprecedented title making Mortimer earl of all the English–Welsh borderlands. The *Brut* says that this was done against the will of all the barons of England and to the prejudice of Edward III and his crown, and says 'and evermore the queen Isabel so much procured against her son the king'.[21] Isabella's uncle Henry of Lancaster was unimpressed. Ignored and partly disinherited by his cousin Edward II, Lancaster had joined Isabella in the hope of regaining his lands and his rightful position at court, but over the previous two years had been prevented from exercising any influence. He made his displeasure known, and led a rebellion against Isabella and Roger Mortimer that, though unsuccessful, demonstrated how rapidly they had lost the support of many of the men who had enthusiastically supported them just two years earlier. A further rift between Isabella and her uncle came about when Lancaster either condoned the murder of Sir Robert Holland, or at least protected the murderers. Holland had been a close friend and ally of Lancaster's older brother, Thomas, for many years, but had betrayed Thomas before the battle of Boroughbridge in March 1322 and joined Edward II with an armed force (in fairness, Holland's decision must have had something to do with the fact that Edward was holding one of his daughters hostage). Edward II imprisoned Holland, but Isabella released him and seems to have shown him much favour, greatly to the annoyance of Henry of

Lancaster. In early October 1328, Robert Holland was waylaid in a wood in Essex by some Lancastrian knights, who decapitated him and sent his head to Earl Henry.

The earl of Lancaster was joined by former important allies of Isabella such as Hugh Audley, the only favourite of Edward II who survived his reign and who had been imprisoned for years after the battle of Boroughbridge in March 1322, and who was also a close relative of Roger Mortimer; Henry, Lord Beaumont, imprisoned by Edward II in 1326 supposedly for refusing to swear an oath to Hugh Despenser the Younger; the earl of Lancaster's son-in-law Thomas Wake, Mortimer's first cousin, who had played a vital role in the parliament of January 1327 which deposed Edward II and who had been one of Isabella's staunchest supporters after she returned to England in September 1326; and men who had been on the Continent with Mortimer before the invasion such as Thomas Roscelyn and even William Trussell, who had pronounced the death sentence on both Hugh Despensers.[22] Henry Beaumont, who was the titular earl of Buchan by right of his wife Alice Comyn, and his son-in-law David de Strathbogie, titular earl of Atholl, were motivated by dissatisfaction at the settlement with Scotland, which meant that they would never be able to hold the lands they claimed in that country, but the others were motivated perhaps by disgust and disillusionment that they had risked so much to overthrow a king and replaced him with a regime which was no better.

After the end of parliament on 1 November 1328, Isabella, her son the king, daughter-in-law Queen Philippa and the rest of the royal party travelled to Winchester, where the earl of Lancaster was staying with his forces. Lancaster left the city, Thomas Wake and Hugh Audley with him, without incident, though his men jeered at the royal household.[23] On 28 November, Isabella's and Edward III's sergeants-at-arms were exempted from a general order to the populace not to carry weapons in London, and the mayor was ordered to imprison anyone 'disobedient to authority' in the city, indications of the rising tensions.[24] Still afraid of the earl's intentions, however, and knowing that he had returned to his Midlands strongholds of Kenilworth and Higham Ferrers supposedly to raise more men in order to attack the king, Isabella and her son spent the festive season somewhat out of the way in the west of England, at Gloucester and Worcester. Whether by accident or design, Isabella was in Gloucester on 20 December 1328, exactly a year since her husband's funeral had taken place there.[25] On the anniversary, an entry on the Patent Roll – perhaps issued at Isabella's request or command – records a special licence granted to the abbot of St Peter's to appoint general attorneys in all the courts of England, which was 'done for the special reason that the late king's body lies buried in that church' and because Edward II himself had allowed the same licence to the abbot's predecessor.[26] On 15 December, Roger Mortimer, acknowledged as he so often was in the chancery rolls of this period as 'the king's kinsman' even though he and Edward III were only fairly distantly related, gave 100 marks to nine chaplains at the church of his Herefordshire manor of Leintwardine to 'celebrate divine service daily' for the souls of himself, his wife, the king, Queen Philippa, Queen Isabella, his ally the bishop of Lincoln and their ancestors, children and successors.[27]

What happened next is not entirely clear, but the earl of Lancaster and his fellow rebels went to Bedford where, abandoned by his allies the earls of Norfolk and Kent, Lancaster gave in; his brief rebellion was over. The *Brut* says that Edward III, with Isabella beside him dressed 'as a knight armed' (i.e. in armour), rode twenty-four miles through the night towards Bedford, 'for dread of death'.[28] According to the later chronicler Henry Knighton, a strong Lancastrian sympathiser and thus probably not the most reliable source, Roger Mortimer spent eight days in January 1329 devastating Henry of Lancaster's town of Leicester in order to force the earl to submit.[29] On 9 February 1326, the earl of Lancaster was made to acknowledge a liability to pay £30,000 to the king, an impossibly huge sum, 'by reason of the riding with horses and arms at Bedford'. His allies were also made to acknowledge huge debts: 15,000 marks for Thomas Wake, £10,000 for Hugh Audley, and anything between £100 and £5,000 for the rest.[30] The debts were in fact never paid. Two of Lancaster's complaints had been that Edward III was badly advised and had no good council around him, a pointed dig at Lancaster's niece Isabella, and that the king had not the wherewithal to live and did not (or more likely could not) pay for the expenses of his household. Queen Philippa, meanwhile, 'ought to have her dowry on which to live without grieving the people'. To these points Edward III, or more likely Isabella or someone else close to him, made the flippant reply that 'it was impossible for him to be any richer, since both he and his people were impoverished by the present disturbances, but if any man knew how to make him richer, it would give him and his advisers great satisfaction'.[31] One entirely unintended and undesired consequence of the earl of Lancaster's rebellion was to entrench the power of the dowager queen's favourite Roger Mortimer, earl of March and to increase the young king's forced dependence on him.[32]

Isabella and Roger Mortimer quickly dealt with her uncle Lancaster's abortive rebellion, but things were going badly wrong for them very quickly, and soon they had to contend with something extraordinary: plots to free Isabella's supposedly dead husband.

13

More Plots

1329–1330

Isabella's twenty-eight-year-old first cousin and brother-in-law Edmund of Woodstock, earl of Kent had attended his half-brother Edward II's funeral in Gloucester on 20 December 1327. Astonishingly, in March 1330, Kent was put on trial before parliament for treason against his nephew Edward III, on the grounds that he had tried to rescue Edward II from captivity at Corfe Castle, long after his supposed death. The earl of Kent was not the only man who strongly believed that the former king was still alive. Edward II's old friend Donald, earl of Mar, now returned to his native Scotland and a first cousin of the new child-king David II, told the archbishop of York in October 1329 that he would willingly bring an army of 40,000 men to England to help secure Edward's release.[1] The archbishop of York himself, William Melton, sent an astonishing letter to his kinsman Simon Swanland, mayor of London, on 14 January 1330. Melton stated outright that 'our liege lord Edward of Caernarfon [Edward de Karnarvan] is alive and in good health of body, and in a safe place'. Melton asked Swanland, a draper who had often supplied cloth to Edward II and his household, to purchase a number of provisions for the former king, including twenty ells of linen cloth, two belts and two bags 'the best you can find for sale', riding clothes lined with miniver fur and three hoods with the same, six pairs of shoes, two pairs of leather boots, and cushions. He begged him to keep the matter secret, which Swanland did; his involvement in the curious events of 1329/30 was never discovered or apparently even suspected.[2] Melton also pledged the astonishingly large sum of £5,000 to do whatever he could to help effect Edward's release.[3] The earl of Kent suffered the ultimate penalty for his attempt to free his half-brother: he was beheaded in Winchester on 19 March 1330. Isabella and Roger Mortimer, or whoever else issued the order for his execution, showed considerably more concern for the fate of the jewels and other goods belonging to the earl's widow, Mortimer's first cousin Margaret Wake, than for the almost nine months pregnant Margaret herself. The jewels were to be delivered to two of the king's men while other men were ordered to search for any goods belonging to Margaret and have them taken away from Arundel Castle. The countess, meanwhile, was ordered to be imprisoned at Salisbury Castle with her young children – one of whom was Joan of Kent, mother of Richard II and then merely a toddler – and only two attendants.[4] Countess Margaret gave birth to her son John on 7 April, nineteen days after her husband's death. Edmund, earl of Kent, the son, brother, nephew and uncle (and grandfather, though he could not have known it) of kings, was forced to wait around all day on the scaffold, as the Winchester executioner, unwilling to participate in the judicial murder of a man so highly born, had fled. Finally, a latrine cleaner under sentence of death himself was persuaded to wield the axe in exchange for a pardon. Kent, unable to believe that he was to die for the 'crime' of attempting to free a supposedly dead man from prison, had sworn that he would walk from Winchester to London barefoot with a halter around his neck if it would save his life, but to no avail.[5] His death was a foregone conclusion: four days before his execution and the day before he confessed to parliament, he was already being named as 'the late earl of Kent'.[6]

The plot of the earl of Kent is well known to historians, and it is often stated as 'fact' that he was gullible, stupid and inconsistent and that this is the only reason why he came to believe that his half-brother was still alive two and a half years after Edward II's death.[7] It is also often stated, however, that Kent was such a dangerous threat to Isabella and Roger Mortimer's continued political survival that they felt they had no other choice but to manufacture a reason to force him into treason so that they had an excuse to execute him, and thus protect themselves and their regime from him.[8] They therefore came up with the story, so the argument goes, that Isabella's husband was still alive, intending that Kent would stupidly believe the rumours they were spreading, try to rescue the dead Edward II and fall into their clever trap. The contradiction that Kent was both a stupid, credulous man willing to believe in the continued existence of his dead half-brother on the strength of mere rumours and a serious threat to Isabella and Mortimer's continued political survival notwithstanding, pretending that Edward II was still alive in 1329/30 was in fact the last thing Isabella and Mortimer would have wanted to do. Supposedly, they had wanted him dead in the first place to put an end to the 1327 plots to free him and restore him to the throne, and it makes no sense that they would have wished all these plots and rumours (which had come to an abrupt end on the announcement of Edward's death) to start up again, and have to deal with possible pretenders to the throne. This would have threatened their position far more than the earl of Kent could possibly have done. Kent had taken part at first in the rebellion of his cousin the earl of Lancaster in late 1328, but soon returned to Edward III and Isabella. He was not personally hostile to them, and began his attempts to free Edward II from Corfe Castle after being reconciled to their regime.

The earl of Kent was not stupid, and the notion that he was is merely a transparent attempt by modern historians convinced that Edward II died in 1327 to make Kent's plot to free him in 1330 fit into that worldview. Even if the earl were stupid, then Archbishop William Melton, a man then probably in his fifties, often considered to be one of the greatest archbishops in English history and widely admired both by his contemporaries and ever since, certainly was not. And Melton stated outright in 1330 his belief that Edward II was still alive, despite having also most probably attended his funeral more than two years previously. Donald, earl of Mar, another firm believer in Edward's survival, was not stupid, and neither were the many dozens or, more probably, hundreds of men who flocked to Kent and Melton's cause in 1330. They included the bishop of London Stephen Gravesend, several sheriffs, several lords including Fulk Fitzwarin and John Say, Edward II's nephew Edward Monthermer and his great-nephew Huchon Despenser (still in prison), former adherents of the Despensers such as Sir Ingelram Berenger, Sir William Spersholt, Benet Braham, Malcolm Musard and William Cliff, and numerous former members of Edward II's household including clerks, his squires Giles of Spain and John Harsik, his tailor Henry de Cantebregge, and Peter Bernard, usher of his chamber.[9] Rhys ap Gruffudd, the Welshman who had tried to free Edward II from Berkeley Castle in September 1327 and who subsequently fled to Scotland, also joined the earl of Kent, as did William la Zouche, who had been one of the men who captured Edward II and Hugh Despenser the Younger in south Wales on 16 November 1326 and who subsequently married Edward's niece and Despenser's widow Eleanor de Clare. Stephen Dunheved, who with his brother Thomas the Dominican friar had led the attack on Berkeley Castle in the summer of 1327 which temporarily freed Edward, was another man who joined the earl, having escaped from Newgate prison in London a few months before. Another was Ieuan ap Gruffudd, whose father Gruffudd Llwyd had demonstrated great loyalty to Edward II for many years and who spent eighteen months in prison at Caernarfon Castle from September 1327 after joining Rhys ap Gruffudd's plot to free Edward that month. Close friends and allies of Edward II such as William Aune, who had served as constable of Tickhill Castle for most of Edward's reign, and William, abbot of Langdon, also joined the earl of Kent in 1329/30. Two more of the earl's adherents were Sir John Pecche, lord of Hampton-in-Arden in Warwickshire, and his son Nicholas. John Pecche's willingness to join the earl, presumably because he believed in Edward of Caernarfon's survival, is significant: he was the constable of Corfe Castle until replaced by John Maltravers on 24 September 1329, and was thus in an excellent position to know whether Edward of Caernarfon was alive and being held there or not, as the earl of Kent believed. Pecche also had connections with John Dunheved, brother of Thomas and Stephen Dunheved.[10] The association of Edward of Caernarfon with Corfe Castle is very strong: Adam Murimuth and Geoffrey le Baker both thought he was held in captivity there at some point, the author of the *Brut* believed he was murdered there rather than at Berkeley, and his joint custodian John Maltravers was at Corfe in September 1327 around the time of Edward's alleged murder, when the other custodian, Thomas Berkeley, sent him letters there. Maltravers also received £258 in September 1327 for 'services to the king's father in Dorset'.[11]

Inquisitions were ordered across England and Wales within days of the earl of Kent's execution to discover his adherents, and they were believed to be particularly numerous in East Anglia and in Wales.[12] On 13 April, it was proclaimed in all the counties of England that anyone who said in public that 'the king's father is yet alive' or that the earl of Kent had been executed for any other reason than his 'treasons and wickedness' would be arrested.[13] Kent's brother Thomas of Brotherton, earl of Norfolk did not join his plot, either because he did not believe their half-brother was alive, or because his son and heir Edward of Norfolk was now married to Roger Mortimer's daughter Beatrice and the earl felt tied to the regime of Mortimer and Isabella. It is extremely likely, however, that Norfolk knew of the plot and may have been his brother's confidant.[14] Isabella's uncle and Kent's cousin Henry, earl of Lancaster may also have known about the plot and Kent's suspicions that Edward II was alive: on 5 November 1328, Lancaster told the mayor and citizens of London that Kent had told him something he did not dare to put into writing, but that his messenger would inform them of it orally instead.[15] The city of London had violently rejected Edward II after Isabella's 1326 invasion, and it is curious and interesting to note that some prominent Londoners turned against Isabella in 1329/30 and supported the release and, one imagines, the restoration to the throne of her husband. As well as the bishop and mayor of London, the earl of Kent's co-conspirators of 1329/30 included John Hauteyn, an alderman of the city who had been one of its sheriffs in 1328, and several important merchants.[16]

Kent was said to have made 'confederacies and alliances' both in England and abroad.[17] His plot to free Edward II was not, as modern historians commonly claim, one gullible, foolish person acting alone, but a large number of men. To what extent the men who joined Kent truly believed in Edward's survival is hard to say; perhaps some of them were expressing their dissatisfaction with the regime of Isabella and Mortimer, though many had been loyal to and close to Edward II, even at the end of his reign when most of his followers had abandoned him. Many of the men were low ranking, and it hardly seems plausible that Isabella and Mortimer would go to all the trouble of pretending that her husband was still alive in order to catch a glover, a few friars, clerks and squires and a tailor; besides, many of them had been released by the time Isabella and Mortimer fell from power later in 1330, which hardly suggests that their aim was to keep their dangerous political enemies safely in prison. Very few if any of Kent's followers had suffered under the regime of Isabella and Mortimer or had demonstrated antipathy to the regime, and even long-term Despenser adherents such as Ingelram Berenger had been allowed to go unpunished and unmolested after the Despensers' downfall. It is hard to see how revenge against the queen mother and her favourite might have been their motive, even if they were, like so many others, becoming disgusted with Isabella and Mortimer's greed and ostentation. If removing Isabella and Mortimer from power were the motive of the conspirators of 1329/30, pretending that Edward II was still alive seems an odd way to go about it. The earl of Lancaster in late 1328 had not felt the need to mention his cousin's name when leading his abortive rebellion, and had the earl of Kent's adherents wished to remove Isabella and Mortimer from their position, joining the rebellion of the earl of Lancaster – the only man with the wealth and power base to mount a serious challenge to the pair – would have made far more sense than pretending that Edward II was alive. The merciless speed with which the earl of Kent was arrested, tried and executed suggests rather that Isabella and Roger Mortimer knew that the plot to free Edward was a genuine one, and nearing fruition.

The plan was to take Edward to the earl of Kent's castle of Arundel in Sussex – boats had been arranged with the aid of John Gymmynges, formerly a Despenser adherent – and then apparently abroad somewhere, either as a permanent sanctuary outside England or for him to try to raise an army to reclaim his throne from his son. This would inevitably lead to civil war, and Kent's plot thus not only threatened the position of Isabella and Roger Mortimer, but her son the king's too. It is difficult to understand the plot of the earl of Kent and his many associates without assuming that either Edward II was still alive in 1329/30, or at the very least that many influential people strongly believed that he was. They must have had convincing evidence to risk so much in order to save him. According to several chroniclers, the earl of Kent told parliament that a friar came to him, telling him he had raised a demon who informed him that Edward II was still alive.[18] This is either a desperate fabrication by Kent to protect his real source, or an invention inserted into his confession to discredit him. It is impossible that so many people, including an archbishop, a bishop, lords and sheriffs – politically astute men who had survived Edward's downfall – would have risked exile, imprisonment, forfeiture of their lands and goods and perhaps even execution because a demon-raising friar said Edward was alive. Many of the earl of Kent's adherents were imprisoned and their lands and goods seized (Sir William Cleydon died in prison later that year), others fled from the country (Sir Fulk Fitzwarin was one, and his two sons were imprisoned instead), and some were indicted before King's Bench. Many men took huge risks which, for all they knew, might even have included execution, and would not have done so if the only evidence they had of Edward II's survival was the word of a demon-raising friar. Nor did they take this risk because they were all stupid and gullible.

Some of the men named as Kent's adherents fled to the Continent and plotted an invasion of England: the plan was to land near Scotland with the aid of Donald, earl of Mar. Kent himself met his co-conspirators in the Paris chamber of Duke John III of Brabant, his and Edward II's nephew, who allowed the English exiles refuge in his territories (Edward II's sister Margaret, the dowager duchess, was still alive).[19] The impending invasion caused panic in England, and in mid-July 1330 Isabella and Roger Mortimer (presumably it was they, though the writs as always were issued in Edward III's name) ordered all the sheriffs in the country to array knights, squires and all other men who bore arms. The men should prepare themselves as speedily as possible to 'set out against certain Contrariants and rebels who lately withdrew secretly from the realm and who have assembled a multitude of men in parts beyond the sea and have prepared ships of war and other things and who purpose entering the realm to aggrieve the king and his people'.[20] In late July and early August 1330, mayors, sheriffs and bailiffs in London and more than thirty other towns were ordered to array knights and men-at-arms against the rebels overseas who intended to 'do what mischief they can'. Roger Mortimer himself was to array knights and other armed men in Gloucestershire, Herefordshire, Worcestershire and Shropshire, while Louis Beaumont, bishop of Durham (and brother of Henry Beaumont, one of the rebels), was ordered on 10 August to have knights, squires and others to be ready to 'set out against the said rebels if they invade the realm'.[21] Isabella and Roger Mortimer's enemies were doing to them what they had done to Edward II and the Despensers. The invasion in fact never came about, perhaps because Isabella and Mortimer's enemies did not want to seen to be rebelling against Edward III himself, with whom they had no quarrel. Richard Fitzalan, teenaged son of the earl of Arundel who had been murdered on Roger Mortimer's orders in November 1326, also took part in some kind of plot against Mortimer and Isabella in the summer of 1330, either the earl of Kent's conspiracy or one of his own: on 4 June 1330, two men were commissioned to find his adherents in Shropshire and Staffordshire.[22] It failed, and Fitzalan fled to the Continent, presumably to join the growing number of enemies to Isabella and Mortimer's regime there. Thomas, Lord Wake, Mortimer's cousin, the earl of Lancaster's son-in-law and the earl of Kent's brother-in-law, was another of those who fled the country sometime before 4 April 1330, 'fearing the cruelty and tyranny of the earl of March'.[23]

There is other evidence that Edward II did not die at Berkeley Castle in September 1327. Some years later, in the late 1330s or thereabouts, an Italian priest named Manuele Fieschi wrote a letter to Edward III. Fieschi was a nobleman by birth (some of his cousins were related to the English royal family, though Manuele himself was not), member of a family which produced two thirteenth-century popes and any number of cardinals and bishops, and the future bishop of Vercelli. The letter was discovered in a French archive in the late nineteenth century. In it, Fieschi explained how Edward II told him in person how he had escaped from Berkeley Castle with an attendant, killing a porter on his way, having been told that Sir Thomas Gurney and Sir Simon Bereford, an ally of Roger Mortimer, were coming to kill him. He made his way to Corfe Castle in Dorset, and on hearing much later of the execution of his half-brother the earl of Kent after trying to free him from Corfe, made his way to Ireland. Following Mortimer's execution a few months after this, Edward travelled to the Continent, met Pope John XXII at Avignon, went to Cologne, and finally to Italy, where he spent his time at a remote hermitage identifiable as Sant'Alberto di Butrio high in the hills between Milan and Genoa in northern Italy. On the other side of the valley from the hermitage stood the castle of Oramala, which in the 1330s was owned by a nephew of Cardinal Luca Fieschi, a kinsman of both Manuele Fieschi and Edward of Caernarfon himself. According to Manuele Fieschi, Edward lived at Sant'Alberto, devoting himself to good works and prayer. It is not clear from the letter whether Edward had died before Fieschi wrote it, or was still alive (as far as Fieschi knew it).

As hilariously implausible as it sounds that a king of England might escape from captivity at Berkeley Castle by the simple expedient of killing a porter, then make his way to Italy and live out the remaining years of his life after his supposed death and funeral in secret, silent contemplation, it is difficult to discount the letter entirely, or to understand why Manuele Fieschi would have sent it to Edward III unless he thought it were true. There is much in the letter about Edward II's movements in south Wales after Isabella's invasion and before his forced deposition which is accurate and could only have been known to a handful of people, such as the king's attempting to sail from his half-brother the earl of Norfolk's castle of Chepstow in October 1326, and being at sea for several days. This latter fact appears neither in any chronicle nor in the chancery rolls, and is only known to historians thanks to the fortunate survival of Edward's last chamber account. The letter does at the very least imply that there was some doubt in Europe in the 1330s as to whether Edward II had really died in September 1327: if this were a known and certain fact, Fieschi would not have been taken in by an impostor pretending to be the king of England's father (and Fieschi refers throughout the letter to the man he met as 'your father', i.e. Edward III's, as though he is sure of the identification, not 'the man claiming to be your father'). Fieschi's first cousin Percivalle Fieschi was bishop of the town of Tortona just a few miles from Sant'Alberto, and had accompanied Cardinal Luca Fieschi to England when he met Edward II in 1317. It was thus easily within Manuele Fieschi's power to check the identity of the man he met – it is unclear whether he himself had ever seen Edward in person during his reign, but certainly he knew and was closely related to people who had – and it is thus difficult to imagine how he could have been deceived by an impostor. Neither would blackmail, frequently Fieschi's suggested motive for inventing a story to tell Edward III about his father's escape, have worked if the young king had known for certain that his father had died in 1327. Additionally, Fieschi was a member of a wealthy, extremely well-connected and powerful noble family, not a humble or ignorant parish priest who had no means of checking the identity of the man who said he was Edward of Caernarfon, and he had no reason to try to blackmail anyone for position and influence.[24]

It is entirely possible, even likely, that Edward III did not know for certain in the 1330s whether his father had died in 1327. He began disseminating the news of Edward II's death before he could possibly have verified it (and indeed seems never to have sent men to Berkeley Castle to verify it), and neither he nor anyone else saw Edward II's face before his funeral, as the body lay in a coffin topped by a wooden effigy. It is also impossible that the earl of Kent, who attended the funeral, would have later come to believe that Edward was still alive if he had seen the body properly, and if Edward's own son and brother were not able to see and identify him, it seems most unlikely that anyone else was either. It is extremely probable that William Melton, archbishop of York, also attended Edward II's funeral, as he had long been a friend and ally of the king (whom he had known since 1297 or earlier when Edward was barely into his teens), had spoken out against the king's deposition at the parliament of January 1327 and refused to attend Edward III's coronation out of loyalty to the young king's father. And Melton stated outright in January 1330, more than two years after the funeral, that Edward II was then alive and in good health.

When Edward III was at Koblenz in Germany in early September 1338 to meet the Holy Roman Emperor Louis or Ludwig of Bavaria, he met a man named in his accounts as William *le Galeys*, William the

Welshman. William Norwell, keeper of Edward III's wardrobe, who had served Edward II from 1313 onwards as well as his son, described this man in the royal wardrobe account as 'William le Galeys, who asserts that he is the father of the present king' and 'who calls himself king of England, father of the present king'.[25] Royal pretenders were almost invariably executed, but William the Welshman was not, and spent time with Edward III. Edward II was born in Caernarfon in north Wales and was the first heir to the English throne to receive the title of prince of Wales – the only title he never gave up to his son. As with the Fieschi Letter, Edward III's account does not say that William 'falsely' claimed to be the king's father. It seems as though William was brought to Edward III the fifty-five miles to Koblenz from Cologne at the king's own command.[26] The Fieschi Letter also states that Edward of Caernarfon went to Cologne before he ended up in Italy. A now empty tomb at the hermitage of Sant'Alberto di Butrio is claimed as Edward II's, and many Italians remember being told the story of a fugitive English king who died in Italy as children.

And finally, there are the curious words of Edward II's 1327 custodian Thomas, Lord Berkeley, to parliament in November 1330, after Isabella and Roger Mortimer's downfall. This was the parliament which condemned Lord Berkeley's father-in-law Mortimer to death, one of the fourteen charges against him being that he had had Edward taken to Berkeley Castle in order to have him killed. Thomas Gurney and William Ockley were also sentenced to death in absentia for Edward's murder (John Maltravers, Edward's joint custodian of 1327, was given a death sentence in absentia for his role in the earl of Kent's execution a few months earlier, but he was never accused of any complicity in Edward II's death or of mistreating him in any way). When asked how he wished to acquit himself of involvement in the former king's death, Lord Berkeley said '*quod ipset nunquam fuit consentiens, auxilians, seu procurans, ad mortem suam, nec unquam scivit de morte sua usque in presenti parliament isto*', 'that he was never an accomplice, a helper or a procurer in his death, nor did he ever know of his death until this present parliament'.[27] These words, Berkeley stating that he had not heard of Edward II's death until the parliament of November 1330 more than three years after Edward's alleged murder, are peculiar given that it was a letter sent by Lord Berkeley himself which informed Edward III of his father's death during the night of 23/24 September 1327, and especially as Edward III had immediately begun disseminating news of the death on receipt of this letter. Berkeley's speech has generally been over-elaborately translated by modern historians to mean that he was saying he did not know that Edward II had been murdered, or that he knew nothing of the circumstances of the death, even though it happened in his own castle. But his words say that he did not know of

Edward's death until he attended the Westminster parliament three years later, no more, no less.

So did Edward II die at Berkeley Castle in September 1327 or not? This is a question of paramount importance to a consideration of Isabella of France and her life, as she has so often been assumed to have ordered her husband's murder, or at least to have been delighted to hear of it and to have continued to live with the murderer in the full knowledge of what he had done. Isabella did not hate her husband, which is usually a reason given for her acceptance of his murder or even her ordering of it. She must have been furious with Edward for his excessive favouritism towards the hated Hugh Despenser and his tolerance of Despenser's edging her out of her rightful position as Edward's consort, and she grieved for what she saw as the loss of her marriage, but it would have been a long step from anger and grief to tolerating or ordering the murder of her own husband and king, the father of her children. Isabella's referring to Edward even in 1325/26 as her 'very sweet heart' and 'very dear and very sweet lord and friend', trying to reconcile with him, telling Roger Mortimer she wished to return to him, avenging herself savagely on the man she held responsible for the destruction of her marriage, sending Edward letters and gifts even after the deposition for which she had been primarily responsible, suggest that she still loved him, not that she loathed him and wished him dead. Isabella rebelled against Edward's favourite and ultimately against the king himself, and brought him down whether she had wished for this or not; it does not necessarily follow that her actions against the king means that she loathed the man, her husband. It is hard to imagine that Isabella, daughter of an autocratic king of France and a queen regnant, sister of three kings and mother of another, a woman with a profound and sacred sense of royalty, could have tolerated the murder of a man as royal as she herself was, particularly by a method as foul and agonising as the mythical red-hot poker. History has done Isabella of France an injustice by holding her responsible for something so evil. Edward II's ultimate fate remains one of the greatest mysteries of English history, but given that so many influential people in the late 1320s and 1330s strongly believed that he was still alive and acted on it, we should take the notion seriously. Pretending that Edward was dead in September 1327 but secretly keeping him alive would have given Isabella and Mortimer, if they were the ones responsible, all the advantages of a dead king – putting an abrupt end to the plots to free him and restore him to the throne and thus safeguarding their own position – without having to kill Isabella's own royal husband. What Isabella knew about her husband's fate, when she knew it and what role she played in the conspiracy to present him as dead when he was not, must remain part of the mystery; we cannot, unfortunately, come to any firm conclusions. If the man buried at Gloucester in December

1327 was not Edward II, someone was killed and buried in his place, and his identity remains unknown. But there is a strong possibility that Edward was not murdered, and therefore, Isabella was no regicide and mariticide.

14

Downfall

1330

Just a month before the earl of Kent's execution on 19 March 1330, Isabella finally consented to the coronation of her daughter-in-law Philippa of Hainault as queen of England. Philippa was now about fifteen or sixteen and five months pregnant with her first child – the child who if male would be the next king of England – and it was becoming scandalous that she had not yet been crowned. A shortened ceremony, to take account of her pregnancy, took place at Westminster Abbey. A few weeks before she herself gave birth, Philippa received news that her sister Joan, countess of Jülich had borne a child, and Joan's messenger Colard Maloysel was given a generous gift of 25 marks for travelling to England with the news.[1] On 15 June 1330, at the royal palace of Woodstock near Oxford, Queen Philippa gave birth to Isabella's first grandchild, named Edward after his father, grandfather and great-grandfather. Known to history as the Black Prince, Edward of Woodstock would grow up to be a great warrior in the mould of his father. He famously fought at Crécy at the age of only sixteen in 1346, and captured King John II of France at the battle of Poitiers in 1356, but died a year before his father and thus never succeeded as king. Edward III was still only seventeen in June 1330, and Isabella, who had borne Edward probably shortly before she turned seventeen herself, was only thirty-four when she became a grandmother. She was at Woodstock on 30 May when she wrote to the chancellor of England (who was her ally Henry Burghersh, bishop of Lincoln), and presumably stayed there for a while longer until Philippa gave birth.[2] After the birth, Isabella and Edward III travelled to Gloucester and Tewkesbury, and made a formal visit to Edward II's burial place.[3]

Isabella may not have realised it, but her son the king, chafing at her tutelage, was plotting against her. Sometime in 1329 or 1330, he sent his friend and trusted ally William Montacute – whose father of the same name had been powerful at Edward II's court and a close friend of the king in the mid- to late 1310s – to Pope John XXII with a letter. It contained the words *Pater Sancte* ('Holy Father' in Latin) in Edward III's own hand, the earliest extant example of a king of England's handwriting. Any future letters sent by the king himself would include these words written in his own hand as a code, which John XXII would now be able to recognise. Any which did not could be assumed to have been sent in the king's name by his mother or Roger Mortimer or others, and could be discounted.

Edward III's problem was that he could not simply go off and raise an army against his mother without her noticing. He had to find considerably more subtle ways of ridding himself of her and her hated favourite Roger Mortimer, who by this point was becoming unbearably arrogant and behaving as though he himself were king. He was appallingly discourteous to Edward, walking alongside him or even ahead of him, remaining seated in his presence, and going around everywhere with a retinue greater than the king's. Astonishingly, he even ordered that his word was to be obeyed above the king's, and there was a rumour, reported by Geoffrey le Baker much later so possibly not entirely accurate, that Mortimer wished to destroy the royal blood and usurp the throne. Baker calls Mortimer *amasius regine et regis magister*, 'the lover of the queen and the master of the king'.[4] Mortimer's own son Geoffrey openly mocked him as the King of Folly, because he was 'so full of pride'.[5] Isabella herself apparently tolerated her favourite's rudeness towards her royal son; as her husband had allowed his favourite Hugh Despenser the Younger to treat her with blatant disrespect, so she allowed Mortimer to do the same to her son the king. This probably indicates that she was dependent on Mortimer in some way, either politically or emotionally or both; had she not been, she would presumably not have tolerated his rudeness towards her son. Edward III himself, however, could no longer be expected to endure such disrespect. In the autumn of 1330, matters came to a head.

It was the evening of Friday 19 October 1330. Isabella, Roger Mortimer, Edward III and numerous members of the English nobility and episcopate were staying at Nottingham to attend a session of parliament. Mortimer, wary, lodged in the castle, as did Isabella, who took personal possession of the castle keys.[6] They badly insulted Isabella's uncle Henry, earl of Lancaster by insisting that he lodge outside the city and be chaperoned by the king's first cousin John de Bohun, earl of Hereford and constable of England, having firstly rebuked a servant for daring to lodge an enemy of Queen Isabella's so close to her.[7] Suspicious, and rightly so, that the young king was plotting against him with Sir William Montacute and other close friends such as Sir William Clinton, Sir Robert Ufford and

Sir Ralph Stafford, Mortimer had them all questioned before his council. All of the young men remained silent except Montacute, who vigorously denied any plot against the royal favourite. Montacute, according to the later *Scalacronica*, advised Edward III to act against Mortimer on the grounds that 'it is better to eat the dog than be eaten by the dog'.[8] Edward III was not quite eighteen years old. He was father to a son and had thus secured the succession to his throne. His wife had been humiliated by his mother, as he had himself, and both would have felt suffocated and had been kept short of money, a tactic Edward II had inflicted on Isabella herself in 1324. Despite her utter rage at being deprived of her lands and income, she did the same thing to her son and daughter-in-law, who had no more mind to tolerate it than she had. Isabella and Mortimer also filled Edward III's household with spies, which made the king absolutely furious: he later accused Mortimer of making him feel like he was a man living in captivity.[9] When William Eland, a man who knew Nottingham Castle well – though was not, as sometimes stated, its constable – informed Edward of a secret tunnel leading into the stronghold, the young king realised he would never have a better time to act.

Isabella was in her bedchamber in the castle with Mortimer, a situation not nearly as intimate as it might sound to modern ears: in the Middle Ages the royal bedchamber was frequently used as a place to hold meetings, and also present were Henry Burghersh, bishop of Lincoln, Sir Hugh Turplington, Sir Oliver Ingham, Sir Simon Bereford and Mortimer's son Geoffrey, most of the few remaining allies the dowager queen and the earl of March still had. Meanwhile, Edward III was feigning illness, possibly with the connivance of his Italian physician Pancio Controne (who had previously served his father). With him were a small number of young knights, including Montacute, Clinton, Ufford, Stafford, John Neville of Hornby and the king's first cousin Edward de Bohun, and a squire called John Molyns, formerly an adherent of the Despensers and Hugh the Younger's valet.[10] Edward III clearly took advantage of a situation which conveniently presented itself, and the attack was probably carried out fairly spontaneously with at most a few hours' preparation, but equally clearly, the young king had been planning some kind of action against his mother and Mortimer for a considerable time. It was no coincidence that he had gathered a group of young knights around him whom he knew he could trust and who would support him, and his sending William Montacute to Pope John XXII with a secret coded letter earlier in 1330 or in 1329 also shows that he was intending to assert himself against Isabella and Mortimer.

The young knights and the king made their way quietly through the secret passage into the castle and burst into Isabella's chamber. John Neville of Hornby killed Sir Hugh Turplington, the steward of Edward III's household and a Mortimer ally, who was shouting, 'You shall all die an evil death here!'[11] Mortimer's squire Richard de Monmouth, who had escaped from the Tower with him in 1323, was also killed.[12] According to Geoffrey le Baker, Isabella, realising what was happening, cried out to her son, '*Beal fitz, beal fitz, eiez pitie de gentil Mortymer!*'[13] This is usually translated as 'Fair son, fair son, have pity on gentle Mortimer!', though *gentil* means 'noble' in the sense of being of high birth, not 'gentle' in the modern English sense. The *Brut* chronicle also has her saying, rather wordily, 'Now, fair sires, I pray you that you do no harm unto his body; [he is] a worthy knight, our well beloved friend and our dear cousin.'[14]

Roger Mortimer was seized, bound and gagged, and hustled out of the castle. Meanwhile, the bishop of Lincoln tried, humiliatingly and unsuccessfully, to escape down a latrine chute, and Geoffrey Mortimer, Sir Oliver Ingham and Sir Simon Bereford were also arrested. Geoffrey and Ingham were soon released; Bereford was not. Isabella, helpless, her power and influence suddenly, shockingly gone, was treated with consideration by her son but held in temporary captivity with guards placed on her room, and if she continued to plead on behalf of Mortimer it had no effect whatsoever. Mortimer was taken from Nottingham to imprisonment at the Tower of London via Loughborough and Leicester, two towns belonging to Henry, earl of Lancaster, one of which had been sacked by Mortimer less than two years before.[15] This is surely no coincidence. Isabella, meanwhile, was sent under guard to Berkhamsted Castle twenty-five miles from London.

On 25 November 1330, parliament began at Westminster. Roger Mortimer, still gagged and bound and thus not able to speak in his own defence, was accused and convicted of the murder of Edward II and thirteen other charges, mostly of usurping Edward III's royal power, and of causing discord between Edward II and Isabella and persuading the queen that she would be killed if she returned to her husband. Otherwise, Isabella was not mentioned, and Mortimer was made the scapegoat for the disasters of the past few years, as Hugh Despenser had been for Edward II's failed reign. Only four days later, on 29 November, Mortimer was dragged from the Tower to The Elms at Tyburn wearing the black tunic he had worn to Edward II's funeral three years before; someone, probably Edward III himself, who remembered that piece of hypocrisy, sent for the tunic and forced Mortimer to wear it. On the scaffold, Mortimer admitted his responsibility for the death of the earl of Kent eight months before, but did not mention Isabella or the death of Edward II. His tunic was stripped off leaving him naked, and Psalm 52, which had been carved or scrawled on the body of Hugh Despenser the Younger four years earlier, almost to the day, was read out to him.[16] Edward III spared Mortimer the full horrors of the traitor's death and he was merely hanged, though Tyburn had been a place of execution for common criminals since the 1190s and noblemen could normally expect to be beheaded rather than hanged – a privilege of rank as it was generally a much quicker death (with the notable exception of the horribly slow and painful beheading Mortimer inflicted on his cousin Arundel in 1326). The king was definitely making a point.

Roger Mortimer's body was buried in the Greyfriars or Franciscans' church in Coventry, not, as the chronicler Adam Murimuth states and as many people still believe today, in the Greyfriars church in London where Isabella was buried many years later. It is possible, though, that the Franciscans of London took temporary charge of the body until their Coventry brethren came to claim it or it could be transported there, hence Murimuth's confusion on this point. On 7 November 1331, just under a year after the execution, Edward III gave Mortimer's widow, Joan Geneville, permission to have his body moved from the Greyfriars in Coventry to Wigmore in Herefordshire, the Mortimers' ancestral home. It is not clear, however, if his remains were indeed moved – Joan petitioned the king for permission to let her husband be 'interred amongst his ancestors' in Wigmore again sometime in 1332 because the Coventry brethren had refused to do anything about her request – and therefore it is unfortunately impossible to determine where Roger Mortimer's remains lie today.[17] At Christmas 1330, Mortimer's ally Sir Simon Bereford was also hanged, the only other man besides Mortimer to suffer the death penalty. Bereford is rather obscure and his role in Mortimer's misdeeds not entirely clear, though the November 1330 parliament declared him guilty of aiding Mortimer in all his felonies. The Fieschi Letter states that he was one of the two men who went to murder Edward II at Berkeley Castle, which may be true but is unconfirmed by other sources (no chronicler mentions him in this context). Presumably, Edward III thought he had good reasons to hang him, even if they and Bereford himself remain somewhat obscure to modern historians.

The claim by the later chronicler Jean Froissart that Isabella was pregnant when she and Mortimer fell from power is unlikely to be true, and is not supported by any other evidence. If Isabella were indeed pregnant and miscarried a child, it is unclear how Froissart could have known this when no English chronicler so much as hinted at the possibility, or why anyone in her family or retinue would have told him something so private and scandalous. Even if she were, the pregnancy did not result in a living child, though the strange and wildly improbable notion that the dowager queen secretly gave birth to a son called William Alfred or William Knight (or William Alfred Knight) who was smuggled out of court by one of her allies and who later married and had children has become inexplicably popular on genealogy websites of the twenty-first century. There is not a shred of evidence for this story. Isabella made some arrangements regarding her will in 1329, for example requesting on 1 September that year that 'whenever she shall happen to die, her executors may dispose of all her jewels and goods and execute her testament as may seem to them best for the good estate of her soul without interference from the king'.[18] She had first made her will (which does not survive) in October 1312 when eight months pregnant with her first child, and therefore modern writers have sometimes speculated that she was pregnant again seventeen years later. This is not impossible, but there were other reasons besides pregnancy why the minds of thirteenth and fourteenth-century people turned to their testaments and the arrangements they wished to be made after their death. Perhaps Isabella was ill, or perhaps her preparations are an indication of her inner turmoil or her realisation of the turbulence and political dangers of the period. Still only in her mid-thirties, she had already lost the last of her siblings in 1328; two of her sisters-in-law, Clemence of Hungary and Joan of Burgundy, also died during the period 1328–30; she probably already knew in the autumn of 1329 that her brother-in-law the earl of Kent and others were plotting to release her supposedly dead husband from captivity and perhaps also that her son the king was growing restless and dissatisfied. Anticipating that her situation might change for the worse in the not too distant future might have been reason enough for Isabella to wish to update her will, rather than the assumption that she was pregnant. People often made wills when they were ill or in some way involved in a risky situation: Edward II's father Edward I, for example, made his when on crusade in the Holy Land in 1272 (and never updated it for the remaining thirty-five years of his life), and Isabella's father Philip IV first made his in May 1311, three and a half years before he died, perhaps because of illness.[19] In the final reckoning, the true nature of Isabella's relationship with Roger Mortimer from late 1325 until October 1330 is unknown and forever unknowable.

Edward III surveyed the damage: his treasury was empty, the almost £80,000 it had held four years previously now reduced to the paltry amount of a little over £40, and much of his inheritance in Gascony and Scotland had been given away. On 20 October 1330, the day after Mortimer's arrest, he ordered all his sheriffs to issue a proclamation which demonstrates how unimpressed he was with events of the past four years, stating that the affairs of the kingdom 'have been directed until now to the damage and dishonour of him and his realm'.[20] He called a parliament to be held at Westminster to put right 'the matters touching the king and his realm after his accession [which] have been hitherto conducted to the king's damage and to the shame and impoverishment of his people,' and also had it proclaimed that 'the king understands that diverse oppressions and hardships have been inflicted upon many men of his realm by certain persons who have been his ministers', asking his subjects to bring their grievances to parliament.[21] And so fell a regime which had equalled, and surely exceeded, even that of Edward II and Hugh Despenser the Younger in rapacity and unpopularity. So precarious had Isabella and Mortimer's position become, so tiny their circle of allies, that it took Isabella's son and barely twenty other men a matter of minutes to overthrow them.

At the parliament of November 1330, Edmund of Woodstock, earl of Kent was pardoned seven months after his judicial murder, and his small son and heir, Edmund, restored to his inheritance (young Edmund died as a child sometime before 13 October 1331 and Kent's other son, the posthumous John, died childless in December 1352, and so Kent's ultimate heir was his daughter Joan, princess of Wales).[22] Kent's co-conspirators who had fled the kingdom were invited to return and restored to their lands and goods, including Richard Fitzalan, son of the earl of Arundel killed in 1326, who became one of the richest men in England and lived until 1376.[23] Thomas Wake and William la Zouche, who had joined the earl of Kent, also returned and were appointed as the mainpernors of Roger Mortimer's son Geoffrey in 1331.[24] The parliamentary record pardoning the earl of Kent is hilariously keen to state that Edward II was, in fact, dead; it states no fewer than four times within a few lines that it had been impossible for the earl to rescue a dead man, a man who was dead, really truly dead, and who had been dead for a long time. Whether Edward III really believed that his father was dead or not, he had no choice but to continue the pretence that he was.

After Mortimer's arrest, Isabella was sent to live at the castle of Berkhamsted. On 21 December 1330, Edward III ordered four men to bring his mother from there to spend Christmas with him (and presumably his queen and baby son) at Windsor. The men were Thomas Wake, Roger Mortimer's first cousin, recently returned to England; Eubolo Lestrange, second husband of Isabella's aunt by marriage Alice Lacy, countess of Lincoln; and Isabella's nephews-in-law William and Edward de Bohun, who were twins, the sons of Edward II's sister Elizabeth and younger brothers of the earl of Hereford.[25] Isabella remained under a kind of honourable house arrest at Windsor Castle for a while: on 6 March 1332, the castle constable was reimbursed the 'expenses incurred by him in safe-keeping Queen Isabella in that castle for some time by the king's order'.[26] Edward III even put guards on his mother's jewels and other possessions stored at the Tower of London.[27] Her lands were taken into her son's hands on 1 December 1330 (this seizure was presented as a voluntary surrender, which it certainly was not) in exchange for an annual income of £3,000 from the exchequer, and the king appointed keepers to look after them. Most of them were restored to her a year later in November 1331, though she only received the northern French county of Ponthieu – which had been Edward

II's inheritance from his mother Eleanor of Castile and which he later granted to his wife – in September 1334, 'in remembrance of the divine precept that sons should reverence their parents and of filial duty, and that she may have such increase of honour as becomes her estate'.[28] In the nineteenth century Agnes Strickland suggested that Isabella became insane with grief after Mortimer's execution and thereafter suffered periodic bouts of madness, but as she believed that Isabella was confined for the rest of her life at Castle Rising and that her son 'forbade her ever to go out', which is nonsense, this opinion does not count for very much, for all that it has often been repeated ever since.[29]

John XXII, 800 miles away from Nottingham in Avignon, received the news of Mortimer's arrest ('the pope has heard that on 19 October, about the middle of the night, the king suddenly seized some princes and nobles of the realm') on 3 November 1330, fifteen days after it had happened. Keen to protect Isabella and having heard that Edward 'was not showing signs of filial affection towards her', the pope sent two letters to the king, one a duplicate in case the other got lost, begging him to 'remember what his mother has done for him and what enmity and ill-will she has provoked against herself in his service'. John 'begs him [Edward III] to show mercy [to Isabella], so that he himself may find it in the day of judgement', and also wrote to the young Queen Philippa asking her to insist that her husband renewed his goodwill towards his mother. Having sent these letters, the pope then heard from an English merchant passing through Avignon that Edward III 'is behaving with humanity and reverence towards his mother', and wrote another letter to commend him (this gives an interesting insight into how news travelled around Europe in the fourteenth century).[30] John XXII wrote again to Edward and Philippa in the summer of 1331, exhorting them to reverence and honour Isabella and visit her often, 'so that her good fame may remain intact, and evil report be silenced'.[31] He took the line that Isabella's actions from 1326 to 1330 had been motivated out of selfless devotion to her son's interests rather than her own, which was a rather positive spin to put on it.

Isabella of France lived for another twenty-eight years, but the drama, excitement and perhaps passion of her life was now over. She had lost control of her own destiny, and the remainder of her life would pass entirely conventionally, as though the years 1325 to 1330 had never happened.

PART THREE

The Dowager Queen

15

A Conventional
Queen Again
1330–1358

There are numerous tall tales often repeated about Isabella of France and the last twenty-eight years of her life after her son removed her from power. She did not go mad; she was not incarcerated in Castle Rising; she was not immured in a nunnery. In fact, Isabella lived a purely conventional life as a dowager queen, travelling around her estates, making pilgrimages, entertaining numerous members of the English nobility and her own family for dinner, listening to music, and – as always – spending vast amounts of money on clothes and jewels. Isabella did spend a lot of time at Castle Rising in Norfolk, but only because it was her favourite residence, and the notion that her son imprisoned her there is disproved by the fact that she died at Hertford Castle in 1358. The story that her mad, screaming ghost haunts Castle Rising to this day is often repeated on websites. She survived the first horrendous outbreak of the Black Death in 1348/49, as other members of the English nobility and royalty did not: Isabella's thirteen-year-old granddaughter Joan, second daughter of Edward III and Philippa of Hainault, died in the south of France in the summer of 1348 on her way to marry Pedro, king of Castile. Other possible victims of the Black Death, members of the nobility who died in 1348/49, included Isabella's former ward Thomas, Lord Wake, his sister Margaret, countess of Kent and widow of Edmund of Woodstock, Isabella's goddaughter Isabella Verdon, Hugh Despenser the Younger's son Hugh, or Huchon, and Isabella's aunt by marriage Alice Lacy, countess of Lincoln.

In June 1345, Isabella gave a parcel of land called 'Babbelake' to the gild of St John the Baptist in Coventry, for them to build a chapel in which 'to celebrate divine service daily for the good estate of the king, the said queen [Isabella], Queen Philippa, Edward, prince of Wales ... and for the souls of Edward II and John de Eltham, late earl of Cornwall, the king's brother'. This is evidence that Isabella knew her husband was dead by then; an earlier grant of land by Isabella in May 1343 to the Coventry gild of St John the Baptist in exchange for their prayers on behalf of the royal family refers to praying for the soul of her younger son, the late John of Eltham, but not Edward II's.[1] At some unspecified date perhaps as early as the 1360s, this chapel expanded to include a college, and the prestigious Bablake School still exists to this day.

From the early 1340s onwards, Edward III's visits to his mother became more regular, but the king's biographer believes that 'theirs is hardly likely to have been an affectionate relationship ... Edward III could never quite free himself from the embarrassment of his parents'.[2] Edward showed himself to be considerably more forgiving and less vindictive than his parents, especially his father: Hugh Despenser the Younger's son Huchon, imprisoned from early 1327 until after Isabella's downfall, made a good career at his court and made an excellent marriage to the earl of Salisbury's daughter, and Edward allowed Roger Mortimer's namesake grandson to have the contentious earldom of March in 1354. The younger Roger Mortimer's son and heir, Edmund, married Edward III's own granddaughter Philippa of Clarence, only child and heiress of the king's second son, Lionel, which in the 1390s during Richard II's reign brought the Mortimers close to the throne. Edward III was not a man to blame the son for the sins of the father, and he showed a similar lack of anger and vindictiveness towards his mother and regularly sent her letters and gifts at the end of her life (and presumably earlier as well, but her accounts do not survive). It is always difficult to ascertain people's affection, or otherwise, for their family members from fourteenth-century sources, but it may be revealing that when Edward III founded a chapel at Westminster in 1348, he dedicated it to the Virgin Mary and described her as a 'better mother'.[3] Edward III did shield Isabella from criticism and attack, and put all the blame for the disasters of the period from 1327 to 1330 on Roger Mortimer, at least in public. To what extent he did this out of genuine affection and filial loyalty, or because he derived his claims to the throne of France from Isabella as his royal mother and found it unwise to treat her too harshly and perhaps jeopardise those claims, is impossible to say.

Isabella of France's household accounts for the last few months of her life in 1357/58 fortuitously survive, as they do not for the previous twenty-seven years following her downfall. On 15 December 1357, she was visited by 'the countess of Pembroke', with whom she also exchanged letters and gifts. It is usually assumed that this woman was Roger Mortimer's daughter Agnes, widow of Laurence Hastings, earl of Pembroke, and it has thus been romantically stated that the dowager queen and her dead lover's daughter 'became close friends and hardly ever separated', a rather bold assertion to make on the strength of one visit and several letters exchanged.[4] The countess of Pembroke in contact with Isabella, however, was not Agnes Hastings née Mortimer but Marie de Châtillon – also sometimes known as Marie of St Pol – who was a great-granddaughter of King Henry III and the widow of Aymer de Valence, Laurence Hastings' great-uncle and predecessor as earl of Pembroke. (Marie's older sister Mahaut was the third wife of Isabella's uncle Charles of Valois.) Countess Marie and Queen Isabella formed half of a circle of four ladies, friends and relatives of similar age who kept in frequent touch for many years, the other two being Edward II's nieces Joan of Bar, countess of Surrey and Elizabeth de Clare. These three ladies all survived Isabella. Elizabeth died in 1360, Joan in 1361 – her husband John de Warenne's long and increasingly desperate attempts to have their marriage annulled had failed – and Marie in 1377, having outlived her husband Aymer de Valence by a remarkable fifty-three years. Elizabeth and Marie both founded colleges at Cambridge University: Clare and Pembroke. There seems no particular reason why Roger Mortimer's daughter Agnes would become a close friend of the dowager queen, and in fact she did not. Mortimer's widow, Joan Geneville, meanwhile, died at the age of seventy on 19 October 1356, twenty-two months before Isabella and on the twenty-sixth anniversary of her husband's arrest at Nottingham. Joan was a great-grandmother many times over by 1356, and at the time of her death was the grandmother of the earls of March and Pembroke and the mother-in-law of the earl of Warwick. She outlived eight of her and Roger's twelve children.

Isabella was visited three times in 1357/58 by the *comes de la March* (earl or count of March), who is usually assumed to have been Roger Mortimer's namesake grandson and heir, Roger Mortimer, born in 1328 as the only son of Roger's eldest son, Edmund, and made second earl of March in 1354. On one occasion, the *comes de la March* dined with Isabella in the company of her son the king and grandson the prince of Wales. In yet another example of the romanticising which bedevils much modern writing about Isabella and her association with the elder Roger Mortimer, it has been stated that this man 'was the grandson of her lover and was specially favoured by the old Queen', with no evidence cited for this alleged 'special favour' except that he dined with her three times, as did plenty of other people.[5] The *comes de la March* who visited Isabella in the last few months of her life was not, in fact, Roger Mortimer the English earl of March but Jacques de Bourbon, the French count of La Marche, who was a great-grandson of Saint Louis IX and Isabella's second cousin.[6] Jacques de Bourbon was taken prisoner by Isabella's grandson the prince of Wales at the battle of Poitiers in 1356, as was

King John II (son of her first cousin Philip VI). Isabella kept in touch with the French king while he was in captivity in England – she lent him two books, French romances about the Holy Grail and Lancelot – and was regularly visited by members of his entourage who accompanied him there or who visited him regularly, including the counts of Tancarville and La Marche and the lords of Audrehem and d'Aubigny.[7] The identification of the *comes de la March* with the English earl of March has been made since the nineteenth century, but is incorrect.

Isabella was not visited by or otherwise in contact with any of Roger Mortimer's family in 1357/58, contrary to common belief, and she did not mark the anniversary of his execution on 29 November. We should not infer evidence of absence from absence of evidence regarding the queen's sentiments towards her late husband, Edward II, as one modern historian has done, claiming that Isabella's accounts are 'silent on any memory of or regret for' Edward of Caernarfon, apart from donating food to the poor on the anniversary of his supposed death on 21 September.[8] There is no evidence that Isabella remembered or regretted her favourite Roger Mortimer of almost three decades previously, either – something he fails to mention. Using this argument, we could 'prove' that Isabella never gave Mortimer a second thought after his 1330 execution, given that neither he nor his family are mentioned in her last account (for all the romanticising that Isabella and Mortimer's daughter Agnes became close friends, which they did not, and that Isabella specially favoured Mortimer's grandson, which she did not). Isabella's elder daughter, Eleanor of Woodstock, who died in 1355, does not appear in her account of 1357/58 either, which cannot be and is not used as evidence of Isabella's lack of 'memory of or regret for' her dead child. People in the fourteenth century did not keep diaries expressing their feelings, and it is not as though we have a full record of the last twenty-eight years of Isabella's life in which Edward II is never mentioned. Household accounts, with their business-like entries detailing expenditure on food, gifts, clothes, charitable donations and so on, are extremely useful in their way but are a highly dubious method of gauging people's private sentiments towards their loved ones and family members. Isabella herself, for example, hardly ever appears in her husband's own chamber accounts of the 1320s. Confirmation bias can be a problem in historical writing: authors convinced that Isabella was 'delighted' when Edward II died will see the lack of many references to him in her household account at the end of her life as proof of her apathy towards or even hatred of him, while assuming that a few references to people they wrongly think were members of Roger Mortimer's family must be evidence of their belief that Isabella was passionately in love with Mortimer.

Isabella outlived two of her four children. Her second son, John of Eltham, earl of Cornwall, died unmarried and childless at the age of only twenty, in Scotland in September 1336. His tomb in Westminster Abbey still exists, carved with statues of crowned 'weepers', one of whom certainly represents Isabella, though it is unclear which.[9] Isabella's elder daughter, Eleanor of Woodstock, married the decades-older Reynald II, count and later duke of Guelders in the modern-day Netherlands, the month before her fourteenth birthday in May 1332. Eleanor gave birth to her first son a year after her wedding, before she even turned fifteen, and bore her second three years later. Her marriage was unhappy, her sons fought against one another and one imprisoned the other, both died without legitimate children, and the widowed Duchess Eleanor died in poverty on 22 April 1355. She was not yet thirty-seven. Isabella's second daughter, Joan of the Tower, also endured an unhappy and childless marriage to David II of Scotland, who allowed his English mistress or favourite Katherine Mortimer (no relation to Isabella's own favourite Roger Mortimer) to wield considerable power, echoing the behaviour of his parents-in-law with Piers Gaveston, Hugh Despenser and Roger Mortimer. Katherine was killed by some of David's exasperated barons in 1360, which also echoes the fate of Piers Gaveston. An offended Queen Joan returned to England in the late 1350s, and spent much time with her mother in the months before Isabella's death. Joan died on 7 September 1362 at the age of forty-one. Her widower, David II, married again but fathered no children with his second wife, Margaret Drummond, either, and when he died in February 1371 he was succeeded by his half-nephew Robert II, first of the house of Stewart, who rather curiously was eight years older than he. Isabella's eldest child, Edward III, was by far the longest lived of her children and also by far the happiest in his personal life: he had a long and extremely fruitful marriage with Philippa of Hainault. Edward III's eventful reign of half a century, the fifth longest in English history behind Elizabeth II, Victoria, George III and Henry III, ended on 21 June 1377 when he died at the age of sixty-four.

Isabella was active in the last months of her life: in October 1357 and again in early June 1358 she went on her final pilgrimages to Canterbury and the shrine of St Thomas Becket, and on both occasions visited Leeds Castle, where she had taken part in her husband's plot against Bartholomew Badlesmere and the Marcher lords in 1321. On 10 February 1358, messengers brought her news that Charles II 'the Bad', king of Navarre, her brother Louis X's grandson, had escaped from captivity at the castle of Arleux, where he had been imprisoned by his father-in-law John II of France. Isabella's son Edward III; her eldest two grandsons, the prince of Wales and the earl of Ulster (Lionel, born in 1338 and later duke of Clarence); and other members of her family visited her or sent gifts in the last few months of her life, including her first cousin Henry of Grosmont, first duke of Lancaster, son and heir of her uncle Henry, earl of Lancaster. There is nothing to show that anyone believed Isabella to be a notorious adulteress and murderess, to be shunned and reviled. On 26 October 1357, Edward III, Queen Philippa and the prince of Wales visited the dowager queen at her house in Lombard Street in London, where four minstrels performed for them, and Edward III visited her again on 20 March 1358 and also wrote to her on occasion with gifts of wine, wild boar and caged birds. As extravagant as ever, Isabella spent just under £1,400 on clothes, a falcon and jewels in the last months of her life – though in fairness, royals were expected to be profligate and to dress and look the part – including a chaplet of gold set with rubies, sapphires, emeralds, diamonds and pearls, and a crown of gold set with sapphires, rubies and pearls. She gave her daughter Joan, queen of Scotland, a black palfrey horse with an embroidered saddle with gold fittings, and repaid £200 she had borrowed from, of all people, Richard Fitzalan, son of the earl of Arundel killed on Roger Mortimer's orders in 1326 and who had rebelled against her in the summer of 1330. Still extremely keen on her books, Isabella paid Richard the Painter for buying azure paint to illustrate one or more and paid another man for six sheets of vellum to make her another. Also keen on music, she sent Walter Hert, one of her vielle-players (a vielle was a stringed instrument), to London to learn his craft at a 'school of minstrelsy', an entry which reveals the fascinating fact that there was some kind of school of music and performance in the English capital in the mid-fourteenth century. She became ill in February 1358 and sent a man to London to buy medicines for her, and paid her apothecary Nicholas Thomasyer for more medicines and her physician Master Laurence for attending her and her daughter Queen Joan for a month.

Isabella of France, dowager queen of England, died at Hertford Castle on Wednesday 22 August 1358 at the age of sixty-two. Her body remained in the castle chapel until 23 November, watched over day and night by fourteen 'poor persons' who each received 2*d* a day plus food for their services. She was one of the last surviving members of the Capetian dynasty, outlived only by some of her cousins including her sister-in-law the dowager queen of France Joan of Evreux, and her nieces Blanche, duchess of Orleans and Marguerite, countess of Flanders. Isabella's funeral took place on 27 November 1358, a little over three months after she died, a long delay between a royal death and burial being entirely normal in the fourteenth century. (Edward I died on 7 July 1307 and was buried on 27 October; Edward II supposedly died on 21 September 1327 and was buried on 20 December; Philippa of Hainault died on 15 August 1369 and was buried on 9 January 1370.) There is no reason to suppose that the date of 27 November was significant – it was two days before the anniversary of Roger Mortimer's execution on 29 November 1330 – as Edward III presumably decided the timing of the ceremony, not Isabella, and it doesn't seem terribly likely that she had asked her son to bury her almost but not quite on the anniversary.[10] In 1345, Isabella had obtained permission from the pope for her body to be divided after death and buried in three places, though this did not in fact happen.[11] The king met her funeral cortège when it arrived in London on 24 or 25 November 1358, and a man called John Galeys received £10 for the use of his house at Mile End 'for the time the body of Isabella, late queen of England, remained there with the king and his household'. On arrival at church, Isabella's body was covered with two cloths of fine white silk.[12]

Isabella was not buried next to her husband in distant Gloucester or with his parents Edward I and Eleanor of Castile in Westminster Abbey, but in the fashionable Greyfriars or Franciscans' church in London, where her aunt Queen Marguerite had also been buried in 1318. It is not clear whether this was her own choice or Edward III's; perhaps either she or her son thought it would be inappropriate for her to be lain to eternal rest next to Edward II, and Isabella had always favoured the Franciscan order. It is a romantic myth that she chose to lie next to Roger Mortimer or with his heart on her breast: Mortimer was buried over a hundred miles away at the Greyfriars church in Coventry, and his body may have been removed to Wigmore in Herefordshire. Besides, Edward III would never have permitted his royal mother to be buried next to a man whom he had executed for treason, even if she had wished and asked for it (and there is no evidence that she did). Isabella was, according to a rather later tradition, buried with a heart, but it was her husband Edward II's, not Mortimer's, placed on her chest in a silver casket. Separate heart burial was entirely normal in the royal family in the Middle Ages – the hearts of Edward II's mother, Eleanor of Castile, and her third son, Alfonso, were given to the Dominicans of London in 1290, for example, and that of Edward II's paternal grandmother, Eleanor of Provence, lay in the Franciscan church where Isabella was buried – so this was not as morbid or strange as it sounds. Isabella also asked to be buried with the clothes she had worn at her wedding to Edward II on 25 January 1308, fifty years and seven months before her death. Whether her body was dressed in them or if they were merely placed in the tomb with her is unclear; it would have been quite an achievement if she still fitted into clothes she had worn when she was twelve.[13] Her daughter Joan of the Tower, queen of Scotland, was buried in the same church four years later.[14] Edward III attended his mother's funeral. In contrast to later tradition, kings did visit funerals in the fourteenth century; Edward had also attended his father's in Gloucester in December 1327, and Edward II attended his own father's in 1307 as well as his sister Elizabeth's in 1316 and his stepmother, Marguerite's at the London Greyfriars church in 1318.[15] Isabella's tomb, sadly, was later lost: the sepulchral monuments of the Greyfriars church were sold during the Reformation in the sixteenth century, and the church itself was destroyed during the Great Fire of London in 1666, was rebuilt by Christopher Wren, and destroyed again by bombs during the Second World War. Roger Mortimer's final resting place is also uncertain. In this respect, Edward II and Hugh Despenser the Younger have fared better: Edward's magnificent tomb in Gloucester Cathedral is one of the great glories of medieval England, and Despenser's tomb still exists at Tewkesbury Abbey, just ten miles from Gloucester, as do those of many of his family. Isabella left her numerous books to her two surviving children, King Edward and Queen Joan, and her inquisition post mortem solemnly records that 'Sir Edward, now king of England, of full age, is her heir' and that she had died 'on the Wednesday before St Bartholomew last' in the thirty-second year of her son's reign.[16]

Isabella's dire reputation in the centuries after her death rests mostly on her assumed involvement with the murder of her husband, or at least on suspicion of standing by without protest as it happened, and on her assumed sexual 'immorality' because she had an affair with Roger Mortimer. However, there is a very good chance that Edward II was not murdered at all, and also a chance that Isabella's association with Mortimer was not a love affair (it may have been, but the notion is speculation and inference, not fact). So much of what we think we know about Isabella simply melts away when we examine the primary sources, and reveals itself as assumption, myth and pure fiction which over time has resolved itself into a certain narrative about the queen. Modern books about her follow a fixed storyline: Isabella marries a gay man who heartlessly neglects her, despite her yearning for his affection; sees her jewels or gifts given to his lover; is abandoned weeping and pregnant as her husband takes his lover instead of her to safety; comes to hate her husband and his lover; is delighted when the lover is killed; manages to create children with her husband despite her growing hatred and contempt for him (or in some cases sleeps with another man who fathers them); sees her children cruelly taken away from her; highly sexed and frustrated, falls deeply in love with a man vastly superior to her husband and schemes to help him escape; schemes some more in order to be reunited with her lover and to act with him against her husband; orders her husband's murder, continues living in sin with her lover and thus becomes a She-Wolf *par extraordinaire*; mourns her executed lover for many years, keeps in touch with his family and asks to be buried next to him; and so on. There is little if any evidence for any of this, but it has become the standard tale of Isabella of France's life, endlessly repeated and recycled in both fiction and (unfortunately) non-fiction with new myths and inventions added on occasion, such as the fabrication of the late 1970s that her children were removed from her care in 1324, a story found in no fourteenth-century source. The events of Isabella's life have all too often been examined with the benefit of centuries of hindsight and it is sometimes forgotten that she was living through those events, and did not know beforehand how things would work out. It is far too frequently assumed that because her marriage to Edward II ended badly, it must always have been a doomed, unhappy tragedy; that because she ended up rebelling against Edward she must have been planning and plotting to achieve this for a long time; that because she began some kind of relationship with Roger Mortimer in about late 1325 she must have been in love with him and scheming with him against Edward for years, and so on. This is looking at where Isabella ended up and then writing her life backwards, treating her as though she is a fictional character whose experiences can neatly be made to fit a pre-conceived plot.

Isabella was not a 'she-wolf' or a 'whore' or a 'bitch' or any of the other ugly, judgemental insults hurled at her. She did not kill her husband or hate him or feel repulsed by him, and was his loyal, affectionate supporter and ally for many years until finally his confiscation of her lands, excessive favouring of a man she loathed and removal of her from her rightful position at his side drove her into opposition – an opposition she did not wish for and found painful and difficult. Even then, Isabella gave Edward chances to put things right between them, but he refused and thus gave her no option but to act against him and ally herself with his greatest enemy, the only man with the will and the ability to remove the hated Despensers from Edward's side. Edward's subsequent rapid downfall may not have been something Isabella had desired or planned for, and the notion that she had been conspiring with his enemies for years to bring him down is sheer assumption without a scrap of evidence and most unlikely to be true. For all that Edward loved men, his and Isabella's marriage was far more successful for far longer than is generally supposed, and Isabella accepted her husband's favourites or lovers (if they were) without complaint until he allowed the last of them to destroy her position as queen, wife, landowner, intercessor and perhaps even as mother, given that the royal couple had no more children once Hugh Despenser the Younger had become dominant at court and in her husband's life.

Both Isabella and Edward II have been poorly served by writers, and were as far removed from their reputations in popular culture as any two people possibly could be. Edward was a million miles from being a cowardly, feeble but vicious, effeminate fop loathed by his wife; Isabella was a million miles both from being an evil, manipulative, vengeful, murderous she-wolf and a desperate housewife stuck in a supposedly hateful marriage on the search for true love who allowed herself to become the passive victim of unscrupulous men. The myths and inventions about them have become far better known than the reality, which is a pity, because their lives are fascinating and vivid enough without the tawdry melodramatic tales invented and embroidered in later times.

Abbreviations in Notes and Bibliography

AL: Annales Londonienses 1195-1330
AP: Annales Paulini 1307-1340
Anonimalle: The Anonimalle Chronicle 1307 to 1334
Baker: Chronicon Galfridi le Baker de Swynbroke (ed. Thompson)
BIHR: Bulletin of the Institute of Historical Research
Brut: The Brut or the Chronicles of England
Chaplais, *Gaveston:* Pierre Chaplais, Piers Gaveston: Edward II's
 Adoptive Brother
CCR: Calendar of Close Rolls
CChR: Calendar of Charter Rolls
CCW: Calendar of Chancery Warrants 1244-1326
CDS: Calendar of Documents Relating to Scotland 1307-1357
CFR: Calendar of Fine Rolls
CIM: Calendar of Inquisitions Miscellaneous 1308-1348
CIPM: Calendar of Inquisitions Post Mortem
CMR: Calendar of Memoranda Rolls Michaelmas 1326-Michaelmas
 1327
CPL: Calendar of Papal Letters 1305-1341
CPR: Calendar of Patent Rolls
Croniques: Croniques de London depuis l'an 44 Hen III jusqu'à l'an 17
 Edw III
Doherty, *Death*: Paul Doherty, Isabella and the Strange Death of
 Edward II
EHR: English Historical Review
Flores: Flores Historiarum, vol. iii
Foedera: Rhymer's Foedera, Conventiones, Litterae, 1307-1327
Gesta: Gesta Edwardi de Carnarvon Auctore Canonico Bridlingtoniensi

Haines, Edward: Roy Martin Haines, King Edward II

HB: The Household Book of Queen Isabella of England, ed. Blackley and Hermansen

Intrigue: Ian Mortimer, Medieval Intrigue

Itinerary: Elizabeth Hallam, The Itinerary of Edward II and his Household

JMH: Journal of Medieval History

Lanercost: The Chronicle of Lanercost 1272-1346

Livere: Le Livere de Reis de Britanie e le Livere de Reis de Engletere

Murimuth: Adae Murimuth Continuatio Chronicarum

ODNB: Oxford Dictionary of National Biography

Opposition: James Conway Davies, The Baronial Opposition to Edward II

Phillips: Seymour Phillips, Edward II

Polychronicon: Polychronicon Ranulphi Higden, vol. viii

PROME: The Parliament Rolls of Medieval England

RENP: Reign of Edward II: New Perspectives, ed. Dodd and Musson

SAL MS: Society of Antiquaries of London, manuscript

Scalacronica: Scalacronica by Sir Thomas Gray of Heton, knight (ed. Stevenson)

Three Medieval Queens: Lisa Benz St John, Three Medieval Queens

TNA: The National Archives (C: Chancery; DL: Duchy of Lancaster; E: Exchequer; SC: Special Collections)

Tout, Chapters: T. F. Tout, Chapters in the Administrative History of England

TRHS: Transactions of the Royal Historical Society

Trokelowe: Johannis de Trokelowe et Henrici de Blaneforde Chronica et Annales

Tyranny: Natalie Fryde, The Tyranny and Fall of Edward II 1321-1326

Vita: Vita Edwardi Secundi (ed. Denholm-Young)

Warner: Kathryn Warner, Edward II: The Unconventional King

Weir: Alison Weir, Isabella, She-Wolf of France, Queen of England

Endnotes

Introduction

1. SAL MS 122, 87. For the 1326 drought, see *AP*, 312, and *Croniques*, 50, which says that there was a 'great drought in rivers and springs, and a great want of water,' and that towns and abbeys burned and that other 'conflagrations' occurred because of the heat and dryness.
2. Agnes Strickland, *Lives of the Queens of England,* vol. 2, 122.
3. Thomas Costain, *The Three Edwards*, 292.
4. Buck, *Politics, Finance*, 223, says that in 1326 England was 'delivered into the hands of Roger Mortimer and his whore'; Doherty, *Death*, 108, 133, 141. Doherty's novels featuring Isabella, such as *Death of a King* (New York: St Martin's Press, 1985), *A Tapestry of Murders* (London: Headline, 1994) and *The Cup of Ghosts* (Headline, 2005), depict Isabella in much the same way: she is called an 'old bitch', a 'whore' and an 'evil woman'.
5. For example, Weir, 214: Isabella convinced herself in 1326 that she 'would be liberating an oppressed and resentful people from tyranny, and herself from a hateful marriage'.
6. Doherty, *Death*, 171. Weir, 376, says that 'Isabella's downfall lay in her involvement with Mortimer'.
7. Weir, 5.

1 My Lady Yzabel, Queen of England, 1295–1308

1. Phillips, 134.
2. Doherty, 'Date of Birth', 246-7; Brown, 'King's Conundrum', 133-4.
3. *AP*, 262. Doherty, *Death*, 11, claims that Isabella, whom he calls 'a fairy-tale Princess,' had 'beautiful blonde hair' inherited from her father and 'slightly arabic [*sic*, with a small 'a'] features' inherited from her mother, but cites no evidence and doesn't explain what 'slightly Arabic' features are or how they came to exist in a woman, Joan of Navarre, who was of mostly French and northern European origin. He also says that her features are 'faithfully represented' on the statue of her which adorns the tomb of her son John of Eltham in Westminster Abbey, but it is unclear which of the statues of weepers carved on the tomb is intended to be Isabella, and Doherty fails to clarify how

he knows one of the statues 'faithfully' represents what she looked like and what he is comparing it to.

4. J. A. Buchon, ed., *Chronique métrique*, 182, 196, 244.

5. The first quotes are from Weir, 196: Mortimer 'appears to have been everything that Edward II was not: strong, manly, unequivocally heterosexual, virile, courageous and decisive'. Given the unanimity of contemporary chroniclers' statements about Edward II's enormous strength, this is a peculiar remark. 'Manly' and 'virile' in particular appear simply to be modern value judgements assigned to a man assumed, whether correctly or not, to have been 'unequivocally heterosexual' as opposed to a man who can safely be assumed not to have been, and are not based on any historical source. Elsewhere on the same page, Weir calls Mortimer a 'strong and lusty adventurer' to whom Isabella 'succumbs', and claims that 'after surrendering herself to his embraces, she could feel nothing but profound revulsion for her husband'. No evidence is given for this statement either. On pp. 20 and 148, Weir states that Edward II and Piers Gaveston both marrying women and fathering children proves that 'each man was capable of normal sexual relations' and that Hugh Despenser's 'power over the king was rooted in a perverted sexual dominance'. On p. 62, there appears the rather astonishing statement that when Edward consummated his marriage with Isabella, he 'had at last played the man'. The 'smooth girlish hands' and 'heated warrior' quotes are taken from Eleanor Herman's *Sex With The Queen* (New York: Harper Perennial, 2006), 59, and again are not based on any historical evidence but apparently only on an assumption that a homosexual or bisexual man must necessarily be 'girlish'. Three modern novels which present a particularly egregious depiction of Edward II as a shrieking, snivelling, foot-stamping caricature are Brandy Purdy's *The Confession of Piers Gaveston* (iUniverse, 2007), N. Gemini Sasson's *Isabeau* (Cader Idris, 2010) and Virginia Henley's *Notorious* (Signet, 2007), though there are plenty of others.

6. Warner, 26.

7. Gaveston is sometimes said to be French, which is not strictly accurate; as he came from Gascony, the area of France then ruled by the English kings, Gaveston was a subject of the English Crown.

8. Strickland, *Lives of the Queens*, vol. 2, 123.

9. Doherty, *Death*, 42–3, claims that Edward was playing games in 1307 and trying to repudiate his impending marriage and the treaty which had arranged it. On the next page, however, he contradicts himself by stating that Edward neglected the war in Scotland 'because of his desire to marry the beautiful Princess [*sic*] as soon as possible', and the contradictions continue: also on p. 44, Edward is 'captivated' when he meets Isabella, but on p. 46 'chose the occasion [their coronation] to publicly insult both his bride and his guests'.

10. *Foedera 1272–1307*, 954.

11. Brown, 'Political Repercussions', 576, 578-9; Phillips, 132.

12. As suggested by Doherty, *Death*, 43.

13. CPR 1307–1327, 31; *Foedera 1307–1327*, 24.

14. One notable exception is Edward II and Isabella's daughter Eleanor, who married the much older Reynald II, count of Guelders the month before her fourteenth birthday in 1332 and gave birth to her first child a year later, before she had even turned fifteen. Neither Edward nor Isabella had anything to do with this marriage, however, which was arranged by their son Edward III.

15. Rhodes, 'Inventory of the Jewels', 518–21.

16. AP, 258, which says *Rex Franciae dedit regi Angliae genero suo annulum*

regni sui, cubile suum quam pulcrum not vidit aliud, destrarios electos et alia donaria multa nimis. Quae omnia rex Angliae concito Petro misit: 'The king of France gave to his son-in-law the king of England a ring of his kingdom, the most beautiful bed (or couch) ever seen, select war-horses, and many other extravagant gifts. All of which the king of England straight away sent to Piers [Gaveston].' This is all the annals have to say on the matter. As is apparent, Isabella and her possessions are nowhere mentioned, and it is curious that the tale of Edward giving away her gifts or jewels to Gaveston has taken such a firm hold. See Strickland, *Lives of the Queens*, vol. 2, 128; she wrongly claims that Gaveston was exiled to his native Gascony in 1308 when Edward gave him jewels, when in fact he was appointed the king's lieutenant of Ireland and it is nowhere stated that Edward gave him jewels at this time, let alone Isabella's. Weir, 30, claims that after Isabella arrived in England she saw Gaveston wearing some of the jewellery she had brought from France as part of her dowry, citing *Annales Paulini*, which (as can be seen above) it does not say.

17. Phillips, 135.
18. *Itinerary*, 28.
19. *Vita*, 3.

2 Three People in the Marriage, 1308–1311

1. *Itinerary*, 28. Doherty, *Death*, 44–5, makes the odd claim that Piers Gaveston deliberately brought the king's sisters, cousin and other members of the nobility to Dover at least four days too early in order to make them suffer uncomfortably in a cold and bleak port and gained 'great pleasure' from doing so, as though it were possible to plan winter travel in the early fourteenth century reliably to a specific day and as though anyone could possibly have known beforehand that Edward and Isabella would be delayed for a few days in Wissant. The writ ordering Henry of Lancaster and others to attend the king on his return was issued on 22 January, the day Edward left England, officially by Piers Gaveston as regent of the kingdom but most probably at Edward's own command before he departed (*CCR 1307–13*, 51). This is an excellent example of the way some modern historians choose to interpret everything Edward II and Gaveston did in the most critical and negative way possible, even when the interpretation makes no sense.
2. *Baker*, 4 (graceful); *Scalacronica*, 48 (magnificent); *Vita*, 16–17 (the rest); for Gaveston's age see Hamilton, *Gaveston*, 19–28, and Warner, 27–28.
3. John Stow, *Annales, Or a Generale Chronicle of England* (London: Richard Meighen, 1631, first published 1580), 213, who also claims that Gaveston was banished from Gascony because of his mother's witchcraft. Gaveston in fact arrived in England with his father Arnaud in 1296/97; Hamilton, *Gaveston*, 29, and 25 for Claramonde.
4. One self-published 2007 novel about Gaveston, for example (*The Confession of Piers Gaveston*), portrays him as a male prostitute with an uncle who is an innkeeper and sells him into the sex trade. It is absurd to imagine that the king of England in 1300 would have allowed such a person anywhere near his son.
5. Burgtorf, 'With My Life', 46–7.
6. *CFR 1307–19*, 14.
7. Cited in Weir, 51.
8. *Three Medieval Queens*, 39.
9. *CPR 1307–13*, 74.

10. Doherty, *Death*, 47; Helen Castor, *She-Wolves*, 234–5.
11. *CPR 1307–13*, 55, 58, 63, 78; CCW, 271.
12. Carmi Parsons, 'Intercessory Patronage', 153.
13. *CPR 1307-13*, 92; TNA SC 1/35/64 and 65, 1/35/111, 1/36/77.
14. *Flores*, 141–2; *AP*, 258–62.
15. *AP*, 261.
16. *AP*, 262; Hamilton, *Gaveston*, 48; Phillips, 146.
17. *AP*, 262: *rex plus exerceret Petri triclinium quam reginae.*
18. Maddicott, *Thomas of Lancaster*, 86.
19. Chaplais, *Gaveston*, 61ff, 115ff; Maddicott, *Lancaster*, 85–6.
20. *Three Medieval Queens*, 39.
21. For example, Maddicott, *Lancaster*, 84.
22. *Vita*, 15; *AP*, 262; *Gesta*, 33.
23. *AP*, 262; *Vita*, 15.
24. *CPR 1307–13*, 101, 158; *Foedera*, 68–9; *CCR 1307–13*, 106.
25. *CPR 1307–13*, 114, 138, 150–51, 158, 177, 190 etc.
26. Cockerill, *Eleanor of Castile*, 233.
27. *Vita*, 8.
28. *AL*, 169–74; Phillips, 166–7; Maddicott, *Lancaster*, 111–12.
29. *Foedera 1307–1327*, 79; Warner, 56.
30. Prestwich, *Three Edwards*, 81.
31. Devon, *Issues of the Exchequer*, 124–5; CDS, 33.
32. CDS, 40.
33. CDS, 48; HB, 147.
34. *CPR 1307–13*, 333.
35. CDS, 41.
36. HB, 17.
37. HB, xiii, 103, 121; Bullock-Davies, *Menestrellorum Multitudo*, 116.
38. HB, xiii, 207, 235.
39. Devon, *Issues of the Exchequer*, 124.
40. *CPR 1301–07*, 431.
41. HB, 19, 127–9.
42. *CCR 1307–13*, 581.
43. HB, xiv-xv; *CPR 1307-13*, 362, 378. £300 was such a staggeringly enormous sum for people of Margaret and Odin's rank, far more than both of them together would have earned in their entire lifetimes, that this amount is likely to be a clerical error or a misprint by the modern editors of the Patent Roll. Isabella's damsel Joan Villiers was granted £5 a year out of the queen's revenues of Ponthieu, a much more reasonable amount (*CPR 1321–4*, 10).
44. HB, 149.
45. *Vita*, 17.
46. HB, xxi, 227.
47. HB, 208; Chaplais, *Gaveston*, 75.
48. HB, 144.
49. *CPR 13-7-13*, 395, 398, 403, 452.
50. HB, 36, 43, 115, 209–11.
51. *CFR 1307–19*, 107.
52. Trokelowe, 68–9; *Vita*, 21; *AP*, 271; *CPR 1307–13*, 405.
53. *Vita*, 21.
54. *AL*, 202; *Gesta*, 41; *Vita*, 21; Hamilton, *Gaveston*, 93.
55. HB, 115; 'Brief Summary', 342.

56. The older Margaret, who was to die in 1312, was the widow of Edward I's cousin Edmund, earl of Cornwall, who died in 1300.
57. *HB*, xxiv, 133, 139, 209, 215.
58. *HB*, 143.
59. *Itinerary*, 81; *CCW*, 382; Chaplais, *Gaveston*, 77–8.

3 An Heir is Born, 1312–1314

1. *CCR 1307-13*, 448–9; *Foedera 1307–1327*, 153.
2. *AL*, 203.
3. *HB*, 149.
4. *HB*, xxiv, 11, 137, 139, 143 etc.
5. *HB*, 17, 25.
6. *Vita*, 22–3; *HB*, 139.
7. *HB*, 25, 27, 137.
8. *HB*, 13.
9. Bullock-Davies, *Register of Minstrels*, 218; Brown, 'King's Conundrum', 134 note 45.
10. Mortimer, *The Greatest Traitor*, 49–50, 69–70, 100–1, 305–9.
11. *Death of a King* by Paul Doherty (New York: St Martin's Press). The author's foreword and Historical Note at the end claim historical accuracy, but the altered date of birth for Edward III and his impossible fathering by Roger Mortimer (which appear on pp. 10 and 170 of the novel) are not mentioned.
12. A self-published novel of 2006, Charles Randolph Bruce and Carolyn Hale Bruce's *Rebel King: Bannok Burn* (Bruce & Bruce Inc., 2006), makes Roger Mortimer Edward III's real father, though Isabella manages to convince Edward that his own lover Piers Gaveston is in fact her child's father. Edith Felber's *Queen of Shadows: A Novel of Isabella, Wife of King Edward II* (New York: New American Library, 2006) curiously and coyly hints throughout that Isabella conceives Edward III with a Scottish lover who is never named, whom Isabella meets and has an affair with when Edward abandons her behind Scottish lines. The webpage **http://www.relaxorium.com/mindspringbs/angusdebate.html** states 'most historians DO believe it was Edward Longshanks [Edward I] that fathered the child, and not Edward II'. There are numerous other websites, forums, blogs, posts on social media and book reviews which claim that Edward II was not or was probably not Edward III's father.
13. Howell, 'Children of Henry III', 57–72.
14. Weir, 321.
15. *HB*, 219.
16. *HB*, xxv, 235–7.
17. *HB*, 43, 53, 149.
18. Hamilton, *Gaveston*, 95.
19. *HB*, 221.
20. *CCR 1307-13*, 426; Bullock-Davies, *Register of Minstrels*, 143.
21. *Vita*, 22–4.
22. *Flores*, 149; *Vita*, 22.
23. *Vita*, 23.
24. *Trokelowe*, 75-6; Phillips, 203 note 66.
25. *HB*, xxvi, 15.
26. *HB*, xxvi, 131.

27. *Trokelowe*, 75–6; Doherty, *Death*, 51.

28. Phillips, 203; *HB*, xxv-xxvi. For further refutation of the chronicler's claim, see Haines, *Edward II*, 84: 'This has the appearance of a fictitious tale'; Doherty, *Death*, 51: Isabella 'adhered to her husband'; Burgtorf, 'With my Life, his Joyes Began and Ended', 49, points out that the life of the heir to the throne was at stake. Alison Weir (*Isabella*, 63–4), is the only modern writer who repeats the story as though it is certain fact, despite having read Isabella's Household Book which demonstrates that the story is completely unsupported by the queen's own accounts, and that the itineraries of the king and queen show that they either travelled together or met in York within a few days.

29. *HB*, 121; *Foedera*, 170.

30. *Vita*, 25-6.

31. *Vita*, 26.

32. *Foedera 1307–1327*, 204.

33. *HB*, 45, 63, 221; *Itinerary*, 86.

34. *CFR 1307–19*, 136–7; *CCR 1307–13*, 427–8; *CPR 1307–13*, 465.

35. *Scalacronica*, 51.

36. *HB*, 227.

37. *HB*, 221; Bullock-Davies, *Menestrellorum Multitudo*, 116–17.

38. *CPR 1307–13*, 490.

39. Phillips, 196; *CPR 1307–13*, 498; *CCR 1307–13*, 481; Bullock-Davies, *Register of Minstrels*, 32.

40. *Foedera 1307–1327*, 191–2, 203–5; *AL*, 221–25; *CPR 1307–13*, 517; Roberts, *Jewels and Horses*, 1-22.

41. Phillips, 203–4; Weir, 69.

42. *Itinerary*, 90–91.

43. For Moderville, Ormrod, *Edward III*, 6.

44. Bullock-Davies, *Register of Minstrels*, 31–32; *CPR 1307–13*, 508; *Foedera 1307–13*, 184; Phillips, 204.

45. Strickland, *Lives of the Queens*, vol. 2, 130, and see the memo in *Foedera 1307–1327*, 187 (the original French) and *CCR 1307–13*, 558 (English translation). Weir, 430 note 34, claims 'This was the first occasion on which the time of the birth of an English king was recorded.' It wasn't recorded, and if it had been, it would have been noted as taking place at around Prime or 6 a.m.; Terce or the third hour or about 9 a.m.; the sixth hour or about midday; the ninth hour or mid-afternoon; or Vespers, i.e. sunset. This was how people in England told the time in the early 1300s. *CFR 1307–19*, 14, for example, has a memorandum that 'on Wednesday after the Purification, 1 Edward II' (7 February in the first year of Edward's reign, which ran from 8 July 1307 to 7 July 1308), the king landed at Dover 'about the ninth hour' (roughly mid-afternoon) when he returned to England with Isabella. *CCR 1313–8*, 66, says that Edward and Isabella returned to England from their long visit to France on 'Monday before St Margaret the Virgin, at vespers, in the seventh year of his reign', which means around sunset or simply just 'evening' on 16 July 1313.

46. *CPR 1307–13*, 516, 519; *CCR 1313–8*, 54.

47. *CChR*, 202–3; *CCW*, 392.

48. *Vita*, 36; *Trokelowe*, 79–80.

49. *Vita*, 39–40.

50. *AL*, 220–21; Ormrod, *Edward III*, 6–7.

51. *Vita*, 36–7.

52. *Trokelowe*, 79; Mortimer, *Perfect King*, 443 note 26.
53. Mortimer, *Perfect King*, 25–6.
54. *CFR 1307-19*, 158, for the cloth; *Itinerary*, 93–4.
55. *Itinerary*, 95.
56. TNA E 101/375/2.
57. *Foedera 1307–27*, 203–5.
58. Mortimer, *Perfect King*, 23–4, 26; *Itinerary*, 103.
59. *CPR 1307–13*, 579–84.
60. *Foedera 1307–27*, 218; *CPR 1307–13*, 594.
61. *CPR 1313–7*, 12; *CCR 1313–8*, 45–6.
62. *Foedera 1307–27*, 218.
63. *CCR 1307–13*, 583.
64. *CPR 1307–13*, 588; *Vita*, 39.
65. *CPR 1307–13*, 585; *CCR 1307–13*, 537; CCW, 389; Chaplais, *Gaveston*, 111–12.
66. Brown and Degalado, 'La grant feste', 59–60.
67. Buchon, *Chronique métrique*, 183.
68. Brown and Degalado, 56–7, 59. Edward II had also been knighted at Pentecost, 22 May 1306.
69. *Chronique métrique*, 186–7.
70. Brown and Degalado, 59–63.
71. *Chronique métrique*, 194.
72. *Chronique métrique*, 196–7.
73. Doherty, *Death*, 56; Hamilton, 'Notes on 'Royal' Medicine', 36–7.
74. TNA E 163/4/11; Chaplais, *Saint Sardos*, 199–200; Crawford, *Letters of the Queens of England 1100–1547*, 87; Phillips, 491.
75. *Three Medieval Queens*, 38–9, 70.
76. *CCR 1307–13*, 583–4.
77. Brown and Degalado, 72.
78. Vale, *Princely Court*, 144, 229, 280.
79. CCW, 392. Philip of Taranto was a second cousin of both Edward II and Philip IV: their paternal grandmothers Marguerite, Eleanor and Beatrice of Provence were sisters.
80. 'Brief Summary', 342; Bullock-Davies, *Register of Minstrels*, 39.
81. *CCR 1313–8*, 66 (return); *CPR 1313–7*, 5 (Woodstock).
82. Crawford, *Letters*, 87; SC 1/35/29.
83. Trease, 'Spicers and Apothecaries', 37, 46; Hamilton, 'Medicine', 40 and note 26. The modern French word for pennyroyal is *pouliot*, and in the document Trease cites, it is called *pewleus* and appears first on the list of medicines given to Isabella. Paul Doherty's doctoral thesis, 53, Hamilton, 'Medicine', 36 note 26 and Brown, 'Diplomacy', 65 note 49, dismiss Trease's notion that Isabella had a miscarriage, but seem to assume he thought she had suffered one because of the breast milk bought for her, when surely it was on account of the pennyroyal.
84. *CPR 1313–7*, 38.
85. *CPR 1313–7*, 12-13, 15, 17, 20, 44–5, 80, 82 etc.; *CCR 1313–8*, 4.
86. *CPR 1313–7*, 81.
87. *CPR 1313–7*, 21-6, 35–6; *Foedera 1307–27*, 230–3; AL, 222–9.
88. *Vita*, 43–4; *Lanercost*, 203.
89. *Foedera,* 238; Phillips, 221.
90. *CCR 1313–8*, 33–4.

91. Phillips, 214; *Itinerary*, 98.
92. Phillips, 221.
93. *CPR 1313–7*, 85–7; Phillips, 221 note 172; Doherty, *Death*, 57.
94. *CPR 1313–7*, 111; *CCR 1313–8*, 607; TNA E 40/5298.
95. Brown, 'Diplomacy, Adultery', 55, 66.
96. *CCR 1307–13*, 14, 90.
97. Brown, 'Diplomacy', 66 note 61.
98. Phillips, 222.
99. Cited in Brown, 'Diplomacy', 75.
100. Hallam and Everard, *Capetian France*, 282–3; Bradbury, *The Capetians*, 277–8, who claims that Isabella's relationship with Edward had 'embittered' her, which in 1314 was certainly not true. In April 1314 Isabella was a beautiful young queen, mother of the future king of England, in a seemingly perfectly satisfactory marriage, and was surely not 'bitter' about anything.
101. *Scalacronica*, 46.
102. *Capetian France*, 366.

4 The King's Defeat, 1314–1316

1. Brown, 'Diplomacy', 67, 77.
2. Brown, 'Diplomacy', 67.
3. Brown, 'Diplomacy', 67.
4. Barrow, *Robert Bruce*, 336.
5. *Vita*, 50; Reese, *Greatest Victory*, 115–19; Nusbacher, *Bannockburn 1314*, 85–114.
6. Derek Birley, *Sport and the Making of Britain* (1993), 32.
7. Vale, *Princely Court*, 221–2.
8. Vale, *Princely Court*, 236–7.
9. Ormrod, 'Personal Religion', 855–6; Prestwich, *Edward I*, 111–14; Mortimer, *Perfect King*, 109–13; *CPR 1327–30*, 440.
10. Baker, 9; Trevor Henry Aston et al, *The Early Oxford Colleges* (1984), 195; *CPR 1317–21*, 75, 103–4, 168–9, 237; *CPR 1321–4*, 423.
11. Phillips, 240.
12. At least, according to a source written in the fifteenth century: Phillips, 235 note 264.
13. *Vita*, 56; *Lanercost*, 207.
14. *Vita*, 40.
15. Johnstone, *Edward of Carnarvon*, 129–30; Johnstone, 'Eccentricities of Edward II', 265-7; Phillips, 277.
16. Phillips, 15, 277-8.
17. *Trokelowe*, 86.
18. Doherty, *Death*, 60.
19. Vale, *Princely Court*, 108–9.
20. *Itinerary*, 114–6.
21. Mortimer, *Greatest Traitor*, 64, 275–6.
22. Tout, *Place*, 93; *Vita*, 57-8; *Lanercost*, 210.
23. Vale, *Princely Court*, 215.
24. Phillips, 223.
25. *CCR 1313–8*, 204.
26. Bradbury, *The Capetians*, 278.
27. Vale, *Princely Court*, 171, 245.

28. *Murimuth*, 17; C. F. R. Palmer, 'The Friar-Preachers of King's Langley', *The Reliquary* 23 (1882–3), 156; *Foedera*, 259.
29. *CPR 1313–7*, 206.
30. *Vita*, 58.
31. Hamilton, *Gaveston*, 100, 166–7.
32. TNA SC 8/197/9804; *CCR 1313–8*, 463.
33. TNA SC 8/279/13911; *CPR 1313–7*, 672.
34. TNA E 101/375/15; *CCR 1313–8*, 139.
35. *Scalacronica*, 65.
36. Devon, *Issues*, 136; *AL*, 157; *AP*, 267.
37. High Peak: *CPR 1313–7*, 276; requests: *CPR 1313-7*, 162, 165, 168, 169, 201, 223, 254, 287 etc; also CCW, 411, 418.
38. *Trokelowe*, 95; *Vita*, 70.
39. *CDS*, 85, 89–91; CCW, 438–9.
40. *Vita*, 70.
41. *CCR 1313–8*, 306; *Foedera*, 263, 266, 274-5; *Anonimalle*, 288, 290; *Vita*, 69; PROME.
42. Bradbury, *The Capetians*, 277.
43. *Flores*, 173; *Itinerary*, 132-3.
44. *Brut*, 208.
45. Bullock-Davies, *Register of Minstrels*, 19, for Bussard.
46. Weir, 150. Wat Cowherd, Robin and Simon Hod and Robin Dyer are the men she names with whom she wonders if Edward was 'being promiscuous', but did not research further and discover that these men were among the king's chamber valets throughout the 1320s and that their names appear as such over and over in Edward's extant accounts; see SAL MS 122 and TNA E 101/379/7, for example.
47. *Polychronicon*, 299.
48. *Lanercost*, 222.
49. Cited in Johnstone, *Edward of Carnarvon*, 130.
50. *CCR 1313–8*, 367, 440–41; *CCR 1318-23*, 4, 269; *CDS*, 86; *CPR 1313–7*, 422, 551; *CFR 1307–19*, 266; TNA SC 8/317/E267.
51. *CPR 1313–7*, 372, 378, 384, 525, 598, 609, 615 etc.; *CFR 1307–19*, 225, 294, 316–17.
52. *CPR 1327–30*, 439.
53. CCW, 485.
54. *Flores*, 178.
55. *Itinerary*, 136; *Flores*, 173.
56. McKisack, *Fourteenth Century*, 47.
57. PROME.
58. *CPR 1313–7*, 398.
59. Devon, *Issues*, 131; 'Brief Summary', 342–3.
60. Vale, *Princely Court*, 109–10.
61. *Itinerary*, 140; *AP*, 279; Verity, 'Children of Elizabeth, Countess of Hereford', 3.
62. *Foedera*, 290.
63. Bradbury, *The Capetians*, 280.
64. Chaplais, *English Medieval Diplomatic Practice*, part 1, vol. 2, 820; Brown, 'King's Conundrum', 130 note 30.
65. Michael Walsh, *The Conclave: A Sometimes Secret and Occasionally Bloody History of Papal Elections* (Norwich: Canterbury Press, 2003), 95.

66. 'Brief Summary', 322–3; Devon, *Issues*, 133; *CPR 1313–7*, 608.
67. *Foedera*, 293; *CPR 1313–7*, 527.
68. TNA SC 1/35/152.
69. *Lanercost*, 217.
70. Maddicott, *Lancaster*, 187.
71. *CCR 1313–8*, 430; *Foedera*, 296.
72. *Trokelowe*, 95.
73. 'Brief Summary', 336.
74. *Flores*, 176–7.
75. *CPR 1313–7*, 621 (Buntingford); 'Brief Summary', 320 (messenger).
76. *CPR 1313–7*, 563; *Foedera*, 301.
77. Phillips, 281-2; Maddicott, *Lancaster*, 204; *Foedera*, 310–6; *CCR 1318–23*, 697, 'stone wall'; Edwards, 'Political Importance', 342.
78. *Lanercost*, 217.
79. Edwards, 'Political Importance', 342.
80. *CCR 1323–7*, 580; *Foedera*, 615.
81. Haines, *Edward*, 406 note 79; *CPR 1313–7*, 401, 434.
82. *CPR 1313-7*, 528-9.
83. 'Brief Summary', 341.
84. *Foedera*, 304.
85. *CCW*, 460–61.
86. Phillips, 356; Vale, *Origins of The Hundred Years War*, 72.
87. 'Brief Summary', 343–4.
88. Hallam and Everard, *Capetian France*, 365.

5 The Impostor, 1317–1319

1. *CIPM 1327–36*, 296–7.
2. *Flores*, 178–9; *Vita*, 80, 87; *Gesta*, 54; *Anonimalle*, 92.
3. *Foedera*, 322; TNA SC 7/24/10.
4. PROME.
5. Phillips, *Valence*, 111–7; Phillips, 288-9; *Scalacronica*, 144.
6. *Foedera*, 329–30; *CCR 1313–8*, 469–70.
7. Phillips, *Valence*, 116.
8. Barrow, *Robert Bruce*, 340–41.
9. *Foedera*, 308, 317.
10. *Foedera*, 320–21, 364; *CCR 1313–8*, 466.
11. Phillips, *Valence*, 131; Maddicott, *Lancaster*, 224.
12. *Vita*, 87; *Flores*, 176–7.
13. *CPL*, 415, 431, 434, 438–9, 444.
14. *CCR 1313–8*, 462; Devon, *Issues*, 132.
15. *CPR 1313–7*, 642, 668; *CPR 1317–21*, 5, 8–9.
16. *CPR 1324–7*, 281.
17. 'Brief Summary', 342–3.
18. Charles Henry Cooper, *Memorials of Cambridge, volume 2* (1861), 193–4; Cavanaugh, 'Royal Books', 308 note 24.
19. McKisack, *Fourteenth Century*, 2.
20. Warner, 21–22, 110–11.
21. Cavanaugh, 'Royal Books', 305–9; Johnstone, *Edward of Carnarvon*, 18, 86; Warner, 115.
22. 'Royal Books' 309–13, and for 'bibliophile'.

23. Bullock-Davies, *Register of Minstrels,* 47; SAL MS 122, 51.
24. 'Brief Summary', 330; *Scalacronica*, 60.
25. *Gesta*, 50–52; *Murimuth*, 271–6.
26. 'Brief Summary', 341.
27. *Foedera*, 479.
28. Phillips, *Valence*, 123–4; *Vita*, 81–2; *Flores*, 180.
29. *Vita*, 81–2; *Flores*, 180–81; Maddicott, *Lancaster*, 210; Haines, *Edward*, 109.
30. *CPR 1317–21*, 46; *CCR 1313–8*, 575; *Foedera*, 345–6; *CFR 1307–19*, 225, 316, 346–7; *CIM*, 98–9; 'Brief Summary', 329; Maddicott, *Lancaster,* 207–8.
31. *CPR 1317–21*, 53; 'Brief Summary', 344.
32. *CPR 1313–7*, 611, 639, 644, 656; *CPR 1317–21*, 21, 25, 27, 42.
33. Prestwich, 'Court of Edward II', 66–7.
34. *Foedera*, 353.
35. *CPR 1317–21*, 66–7.
36. *CPR 1317–21*, 66.
37. *Foedera*, 360.
38. 'Brief Summary', 337; *Itinerary*, 165.
39. *CCR 1313–8*, 527.
40. *CPR 1317–21*, 115–6, 131–2, 201–2; TNA E 42/544; *CCR 1313–8*, 57.
41. *CPR 1317–21*, 112.
42. *CPR 1317–21,* 130.
43. 'Brief Summary', 338.
44. 'Brief Summary', 337.
45. *CPR 1327–30*, 163; *CFR 1307–19*, 389.
46. *CPR 1317–21*, 222–3.
47. *CPR 1317–21*, 170–72.
48. *CPR 1317–21*, 270–71.
49. *Lanercost*, 221–4; *Vita*, 86–7; *Gesta*, 55; *Scalacronica*, 65.
50. *Anonimalle*, 94.
51. Childs, 'Welcome my Brother', 151–3; Phillips, 323–4; *CPR 1317–21*, 273.
52. *Vita*, 86.
53. *Vita*, 86; *Lanercost*, 222 (quotation).
54. *Vita*, 89.
55. *Vita*, 88.
56. Haines, *Edward*, 112–3.
57. *CPR 1317–21*, 237.
58. *Foedera*, 362, 364; *Lanercost*, 221.
59. *CPR 1301–07*, 244.
60. Tout, *Place*, 241–81; Warner, 127–9, 206–7.
61. *CIM*, 34.
62. *CIM*, 50–51.
63. *CIM*, 20; CCW, 308; *CFR 1307–19*, 54; *CCR 1307–13*, 198; Barker, *Tournament in England*, 133.
64. *AL*, 200.

6 The Contrariants, 1319–1321

1. *CCR 1313–8*, 422.
2. *Foedera*, 380–1, 405; *CCR 1318–23*, 118, 132.
3. Mortimer, *Perfect King*, 403–4.
4. Cited in Mortimer, *Perfect King*, 403–4; Prestwich, *Plantagenet England*, 215.

5. *CDS*, 124.
6. Saaler, *Edward II*, 97.
7. Cited in Maddicott, *Lancaster*, 249.
8. Maddicott, *Lancaster*, 248–9.
9. *Trokelowe*, 103; *Vita*, 95–7; *Flores*, 189; *AP*, 287.
10. *Vita*, 95–8.
11. Haskins, 'Chronicles of Civil Wars', 77.
12. *Flores*, 188; Maddicott, *Lancaster*, 247.
13. *Vita*, 104; *Flores*, 188.
14. Saaler, *Edward II*, 97.
15. Phillips, 347 note 117; Prestwich, 'Unreliability of Household Knights'. 8–9.
16. Doherty, *Death*, 64.
17. *CPR 1317–21*, 400–01, 407–8; *CCR 1318–23*, 153–4.
18. *Lanercost*, 227–8.
19. *CPR 1317–21*, 414, 416; *Foedera*, 409–11; TNA C 47/22/12.
20. *CPR 1307–13*, 473.
21. PROME; *Foedera*, 417–8.
22. *AP*, 288.
23. Phillips, *Valence*, 189; Phillips, 355.
24. *Foedera*, 421; *CPR 1317–21*, 425.
25. PROME; Sayles, *Functions of Medieval Parliament*, 354.
26. *CPR 1317–21*, 448–55; Phillips, 356.
27. 'Brief Summary', 338–9.
28. *CPR 1317–21*, 453.
29. Ormrod, 'Royal Nursery', 400–01.
30. Marshall, 'Childhood and Household of Edward II's Half-Brothers', 191–2.
31. Pole Stuart, 'Interview', 412–5; Vale, *Origins of Hundred Years War*, 51; Phillips, 358–9.
32. Cited in Haines, *Edward*, 45.
33. Cited in PROME.
34. PROME; Sayles, *Functions of Medieval Parliament*, 354.
35. *Scalacronica*, 74–5.
36. Phillips, 360.
37. Bullock-Davies, *Register of Minstrels*, 144.
38. *AP*, 290.
39. Phillips, *Valence*, 190–91.
40. Chaplais, *English Medieval Diplomatic Practice*, part 1, vol. 1, 64–6.
41. TNA SC 1/37/36, SC 1/36/72 and 73; CCW, 513.
42. *AP*, 292; *Trokelowe*, 107.
43. *CCR 1318–23*, 268.
44. *Vita*, 108.
45. *Lanercost*, 229; *Flores*, 164–6.
46. Goronwy Edwards, *Calendar of Ancient Correspondence*, 219–20.
47. Cited in Haines, *Edward*, 124.
48. *Brut*, 212; *Anonimalle*, 92.
49. *Lanercost*, 230; *Vita*, 115.
50. *CCR 1313–8*, 531–2; *CPR 1317–21*, 60.
51. *CPR 1317–21*, 456.
52. *Flores*, 342; *CCR 1318–23*, 494.
53. *CCR 1313–8*, 268.
54. *Vita*, 111.

55. *Vita*, 109.
56. Vale, *Princely Court*, 308.
57. *Scalacronica*, 75; *Polychronicon*, 298–300.
58. Goronwy Edwards, *Ancient Correspondence*, 219.
59. *CPL 1342–62*, 164; 'Brief Summary', 338.
60. *CCR 1318–23*, 366.
61. *Vita*, 109.
62. *CCR 1318–23*, 367–8.
63. *CCR 1318–23*, 363, 366.
64. *Foedera*, 437.
65. *CCR 1318–23*, 363–5; *Foedera*, 446.
66. *CCR 1318–23*, 365.
67. *CPR 1317–21*, 576.
68. *CPR 1317–21*, 578.
69. *Vita*, 110.
70. *CCR 1318-23*, 541–4; *CCR 1323–7*, 118; Davies, 'Despenser War in Glamorgan', 55–6.
71. TNA SC 8/6/298; Davies, 'Despenser War', 58.
72. *Brut*, 213.
73. 'Brief Summary', 338.
74. *Vita*, 116, says that 'the earl [of Lancaster] hated this Bartholomew, and laid many trespasses at his door'.
75. TNA SC 8/7/301; SC 8/92/4561.
76. TNA SC 8/1065268.
77. *CPR 1321–4*, 23.
78. *Foedera*, 452.
79. *CCW*, 522.
80. *AP*, 296–7.
81. *AP*, 297.
82. Cited in PROME.

7   Three People in the Marriage (Part 2), 1321–1322

1. *CCR 1318–23*, 477–8.
2. *AP*, 299.
3. *CPR 1317–21*, 467–8, 473.
4. *CPR 1321–4*, 29.
5. *Anonimalle*, 102–4; *Calendar of Letter-Books of London 1314–37*, 155. See also *AP*, 298–9; *Flores*, 199–200; *Livere*, 339; *Murimuth*, 35; *Trokelowe*, 110–11; *Vita*, 116.
6. *Tyranny*, 51.
7. *Murimuth*, 34; *Scalacronica*, 67.
8. *Vita*, 116.
9. *Vita*, 116. The names of the thirteen men executed are given in *CFR 1319–27*, 76.
10. Maddicott, *Lancaster*, 304.
11. *Livere*, 339.
12. *CPR 1321–4*, 40.
13. *CPR 1321–4*, 45.
14. *Letters of the Kings of England*, 23–4.
15. *Vita*, 118; see also *Gesta*, 74.

16. *CCR 1318–23*, 511–14; *Foedera*, 471.
17. *Vita*, 121.
18. *Vita*, 119.
19. Maddicott, *Lancaster*, 306.
20. *Croniques*, 43; *Vita*, 119.
21. *Murimuth*, 35; *Anonimalle*, 104–5.
22. TNA SC 8/6/255; CCW, 556–7.
23. *CPR 1321–4*, 249; see also *Anonimalle*, 110.
24. *Tyranny*, 63.
25. *CPR 1321–4*, 77; *CCR 1323–7*, 106.
26. *Tyranny*, 63; Mortimer, *Greatest Traitor*, 121.
27. *CCR 1318-23*, 525.
28. Sayles, 'Formal Judgements', 58.
29. Holmes, 'Protest', 210.
30. Ward, *Elizabeth de Burgh*, xvii note 14, citing TNA SC 6/927/31.
31. *CCR 1318–23*, 428.
32. *CCR 1318–23*, 578, 651; *CCR 1323–7*, 65.
33. *Flores*, 346.
34. *Vita*, 124–5. The 'calamity' statement is often misquoted in modern literature to make it seem as though the author was condemning Edward II for making noblemen wear rags during their imprisonment, when in fact they had donned them themselves in an attempt to escape after the battle, and the fact that the *Vita* author approved of the royalist victory over the rebels is usually not cited. See *Tyranny*, 58; Doherty, *Death*, 73–4; and especially Weir, 141, who quotes passages from the *Vita* several pages apart and relating to different years as though they are all one continuous text. Various entries in the chancery rolls confirm that many knights and noblemen tried to escape after Boroughbridge by throwing away their fine clothes and possessions: *CCR 1318–23*, 535; *CIM*, 131ff.
35. For a full list with sources, see **edwardthesecond.blogspot.com/2009/06/edward-iis-executions-of-1322.html**
36. The numbers of those executed have often been grossly inflated in modern literature, generally by including the names of men killed fighting at Boroughbridge, and are frequently described in highly emotive terms: see for example Doherty, *Death*, 73–5, who calls the executions 'a reign of terror,' 'blood-letting,' 'these horrors' and 'dreadful events.' He also calls them 'horror piled upon horror,' citing Maddicott, *Lancaster*, 310–12, who does not use this expression or anything like it.
37. *Brut*, 216–21.
38. *Anonimalle*, 106.
39. *Vita*, 125.
40. *CCR 1318–23*, 525–6; *Foedera*, 474, and see also 459, 463, 472.
41. *Vita*, 126.
42. *Brut*, 222; *Lanercost*, 234; *Anonimalle*, 108.
43. *Brut*, 223; *Vita*, 126; *Lanercost*, 234; *AP*, 202–3.
44. *Vita*, 126; *Livere*, 341–2; *Brut*, 222.
45. *Foedera*, 481; *CPL*, 448; TNA SC 7/25/14. Doherty, *Death*, 74, claims that John XXII begged Edward to 'show some restraint' regarding his executions of the Contrariants; Weir, 141, claims that the pope 'begged the King to desist from his tyrannical course'. Neither writer cites a source for this assertion, and I have been unable to find it.

46. Weir, 139–40, states that the queen was staying at the Tower of London at this time, but cites no source. Oliver's letter is in *CDS*, 140.
47. *Vita*, 135; Doherty, *Death*, 75, for 'bystander'.
48. TNA SC 8/55/2731; *CPR 1324–7*, 200. Weir, 141, cites the chronicle of Jean Froissart, who claims Isabella's 'displeasure' at the executions. Froissart was not even born until about 1337 and died in the early 1400s, never met Isabella (he arrived in England in the early 1360s, after her death), and cannot possibly be used as a reliable source for her private feelings in 1322.
49. *CCR 1318–23*, 433–4, 448–51; *CCW*, 528–30.
50. *CCR 1318–23*, 569, 604, 627; *CCR 1323–7*, 46, 48, 120, 236.
51. *Anonimalle*, 80; *Lanercost*, 235.
52. *Livere*, 345; *CCR 1318–23*, 44–5; Underhill, *Good Estate*, 33–4.
53. Parsons, 'Intercessory Patronage', 153–5.
54. *CPR 1321–4*, 227, 251, 315, 371.
55. TNA DL 42/11 fo. 66v; *CCR 1318–23*, 564, 574–6; *CPR 1321–4*, 141.
56. *CPR 1348–50*, 122; *CCR 1323–7*, 357; TNA E 40/4962, SC 8/310/15484, SC 8/160/7956, SC 8/163/8132.
57. Warner, 161; Holmes, 'Judgement on Despenser', 265, which says that Lady Baret *est touz jours afole et perdue*, 'is forever more driven mad and lost', because Despenser's 'rascals' had had her legs and arms broken.
58. TNA E 101/379/7, 7.
59. Phillips, 98.
60. *Polychronicon*, 314.
61. Phillips, 428–9.
62. Blackley, 'Bastard Son', 76–7.
63. Phillips, 429.
64. Valente, 'Lament of Edward II', 432–3; Ormrod, *Edward III*, 124.
65. *CCR 1318–23*, 680.
66. *Flores*, 224–5.
67. *Foedera*, 498.
68. *Flores*, 210; *Lanercost*, 240.
69. Haines, *Edward*, 84 and 394 note 142; Doherty, *Death*, 75–8.
70. Holmes, 'Judgement on Despenser', 265.
71. *CDS*, 146.
72. Barrow, *Robert Bruce*, 346.
73. Doherty, *Death*, 75.
74. Saaler, *Edward II*, 116.
75. *CPL*, 457.
76. Davies, 'First Journal', 678.
77. *CPR 1321–4*, 227, 229.
78. Doherty, *Death*, 100–102; the letter is in *CCR 1323–7*, 580–81.
79. Doherty, *Death*, 101–2.
80. Weir, 149. The idea that Despenser raped Isabella appears to have been first suggested in Susan Howatch's 1974 novel *Cashelmara*, a re-telling of Edward II's story set in nineteenth-century Ireland.
81. Cited in Phillips, 491.
82. *CPR 1321–4*, 229.
83. Davies, 'First Journal', 676, 678; TNA E 101/379/17.
84. *Scalacronica*, 70; SAL MS 122, 57.
85. *Flores*, 229; Prestwich, 'Court', 71.

8 War with France, 1323–1325

1. *Foedera*, 527; Haines, *Archbishop John Stratford*, 139.
2. CCR 1323–7, 147-8, 198; CCW, 546; *Foedera*, 541; Chaplais, *English Medieval Diplomatic Practice*, part 1 vol. 1, 336–43; Fryde, 'Deposits', 349.
3. Isabella's letter: TNA SC 1/37/45; Eleanor's: SC 1/37/4.
4. *Lanercost*, 241–5; *Brut*, 228; *Foedera*, 502, 504; CDS, 148; CCR 1318–23, 692; CPR 1321–4, 234.
5. *Vita*, 129–31; *Livere*, 347; *Brut*, 231; CPR 1321–4, 234, 257, 314.
6. CCR 1323–7, 133; CPR 1321–4, 257, 314, 349.
7. Maddicott, *Lancaster*, 329–30; *Tyranny*, 153; CCW, 543.
8. CCR 1323–7, 13, 132; CPR 1321–4, 335.
9. *Flores*, 217; Gransden, *Historical Writing*, 20; and see also *Brut*, 231; *Murimuth*, 40; *Scalacronica*, 72; *Lanercost*, 251; *Anonimalle*, 116; AP, 305–6, etc.
10. *Foedera*, 536.
11. CCR 1323–7, 87–8, 106; *Livere*, 351.
12. As suggested by Doherty, *Death*, 87.
13. *Tyranny*, 134.
14. CCR 1318–23, 713–4; *Sardos*, 15–17. The proposals were that Edward of Windsor would marry one of Valois's many daughters, while Eleanor of Woodstock and Joan of the Tower would marry Valois's youngest son with his third wife Mahaut de Châtillon (Louis, count of Chartres, who died as a child) and the son of his son with his first wife Marguerite of Anjou-Naples (which probably means the future King John II of France, born in 1319).
15. Blackley, 'Bishop of Exeter', 225.
16. Cited in Blackley, 'Bishop', 221–2.
17. Haines, *Church and Politics*, 108–9; Haines, *Edward*, 154.
18. *Sardos*, 5; CCW, 548.
19. Phillips, 460 note 39.
20. Weir, 154–5.
21. 'Secular Musicians', 71; CPR 1321–4, 333.
22. CPR 1321–4, 277–9, 333; CDS, 150; *Foedera*, 510–11, 520–23; CCR 1318–23, 717; *Gesta*, 84; *Flores*, 215–16; *Lanercost*, 246–7.
23. *Sardos*, 176–7.
24. *Sardos*, 176–81.
25. Hamilton, *Gaveston*, 167 note 85.
26. There is much confusion in modern books and articles over the date of Charles and Joan's wedding, and it is often wrongly placed in 1325 instead of 1324, but we know the date from a letter to Edward II by his envoys to Charles, written on 10 July 1324. Cited in *Sardos*, 189–90. Joan was already called 'queen of France' in September 1324 in a letter from Pope John XXII, so clearly her marriage cannot have taken place in 1325: CPL, 455.
27. Phillips, *Valence*, 234–6.
28. *Sardos*, 188–90; *Foedera*, 547.
29. *Sardos*, 186 (my translation).
30. *Sardos*, 131–2, 191.
31. CPR 1324–7, 103–4; CCR 1323–7, 253–4; *Sardos*, 140–2.
32. *Sardos*, 130.
33. *Sardos*, 61–3, 92.
34. *Tyranny*, 143.
35. *Sardos*, 16, 50–2, 212, 229–30.

36. *Sardos*, 10–11, 130, 143, 179–80, 183–4, 193.

37. *CFR 1319–27*, 300–2, 308; *CCR 1323–7*, 223, 260; *Foedera*, 569.

38. Holmes, 'Judgement on Despenser', 266.

39. *Lanercost*, 249; Buck 'Reform of the Exchequer', 251, Tout, *Place*, 140; Blackley, 'Bishop', 225; Tout, *Chapters*, vol. 5, 274.

40. Menache, 'Isabelle of France', 110; Tout, *Chapters*, vol. 3, 275.

41. *CCR 1323–7*, 204, 206–7, 209–11, 216.

42. *Lanercost*, 249; *Flores*, 226.

43. Haines, *Edward*, 43, 375.

44. The story was invented by Paul Doherty in his doctoral thesis about Isabella, 103, repeated in his *Death*, 80 and endnote 26 on p. 245.

45. TNA E 101/382/12; SAL MS 122, 66.

46. As suggested in *Three Medieval Queens*, 111.

47. Underhill, *Good Estate*, 40–41.

48. *CCR 1323–7*, 260; *CPR 1324–7*, 88, 157, 243; SAL MS 122, 2, 78, 81; *Notes and Queries*, 7th series (Sept 1886), 258.

49. Marshall 'Childhood and Household', 191–2.

50. *CPR 1292–1301*, 592, 606; *Three Medieval Queens*, 109–10.

51. Ormrod, 'Royal Nursery', 400–11; Ormrod, *Edward III*, 125.

52. *CPR 1317–21*, 453; *Three Medieval Queens*, 111.

53. Doherty, *Death*, 79.

54. *Livere*, 354–5; *CCR 1323–7*, 593; *CFR 1319–27*, 418; *Croniques*, 49.

55. Doherty, *Death*, 81.

56. *CPL*, 475.

57. *Vita*, 136.

58. *CPR 1321–4*, 349.

59. *Croniques*, 51; *Scalacronica*, 156, 158.

60. Vale, 'Ritual Ceremony', 25.

61. *CCR 1323–7*, 579–81.

62. *Vita*, 143.

63. Cited in Sponsler, 'King's Boyfriend', 153, 163.

64. Holmes, 'Judgement on Despenser', 266.

65. Retinue: *CPR 1324–7*, 91–2, 96, 100, 102, 116, 120 etc. Expenses: Blackley, 'Bishop', 228; *Tyranny*, 96.

66. Weir, 170.

67. Blackley, 'Bishop', 233–4.

68. *Tyranny*, 147.

69. For example, *Greatest Traitor*, 136, 138–9, 283 note 14; Michael Packe, *King Edward III* (London: Routledge and Kegan Paul, 1983), 19 ('Mortimer's escape was the overture to a deep and wide conspiracy in northern Europe').

70. *Brut*, 237.

71. Menache, 'Isabelle of France', 115.

72. *Sardos*, 42–3.

73. *Sardos*, 195–6.

74. *CPL*, 458, 462, 465, 467–8.

75. *Foedera*, 599.

76. *Vita*, 135.

9 The Queen and the Baron, 1325–1326

1. *Sardos*, 196.

2. *Sardos*, 267.

3. *Sardos*, 199–200.

4. CCR 1323–7, 385; *Foedera*, 602–3.

5. PROME; *Tyranny*, 148.

6. *CPL*, 466.

7. *Sardos*, 267–70.

8. Blackley, 'Bishop', 228, says 'It is difficult to imagine that Isabella was plotting against anyone' during the first few months of her trip.

9. *Lanercost*, 249; AP, 337.

10. *CPL*, 474; Blackley, 'Bishop', 226.

11. Blackley, 'Bishop', 226.

12. *Croniques*, 50; *Anonimalle*, 120; *Brut*, 233.

13. CCW, 582; SAL MS 122, 89ff.

14. *Vita*, 140, 142; Buck, *Politics, Finance*, 156 note 199, for Edward's fear of indictment.

15. *Vita*, 137–8.

16. CCR 1323–7, 580; *Foedera*, 615.

17. Warner, 194–5.

18. CPR 1324–7, 267–70, 273–5.

19. SAL MS 122, 20–22, 65; Warner, 195.

20. Denholm-Young, 'Bermondsey Priory', 433 note 1.

21. *Murimuth*, 44; *Vita*, 138; *Anonimalle*, 120.

22. *Sardos*, 243, 269; CCR 1323–7, 507; CPR 1324–7, 175.

23. *Vita*, 142–3; *Croniques*, 49.

24. *Vita*, 143.

25. Weir, 196, for 'profound revulsion'.

26. For example Castor, *She-Wolves*, 287.

27. Blackley, 'Bishop', 230–35; Buck, *Politics, Finance*, 156–8.

28. *Vita*, 142.

29. SAL MS 122, 40ff, 48, 59, 75.

30. CPR 1324–7, 213.

31. *Vita*, 143–5.

32. *Foedera*, 615, is the full letter in the original French; CCR 1323–7, 580, is a rather inadequate English translation.

33. SAL MS 122, 40, 43.

34. SAL MS 122, 28, 34, 38.

35. SAL MS 122, 7, 15, 28–9, 36, 41, 46, 92.

36. Vale, *Princely Court*, 159, 339.

37. CPR 1324–7, 171, 193; CCR 1323–7, 505–6, 508, 527–8, 540–1, 569.

38. *Foedera*, 612.

39. *Foedera*, 617–8 (Edward's letters); *CPL*, 260 (dispensation).

40. CCR 1323–7, 576–7.

41. Phillips, 493, citing TNA SC 1/49/91.

42. Haines, *John Stratford*, 166.

43. CCR 1323–7, 552; CFR 1319–27, 383, 388.

44. AP, 310.

45. *CPL*, 246.

46. Not 1328, as is almost inevitably stated; the Inquisition Post Mortem of her younger brother John, earl of Kent taken shortly after his death on 27 December 1352 says that Joan had turned either twenty-five (according to the Nottinghamshire jurors) or twenty-six (according to the Leicestershire jurors)

the previous September, so she was born in September 1326 or September 1327. If 1326, she must have been conceived almost immediately after her parents' marriage and been their eldest child. Joan was old enough to act as her brother John's godmother in April 1330 and to lift him from the font during his baptism, which suggests that she was then older than nineteen months (as her frequently given date of birth of September 1328 would indicate). *CIPM 1347–52*, 455–6; *CIPM 1352–60*, 41–57.

47. *CCR 1323–7*, 464.

48. Grassi, 'William Airmyn', 559–60; Haines, *Edward*, 328–9; Chaplais, *English Medieval Diplomatic Practice*, part 1, vol. 2, 345.

49. Grassi, 'William Airmyn', 556–8.

50. *CCR 1323–7*, 543.

51. Castor, *She-Wolves*, 288, says of their association: 'Physical attraction there clearly was … this was no idle dalliance but an all-consuming personal bond.' Mortimer, *Greatest Traitor*, 145, says that Roger Mortimer 'was the man she [Isabella] loved more passionately than any other in her life. The relationship between Roger and Isabella is one of the great romances of the Middle Ages.' Possibly, but all of this is assumption. Phillips, 490, states more soberly 'It did not automatically follow … that they were also involved romantically. Initially at least, their relationship may have been solely one of business.'

52. *Murimuth*, 45–6. Fryde, *Tyranny*, 180, claims that Murimuth says Isabella became Mortimer's 'mistress'. He does not. Weir, 195, says that Isabella and Mortimer 'plunged headlong into an adulterous affair', citing the *Vita Edwardi Secundi* and *Murimuth*. The *Vita* does not say a single word about Isabella and Mortimer and indeed ends abruptly with the queen's refusal to return to England before her association with him began (presumably because the author died or became incapacitated around the end of 1325), and Adam Murimuth talks merely of an 'excessive familiarity,' *nimiam familiaritatem*, between the two. This part of his chronicle is hedged about with 'it is said' and 'others assert', and this is his only comment on Isabella and Mortimer's relationship. Weir, 214, also claims without citing a source that Pope John XXII wrote to Charles IV of France 'censoring him for harbouring adulterers' and commanding him to shelter them no longer, because of 'the scandal that the Queen's affair with Mortimer was causing'. I have scoured the *Papal Letters 1305–41* and have found no letter from John to Charles even remotely along these lines, and the word 'adulterer' does not appear in the document.

53. *Lanercost*, 266–7; Haines, *Edward*, 169.

54. Haines, *Edward*, 216 and 462 note 214; Burgtorf, 'With my Life', 40.

55. *Scalacronica*, 72; *Croniques*, 51, 61; *Brut*, 233, 246–7.

56. *CCR 1323–7*, 578–9; *Foedera*, 622–3.

57. For example, *Sardos*, 2, 5, 72, 179, 196.

58. Mortimer, *Perfect King*, 45.

59. *CCR 1323–7*, 578; *Foedera*, 623.

60. Cited in Phillips, 491.

61. *PROME* (November 1330 parliament).

62. Haines, 'Bishops and Politics', 605–6.

63. For example, Weir, 202.

64. *CPL*, 473, 475.

65. Haines, *John Stratford*, 168.

66. Weir, 214, for example.

67. *CCR 1323–7*, 578–9; *Foedera*, 623.

68. *Foedera*, 625. For Edward's proclamations, see for example *CCR 1323–7*, 543, 650.
69. Lord, 'Isabella at the Court', 49 and note 31.
70. Lord, 'Court', 49–50; *Foedera*, 631; *CCR 1323–7*, 576.
71. SAL MS 122, 63, 78.
72. *Foedera*, 629; Phillips, 497.
73. *CPL*, 476–7.
74. Haines, 'Bishop and Politics', 605–6.
75. *Foedera*, 631; *CCR 1323–7*, 577.
76. *Foedera*, 640; Haines, *Edward*, 174; Phillips, 500.
77. Holmes, 'Judgement', 266 (my translation).
78. *Brut*, 234–5.
79. Phillips, 500.
80. *Flores*, 231.
81. Phillips, 500.
82. *Tyranny*, 180–82; Ormrod, *Edward III*, 38.
83. Ormrod, *Edward III*, 39.
84. Cited in Mortimer, *Perfect King*, 47.
85. *CFR 1319–27*, 404, 410; *CCR 1323–7*, 636, 642; *CPR 1324–7*, 296 (Charles IV); *CCR 1323–7*, 643 (prayers).
86. *CCR 1323–7*, 640–5 (p. 642 'malice'); SAL MS 122, 83; *Tyranny*, 184–5; Haines, *Edward*, 172.
87. *Foedera*, 632–3, 637–8, 640–41.
88. Phillips, 501.
89. *CCR 1323–7*, 593; *CFR 1319–27*, 418.
90. Phillips, 501–2; *Tyranny*, 185; Ormrod, *Edward III*, 41.

10 Invading England and Deposing a King, 1326–1327

1. Haines, *Edward*, 177.
2. *Sardos*, 72.
3. Phillips, 504; Ormrod, *Edward III*, 42.
4. Phillips, 503–4.
5. *Croniques*, 51; Haines, *Edward*, 178.
6. *CCR 1327–30*, 189, 249; *AP*, 314.
7. Haines, *Edward*, 178; *Tyranny*, 187–8, 194.
8. *CCR 1323–7*, 650–51.
9. *CPR 1324–7*, 328, 335; *CCR 1323–7*, 650–51.
10. *CPR 1324–7*, 325–7.
11. *Tyranny*, 188.
12. *CFR 1319–27*, 418, 421.
13. Ward, *Elizabeth de Burgh*, 3.
14. *Tyranny*, 183–4.
15. *CCW*, 582.
16. Haines, *Edward*, 178.
17. Haines, *Edward*, 178.
18. *Foedera*, 645–6; Phillips, 509–10.
19. *Intrigue*, 47–50; Phillips, 510; Haines, *Edward*, 179; Haines, *Church and Politics*, 165.
20. Phillips, 506.
21. *Croniques*, 54.

22. Buck, *Politics, Finance*, 220-21; Haines, *John Stratford*, 173; *Croniques*, 52.
23. Haines, *Edward*, 179; Phillips, 506–7.
24. Phillips, 507; Buck, *Politics, Finance*, 222.
25. Buck, *Politics, Finance*, 218–9 (my translation).
26. SAL MS 122, 89.
27. *Foedera*, 646; CCR 1323–7, 655.
28. *AP*, 317–18; *Brut*, 240; Haines, *Edward*, 181; Phillips, 513.
29. Cited in Weir, 236.
30. Cited in Doherty, *Death*, 91.
31. Phillips, 507 note 320.
32. *Lanercost*, 252; CFR 1327–37, 3.
33. *Murimuth*, 50.
34. Weir, 238, for 'henchmen'. Micheldever's first name is given in two chronicles and in many modern books as Thomas, but it was certainly Robert. Warner, 225 and 296 note 64.
35. *ODNB*.
36. CFR 1319–27, 430; CFR 1327-37, 12–13; CPR 1324-7, 341, 344; CPR 1327-30, 12, 14, 18, 37–9.
37. Rees, *Caerphilly Castle*, 109–21.
38. CPR 1324–7, 339–40; CCR 1323–7, 621.
39. CFR 1329–27, 422; CPR 1324–7, 337; Phillips, 514.
40. CPR 1324–7, 336.
41. SAL MS 122, 90.
42. CPR 1324–7, 338.
43. *AP*, 319; *Murimuth*, 49; *Flores*, 234.
44. Phillips, 515.
45. CCR 1323–7, 655.
46. CPR 1324–7, 337, 340–43; CCR 1323–7, 622.
47. Haines, *Edward*, 185; *Tyranny*, 193.
48. *Brut*, 240; *Anonimalle*, 130; *Croniques*, 56.
49. Fryde, *Tyranny and Fall*, 77, 191–3, claims that Reading was one of Despenser's closest friends, his marshal and his loyal knight; Doherty, *Death*, 106, says he was Despenser's 'principal henchman' (as Weir, 238, describes the two men killed with the earl of Arundel, 'henchman' apparently being the nicely sinister word of choice to describe Isabella's executed enemies). I have found no evidence to support any of this. Reading was not a knight but a sergeant-at-arms, as Edward's last chamber account, SAL MS 122, makes clear.
50. *Brut*, 339–40 (quotation); *Froissart*, 43–4; Haines, *Edward*, 185; Mortimer, *Traitor*, 241.
51. Holmes, 'Judgement', 261–7, prints them in the original French, and see my translation at **http://edwardthesecond.blogspot.com/2009/04/charges-against-hugh-despenser-younger.html**
52. CCR 1330–3, 175.
53. CCR 1323–7, 624.
54. Underhill, *Good Estate*, 39–40. Weir, 241, states that the girls were placed in convents while their mother was in the Tower and that they 'later became nuns'.
55. CCR 1327–30, 169, 187–8.
56. *CPL*, 482.
57. *Brut*, 252–3.

58. Doherty, *Death*, 108–9, 133. No evidence is cited in support of these extremely unlikely statements.
59. Haines, 'Stamford Council', 143; *Phillips*, 521.
60. Haines, *Edward*, 187.
61. *CPR 1324–7*, 346.
62. *Murimuth*, 52.
63. Doherty, *Death*, 113; Weir, 256–7.
64. *Tyranny*, 196, 209.
65. *Tyranny*, 209, 212–16, 223–4.
66. *CPR 1327–30*, 12, 14, 26, 33, 37, etc; *CCR 1327–30*, 15–16, etc.
67. *CPR 1327–30*, 14, 20.
68. *CPR 1327–30*, 9–14.
69. *CFR 1327–37*, 19; *CPR 1327–30*, 14; *CCR 1327–30*, 98.
70. *CPR 1327-30*, 22; *CFR 1327–37*, 20.
71. Valente, 'Deposition', 862.
72. Valente, 'Deposition', 862–3.
73. *English Historical Documents*, ed. Rothwell, 287.
74. *Lanercost*, 254.
75. Dryburgh, 'Roger Mortimer', 107–8.
76. Lyon, *Constitutional History of UK*, 95–6.
77. McKisack, *Fourteenth Century*, 91–2.
78. *Tyranny*, 195–6.
79. Ormrod, *Edward III*, 50–51.
80. Cited in Mortimer, *Perfect King*, 53.
81. Valente, 'Deposition', 869.
82. *Flores*, 235.
83. Valente, 'Lament', 428.
84. Cited in Mortimer. *Perfect King*, 59; Weir, 200–01.
85. Sumption, *Trial by Battle*, 102; SAL MS 122, 70.
86. Ormrod, *Edward III*, 64; Sumption, *Trial by Battle*, 102.
87. Childs, 'Chronicles and Politics', 46.
88. Phillips, 537 note 95, 607–9; Valente, 'Deposition', 855–6.
89. Haines, *Edward*, 194.
90. *CCR 1327–30*, 100.
91. *Tyranny*, 213.
92. Ormrod, *Edward III*, 55; Mortimer, *Perfect King*, 55.
93. Ormrod, *Edward III*, 57.
94. *CCR 1327–30*, 98.

11 Captivity and Death of a King

1. Phillips, 541.
2. *PROME*, November 1330 parliament; *CCR 1327–30*, 77.
3. Mortimer, *Greatest Traitor*, 173–4, 288, note 26; Mortimer, *Perfect King*, 58.
4. Haines, 'Stamford Council', 142–3.
5. *AP*, 333; *Baker*, 31; Tout, 'Captivity and Death', 158–9.
6. *Baker*, 30–31.
7. *Baker*, 31.
8. *CCR 1327–30*, 77; Tout, 'Captivity', 155.
9. Doherty, *Death*, 120.
10. *CCR 1327–30*, 77, 86.

11. *Murimuth*, 52.
12. *Froissart*, 44.
13. Cited in Doherty, *Death*, 120.
14. *Murimuth*, 52.
15. *CFR 1319–27*, 185.
16. *Lanercost*, 258–9; *Brut*, 249.
17. *CPR 1321–4*, 50; *CPR 1324–7*, 326, 336; *CPR 1327–30*, 38.
18. *CPR 1327–30*, 74–99.
19. *Lanercost*, 257.
20. *Bridlington*, 96; *Lanercost*, 256–7; *CCR 1327–30*, 157, 212 (quotation); *CPR 1327–30*, 139, 180, 183, 191.
21. *CCR 1327–30*, 157.
22. *CCR 1327–30*, 142; *CPR 1327–30*, 153, 183.
23. *CCR 1327–30*, 169, 187–8.
24. *CPR 1327–30*, 95.
25. Tanqueray, 'Conspiracy', 119–24.
26. *CPR 1327–30*, 156–7.
27. *CCR 1327–30*, 156, 179; TNA SC 8/69/3444.
28. *AP*, 337; *CCR 1327–30*, 146, 158, 549.
29. *AP*, 337.
30. Tout, 'Captivity', 165.
31. *CCR 1327–30*, 182.
32. Tout, 'Captivity', 165, 182–90.
33. *CPR 1324–7*, 249.
34. *CPR 1321–4*, 77.
35. Doherty, *Death*, 221.
36. TNA DL 10/253.
37. *PROME*.
38. For thorough accounts of the chronicle evidence for Edward's death, see *Intrigue*, 55–8; Phillips, 560–5.
39. *AP*, 337-8; *Anonimalle*, 134; Phillips, 561 note 238.
40. *Murimuth*, 53–4; *Gesta*, 97–8.
41. *Lanercost*, 259; *Scalacronica*, 74.
42. Phillips, 561–2.
43. *Brut*, 253.
44. Cited in Haines, *Death of a King*, 49.
45. *Murimuth*, 54.
46. *Intrigue*, 67.
47. As claimed by Doherty, *Death*, 141.
48. Ernst Kantorowicz, *The King's Two Bodies*, 420.
49. Moore, 'Documents', 221–2; *Intrigue*, 67, 69; Phillips, 553.
50. Ormrod, 'Personal Religion', 870 note 120.
51. Moore, 'Documents', 218: 'bringing a certain woman who disembowelled the king to the queen by the king's [Edward III's] order, for two days'.

12 Regency and Rebellion, 1327–1328

1. *Three Medieval Queens*, 139.
2. *Scalacronica*, 84–5.
3. Cited in *Three Medieval Queens*, 149.
4. *Three Medieval Queens*, 151–2.

5. *Three Medieval Queens*, 151–3.
6. These entries are far too numerous to list, but see for example *CPR 1327–30*, 140, 159, 160, 165, 168, 169, 175; *CCR 1327–30*, 127.
7. *Scalacronica*, 83–4.
8. *Croniques*, 61–3.
9. *Brut,* 254–5, 257–9.
10. *CCR 1327–41*, 55.
11. *CPR 1327–30*, 125.
12. *CPR 1327–30*, 125; Mortimer, *Greatest Traitor*, 320.
13. Mortimer, *Greatest Traitor*, 320–21.
14. Dryburgh, 'Roger Mortimer', 182.
15. Mortimer, *Perfect King*, 60.
16. *Three Medieval Queens*, 155.
17. *PROME*.
18. *CPR 1327–30*, 270, 501.
19. Ormrod, *Edward III*, 71.
20. *Foedera*, 743; Ormrod, *Edward III*, 81.
21. *Brut*, 260.
22. *CIM 1308–48*, 274–5; *CCR 1327–30*, 437, 439, 463, 528–9.
23. Haines, *John Stratford*, 199; *CIM*, 258; Holmes, 'Rebellion', 88.
24. *CPR 1327–30*, 355.
25. Holmes, 'Rebellion', 84; *CPMR*, 77–82; Ormrod, *Edward III*, 76.
26. *CPR 1327–30*, 345.
27. *CPR 1327–30*, 343.
28. *Brut*, 260.
29. Haines, *John Stratford*, 203.
30. *CCR 1327–30*, 528–31.
31. *CPMR*, 77–82.
32. Ormrod, *Edward III*, 78.

13 More Plots, 1329–1330

1. Phillips, 567; *Intrigue*, 161.
2. The original letter is held at Warwickshire County Record Office, CR 136/C2027. It is printed in the French original in Haines, 'Sumptuous Apparel', 893–4, and in English translation in *Intrigue*, 154–5.
3. *Murimuth*, 256.
4. *CPR 1327–30*, 499; *CCR 1330–33*, 14.
5. *Brut*, 267; *Murimuth*, 257; *Anonimalle*, 142–3.
6. *CCR 1330–3*, 131.
7. See for example Haines, *Edward*, 212; Doherty, *Death*, 147–8, Haines, *Death of a King*, 113.
8. See for example McKisack, *Fourteenth Century*, 100, who claims that Kent was 'foolish' and guilty of 'weakness', yet was also 'dangerous' to Isabella and Mortimer.
9. Warner, 'Adherents', 782–4, 788–91.
10. *Intrigue*, 86–7, 140.
11. *Murimuth*, 52–4; *Brut*, 253; *Intrigue*, 75.
12. *CPR 1327–30*, 556–7, 571; *CCR 1330–3*, 24, 51, 131.
13. *CCR 1330–3*, 132; *CPR 1327–30*, 557.
14. Lawne, 'Edmund of Woodstock', 44; Marshall, 'Thomas of Brotherton', 119.

15. *Plea and Memoranda Rolls 1323–64*, 72.
16. Warner, 'Adherents', 800–01.
17. *CCR 1330–3*, 24.
18. For example, *Lanercost*, 264–5.
19. *Murimuth*, 256.
20. *CCR 1330–3*, 147.
21. *CPR 1327–30*, 544, 563, 570–72; *CCR 1330–3*, 151.
22. *CFR 1327–37*, 181.
23. *CFR 1327–37*, 175; *Lanercost*, 265–6, for the quotation.
24. Doherty, *Death*, 212, suggests blackmail as Fieschi's motive, in order to gain more lucrative benefices in England. I am grateful to Ivan Fowler, Mario Traxino and the members of the Auramala Project for their superb research into the Fieschi family; see their website **https://theauramalaproject.wordpress.com/**, and Ian Mortimer's 'Edward III, his father and the Fieschi' in *Intrigue*, 175–233. It would be difficult to over-estimate the massive importance of the Fieschi and their relatives the Malaspina family in the region of Italy under discussion in the first half of the fourteenth century.
25. Cited in *Intrigue*, 179.
26. *Intrigue*, 197–202, 226–7; Mortimer, *Perfect King*, 414–5; Phillips, 586–8.
27. *PROME*.

14 Downfall, 1330

1. *CPR 1327–30*, 523.
2. Ormrod, *Edward III*, 88 note 161; TNA SC 1/38/193.
3. Ormrod, *Edward III*, 88.
4. *Baker*, 45–6; *PROME*. Ranulph Higden's *Polychronicon*, 296, is one of the chronicles which calls Piers Gaveston Edward II's *amasius*.
5. *Brut*, 262.
6. Shenton, 'Edward III and the Coup', 16; *Brut*, 268.
7. *Baker*, 45.
8. *Scalacronica*, 157.
9. *PROME*.
10. *CPR 1330–4*, 110; Waugh 'For King, Country and Patron', 40, 53.
11. *Baker*, 46.
12. Mortimer, *Greatest Traitor*, 238.
13. *Baker*, 46.
14. *Brut*, 270–71.
15. *Baker*, 46.
16. Mortimer, *Greatest Traitor*, 241.
17. *CCR 1330–33*, 403; TNA SC 8/61/3027; Mortimer, *Greatest Traitor*, 242, 299.
18. *CPR 1327–30*, 437–8, 442.
19. *Testamenta Vetusta: Being Illustrations from Wills*, vol. 1, ed. Nicholas Harris Nicolas (London, 1836), 7–10; Phillips, 223 note 181.
20. *CCR 1330–3*, 158.
21. *CCR 1330–3*, 160–2.
22. *CFR 1327–27*, 277, 279; *CIPM 1352–60*, 41–57.
23. *CPR 1330–4*, 20; *CCR 1330–3*, 74-7, 79, 81.
24. *CCR 1330–3*, 178.
25. *CPR 1330–4*, 36.
26. *CCR 1330–3*, 434.

27. Ormrod, *Edward III*, 124.
28. *CCR 1330–3*, 256; *CPR 1330–4*, 48; *CPR 1334–8*, 24.
29. Strickland, *Lives of the Queens*, 167–8.
30. *CPL*, 498.
31. *CPL*, 500–01.

15 A Conventional Queen Again, 1330–1358

1. *CPR 1343–5*, 40, 479; TNA C/143/274/14; *CPL 1342–62*, 585.
2. Ormrod, *Edward III*, 125.
3. *Three Medieval Queens*, 127, citing *Foedera*, II, iii, 37.
4. Doherty, *Death*, 177.
5. Doherty, *Death*, 177.
6. Bennett, 'Isabelle of France, Anglo-French Diplomacy', 219. Jacques' father Louis was the first duke of Bourbon, and Jacques, born in 1319, was a direct male-line ancestor of Henry IV of France, first king of the house of Bourbon.
7. Bennett, 'Anglo-French Diplomacy', 219–21.
8. Doherty, *Death*, 177.
9. Doherty, *Death*, 11, claims that Isabella's 'striking features' are 'faithfully represented' by one of the statues, but fails to clarify which statue he thinks is hers and what he is comparing it to in order to know that it is 'faithful' to what she looked like.
10. Doherty, *Death*, 179, says 'her funeral took place almost on the anniversary of the day that Mortimer died on the scaffold at Tyburn,' as though this is significant, and also that she chose to be buried at 'the same church which had received the hanged corpse of her beloved Roger Mortimer' (who was buried in Coventry).
11. *CPL 1342–62*, 168.
12. Blackley, 'Cult of the Dead', 31.
13. Blackley, 'Cult', 26.
14. Ormrod, *Edward III*, 468.
15. Weir, 374, says that 'in mediaeval times, protocol generally precluded English monarchs from attending funerals', which may have been the case in Tudor times but was not in the fourteenth century.
16. *CIPM 1352–60*, 356–9.

Select Bibliography

Primary Sources

Adae Murimuth Continuatio Chronicarum, ed. E. M. Thompson (London: Eyre and Spottiswoode, 1889)

Annales Londonienses 1195–1330, in W. Stubbs, ed., *Chronicles of the Reigns of Edward I and Edward II*, volume 1, Rolls Series, 76 (London: Rolls Series, 76, 1882)

Annales Paulini 1307–1340, in Stubbs, *Chronicles*, volume 1

The Anonimalle Chronicle 1307 to 1334, from Brotherton Collection MS 29, ed. W. R. Childs and J. Taylor (Yorkshire Archaeological Society Record Series 147, 1991)

The Brut or the Chronicles of England, part 1, ed. F. W. D. Brie (London: Early English Text Society, 1906)

Calendar of Chancery Warrants, vol. 1, 1244–1326 (London: HMSO, 1927)

Calendar of the Charter Rolls, vol. 3, 1300–1326 (London: HMSO, 1908)

Calendar of the Close Rolls, eleven vols., 1272–1333 (London: HMSO, 1898–1906)

Calendar of Documents Relating to Scotland vol. 3, 1307–1357, ed. Joseph Bain (Edinburgh: H. M. General Register House, 1887)

Calendar of Entries in the Papal Registers Relating to Great Britain and Ireland: Papal Letters, vol. 2, 1305–1341

Calendar of the Fine Rolls, four vols., 1272–1334 (London: HMSO, 1911–13)

Calendar of Inquisitions Miscellaneous (Chancery) vol. 2, 1308–1348 (London: HMSO, 1916)

Calendar of Plea and Memoranda Rolls of the City of London 1323–1364 (London: HMSO, 1926)

Calendar of the Patent Rolls, *eleven vols., 1272–1334 (London: HMSO, 1891–1903)*

Calendar of Memoranda Rolls (Exchequer): Michaelmas 1326 – Michaelmas 1327 (London: HMSO, 1968)

Chronique métrique de Godefroy de Paris, ed. J.-A. Buchon (Paris: Verdière, 1827)

Croniques de London depuis l'an 44 Hen III jusqu'à l'an 17 Edw. III, ed. G. J. Aungier (London: Camden Society, 1844)

Davies, James Conway, 'The First Journal of Edward II's Chamber', *English Historical Review*, 30 (1915)

Devon, Frederick, *Issues of the Exchequer: Being A Collection of Payments Made Out of His Majesty's Revenue* (London: John Murray, 1837)

Edwards, J. Goronwy, *Calendar of Ancient Correspondence Concerning Wales* (Cardiff: University Press Board, 1935)

Edwards, J. Goronwy, *Calendar of Ancient Petitions Relating to Wales* (Cardiff: University of Wales Press, 1975)

English Historical Documents, vol. 3, 1189–1327, ed. Harry Rothwell (London: Eyre and Spottiswoode, 1975)

Flores Historiarum, ed. H. R. Luard, vol. iii (London: Eyre and Spottiswoode for HMSO, 1890)

The flowers of History, especially such as relate to the affairs of Britain. From the beginning of the world to the year 1307, ed. C. D. Yonge (London: Henry G. Bohn, 1853)

Froissart: Chronicles, ed. Geoffrey Brereton (London: Penguin, 1978)

The Chronicle of Geoffrey le Baker of Swinbrook, translated by David Preest (Woodbridge: Boydell and Brewer, 2012)

Chronicon Galfridi le Baker de Swynebroke, ed. E. M. Thompson (Oxford: Clarendon Press, 1889)

Gesta Edwardi de Carnarvon Auctore Canonico Bridlingtoniensi, in W. Stubbs, *Chronicles of the Reigns of Edward I and Edward II*, volume 2 (London: Rolls Series, 76, 1883)

The Chronicle of Walter Guisborough, ed. Harry Rothwell (London: Butler and Tanner (Camden Society, third series, vol. 89) 1957)

Haskins, G. L., 'A Chronicle of the Civil Wars of Edward II', *Speculum*, 14 (1939)

Historia Anglicana, vol. 1, ed. H. T. Riley (London: Longman, Green, 1863)

The Household Book of Queen Isabella of England: For The Fifth Regnal Year Of Edward II, 8th July 1311 To 7th July 1312, ed. F. D. Blackley and G. Hermansen (Edmonton: University of Alberta Press, 1971)

Hallam, Elizabeth, *The Itinerary of Edward II and His Household, 1307–1327* (London: List and Index Society, 1984)

Johannis de Trokelowe et Henrici de Blaneforde Chronica et Annales, ed. H. T. Riley (London: Longman, Green, 1866)

The Chronicle of Lanercost 1272–1346, ed. Herbert Maxwell (Glasgow: James Maclehose and Sons, 1913)

Letters of the Kings of England, vol. 1, ed. J. O. Halliwell (London: Henry Colburn, 1848)

Le Livere de Reis de Britanie e le Livere de Reis de Engletere, ed. John Glover (London: Longman, Green, 1865)

The National Archives: Chancery, Duchy of Lancaster, Exchequer, Special Collection records, especially E 101/379/17, E 101/624/24, E 101/379/11, E 101/376/15, E 101/379/7 (account books of the chamber in the 1320s)

Polychronicon Ranulphi Higden, monachi Cestrensis, vol. 8, ed. J. R. Lumby (London: Longman, Green, 1865)

The Parliament Rolls of Medieval England, ed. Chris Given-Wilson et al, CD-ROM edition (Scholarly Editions, 2005)

Rhodes, Walter E., 'The Inventory of the Jewels and Wardrobe of Queen Isabella (1307–8)', *EHR*, 12 (1897)

Foedera, Conventiones, Litterae et Cujuscunque Generis Acta Publica, vol. 2.1, 1307–1327 (London: Thomas Rymer, 1818)

Roll of Arms of Caerlaverock, ed. T. Wright (London: John Camden Hotten, 1864)

Scalacronica: The Reigns of Edward I, Edward II and Edward III as Recorded by Sir Thomas Gray of Heton, knight, ed. Herbert Maxwell (Glasgow: James Maclehose and Sons, 1907)

Scalacronica: By Sir Thomas Gray of Heton, knight. A Chronicle of England and Scotland From A. D. MLXVI to A. D. MCCCLXII, ed. J. Stevenson (Edinburgh: Maitland Club, 1836)

Society of Antiquaries of London MS 122 (Edward's chamber account of 1325/26)

Stapleton, Thomas, 'A Brief Summary of the Wardrobe Accounts of the tenth, eleventh, and fourteenth years of King Edward the Second', *Archaeologia,* 26 (1836)

Vita Edwardi Secundi Monachi Cuiusdam Malmesberiensis, ed. N. Denholm-Young (London: Thomas Nelson and Sons, 1957)

The War of Saint-Sardos (1323–1325): Gascon Correspondence and Diplomatic Documents, ed. Pierre Chaplais (London: Camden Third Series, 87, 1954)

Warwickshire County Record Office, CR 136/C2027 (letter of January 1330)

Wright, T., *The Political Songs of England* (London: Camden Society, 1839)

Secondary Sources: Articles, Essays and Dissertations

Bennett, Michael, 'Isabelle of France, Anglo-French Diplomacy and Cultural Exchange in the Late 1350s', *The Age of Edward III*, ed. J. S. Bothwell (Woodbridge: Boydell and Brewer, 2001)

Blackley, F. D., 'Adam, the Bastard Son of Edward II', *BIHR*, 37 (1964)

Blackley, F. D., 'Isabella and the Bishop of Exeter', in T. A. Sandqvist and M. R. Powicke, eds., *Essays in Medieval History Presented to Bertie Wilkinson* (Toronto: University of Toronto Press, 1969)

Blackley, F. D., 'Isabella of France, Queen of England (1308–1358) and the Late Medieval Cult of the Dead', *Canadian Journal of History,* 14 (1980)

Bond, E. A., 'Notices of the Last Days of Isabella, Queen of Edward the Second, drawn from an Account of the Expenses of her Household', *Archaeologia,* 35 (1854)

Bothwell, J. S., 'The More Things Change: Isabella and Mortimer, Edward III, and the Painful Delay of a Royal Majority' (1327–1330)', *The Royal Minorities of Medieval and Early Modern England*, ed. Charles Beem (New York: Palgrave Macmillan, 2008)

Brown, Elizabeth A. R., 'The Political Repercussions of Family Ties in the Early Fourteenth Century: The Marriage of Edward II and Isabelle of France', *Speculum,* 63 (1988)

Brown, Elizabeth A. R., 'The Marriage of Edward II of England and Isabelle of France: A Postscript', *Speculum,* 64 (1989)

Brown, Elizabeth A. R., 'Diplomacy, Adultery and Domestic Politics at the Court of Philip the Fair: Queen Isabelle's Mission to France in 1314', in J. S. Hamilton, ed., *Documenting the Past: Essays in Medieval History Presented to George Peddy Cuttino* (Woodbridge: Boydell Press, 1989)

Brown, Elizabeth A. R., 'The Prince is Father of the King: The Character and Childhood of Philip IV of France', *Mediaeval Studies,* 49 (1987)

Brown, Elizabeth A. R., 'The King's Conundrum: Endowing Queens and Loyal Servants, Ensuring Salvation, and Protecting the Patrimony in Fourteenth-Century France', in J. A. Burrow and Ian P. Wei, eds., *Medieval Futures: Attitudes to the Future in the Middle Ages* (Woodbridge: Boydell Press, 2000)

Brown, Elizabeth A. R., and Degalado, Nancy Freeman, '*La grant feste*: Philip the Fair's Celebration of the Knighting of His Sons in Paris at Pentecost of 1313', in Barbara Hanawalt and Kathryn Reyerson, eds., *City and Spectacle in Medieval Europe* (Minneapolis: University of Minnesota Press, 1994)

Burgtorf, Jochen, 'With my Life, his Joyes Began and Ended: Piers Gaveston and King Edward II of England Revisited', *FCE V*, ed. Nigel Saul (Woodbridge: Boydell and Brewer, 2008)

Cavanaugh, Susan, 'Royal Books: King John to Richard II', *The Library*, 5th series, 10 (1988)

Childs, W. R., 'Welcome, My Brother: Edward II, John of Powderham and the Chronicles, 1318', in I. Wood and G. A. Loud, eds., *Church and Chronicle in the Middle Ages: Essays Presented to John Taylor* (London and Rio Grande: Hambledon Press, 1991)

Childs, W. R., 'England in Europe in the Reign of Edward II', *RENP*

Childs, Wendy R., 'Chronicles and Politics in the Reign of Edward II', in Janet Burton, William Marx and Veronica O'Mara, eds., *Leeds Studies in English: Essays in Honour of Oliver Pickering*, new series, XLI (Univ. of Leeds, 2010)

Cobban, A. B., 'Edward II, Pope John XXII, and the University of Cambridge', *Bulletin of the John Rylands Library*, 47 (1964-65)

Cuttino, G. P., and Lyman, T. W., 'Where is Edward II?', *EHR*, 53 (1978)

Davies, James Conway, 'The Despenser War in Glamorgan', *TRHS*, third series, 9 (1915)

Denholm-Young, N., 'Edward III and Bermondsey Priory', *EHR*, 48 (1933)

Dobrowolski, Paula, 'Women and their Dower in the Long Thirteenth Century 1265-1329', *Thirteenth-Century England VI*, ed. Michael Prestwich, R. H. Britnell and Robin Frame (Woodbridge: Boydell and Brewer, 1997)

Doherty, Paul, 'The Date of Birth of Isabella, Queen of England', *BIHR*, 48 (1975)

Dryburgh, Paul, 'The Last Refuge of a Scoundrel? Edward II and Ireland, 1321–7', *RENP*

Dryburgh, Paul, 'The Career of Roger Mortimer, first Earl of March (c. 1287-1330)', Univ. of Bristol PhD thesis, 2002

Edwards, Kathleen, 'The Personal and Political Activities of the English Episcopate during the Reign of Edward II', *BIHR*, 16 (1938)

Edwards, Kathleen, 'The Political Importance of the English Bishops during the Reign of Edward II', *EHR*, 59 (1944)

Edwards, J. G., 'Sir Gruffydd Llwyd', *EHR*, 30 (1915)

Frame, Robin, 'Power and Society in the Lordship of Ireland, 1272–1377', *Past and Present*, 76 (1977)

Fryde, E. B., 'The Deposits of Hugh Despenser the Younger with Italian Bankers', *Economic History Review*, 2nd series, 3 (1951)

Gibbs, V., 'The Battle of Boroughbridge and the Boroughbridge Roll', *Genealogist*, 21 (1905)

Haines, Roy Martin, 'Bishops and politics in the reign of Edward II: Hamo de Hethe, Henry Wharton, and the 'Historia Roffensis'', *Journal of Ecclesiastical History*, 44 (1993)

Haines, Roy Martin, 'Sir Thomas Gurney of Englishcombe, Regicide?', *Somerset Archaeological and Natural History*, 147 (2004)

Haines, Roy Martin, 'The Stamford Council of April 1327', *EHR*, 122 (2007)

Haines, Roy Martin, 'Roger Mortimer's Scam', *Transactions of the Bristol and Gloucestershire Archaeological Society*, 126 (2008)

Haines, Roy Martin, 'Sumptuous Apparel for a Royal Prisoner: Archbishop Melton's letter, 14 January 1330', *EHR*, 124 (2009)

Hallam, Elizabeth, 'Royal Burial and the Cult of Kingship in France and England, 1066-1330' *JMH*, 8 (1982)

Hamilton, J. S., 'The Uncertain Death of Edward II', *History Compass*, 6, 5 (2008)

Hamilton, J. S., 'Charter Witness Lists for the Reign of Edward II', *Fourteenth Century England I*, ed. Nigel Saul (Woodbridge: Boydell and Brewer, 2000)

Hamilton, J. S., 'Some Notes on 'Royal' Medicine in the Reign of Edward II', *Fourteenth Century England II*, ed. Chris Given-Wilson (Woodbridge: Boydell and Brewer, 2002)

Hamilton, J. S., 'The Character of Edward II: The Letters of Edward of Caernarfon Reconsidered', *RENP*

Hamilton, J. S., 'A Reassessment of the Loyalty of the Household Knights of Edward II', *Fourteenth Century England VII*, ed. Mark Ormrod (Woodbridge: Boydell and Brewer, 2012)

Haskins, G. L., 'The Doncaster Petition of 1321', *EHR*, 53 (1938)

Haskins, G. L., 'Judicial Proceedings against a Traitor after Boroughbridge', *Speculum*, 12 (1937)

Holmes, G. A., *The Estates of the Higher Nobility in Fourteenth-Century England* (1957)

Holmes, G. A., 'The Judgement on the Younger Despenser, 1326', *EHR*, 70 (1955)

Holmes, G. A., 'A Protest Against the Despensers, 1326', *Speculum*, 30 (1955)

Holmes, G. A., 'The Rebellion of the Earl of Lancaster, 1328-9', *BIHR*, 28 (1955)

Howell, Margaret, 'The Children of Henry III and Eleanor of Provence', *Thirteenth Century England IV*, ed. P. R. Coss and S. D. Lloyd (Woodbridge: Boydell and Brewer, 1993)

Hunter, Joseph, 'Measures taken for the Apprehension of Sir Thomas de Gurney, One of the Murderers of Edward II', *Archaeologia*, 27 (1838)

Hunter, Joseph, 'Journal of the Mission of Queen Isabella to the Court of France and of her long residence in that Country', *Archaeologia*, 36 (1855)

Johnstone, Hilda, 'Isabella, the She-wolf of France', *History*, 21 (1936)

Johnstone, Hilda, 'The Eccentricities of Edward II', *EHR*, 48 (1933)

Johnstone, Hilda, 'The Parliament of Lincoln, 1316', *EHR*, 36 (1921)

Johnstone, Hilda, 'The County of Ponthieu, 1279-1307', *EHR*, 29 (1914)

King, Andy, "Pur Salvation du Roiaume': Military Service and Obligation in Fourteenth-Century Northumberland', *FCE II*

King, Andy, 'Bandits, Robbers and *Schavaldours*: War and Disorder in Northumberland in the Reign of Edward II', *Thirteenth-Century England IX*, ed. Michael Prestwich, Richard Britnell and Robin Frame (Woodbridge: Boydell and Brewer, 2003)

King, Andy, 'Thomas of Lancaster's First Quarrel with Edward II', *Fourteenth Century England III*, ed. W. M. Ormrod (Woodbridge: Boydell and Brewer, 2004)

Lachaud, Frédérique, 'Liveries of Robes in England, *c.*1200 – *c.*1330', *EHR*, 61 (1996)

Lawne, Penny, 'Edmund of Woodstock (1301–1330): A Study of Personal Loyalty', in *Fourteenth Century England VI*, ed. C. Given-Wilson (Woodbridge: Boydell and Brewer, 2010)

Lawrence, Martyn, 'Rise of a Royal Favourite: the Early Career of Hugh Despenser the Elder', *RENP*

Lawrence, Martyn, 'Secular Patronage and Religious Devotion: the Despensers and St Mary's Abbey, Tewkesbury', *Fourteenth Century England V*, ed. Nigel Saul (Woodbridge: Boydell and Brewer, 2008)

Lawrence, Martyn, 'Power, Ambition and Political Rehabilitation: the Despensers, *c.* 1281-1400', Univ. of York DPhil thesis, 2005

Lewis, Suzanne, 'The Apocalypse of Isabella of France: Paris, Bibl. Nat. MS Fr 13096', The Art Bulletin, 72.2 (1990)

Linehan, Peter, 'The English Mission of Cardinal Petrus Hispanus, the Chronicle of Walter of Guisborough, and news from Castile at Carlisle (1307)', *EHR*, 117 (2002)

Lord, Carla, 'Queen Isabella at the Court of France', *FCE II*

Lucas, H. S., 'The Great European Famine of 1315, 1316 and 1317', *Speculum*, 5 (1930)

Lumsden, Andrew, 'The fairy tale of Edward II', *The Gay and Lesbian Review Worldwide*, March/April 2004

Maddicott, J. R., 'Thomas of Lancaster and Sir Robert Holland: a Study in Noble Patronage', *EHR*, 86 (1971)

Marshall, Alison, 'The Childhood and Household of Edward II's Half-Brothers, Thomas of Brotherton and Edmund of Woodstock', *RENP*

Marshall, Alison, 'Thomas of Brotherton, Earl of Norfolk and Marshal of England: A Study in Early Fourteenth-Century Aristocracy', Univ. of Bristol PhD diss., 2006

Moore, S. A., 'Documents relating to the Death and Burial of Edward II', *Archaeologia*, 50 (1887)

Menache, Sophia, 'Isabelle of France, Queen of England – A Reconsideration', *JMH*, 10 (1984)

Mortimer, Ian, 'The Death of Edward II in Berkeley Castle', *EHR*, 489 (2005) (reprinted in his *Medieval Intrigue*)

Mortimer, Ian, 'Sermons of Sodomy: A Reconsideration of Edward II's Sodomitical Reputation', *RENP* (reprinted in his *Medieval Intrigue*)

Nicholson, R., 'The Last Campaign of Robert Bruce', *EHR*, 77 (1962)

Ormrod, W. M., 'The Personal Religion of Edward III', *Speculum*, 64 (1989)

Ormrod, W. M., 'The Royal Nursery: A Household for the Younger Children of Edward III', *EHR*, 120 (2005)

Ormrod, W. M., 'The Sexualities of Edward II', *RENP*

Parsons, John Carmi, 'The Intercessory Patronage of Queens Margaret and Isabella of France', *Thirteenth-Century England VI*, ed. Michael Prestwich, R. H. Britnell and Robin Frame (Woodbridge: Boydell and Brewer, 1997)

Parsons, John Carmi, 'The Year of Eleanor of Castile's Birth and her Children by Edward I', *Mediaeval Studies*, 46 (1984)

Phillips, J. R. S., 'The "Middle Party" and the Negotiating of the Treaty of Leake, August 1318: A Reinterpretation', *BIHR*, 46 (1973)

Phillips, J. R. S., 'Edward II and the Prophets', *England in the Fourteenth Century: Proceedings of the 1985 Harlaxton Symposium*, ed. W. M. Ormrod (Woodbridge: Boydell Press, 1986)

Phillips, J. R. S., '"Edward II" in Italy: English and Welsh Political Exiles and Fugitives in Continental Europe, 1322–1364', *Thirteenth Century England X*, ed. Prestwich, Britnell and Frame (Woodbridge: Boydell and Brewer, 2005)

Phillips, J. R. S., 'The Place of the Reign of Edward II', *RENP*

Prestwich, Michael, 'The Court of Edward II', *RENP*

Prestwich, Michael, 'The Unreliability of Royal Household Knights in the Early Fourteenth Century', *FCE II*

Prestwich, Michael, 'An Everyday Story of Knightly Folk', *Thirteenth-Century England IX*, ed. Prestwich, Britnell and Frame (Prestwich, Michael, Britnell, Richard, and Frame, Robin, eds., *Thirteenth-Century England X* (Woodbridge: Boydell and Brewer, 2001)

Prestwich, Michael, 'Gilbert de Middleton and the Attack on the Cardinals, 1317', *Warriors and Churchmen in the High Middle Ages: Essays Presented to Karl Leyser*, ed. T. Reuter (London and Rio Grande: Hambeldon Press, 1992)

Prestwich, Michael, 'The Piety of Edward I', *England in the Thirteenth Century: Proceedings of the 1984 Harlaxton Symposium*, ed. W. M. Ormrod (Woodbridge: Boydell Press, 1985)

Prestwich, Michael, 'English Castles in the Reign of Edward II', *JMH*, 8 (1982)

Pugh, T. B., 'The Marcher Lords of Glamorgan and Morgannwg, 1317-1485', *Glamorgan County History, III: The Middle Ages*, ed. T. B. Pugh (1971)

Rastall, Richard, 'Secular Musicians in Late Medieval England' Univ. of Manchester PhD thesis, 1968

Redstone, V. B., 'Some Mercenaries of Henry of Lancaster, 1327-1330', *TRHS*, 3rd series, 7 (1913)

Saul, Nigel, 'The Despensers and the Downfall of Edward II', *EHR*, 99 (1984)

Sayles, George Osborne, 'The Formal Judgements on the Traitors of 1322', *Speculum*, 16 (1941)

Shenton, Caroline, 'Edward III and the Coup of 1330', *The Age of Edward III* (Woodbridge: Boydell and Brewer, 2001), ed. J. S. Bothwell

Smith, J. B., 'Edward II and the Allegiance of Wales', *Welsh History Review*, 8 (1976)

Sponsler, Claire, 'The King's Boyfriend', in Glenn Burger and Steven F. Kruger, eds., *Queering the Middle Ages* (Minneapolis: University of Minnesota Press, 2001)

Stevenson, W. H., 'A Letter of the Younger Despenser on the Eve of the Barons' Rebellion, 21 March 1321', *EHR*, 12 (1897)

Stones, E. L. G., and Keil, I. J. E., 'Edward II and the Abbot of Glastonbury: A New Case of Historical Evidence Solicited from Monasteries', *Archives*, 12 (1976)

Stuart, E. Pole, 'The Interview between Philip V and Edward II at Amiens in 1320', *EHR*, 41 (1926)

Tanqueray, Frédéric J., 'The Conspiracy of Thomas Dunheved, 1327', *EHR*, 31 (1916)

Taylor, John, 'The Judgement on Hugh Despenser the Younger', *Medievalia et Humanistica*, 12 (1958)

Tebbit, Alistair, 'Royal Patronage and Political Allegiance: The Household Knights of Edward II 1314–1321' in *Thirteenth-Century England X*

Tebbit, Alistair, 'Household Knights and Military Service Under the Direction of Edward II', *RENP*

Tout, T. F., 'The Captivity and Death of Edward of Carnarvon', *Collected Papers of T. F. Tout*, vol. iii (Manchester: Manchester University Press, 1934)

Trease, G. E., 'The Spicers and Apothecaries of the Royal Household in the Reigns of Edward I and Edward II', *Nottingham Medieval Studies*, 3 (1959)

Vale, Malcolm, 'Ritual Ceremony and the 'Civilising Process': The Role of the Court, *c.* 1270-1400', in Steven J. Gunn and A. Janse, eds., *The Court as a Stage* (Woodbridge: Boydell and Brewer, 2006)

Valente, Claire, 'The Deposition and Abdication of Edward II', *EHR*, 113 (1998)

Valente, Claire, 'The "Lament of Edward II": Religious Lyric, Political Propaganda', *Speculum*, 77 (2002)

Verity, Brad, 'The Children of Elizabeth, Countess of Hereford, Daughter of Edward I of England', *Foundation for Medieval Genealogy*, 6 (2006)

Warner, Kathryn, 'The Adherents of Edmund of Woodstock, Earl of Kent, in March 1330', *EHR*, 126 (2011)

Waugh, Scott L., 'For King, Country and Patron: The Despensers and Local Administration 1321–1322', *The Journal of British Studies*, 22 (1983)

Waugh, Scott L., 'The Profits of Violence: the Minor Gentry in the Rebellion of 1321–22 in Gloucestershire and Herefordshire', *Speculum*, 52 (1977)

Westerhof, Danielle, 'Deconstructing Identities on the Scaffold: the Execution of Hugh Despenser the Younger, 1326', *JMH*, 33 (2007)

Wilkinson, Bertie, 'The Sherburn Indenture and the Attack on the Despensers', *EHR*, 63 (1948)

Wood, Charles T., 'Where is John the Posthumous? Or, Mahaut of Artois Settles her Royal Debts', in J. S. Hamilton, ed., *Documenting the Past: Essays in Medieval History Presented to George Peddy Cuttino* (Woodbridge: Boydell Press, 1989)

Secondary Sources: Books

Altschul, Michael, *A Baronial Family in Medieval England: the Clares, 1217–1314* (Baltimore: Johns Hopkins University Press, 1965)

Barber, Malcolm, *The Trial of the Templars* (Cambridge: Cambridge University Press, second edition, 2006)

Barrow, G. W. S., *Robert Bruce and the Community of the Realm of Scotland* (Edinburgh: Edinburgh University Press, second edition, 1976)

Bell, Graham, *Robert the Bruce's Forgotten Victory: The Battle of Byland 1322* (Stroud: Tempus Publishing, 2005)

Benz St John, Lisa, *Three Medieval Queens: Queenship and the Crown in Fourteenth-Century England* (New York: Palgrave Macmillan, 2012)

Bingham, Caroline, *The Life and Times of Edward II* (London: Weidenfeld and Nicholson, 1973)

Boswell, J., *Christianity, Social Tolerance and Homosexuality* (Chicago: University of Chicago Press, 1980)

Bothwell, J. S., ed., *The Age of Edward III* (Woodbridge: Boydell and Brewer, 2001)

Bradbury, Jim, *The Capetians: Kings of France 987–1328* (London: Continuum, 2007)

Brown, Chris, *Bannockburn 1314: A New History* (Stroud: The History Press, 2009)

Brown, Michael, *Bannockburn: The Scottish War and the British Isles 1307–1323* (Edinburgh: Edinburgh University Press, 2008)

Buck, Mark, *Politics, Finance and the Church in the Reign of Edward II: Walter Stapeldon, Treasurer of England* (Cambridge: Cambridge University Press, 1983)

Bullock-Davies, Constance, *Menestrellorum Multitudo: Minstrels at a Royal Feast* (Cardiff: University of Wales Press, 1978)

Bullock-Davies, Constance, *A Register of Royal and Baronial Domestic Minstrels 1272–1327* (Woodbridge: Boydell Press, 1986)

Burtscher, Michael, *The Fitzalans: Earls of Arundel and Surrey, Lords of the Welsh Marches (1267–1415)* (Woonton Almeley: Logaston Press, 2008)

Castor, Helen, *She-Wolves: The Women who Ruled England Before Elizabeth* (London: Faber and Faber, 2010)

Chaplais, Pierre, *English Medieval Diplomatic Practice, Part 1: Documents and Interpretation*, 2 vols. (London: HMSO, 1982)

Chaplais, Pierre, *Piers Gaveston: Edward II's Adoptive Brother* (Oxford: Clarendon Press, 1994)

Chaplais, Pierre, *English Diplomatic Practice in the Middle Ages* (London: Bloomsbury, 2003)

Cockerill, Sara, *Eleanor of Castile: The Shadow Queen* (Stroud: Amberley Publishing, 2014)

Coss, Peter R. and Keen, Maurice Hugh, *Heraldry, Pageantry and Social Display in Medieval England* (Woodbridge: Boydell Press, 2003)

Costain, Thomas, *The Three Edwards* (London: Universal-Tandem, 1973, first published in the US by Doubleday in 1958)

Crawford, Anne, *Letters of the Queens of England 1100–1547* (Stroud: Sutton Publishing, 1997)

Davies, James Conway, *The Baronial Opposition to Edward II: Its Character and Policy* (Cambridge: Cambridge University Press, 1918)

Denton, Jeffrey H., *Robert Winchelsey and the Crown 1294–1313* (Cambridge: Cambridge University Press, 2002)

Dixon, W. H., and Raine, J., *Lives of the Archbishops of York*, vol. 1 (London: Longman, Green, 1863)

Dodd, Gwilym, and Musson, Anthony, eds., *The Reign of Edward II: New Perspectives* (York: York Medieval Press, Brewer, 2006)

Doherty, Paul, *Isabella and the Strange Death of Edward II* (London: Constable and Robinson, 2003)

Frame, Robin, *English Lordship in Ireland, 1318–1361* (Oxford: Oxford University Press, 1982)

Fryde, Natalie, *The Tyranny and Fall of Edward II 1321–1326* (Cambridge: Cambridge University Press, 1979)

Given-Wilson, Chris, ed., *Fourteenth Century England II* (Woodbridge: Boydell and Brewer, 2002)

Given-Wilson, Chris, and Curteis, Alice, *The Royal Bastards of Medieval England* (London: Routledge and Kegan Paul, 1984)

Given-Wilson, Chris, *Chronicles: The Writing of History in Medieval England* (London: Bloomsbury, 2004)

Gransden, Antonia, *Historical Writing in England II: c. 1307 to the Early Sixteenth Century* (London: Routledge, 1982)

Griffiths, John, *Edward II in Glamorgan* (London: W. H. Roberts, 1904)

Haines, Roy Martin, *King Edward II: His Life, His Reign, and Its Aftermath, 1284-1330* (Montreal: MacGill-Queen's University Press, 2003)

Haines, Roy Martin, *Death of a King* (Lancaster: Scotforth Books, 2002)

Haines, Roy Martin, *The Church and Politics in Fourteenth-Century England: the Career of Adam Orleton, c. 1275–1345* (Cambridge: Cambridge University Press, 1978)

Haines, Roy Martin, *Archbishop John Stratford: Political Revolutionary and Champion of the Liberties of the English Church, ca. 1275/80–1348* (Toronto: Pontifical Institute of Mediaeval Studies, 1986)

Hallam, Elizabeth and Everard, Judith, *Capetian France 987-1328* (London and New York: Routledge, second edition, 2001)

Hamilton, J. S., *Piers Gaveston, Earl of Cornwall 1307–1312: Politics and Patronage in the Reign of Edward II* (Detroit: Wayne State University Press, 1988)

Hutchison, Harold F., *Edward II: The Pliant King* (London: Eyre and Spottiswoode, 1971)

Lyon, Ann, *Constitutional History of the UK* (London: Cavendish, 2003)

Maddicott, J. R., *Thomas of Lancaster 1307–1322: A Study in the Reign of Edward II* (Oxford: Oxford University Press, 1970)

McFarlane, K. B., *The Nobility of Later Medieval England* (Oxford: Clarendon Press, 1973)

McKisack, May, *The Fourteenth Century 1307-1399* (Oxford: Clarendon Press, 1959)

Mitchell, Linda E., *Portraits of Medieval Women: Family, Marriage and Politics in England 1225–1350* (New York: Palgrave Macmillan, 2003)

Moor, Charles, *Knights of Edward I* (London: Harleian Society 81–84, 1929–32)

Mortimer, Ian, *The Greatest Traitor: The Life of Sir Roger Mortimer, Ruler of England 1327 to 1330* (London: Pimlico, 2003)

Mortimer, Ian, *The Perfect King: The Life of Edward III* (London: Vintage, 2006)

Mortimer, Ian, *The Time-Traveller's Guide to Medieval England* (London: The Bodley Head, 2008)

Mortimer, Ian, *Medieval Intrigue: Decoding Royal Conspiracies* (London: Continuum, 2010)

Nusbacher, Aryeh, *Bannockburn 1314* (Stroud: Tempus, 2005)

Ormrod, W. M., ed., *Fourteenth-Century England III* (Woodbridge: Boydell and Brewer, 2004)

Ormrod, W. M., *Edward III* (New Haven and London: Yale University Press, 2011)

Oxford Dictionary of National Biography, online edition.

Parsons, John Carmi, *Eleanor of Castile: Queen and Society in Thirteenth-Century England* (Basingstoke: Macmillan, 1995)

Perry, R., *Edward the Second: Suddenly, at Berkeley* (Wotton-under-Edge: Ivy House Books, 1988)

Phillips, J. R. S., *Aymer de Valence, earl of Pembroke 1307–1324: Baronial Politics in the Reign of Edward II* (Oxford: Clarendon Press, 1972)

Phillips, Seymour, *Edward II* (New Haven and London: Yale University Press, 2010)

Prestwich, Michael, *Plantagenet England 1225–1360* (Oxford: Clarendon Press, 2005)

Prestwich, Michael, *Edward I* (London: Methuen, 1988)

Prestwich, Michael, *The Three Edwards: War and State in England 1272–1377* (London: Routledge, 1980)

Prestwich, Michael, Britnell, Richard, and Frame, Robin, eds., *Thirteenth-Century England X* (Woodbridge: Boydell and Brewer, 2003)

Rees, William, *Caerphilly Castle and its Place in the Annals of Glamorgan* (Caerphilly: D. Brown and Sons, new edition, 1974)

Reese, Peter, *Bannockburn: Scotland's Greatest Victory* (Edinburgh: Canongate Books, 2003)

Richardson, Douglas, *Plantagenet Ancestry: A Study in Colonial and Medieval Families* (Baltimore: Genealogical Publishing Company, 2004)

Roberts, R. A., *Edward II, the Lords Ordainers and Piers Gaveston's Jewels and Horses (1312–1313)* (London: Camden Miscellany, xv, 1929)

Rouse Ball, W. W., *The King's Scholars and King's Hall* (printed privately, 1917)

Saaler, Mary, *Edward II 1307–1327* (London: Rubicon, 1997)

Sadler, John, *Bannockburn: Battle for Liberty* (Barnsley: Pen and Sword Military, 2008)

Saul, Nigel, ed., *Fourteenth-Century England 1* (Woodbridge: Boydell and Brewer, 2000)

Sayles, George Osborne, *The Functions of the Medieval Parliament of England* (London: Bloomsbury, revised edition, 1988)

Strickland, Agnes, *The Lives of the Queens of England from the Norman Conquest*, vol. 2 (Philadelphia: Lea and Blanchard, 1848)

Sumption, Jonathan, *The Hundred Years War 1: Trial by Battle* (London: Faber and Faber, 1999)

Tout, T. F., *The Place of the Reign of Edward II in English History* (Manchester: Manchester University Press, second edition, 1936)

Tout, T. F., *Chapters in the Administrative History of England* (Manchester: Manchester University Press, six vols, 1920–1937)

Tuck, Anthony, *Crown and Nobility 1272–1461* (London: Fontana, 1985)

Underhill, Frances A., *For Her Good Estate: The Life of Elizabeth de Burgh* (New York: St Martin's Press, 1999)

Vale, Malcolm, *The Princely Court: Medieval Courts and Culture in North-West Europe* (Oxford: Oxford University Press, 2001)

Vale, Malcolm, *The Origins of the Hundred Years War: The Angevin Legacy 1250–1340* (Oxford: Clarendon Press, 1990)

Ward, Jennifer C., *English Noblewomen in the Later Middle Ages* (London and New York: Longman, 1992)

Ward, Jennifer, *Elizabeth de Burgh, Lady of Clare (1295–1360): Household and Other Records* (Woodbridge: The Boydell Press, 2014)

Warner, Kathryn, *Edward II: The Unconventional King* (Stroud: Amberley Publishing, 2014)

Waugh, Scott L., *The Lordship of England: Royal Wardships and Marriages in English Society and Politics 1217–1327* (Princeton: Princeton University Press, 1988)

Weir, Alison, *Isabella, She-Wolf of France, Queen of England* (London: Pimlico, 2005)

Woodacre, Elena, *The Queens Regnant of Navarre: Succession, Politics and Partnership, 1274–1512* (New York: Palgrave Macmillan, 2013)

Woolgar, C. M., *The Great Household in Late Medieval England* (New Haven and London: Yale University Press, 1999)

Websites

My Edward II site at **http://edwardthesecond.blogspot.com/** has many hundreds of articles about Edward II and Isabella, his reign and its aftermath, going back to 2005.

http://theauramalaproject.wordpress.com/ discusses the possibilities of Edward's survival in Italy, and the team are doing superb and important research into the Fieschi Letter.

British History Online **http://www.british-history.ac.uk/**

The National Archives **http://www.nationalarchives.gov.uk/**

http://www.ianmortimer.com/ contains many essays about Edward II and his survival, and history in general.

http://www.ladydespensersscribery.com/ is an excellent resource for the Despensers, Edward II and the fourteenth century.

The archives of **http://susandhigginbotham.blogspot.com/** contain many great articles about Edward II and Isabella.

Index